GW00649049

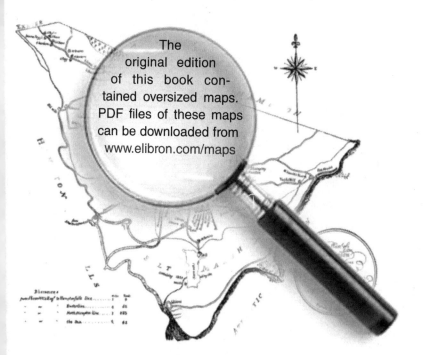

Charles Boswell Norman

ARMENIA
AND THE CAMPAIGN OF 1877

Elibron Classics
www.elibron.com

ARMENIA,

AND THE CAMPAIGN OF 1877.

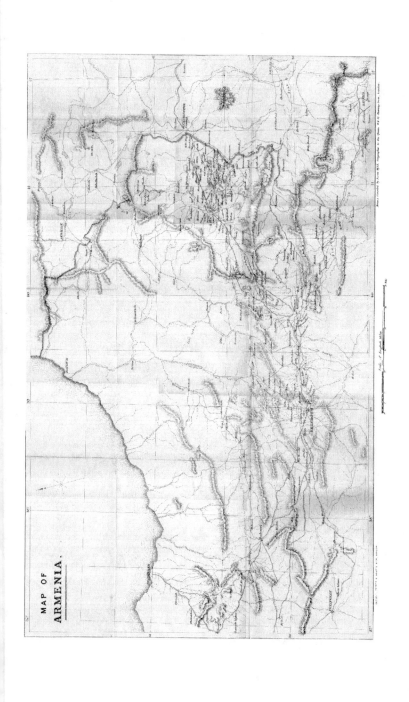

MAP OF
ARMENIA.

ARMENIA,

AND THE CAMPAIGN OF 1877.

BY

C. B. NORMAN,

LATE SPECIAL CORRESPONDENT OF "THE TIMES" AT THE SEAT OF WAR.

WITH SPECIALLY-PREPARED MAPS AND PLANS.

CASSELL PETTER & GALPIN:

LONDON, PARIS & NEW YORK.

TO

LIEUTENANT-GENERAL

SIR ARNOLD KEMBALL, C.B., K.C.S.I.,

ROYAL ARTILLERY,

WHOSE CAREER IN PAST DAYS AS A BOMBAY HORSE ARTILLERYMAN,

IN THESE NO LESS STIRRING TIMES AS A SOLDIER DIPLOMATIST,

TESTIFIES ALIKE TO HIS TACT, ENDURANCE, AND GALLANTRY—WHOSE

NAME ADDS ONE MORE TO THE LIST OF THOSE INDIAN HEROES OF

WHOM EVERY ENGLISHMAN MAY BE JUSTLY PROUD—

THIS VOLUME IS DEDICATED

BY HIS OBEDIENT SERVANT,

THE AUTHOR.

A

PREFACE.

My apology for launching yet another book on the world must be that I am aware the history of the war in Armenia is but imperfectly known in this country. More vivid interest attached to the scenes nearer home, Plevna and Schipka eclipsed Zewin and Kars in both honour and gallantry, and though British interests were more sensibly affected, according to party cry, by the events in Asia, yet popular interest was more visibly affected by the deeds upon European ground.

I landed at Trebizond an advanced philo-Turk, and deeply impressed with the idea that Turkish misrule and Turkish mal-administration had been grossly exaggerated. Being a novice in the profession of journalism, I was not bound to adhere to my former opinions for the sake of consistency in my future articles; and being entirely unfettered in my instructions, I determined to write fairly and honestly what came before me, and endeavour to the best of my ability to uphold the Ottoman cause.

I have seen misrule in native states in India; I have seen Oriental vice and profligacy amongst the higher classes of Her Majesty's Eastern subjects; I

A 2

have studied the Oriental character for some years, and flattered myself I knew a little about it. These pages will show how soon my views changed; how soon I learnt that no words could exaggerate the amount of misrule that exists in Asiatic Turkey, where Christian and Mahomedan alike groan under an intolerable yoke. I learnt, too, that the debauched rajah is an innocent compared with the majority of pashas.

As regards the Turkish army, I never saw a Nizam battalion that could hold its own with our worst-drilled regiment of Bengal Infantry. Our native officers are as a rule infinitely superior to the Ottoman regimental officers, few of whom, in Lord Napier of Magdala's *régime*, could have qualified educationally for promotion to naièk. Some few among the superiors —how few the campaign shows—were good men. It is no exaggeration to say that the success of the earlier portion of the war may be traced to the exertions of less than half a dozen men—Ahmed Mukhtar, Djameel and Faizi Pashas, Halit, and Captain Mahomed Bey.

Remembering what the Ottoman army did in the Crimea, fighting by the side of our own men, and remembering what our native troops in India have done at Lucknow, Delhi, Chillianwallah, Punniar, Jellalabad, Ghuzni, and a hundred other places—comparing these acts with those of the present campaign, we ought, at any rate, to feel satisfied that if with their faulty organisation, bad officers, ignorant staff, and lack of pecuniary resources, the Ottoman armies have been enabled to hold Russia at bay for eight long months, we with our well-trained troops, and

our inexhaustible native reserve (every whit the equal
in physique and gallantry of the Osmanli), need have
no fear should we unfortunately be drawn into war.
If the Czar's armies have taken two-thirds of a year
to march from Alexandropol to Erzeroum, and seven
months from Goomri to Kars, they may abandon all
hope of ever reaching Peshawur, of ever ruling in
Hindostan.

I have not touched on the political view of the
Eastern Question, for I know little about it. I am
aware that the war is entirely due to the machinations
of Russia. I know that her agents fomented rebellion
in Bulgaria; that her ambassador persuaded the Porte
to suppress the revolt with Bashi-Bazouks, and to
repudiate her loans. I am aware that, behind the
flimsy pretence of the amelioration of the Christian
subjects of the Porte, the real reason for the war
was love of aggression, and that the Czar still hopes
to see the Cathedral of St. Sophia the head of the
Greek Church. Thus, though I know the conduct
of Russia to be indefensible on every ground, I cannot
but feel that if the war is the cause of granting a
good government to the subjects of the Porte, if it
strangles the rule of the pasha and the zaptieh, the
Czar will deserve as much credit for the invasion of
Turkey as for the emancipation of the serf.

As for British interests being affected by the annexa-
tion of Armenia, I fail to see the point. Alexandropol
and Erivan are nearer the Persian Gulf than Kars and
Erzeroum, Samarkand and Khokand nearer the Punjaub
than either. Those who advance the theory that the

Mahomedan tribes of Hindostan would join Russia were we involved in hostilities with her, because we failed to support the Sultan in his hour of need, forget the lesson taught in 1857, just one year after the Treaty of Paris, one year after the Crimean War, when we sacrificed 100,000 men and £100,000,000 to bolster up the Ottoman Empire, the Bengal army mutinied, and our bitterest foes in that dire struggle were the Mahomedans of Northern India.*

Before these pages see the light we may be at war with Russia. A large section of the people seem urging the Government to defend "British interests;" but not a man seems able to define the term. Should unhappily we find ourselves called upon to defend either of the two points laid down by Lord Derby as debatable ground, I feel no fear for the result. We know Russia's armed strength : the events of the last few months have thoroughly opened our eyes to the exaggerated views we formerly held of her power. She has no idea of our power; and as this war has proved the value of infantry, the uselessness of un-trained artillery fire, so if we go to war will we prove that our infantry are the finest-trained soldiers in the world, even as they ever have been. I have no doubt in my mind that a battalion of native troops, organised

* I recently read a lecture given by a Lieutenant-Colonel of Volunteers, in which it was deliberately stated that the capture of Kars in '55 weakened our hold of India, and was one of the primary causes of the Mutiny. This is as amusing as the statement gravely made by Sir H. Hoare to Lord Derby, that our first news of the capture of Kars on the 18th November was derived by telegraph from Cabul ! Truly, as Lord Salisbury remarked, the study of large scale maps is most desirable—a little knowledge is a dangerous thing !

as they now are, would prove more than a match for any battalion the Czar could put against them; and, as far as the cavalry of the army of the Caucasus is concerned, our Indian irregular cavalry, I am convinced, could walk round them. If Russia, overpowered by conceit at her recent successes, rushes into war with us, she will, I believe, emerge a crippled and a third-rate Power.

In my correspondence to the *Times* I made it a rule to report nothing but what came under my own personal observation, or facts confirmed by European evidence; in the re-publication of my letters I have adhered to that rule. I have endeavoured to write impartially, neither glossing over the faults of the Turks nor imputing glaring atrocities to the Russians; in truth I may say that I failed to obtain one authenticated case of cruelty committed by the army of the Grand Duke, and in this statement I am borne out by the despatches of Sir Arnold Kemball, published in the recent Blue Books on the Eastern Question.

Of the conduct of the Turkish administration no one could speak too strongly: in making no provision for their sick and wounded; in sanctioning the employment of irregulars; in failing to punish the perpetrators of deeds which roused the indignation of every honest man; and in circulating the most barefaced falsehoods about Russian cruelty, notably the statements of the treatment of prisoners at Ardahan, and of the inhabitants of the Alashgird plain. Such acts as these must inevitably alienate the support of those who feel for a gallant people fighting for *effete* rulers.

In conclusion, I have to offer my heartfelt thanks to many, but for whose kind assistance I should have been unable to lay before the public what I venture to trust will be accepted as a truthful history of the Armenian campaign. To Dr. W. H. Russell, the king of war correspondents, I am indebted for much help—hints as to kit, and warnings as to the danger that besets the unwary correspondent; to Mr. Wylde for his invaluable help in the compilation of the map which accompanies this volume; to Mr. Zohrab, Her Majesty's Consul at Erzeroum; Mr. Biliotti, Consul at Trebizond; Mr. A. Magack, of Erzeroum, all and each of whom vied in kindness and hospitality, placing not only their houses and libraries at my disposal, but aiding me in collecting news of hostilities and facts concerning the history and administration of the country; without their help I should have been powerless. To Sir Arnold Kemball and his indefatigable aide-de-camp, Lieut. Maitland Dougall, R.N., I owe more than words can express. I can only hope that they retain as pleasant a reminiscence of our united efforts to rub along under discomforts of no ordinary kind, on the sunny slopes of Ararat, as I ever shall.

CONTENTS.

CHAPTER I.

LONDON TO TREBIZOND.

PAGE

Austrian Custom House—Travelling Companions—Misseri's Hotel—Search for Horse-flesh—Krikol, Possum, and Mr. Vincent—Early Impressions of the Turkish Army—Defences of the Bosphorus—Redif and Raouf—Turkish Volunteers—Trebizond and Her Majesty's Consul—Trade in the Black Sea—Sport and " Polly "—Djameel Pasha—The Abkhasians   1

CHAPTER II.

TREBIZOND TO ERZEROUM.

Djameel Pasha at Work—The Sword of my Escort—Turkish Troops pushing on to the Front—Anatolian Trout—The Zigana Pass—A Night's Lodging—" Riz-au-gras "—The Pests of Armenia—Guns and Volunteers—Comfortable Quarters—*Esprit de Corps*—Monsieur Magack —Erzeroum—Its People and Defences—Its Drains and Dirt—Its Shepherd—Its Trade   19

CHAPTER III.

THE HOSTILE ARMIES.

The Turkish Army, and its Changes during the Present Century—Thirty Years' Stagnation—Abdul Azeez's Reforms—Equality of Race as regards Military Service—Nizam, Ichtayat, Redif, and Mustahfiz—Military Districts—Administrative Staff—Sappers and Miners—Artillery—Guns—Equipment of Mounted Branch—Horses—Pay of all Grades—Cavalry Equipment—Horses—Men—Pay of all Grades—Infantry Staff—Uniform and Equipment—Arms and Pay—Rations and Quarters—Scarcity of Officers—Mukhtar's Forces—Russian Army—Composition — Artillery — Position of Turkish Army—Position of Russian Army   34

CHAPTER IV.

THE STORY OF ARDAHAN.

PAGE

Ismail Kurd's Invasion of Russia—Discontent in the City—The Petition to the British Consul—Mr. Zohrab—Russian Designs on Armenia—Alacrity in following up the Declaration of War—Capture of Bayazid—City *Canards*—Ardahan—Captain Mehmed Bey—Sabri Pasha—Gallant Defence of the Emir Oghlou—Flight of Sabri—Capture of the Town 59

CHAPTER V.

ON THE WAY TO THE FRONT.

Fugitives from Ardahan—Sabri Pasha again—Conduct of Russians—Retreat from Olti—The Herman Dooz—Kuipri Kui and its Defences—Suspicious Death of a Christian—Khorassan—The Fight at Beghli Ahmed—First Impressions of Circassians—Ahmed Mukhtar Pasha—The Zewin Dooz—Disposition of Turkish Troops—Apathy of Ismail Pasha—The Kurds—Discontent among Troops at Erzeroum—Appeal for Help from England—Visit to the Camp at Delibaba—The Pass—Turkish Officers—Re-occupation of Olti—Our Kurdish Escort—Sortie from Kars—Faizi Pasha's Opinions—Other Versions of Beghli Ahmed—The Head-quarter Camp—Talked-of Court-martial on Sabri Pasha—Want of Cavalry—Position of Russian Forces—Position of Turkish Forces 76

CHAPTER VI.

THE BATTLE OF TAGHIR.

A Fatal Omen!—With Sir Arnold in Search of a "Scrim"—Mahomed Pasha wishes to Fight—Our Breakfast Interrupted—View the Ground—Kurds and Circassians—A Rough Time of it—Russian Intentions—Disposition of our Troops—Description of the Ground—Wild Firing of the Turks—Gallantry of their Gunners—Pluck of the Tcherkess—Excellence of Russian Infantry—Waste of Ammunition—Our Flank Turned—Yahvash! Yahvash! A Run from the Cossacks—Hospital Arrangements—Reflection on the Fight—The Energetic Djameel Pasha—Turkish Losses 104

CHAPTER VII.

A LULL IN THE STORM.

Ismail's Canards—Halit Bey—Disorganised state of Turkish Right Wing—A Russian Scare—A Fish Dinner—Position of the Hostile Armies—

PAGE

Re-occupation of Bayazid by Faik Pasha—Mukhtar Pasha reinforces
and assumes Command of Right Wing—Ismail the Kurd joins Central
Column—Moussa Pasha—News of a Turkish Success at Eshek Khaliass
—Awkward Position of Tergukassoff—Faik Pasha's Division .   . 130

CHAPTER VIII.

THE MOSLEM AT BAY.

Leave Erzeroum once more for the Front—The Battle of Eshek Khaliass—
Conduct of Turkish Cavalry—No Ammunition!—Wounded Men—
German Doctors—Hand-wounds—True Missionaries—Sir Arnold
Kemball—Fresh News of Eshek Khaliass—Turkish Losses—Fate of
Skirmishers against Shelter Trenches—More Fighting—Another
Stampede—Tcherkess Heroes—A Christian Village—Reinforcements
for Zewin—Rumours of a Fight—"*Perish India*"—Outrages on
Christians—Faizi Pasha's Victory—Enthusiasm of the Turks—Ismail
and the Koran—Russian and Turkish Losses—Value of Turkish
Cavalry—Value of Turkish Casualty Returns—Melikoff's Returns . 143

CHAPTER IX.

IN PURSUIT OF THE RUSSIANS.

Visit from the Mushir—Complications in Daghestan—An Advance on the
Enemy—A Cold Night—Inefficient Quartermaster-General's Depart-
ment—The Bivouac on the Mellidooz—Treatment of Sir Arnold Kemball
—March to Sara Kamysh—A Turkish Camp—Turkish Hospitals—
Rations of the Turkish Soldier—Discipline on the Line of March—The
Peabody-Martini Rifle—Russian Letters—The Opinion expressed in
them of the Conduct of the War—Russian Retreat from Zaidikan—
Desecration of the Graves of Russian Dead—Stripping the Dead—Dis-
position of the Army—Rumour of Russian Retreat—Turkish Reverse
near Ardanutsch—Kurdish Atrocities—Lawlessness of the Circassians
—Russian Wounded killed on the Field—Murder of Two Karapapak
Irregulars—A new Mushir with Reinforcements—Detail of our Army—
Officers of Redif Battalions on the Line of March—Stories of Russian
Cruelty—Not borne out by Facts—Plunder of Christian Villages by
Circassians—Vairan Kale—A Late Dinner 174

CHAPTER X.

THE RELIEF OF KARS.

We enter the Fortress—The old familiar Names—Turkish Forts and Turkish
"Obstacles"—Losses during Bombardment—Round-headed Shell—
Russian Siege Batteries—Changes in our Staff—The Town well supplied
with Provisions—Fortress with Ammunition—Description of the place
from the *Moskovskiya Vêdomosti* 204

CHAPTER XI.

CAMP LIFE IN FRONT OF KARS.

PAGE

Massacre at Bayazid—Kurdish Atrocities—Conduct of Faik Pasha—Murder
of a Russian Doctor near Kars—His Diary—Russian Opinion of Battle
of Khaliass—Strictures on Heimann—The Siege raised—Yet one more
instance of the value of Turkish Cavalry—Siege Batteries—Move our
Camp to Vezinkui—Beggars on Horseback—Success of the Turks
deemed only Temporary—Conduct of the Officer in charge of Hospitals
—An Interruption to our Breakfast—An Interchange of Civilities on
the Slopes of the Yagni—Kindness of the Consul at Erzeroum—Energy
displayed by the new Governor there—News from Van—Treatment of
Christians throughout Armenia—Russians change their Camp—Their
Kindness to Turkish Prisoners at Ardahan—A Flag of Truce fired on,
and Bearer killed, by the Russians—The Polish Legion—Cavalry
Skirmish near Sabatan—Turkish Opinion of Kurds   220

CHAPTER XII.

ON THE WATCH.

Shift our Camp once more—Strength of our Forces—Stoppage of Telegrams
—Hospitals in Erzeroum—Relief of Bayazid by Tergukassoff—That
General's Operations during the War—The Kurds once more—Court-
martials on Faik and Sabri Pasha—Turkish Accounts of the Relief of
Bayazid—Circassian Account of same Affair—Losses in the Engagement
—Russian Punishment of Kurds—Pleasures of Camp Life—Expec-
tations of a "Scrim" disappointed—Turkish Reconnaissance into
Russian Territory—The Enemy's Attempts to cut it off—Peace and
War—Russian Reinforcements at Tashkale—Hailstones and Pigeons'
Eggs—Spies' Tales of Bayazid—British Officers' Accounts of Scenes in
Bayazid—Sir Arnold Kemball's Endeavours to stop the Kurdish
Atrocities—Mukhtar Pasha's little Affair with the Circassian—His stern
Ideas of Discipline—Russian Atrocities in Armenia—Utterly False—
Disposition of Russian Troops   244

CHAPTER XIII.

HEAD-QUARTERS, FOURTH TURKISH ARMY CORPS.

The Russian Retreat—Machinery of Turkish Staff—Medical Department—
An Amateur Opinion on Russian Reconnaissances—A Skirmish on the
28th—Cossacks left to bear the brunt of the Fight—Dash of the Circassians—More Russian Reinforcements—Story of a Deserter—Strength
of the Invading Army—Demoralisation after Defeat at Zewin—Russian
Casualties—Projected Assault at Kars—Value of our Cavalry—Russians occupy Ani unobserved—Mukhtar attacks them—Fresh Details

PAGE

from Bayazid—The Instigators of the Massacre—Sir Arnold Kemball Demands their Punishment—Positions of Ismail Pasha and Tergukassoff—Turkish Official Telegrams—Their close Adherence to Truth —Interchange of Civilities between Melikoff and Mukhtar—Ahmed Vefyk Pasha and the Stafford House Surgeons 264

CHAPTER XIV.

MOSLEM AND CHRISTIAN.

Return to Erzeroum—Russians evacuate Ani—Incompetency of Commanders of Turkish Right and Left Wings—Christian Harvest and Moslem Reapers—Disinterred Russians—Behaviour of Kurds in Head-quarter Camp, and in the Right Column—English Hospital at Erzeroum—War Preparations at Erzeroum—Ani once more reoccupied—Conduct of the Russians in Armenia—The Kurds of Shoragel, Mehded, and Youssouf Bey—The Kurds in Alashgird—At Moosh—At Bitlis—In Van—The Treatment of American Missionaries—Of Armenian Villages—Apathy or Sympathy of Ismail Pasha—Skirmish at Taouskui—Another at Hiersai Bulak—Engagement on 18th August—Preparations for a Winter Campaign—War Taxes, and prompt Payment of subordinate Officials 281

CHAPTER XV.

TURKISH SUCCESSES.

Battle on the 18th August—Attack on the Nakharji-Tepe unsuccessful— Russians fail to press home any of their Assaults—Turkish Losses— Stripping the Dead—Skirmishes between Ismail and Tergukassoff at Khalifin and Abazgool—Battle of Kizil-Tepe—Successful Assault of the Hill by Mehmed Bey—Gallant Attempt of the Abkhasian Prince to retake it—He is Wounded—Sheremetieff succeeds to the Command— Melikoff arrives with Reinforcements—Defeat of the Russians—Losses on both Sides—Reinforcements called for by both Mukhtar and Ismail Mr. Zohrab's position in Erzeroum—Paper Organisation of the Ottoman Army and its actual Condition—Drill and Discipline—Skirmishes and Sentries—Taxation in Armenia—Movements of Ismail Pasha . . 305

CHAPTER XVI.

ARMENIANS—THE TRUE STORY OF BAYAZID.

Arrival of Stafford House Stores at Erzeroum—State of Hospitals in Main Army and in Right Wing—Turkish Authorities refuse Permission to amputate—Refuse Carriage for Medical Stores—Our Hospitals in Erzeroum—My Ideas of the Armenian—The Exodus to Russian Territory, caused by Kurdish Atrocities—Denial of this by Kurd Ismail

PAGE

Pasha—Changes in the Turkish Staff—Jealousy of General Kohlmann
—Court-martial on Sabri and Faik Pashas—Hussain Avni, and Zarif
Mustafa—The True Story of Bayazid—Ferocity of the Kurds—Supineness of Faik Pasha—Neglect of Ismail to Support—Consequent Defeat
of the Turks at Bayazid by Tergukassoff—Defence of Mr. Zohrab   . 322

CHAPTER XVII.

WINTER PREPARATIONS.

Ghazi Mukhtar Pasha—Promotion of Captain Mehmed Pasha—Further
Plans of the Turkish Commander-in-Chief—Condition of the Erze-
roum Garrison—Prospect of Famine—Komaroff's Measures for the
Defence of Ardahan—Rumoured Reinforcements for Tergukassoff—
Winter Clothing for Turkish Troops—The British Ambulance—Re-
ported Violation of the Geneva Convention by the Russians—Conduct
of the Turks on the Battle-field—Conduct of the Russians in Ardahan—
Explosive Bullets—Desertion of the Circassians—Probability of the
Loss seriously affecting Mukhtar—Difficulty of an Advance on Erivan
—Successful Raid of Arab Cavalry—Force despatched to Natschevan—
Russian Reinforcements—Skirmish at Tcherkgi   344

CHAPTER XVIII.

THE MOSLEM AT THE END OF HIS TETHER.

Skirmish near Zaim—Russians defeated—Plans of the Grand Duke—
Mukhtar preparing for a Winter Campaign—His Position near Kars
—Skirmish at Natschevan—Battle of the Yagnis on 2nd October—
Gallantry of Mehmed Pasha's Brigade—Turkish Success at the Little
Yagni—Attack and Capture of the Great Yagni—Repulse of the
Russians—Heavy Losses—Misery in Kars—Paucity of Doctors—
Hospital Arrangements   357

CHAPTER XIX.

TURKISH ADMINISTRATION IN ARMENIA.

Mahomedans Exempted from War Taxation—Christians Forced to Pay—
Pensioners of Turkish Government—Irregular Imposts—The Discon-
tent they Cause—The Hadji—The Caimakam and the British Consul
—The Police Station at the Mouth of the Ghiurji Boghaz—Mr.
Layard and the Danger to India—American Missionaries' Views on
Christian Oppression—Turkish Reforms—Her Hospitals—Dr. Casson
on Turkish Atrocities—Employment of the Press by the Porte—The
Abkhasian Exodus—Treatment of the Bayazid Refugees by the
Russians and Persians—Treatment of their own Wounded by Turks—
Reduction of Unpaid Salaries   366

CHAPTER XX.

THE TURN OF THE TIDE.

Russian Reinforcements—Mukhtar draws in his Men—The Grand Duke occupies the late Turkish advanced Posts—Mukhtar's Confidence—Despondency of Turkish Soldiers—Increased Desertions—Russians learn the Value of a turning Movement—The Battle of the Aladja Dagh—Gallant Defence of the Little Yagni—Loss of the Olya Tepe—Extraordinary Conduct of Men sent to support the Position—Russians occupy the Nalband Tepe—Panic on the Aladja Dagh—Flight to Kars—Scene in the Fortress—Hassan Bey's Exertions—Sanitary State of Kars—Mehmed Pasha evacuates the Little Yagni—Mukhtar's Plans —He falls back on the Araxes—Ismail Pasha also retires—Russian Trophies—Retreat through the Kose Dagh—Evacuation of Kuipri Kui —Energy of Faizi Pasha—Ismail surprised at Hassan Kale—Capture of Captain Creagh—Treatment accorded to him, and to Dr. Casson— Turks fall back on the Devi-boyun—Reinforcements from Constantinople and Batoum 382

CHAPTER XXI.

OPERATIONS ROUND ERZEROUM.

Turks strengthen both Erzeroum and the Devi-boyun—Heimann attacks Mukhtar—Great Gallantry of Mehmed Pasha—Faizi holds the Turkish Right—Heimann tries a Ruse—Faizi tries to rally the Osmanli—Flight to Erzeroum—Turkish Losses—Mukhtar Pasha encourages his Men— His Refusal to surrender—Russians invest Erzeroum—They construct a Redoubt on the Tope Dagh—Relative defensive Value of Erzeroum and Kars—Heimann's ill-judged Attempt to assault the Place—Gallantry of Tarnaieff—Capture of the Medjidieh Lunette—Mehmed Bey retakes it—Death of Tarnaieff—Failure of the Attack on the Kremedli Fort —Coolness of the English—Mr. Zohrab—Dr. Featherstonhaugh— Reginald and Percy Zohrab—Conduct of Turks to Wounded—The gentle Ladies of Erzeroum—Mutilation of Russian Dead . . 396

CHAPTER XXII.

THE THIRD CAPTURE OF KARS BY THE RUSSIANS.

Siege of Kars—Capture of Fort Hafiz Pasha—Russians move their Headquarters—Projected Assault of the Place—Detail of Attacking Columns —Success of Lazaroff on the Right—Death of Count Grabbe in front of the Kanli Tabia—Capture of all Works on the Plains—Capture of Karadagh and Citadel—Hussain Hami Pasha Escapes—The Majority of the Garrison surrender—Grand Duke enters the Place in Triumph— Melikoff moves towards Erzeroum—His Column forced to fall back from Olti—Komaroff moves to Ardahan—Thence to Ardanutsch—

PAGE

Skirmish there—Condition of Erzeroum—Treachery at Kars—Hussain
Bey, Commandant of Artillery—Osman the Renegade—Hussain's
Visits to the Russian Camp—The Circassian Letter-carrier—His Death
—Abandonment of the Hafiz Pasha Tabia—Escape of Hami Pasha—
The Man whom the Russian General allowed to wear his Sword—
Like Father, like Son   410

CHAPTER XXIII.

PASKIEWITCH'S CAMPAIGN IN 1828–29.

Paskiewitch's Forces—Doubts about Persia—Pankratieff watches her at
Khoi—Brigade for the Circassians—The Russian Plans—Their Three
Columns—Their Strength and Leaders—Inability to Siege Erzeroum in
one Campaign—Cross the Frontier 14th June—Detail of Army of
Czar—Of that of the Sultan—Kars Captured 23rd June—Akhalk-
alaki, 24th July—Hertwitz, 26th July—Akhalzik, 16th August—
Ardahan taken same day—Aitzkui, 18th August—Russian Right
Column captures Bayazid—The Russian General cantons his Army in
Armenia—Turkish Spring Preparations—Endeavour to re-capture
Akhalzik—Massacre of Christians—19th May, 1829, Paskiewitch
rejoins the Army—11th June, he advances—19th, Battle of Zewin
—20th, Battle of Mellidooz—28th, Erzeroum surrenders—Treaty of
Adrianople 422

APPENDIX A.—ORGANISATION OF TURKISH ARMY 439

APPENDIX B.—RUSSIAN ARMY ORGANISATION 459

APPENDIX C.—THE ARMENIAN THEATRE OF WAR 469

APPENDIX D.—HUSSAIN AVNI PASHA   481

LIST OF MAPS AND PLANS.

MAP OF ARMENIA   .   .   .   . *Frontispiece*

PLAN OF THE AFFAIR AT TAGHIR   .   .   .   . *to face page* 104

PLAN OF THE ENGAGEMENT ON THE ZEWIN PLATEAU   .   .   ,,   162

MAP OF THE GROUND BETWEEN KARS AND ALEXANDROPOL   .   ,,   305

PLAN OF BATTLES OF THE ALADJA DAGH .   .   .   .   ,,   366

PLAN OF ERZEROUM .   .   .   .   .   .   ,   .   ,,   386

SKETCH MAP SHOWING CAMPAIGN OF 1828-29 .   .   .   ,,   405

MAP OF THE COUNTRY AROUND ERZEROUM   .   .   .   ,,   437

ARMENIA,
AND THE CAMPAIGN OF 1877.

CHAPTER I.

LONDON TO TREBIZOND.

Austrian Custom House—Travelling-Companions—Misseri's Hotel—Search for Horse-flesh—Krikol, Possum, and Mr. Vincent—Early Impressions of the Turkish Army—Defences of the Bosphorus—Redif and Raouf—Turkish Volunteers—Trebizond and Her Majesty's Consul—Trade in the Black Sea—Sport and "Polly"—Djameel Pasha—The Abkhasians.

TREBIZOND, *May 19th.*

THE evening of Monday, April 30, 1877, was cold and stormy, not such an one as an unfettered traveller would have chosen for the purpose of crossing the Channel; but, with my head towards Kars, and an ardent longing to reach Armenia before the actual outbreak of hostilities, it did not behove me to be too particular about the weather at the commencement of my trip. Breaking my journey to Buda Pesth of a necessity at Vienna, I experienced the annoyance of an Austrian custom-house examination. It was useless affirming that my saddlery was old; that my waterproof sheeting was destined for Armenia, not Hungary; that my note-paper was for my own use; and that I considered soap an indispensable article for my journey. The cadaverous chief carefully examined, weighed, and measured everything, from a spare tooth-brush to a Colt's revolver, and, after a delay of two hours and a

B

half, permitted me to proceed to the Hotel Imperial, where, as usual, everything was most comfortable. At three p.m. on the 3rd of May, I left Vienna for Pesth. A popular colonel of the Scots Guards, bound for Widdin and the theatre of war on the Danube, was my companion. At ten p.m. we parted, he for the Roumanian frontier, I to make some necessary arrangements with a friend, driving straight to the Casino Nationale. I was present during the reception of the Softa Deputation by representatives of the Hungarian nation, the interest of which was much heightened when I was informed that there was not a single Softa in the group of fezzed heads.

At six the following morning I was once more ready for Trieste, and at noon on Saturday, the 5th, embarked on board the Austrian Lloyd's steamer, *Diana*, for Constantinople. Even on a five days' sea-voyage, I think one naturally looks with interest on one's fellow-travellers, amongst whom, no matter of what nationality or creed they may be, an Englishman, I may say invariably, meets with a friend.

Among the passengers were a naval *confrère, en route* to join Hobart Pasha, and relate the doughty deeds of the Ottoman fleet; two ex-naval officers, about to place their services at the disposal of the Sublime Porte; a Scotch peer, travelling in search of information, and seeking it even at the cannon's mouth; an American journalist; a Prussian nun, who lost her heart during that short water-trip; and last, though not least, Turfek Bey, the late *Chargé d'Affaires* at St. Petersburg, returning with his suite to Constantinople. His first-secretary, Aristarchi Bey, was a perfect English scholar, and to him I am much indebted for valuable information on the subject of the Ottoman administration. Though fine and smooth as we steamed out of the Trieste harbour, the breeze outside was decidedly freshening, and as the sun went down behind a thick dirty bank of clouds, the old Scotch engineer on board prophesied a nasty night. A dead head-wind, rising to a fresh gale, accompanied by heavy showers, ushered in the storm, in which the *Diana* showed her rolling powers. I am afraid few of us turned up to breakfast on Sunday, though dinner-time saw most of the male passengers earnestly discussing the very excellent repast furnished by the burly, good-tempered old steward, who must have been sorely tried by the babel of orders and the practical jokes played on him by more than one member of our mess.

Monday afternoon we spent at Corfu, and heard the usual wail of lamentation from shopkeepers and hotel proprietors, at the cession of the isles to Greece. Whether the move was politic or not is very questionable; that it was most unpopular is doubtless the case. Steaming away the same evening, we reached Syra at four p.m. on Wednesday, the 9th, and then we learnt that the Russians had crossed the frontier of Armenia, and captured Bayazid without a struggle. Here we lost the Prussian nun, the charms of her Smyrniote admirer outweighed all other scruples, and, renouncing her intention of joining the Red Cross Hospital on the Danube, she took ship to the coast of Syria.

At dawn on the 11th we awoke to find ourselves steaming into the Golden Horn, and an hour later we were toiling up the hill from the custom-house to Misseri's. Mr. Murray, Mr. Murray! you have much

B 2

to answer for! confiding in your recommendation, the whole of our party went to the hostelry kept by the late dragoman of Eothen; but that any of us would endorse your opinion, or pay it a second visit, I much doubt.

After breakfast, in company with my naval *confrère*, I drove out to Therapia, where his Excellency Mr. Layard kindly promised me his assistance in obtaining the necessary papers to enable me to go to the front. The ambassador's earnest promises were to a great extent nullified by the extreme discourtesy of his Levantine dragoman, who certainly appears to think that the fact of sitting at a Minister's footstool robes him with a Minister's importance. Keeping appointments and answering letters do not seem to be part of the duty of embassy subordinate officials in Pera.

The following day was spent, in company with some of my fellow-passengers, in exploring the streets of Stamboul in search of horse-flesh. I suppose there are some good cattle in the city; we failed, however, to see anything resembling a horse, and returned, hot and thirsty, and somewhat out of temper, to our hotel. Here I heard of two animals, of which I eventually became the purchaser, and two better little beasts I never wish to own. One, a bay Arab, the property of Hobart Pasha; though peculiarly marked, a very handsome horse, and just as good as he looked. The other, a very ugly bay pony, with two big splints, a huge head, and altogether quite as ugly as the "Earl" was handsome; but as good as he was hideous, and that is saying a great deal.

Having overcome the difficulty of horses, the next thing was to obtain servants. Through the kindness of

Hobart Pasha I engaged two Armenian grooms who had been in his employ for some years. Krikol, the father, was a thoroughly trustworthy old gentleman, who spoke nothing but Armenian. "Possum," the son, spoke and read French, Turkish, and Armenian; a smart, willing, intelligent boy, he possessed all his father's reliability, with twice his intelligence. They certainly were the most favourable specimens of their class I have ever met. They did not lie, they did not cheat much; they stood all the hardships which we subsequently went through most cheerfully, and they had no scruples about going under fire.

A dragoman who could also cook, and who would not be above pitching tents, or putting his hand to all work, was the next difficulty, and it was not until just an hour before the boat left for Trebizond that Mr. Vincent Galdies was introduced to me. A Maltese by birth, and consequently a British subject, Mr. Vincent assumed great airs amongst the people with whom he associated in Armenia, and upheld the dignity of our flag in a comical though authoritative manner. His knowledge of the culinary art was limited; but, situated as we often were, it merited, as it received, our warmest encomiums. His knowledge of English was as small; many was the hearty laugh we indulged in at Mr. Vincent's expense. Poor fellow! the hardships of the campaign told on a not too strong constitution, and it is with much regret I have heard since leaving Pera that he now is in a rapid decline.

During my short stay in Constantinople I had interviews with several Turkish gentlemen, who one and all received me most courteously. They seemed impressed with the idea that both England and Austria would be forced to help them, though they felt pretty confident of holding their own without any foreign aid. There was no excitement or passionate declamation concerning the war. Everything was received in the usual Oriental stoical manner. The Volunteer barracks were slowly filling, chiefly with Circassians and Zeibeks, who strolled into the gates to enlist themselves with the same easy *nonchalant* air that the drummer outside was beating his drum. The good people of Stamboul itself seemed supremely indifferent on the subject; hundreds of able-bodied men, well calculated to form food for powder, were collected in groups at corners of streets discussing affairs in a matter-of-fact sort of way, without betraying any enthusiasm whatever.

In spite of the declaration of neutrality, there were several Englishmen seeking employment under the Porte, but the Turkish officials show great jealousy of English interference, and naturally wish to keep all the superior appointments in their own hands.

The Turkish army is divided into seven army corps, having their head-quarters as follows :—

1st	Army Corps,	Constantinople.
2nd	,,	Shumla.
3rd	,,	Monastir.
4th	,,	Erzeroum.
5th	,,	Damascus.
6th	,,	Bagdad.
7th	,,	Yemen.

The strength of each corps differed, and as the fourth is the only one liable to be called upon to play any part in the campaign, I will in a subsequent chapter give a detailed account of its constitution.

The authorised composition of a *corps d'armée* is two divisions of infantry, each consisting of two brigades of four battalions, one regiment of artillery of twelve batteries, two brigades of cavalry of two regiments each, and a company of engineers, the whole under the command of a Mushir or Marshal.

From what I saw of their regiments, they would not be amiss for the importation of a few smart commandants and adjutants; the physique was admirable, but the clothing, drill, setting-up, and discipline left a very great deal to be desired. The artillery seemed the smartest branch of the service, the guns being Krupp's breechloaders, of a similar pattern to those in use in the German army, while the heavy siege guns and guns of position were either Armstrongs or Krupps. The batteries, like ours, had six guns each, and were chiefly four or six pfünders. There were several mountain batteries of 5½-centimeter Krupps. These guns are mounted on mules similar to our Indian mountain batteries, though the carriages are more clumsy, and ammunition boxes not so complete. Each cavalry regiment is commanded by a colonel, with two majors and two adjutants under him; it is divided into six squadrons of 156 sabres, with one captain, one second captain, and three subalterns, as the staff. Each infantry regiment is commanded by a colonel, with a lieutenant-colonel under him. There is a major to each battalion, assisted by two adjutants, and there are eight companies of from 80 to 100 men in each, officered by one captain, one lieutenant, and one sub-lieutenant. To every regiment of cavalry and battalion of infantry there are several doctors and a paymaster. This is the organisation laid down, but I fear the army is far removed from it.

However, it reads well on paper. As there is no published army-list, and as there are no outward and visible
means of distinguishing regiments from each other—for
they are not numbered, nor have they different facings
—it must be almost as difficult for an officer on the staff
of the Turkish army to know the corps one from another
as it is for a stranger.

Leaving the Golden Horn on the afternoon of the
14th, we steamed slowly up the Bosphorus. I thus had
a good opportunity of looking at the new works for the
defence of those Straits. The old Roumeli Hissar is
supplemented by a powerful earthwork battery, mounting
twelve 10-inch Armstrongs, in embrasures, with traverses
between each gun portion, and six 12-inch Armstrongs
en barbette—*i.e.*, two in the centre of the face and two
on either flank; the face of the battery thus has fourteen
guns. The parapets are thirty-six feet in thickness, with
a command of forty feet over the sea-level. So I was
assured by a major on the Turkish staff, a fellow-passenger
of mine. Between the Roumeli Hissar and the Euxine
are four earthworks, each mounting four 10-inch Armstrongs; the Anatole Hissar has a battery of similar
profile and construction to the old fort of Europe, except
that in the centre are mounted four 12-inch guns *en
barbette*, making twenty pieces in all. Between it and
the sea are six earthworks, two mounting six guns and four
four guns each, all 10-inch Armstrongs. Four Turkish
ironclads are moored in the stream, and supplement the
defences considerably. I could not ascertain their names
or armament, but one looked very like the *Messoudieh*
I saw in the Thames in 1875, and I noticed two Gatlings
in the after quarter-deck ports of each of them.

Clearing the Bosphorus at eight p.m., we experienced

brisk wind and dense mist through the Black Sea, reaching Samsoon, half way to Trebizond, late on Wednesday night. Samsoon is a small town on the coast, with some interesting Greek ruins. There are three small masonry works, one at either extremity of the bay and one in the centre of the town; the garrison consists of two battalions of infantry and 200 gunners. The guns in these antiquated forts are old smooth 18-pounders, but the eastern battery has one 7-inch Armstrong, and the western battery two 40-pounders. The regiment which I saw on parade was a disgrace to any army—material excellent, but training, accoutrements, and discipline wanting. The equipment is there, for the greater part of the Turkish army is now furnished with the Henry-Martini rifle, with the Berdan cartridge; but the men have not been instructed in its use, and very few officers even understand the sights of their new weapon. Discipline in one sense of the word seems to be unknown, but I believe crime is very rare amongst the subordinate ranks. Sentries relieve each other at pleasure, lay their rifles down, and converse pleasantly with their officers on various topics, the most general one being abuse of the War Minister. I am sure even Lord Cardwell never suffered from our service half so much as Redif Pasha does from those under his command. In Constantinople the opinion was pretty openly expressed that he would fall in a few days, and that Raouf Pasha, the present Minister of Marine, would take over his portfolio. Raouf is an old St. Cyr cadet, and served in the Crimea. He is well educated, intelligent, and free from the obstinate conservatism so common among Turkish officials, being very popular in his own service, which is the army; and having been successful at the Ministry of

Marine, the military Turks look forward to having the army put on the same efficient footing as the navy is at present, and for their sakes I hope Raouf will soon rule the War Office.

Leaving Samsoon at eight a.m. on the morning of the 17th, we coasted along the mountainous shores of the Black Sea, reaching Ounieh at two p.m. I there went ashore with the correspondents of the *Temps* and *Moniteur*, fellow-passengers of ours, in order to see a battalion of volunteers, which a major on the general staff of the Turkish army had told me was lying here waiting for transport to Batoum. Volunteers, forsooth! The poor fellows were confined in the common jail of the town, and on seeing us clamoured loudly, imploring us to use our influence to obtain their release. They evidently were not fired with that love of country sufficient to induce them to sacrifice all home ties for the sole purpose of fighting the Giaour. Many of the men were fine, smart, intelligent, clean-limbed young fellows, just the stuff to make troops out of ; but there were a great many weeds too, and not a few greybeards quite unfit for work. I was told that the religious enthusiasm of these elders would inspire some of their more faint-hearted comrades with zeal, and so compensate for the lack of bodily vigour. I noticed that many of the men seemed scarcely to enjoy their position, and the wives, mothers, and sweethearts, sitting under the jail windows, fostered their discontent. The pride of taking part in a religious war scarcely seems to deaden human feelings, even in the breast of the Turk.

Although Ounieh is a telegraph station, we could hear no news from the seat of war; the merchants of the place seemed strangely uninterested in the subject.

They had a rumour that the Circassians had risen and massacred the garrison of Poti, but the story was told in such general terms, with such an absence of detail, that I could not credit it. They also said Kars had been relieved by the Erzeroum force; but as you have later and more trustworthy news than these good folk on the shores of the Euxine, I will not repeat their tattle.

One fellow-passenger, a major, who has lately been promoted from a captaincy in the 1st to the post of *chef de bataillon* in the 5th army corps, treated the whole subject with true Oriental indifference. He did not know, nor did he seem to care, to what regiment he was going, but would have preferred staying at Trebizond. He asked no questions as to recent news, but had an idea that the Russians had been driven back on Alexandropol with heavy slaughter. Although a first-class passenger, he did not dine at our table, but mixed entirely with some non-commissioned officers, who are going to Trebizond as deck cargo, took his meals with them, and played draughts with them all day.

The *Ulysses* steamed into the Trebizond Roads at three p.m. on the 18th, having taken ninety-six hours to perform the 540 miles from Constantinople. A fine iron-clad was at anchor, also a Turkish transport, which had just landed a cargo of guns, both heavy and light Krupp breechloaders. The field guns were minus limbers, and were intended for the reserves, which are being called out all over Asia Minor. The heavy pieces were meant for the defence of Ardahan and Erzeroum, but how they will be sent on to Ardahan no one seems to know, as the Russians are between it and the Turkish corps at Erzeroum. A British steamer, the *Florence Trencham,*

was in the harbour, having come in yesterday morning
from Poti, which she found completely abandoned. The
captain told me he had been ashore three days, and
found the custom-house deserted, all merchants' offices
closed, and being unable to find the consignees of his
cargo, had been forced to return. He says the Turkish
bombardment had done no harm. Very few of their
shells had reached the town, but the bombardment had
completely frightened all the inhabitants away. He
heard there of a rising among some hill-men in the
neighbourhood, but could give me no accurate information on any subject except that the town bore no traces
whatever of the recent bombardment. On landing I at
once proceeded to the house of the British vice-consul,
whose kindness and attention deserve my warmest
thanks. M. Biliotti did his utmost to procure horses
for my servants, and baggage animals for my luggage.
His efforts were so far successful that three hours after
touching the shore I had all my traps packed and was
ready to start. In spite of the day being the Mahomedan
Sunday, and all offices being closed, M. Biliotti himself
went to the governor of the town and procured the
necessary passports for me, and, notwithstanding the
order that all horses and mules are to be used solely for
the purpose of transporting war material to the front,
he succeeded in inducing the Pasha to spare me four.

At dinner I met Monsieur Riva, the Italian consul
at Trebizond. The conversation during the evening
was amusing as well as instructive. Our representative
is decidedly Turcophile in his views, whilst M. Riva is
strongly opposed to the continuance of the Ottoman
Empire. As he represents Germany, and, consequently,
is in charge of all Russian subjects, this gentleman has

his hands very full at the present time. He, however, was good enough to spare time to give me much information regarding the tribes in the Caucasus, and the state of feeling with regard to the war amongst the populace at Trebizond.

From the harbour Trebizond presents a view than which it would be hard to find a fairer. The brightly whitewashed houses cluster in groups on the sides of the well-timbered hills, which rise higher and higher until their snow-capped crests cut the deep blue arch of the Armenian sky. To the east the shore stretches away in hills thickly covered with vegetation, whilst to the west a rocky cliff—on which the citadel stands—shuts out a further peep of the same range. The surrounding country is full of ruins, Greek, Roman, Byzantine, and Genoese all bearing witness to the wealth discovered in the Anatolian provinces by its successive rulers. The capital of a kingdom in its earlier days, a port at which Xenophon embarked, and which had survived the fall of many a prouder empire, it was destined on passing into the hands of the Osmanli, in the year 1461, to become a mere fishing village. Closing the Bosphorus to all vessels but their own, the Porte effectually crippled the maritime trade to which Trebizond owed her importance. By the treaty of Adrianople, in 1829, the Dardanelles were once more opened, and by degrees Trebizond regained her trade, but her position, once lost, seems gone for ever. Lines of Russian, Turkish, Austrian, and French steamers now run weekly from Constantinople and the other ports in the Black Sea. The principal imports are Manchester goods for Persia, which here are transferred on to the backs of " the ships of the desert " or of mules, the caravans travelling viâ Erzeroum and Tabreez. Carpets and tobacco are brought in exchange; also skins and furs to a goodly amount. The opening of the Suez Canal, however, has to a great extent ruined this trade. The merchants of Teheran find it cheaper to procure their goods by the Persian Gulf, and eventually, if some other Reuter comes to the front, and actually builds railroads in the dominions of the Shah, the Erzeroum route will be almost entirely superseded.* Even Oriental merchants are well aware that any carriage is preferable to pack-carriage — with the daily lading and unlading, and continual exposure to weather.

In 1831, the first English vessel carried a cargo to Trebizond, the advantages it possessed as a sea-port for trade with Persia being ably pointed out by Mr. Brant, the consul there. Subsequently the Peninsular and Oriental Company ran a fortnightly steamer; but for the last few years our flag has seldom been seen in the roadstead. The decline of the Persian trade, doubtless, is the cause, for, if statistics are reliable, Trebizond is fast sinking into the same position whence she emerged in 1829. Whereas in 1858 the imports amounted to £3,750,529, and exports to £1,280,794, in 1875 they had fallen to £1,253,647 and £598,073, respectively—a decline of upwards of fifty per cent. !

Trebizond possesses many advantages: the climate is glorious, the surrounding hills full of game—hares, woodcock, partridges (the red-legged, much like the

* I am aware there is a general idea that the Persian trade has been diverted from the Trebizond and Erzeroum to the Poti-Tiflis route. A glance at the books of the British India Steam Navigation Company will show that English steamers now convey the greater bulk by the Persian Gulf route direct from London to Bushire.

chikorr of the Himalayas, and a grey bird resembling the common English species), quail in the season, and snipe near the river; the roadstead, too, is plentifully stocked with fish, turbot and sword-fish being the most sought after, whilst in the mountain streams trout abound.

There are many most interesting ruins in the immediate neighbourhood, the finest being the church and monastery of St. Sophia, which contain some magnificent frescoes. I regret that my short stay prevented my visiting these places.

Amongst other points worthy of notice, in these days of Taunus and " Polly," I ought not to forget a very excellent spring of mineral water, which our worthy consul patronises handsomely.

Just before sitting down to dinner, an aide-de-camp arrived from Lieutenant-General Djameel Pasha—who has been sent here to arrange the forwarding of all war material—asking me if I could spare him half an hour, as he wished to forward some letters to his brother, who commands a battalion at Kars, and also to hear the state of public opinion in Pera. I arranged to call on him at nine p.m., but slightly before that hour the general, unaccompanied by any staff officer, appeared at the consulate. I was much struck with him. He is a man of forty-two (so he says), looks about thirty-five, is very intelligent and active, speaks French well, and is very well up in all subjects of general interest. Entering the army at fifteen, he remained in the rank of Kolaghassi, or adjutant-major, for fifteen years, when, in consequence of his conduct in the Syrian and Cretan affairs, he suddenly found himself famous and a major-general; he now is a general of division of some seven years' standing, and hopes to obtain command of one of the corps in Asia Minor. He complains bitterly of the manner in which he is treated by the War Office authorities at Constantinople. Field guns without limbers are sent to him, and siege guns without carriages. He is furnished with no means of transport nor money for the payment of impressed cattle, and yet he is expected to push everything on to Erzeroum without any delay. As he says, he wants money to repair the road, which is practically impassable; and he finds it utterly impossible to get the country people to work cheerfully without prompt payment. It was a pleasure to converse with the general—a thorough soldier, a perfect gentleman, and an enthusiastic patriot. Without despairing of his country, he saw and acknowledged all her faults, and urged that she was not only not so black as she was painted, but that, as her artists were chiefly Russians, we ought not to look on the pictures as very life-like representations. He assured me that the Anaksia, or Abkhasians, as they are occasionally called, a hill tribe dwelling on the southern slopes of the Caucasus from Kertch to Anaklia, near Poti, were in a state of revolt; that they had attacked Soukoum Kaleh, on the Black Sea, killed the general commanding, massacred the garrison, and were flocking into Batoum in thousands. This corresponds with the news I heard at Samsoon, and also with the stories picked up by the captain of the steamer which had arrived from Poti. Djameel Pasha told me he had despatched 15,000 Snider rifles to Batoum to-day to arm these men, and was endeavouring to spread the revolt all down the Caucasus. The rifles were taken by the ironclad we saw in the roads as we entered—an Egyptian vessel, presented by the

Khedive to the Porte two years ago. Should this movement succeed, it will interfere with the Russian advance in Asia Minor somewhat, as they cannot push on with insurrection rife in their rear. The Abkhasians had burnt two towns near Poti, and were to make an attack on that place in conjunction with the ironclads of the Black Sea blockading fleet. The general also informed me that during the success of the Turkish Troops on the Chorouk Su, near Batoum, the Russians were surprised in a mountain pass, and after nine hours' fighting were forced to retire. He divides their estimated loss by ten, and says, from his information, they have lost about 400 killed, while the Turks had one lieutenant-colonel and 140 killed, with a slightly larger proportion wounded. The Russians had no artillery engaged.

The Abkhasians deserve a passing notice. For the following brief description of them I am indebted to Mr. Biliotti, Her Majesty's consul at Trebizond, whose knowledge of the tribes dwelling on the shores of the Black Sea is equalled only by his kindness to all Englishmen visiting them.

The earliest historical notice we have of this interesting tribe is, that in the third century their country was annexed to the Empire of Constantinople, under whose dominion they flourished until the thirteenth century, when they passed into the hands of the Genoese. The ruins of more than forty towns testify to the grandeur of their buildings in those days, the Temple of Pitsnada being a particularly magnificent structure. There are also many Greek and Byzantine ruins, the frescoes on the walls of which are worthy of study.

c

Initiated into the mysteries of Islamism in the early days of that religion, the Abkhasians for some centuries abandoned their idolatrous courses, and became tolerably faithful followers of the prophet, but by degrees the contact with Armenian and Georgian Christians almost effaced all traces of Mahomedanism, and they lapsed into their old superstitions. Their god, whom they name Tsitsinatelli, is all-present, and all-powerful; but sacrifices to him can only be made on the summit of Mount Dudrupeh, near the source of the Bzib river. Baptism is performed according to the rites of the Greek Church. Funeral ceremonies, except in the case of wealthy or great men, are never performed; whilst marriages are conducted in a most primitive manner. When an attachment springs up between a young couple, the man asks permission of her father to marry the daughter. If the parents approve, a dinner is given, to which all mutual friends are asked, and during the entertainment a male infant is brought in and placed on the knees of the bride, as a delicate hint that she now is permitted to be fruitful and multiply, and an expression of hope that her first-born may be a son.

The reigning house is that of Tchawachawadze, and though under the Russian rule they are bereft of power, they are permitted to retain their rank, and are treated with much deference by the Government. In the campaign of 1828-29, the head of the family placed his sword at the disposal of Paskiewitch; and at the present moment the Prince is commanding the regiment of Nijni Novgorod Dragoons, under Loris Melikoff.*

* He was badly wounded at the battle of Kizil Tepe on the 25th August, 1877, but subsequently recovered sufficiently to command the Cavalry Brigade, which under him did most excellent service at the assault on Kars, 18th October.

CHAPTER II.

TREBIZOND TO ERZEROUM.

Djameel Pasha at Work—The Sword of my Escort—Turkish Troops pushing on to the Front—Anatolian Trout—The Zigana Pass—A Night's Lodging —"Riz-au-gras"—The Pests of Armenia—Guns and Volunteers—Comfortable Quarters—*Esprit de Corps*—Monsieur Magack—Erzeroum—Its People and Defences—Its Drains and Dirt—Its Shepherd—Its Trade.

ERZEROUM, *May 23rd*.

ON the morning of the 19th, after bidding farewell to our hospitable consul, M. Biliotti, I went to return General Djameel Pasha's visit, and found him hard at work in a large, scantily-furnished room, endeavouring to arrange for the transport of guns, heavy and light, and of 30,000 cases of ammunition to the front. Strings of peasantry had volunteered to drag the artillery, and, as we conversed, gun after gun was pulled up the steep hill in front of the Pasha's house, the men singing cheerily as they toiled away. Ever and again the general would go into the street and cheer these villagers with a few kind words of encouragement. Little else has he to offer them. His Excellency had no news that he could give me, but very kindly furnishing me with letters of introduction to his brother, who commands a battalion in Kars, as well as to other officers in the 4th army corps, and giving me some sausages of Turkish manufacture, which he highly commended, bid me God-speed, and at noon I set off on my ride to Erzeroum, escorted by two zaptiehs, or mounted police-

c 2

men, kindly provided by Djameel Pasha. These men were dressed in the usual uniform of the Turkish cavalry, and armed with Winchester repeating rifle and sabre. Their accoutrements, both in material and cleanliness, left much to be desired. I was amused, though I cannot say I was surprised, after cantering for a few miles, to hear a clanking sound behind me, denoting the fall of a sword on the metalled road. I pulled up, and saw that the unwonted strain had carried away the slings of one of my escort's sword-belt. He seemed used to such accidents, for quietly tucking the weapon between his leg and the saddle, he announced that he was perfectly ready to proceed.

For the first few miles the road winds along the shores of the Black Sea, and then, turning sharp off to the south, follows the right bank of the Degirmen river, to a place called Djhevizlik, distant sixteen miles. Here post-horses are changed, and seeing my baggage, which had been waiting for me since morning, shifted on to new animals, I selected the best-looking pony in the stables, and at once starting off again, reached the next post stage, Khamsi-kui, in about two hours. Again changing animals, I proceeded, and in about half an hour overtook a battalion of the 5th army corps, commanded by Colonel Ahmed Hamid Bey, to whom Djameel Pasha had kindly given me letters of introduction. I found the colonel had taken up his quarters in a very comfortable little "khan," or guest-house, some short distance from his men. I sat for about half an hour, conversing with the colonel and two or three of his officers, who came into the room on hearing an Englishman was present. One and all seemed perfectly satisfied that England would help them in the coming struggle, not only with an army, as she did in 1854-55, but also with what Turkey needs far more—money. It was with some difficulty I could get away from my new-found friends, who were most anxious that I should march with the regiment to Erzeroum. Time, however, was of vital importance to me, and as I had already learnt that the Turkish watchword, "yahvash, yahvash" (slowly, slowly), is the cry even of troops moving up to the seat of war, I declined their kind hospitality, and, mounting my post pony, started off for Zigana.

The beauties of Kashmir and Kangra pale before the scenery I now passed through. The road—an excellent metalled highway, some fifteen feet in breadth—followed the course of a clear, rippling stream, the banks of which were in many places overhung with thickets of ash and hazel. In the long still reaches more than once I saw the speckled beauty of our English brooks rise greedily to the small blue quill-gnat, which, even in Asiatic waters, is a sure killer; and as I pushed my pony on, I could not help regretting that I had none of Charles Farlow's handiwork with me, wherewith to try my skill on the Matscka trout.

As I ascended the slopes of the Chulat Dagh range, which had to be crossed before reaching my halting-place of Zigana, the roadway wound along a narrow mountain pass, down which the brook dashed and foamed with all the wildness of a Scotch burn. On either side towered huge basaltic columns, giving an air of grandeur to the scenery, which, softened down by the luxuriant vegetation growing on the lower slopes of the mountains, was again brightened by the many-hued flowers, which in wild profusion lent colour to the whole. The sombre tints of the oak, pine, larch, beech, and birch, were thrown into contrast by the rhododendron, peony, and wild rose, which grew in their midst ; whilst on the grassy banks of the stream wild geraniums, tulips, cowslips, and primroses, lent a home-like air to the scene.

It was dark ere I reached the crest of the Chulat Dagh, near 8,000 feet above sea-level. The snow had been cleared from the roadway, but still lay in widespread masses on the neighbouring slopes ; a chill breeze whistling up the pass, grew still more piercing as it gained intensity from the snowy bed it passed over. It was with no small sense of relief that I spurred my pony down the mountain road, and gained the shelter of the thick forests on the southern slopes of the range.

The " bir sat " (one hour) of my zaptieh was not unlike the " ek koss " of an Indian guide, for it was past ten by my watch ere I reached the village of Zigana, which (notwithstanding the noisy greeting accorded me by the numerous dogs my entrance disturbed from their slumbers) seemed locked in everlasting sleep. Not a light was to be seen, not a sound to be heard, except the dreary howl of the village dogs as they accompanied us in our search for a night's shelter. After knocking at the doors of about a dozen khans, my zaptieh broke the news gently to me that he feared there was no help for it, but the Bey must sleep in the post-house stable. It was with some difficulty we could induce the owner of this edifice to open his doors to us, and when, having succeeded in doing so, I looked in, and saw the number and nature of my fellow-lodgers, I could scarcely persuade myself to enter. A sharp rain drove all thoughts of sleeping in the open out of my head, so procuring a light and despatching my zaptieh for some wood, water, and fire, I strolled round my bed-room.

It was the basement floor of the principal khan in the place, in which (it being filled with troops proceeding to the front) I could obtain not even a corner. The stable consisted of a long, low room, measuring forty-eight feet by eighteen feet, scarcely six feet in height. Down the centre was a long heap of manure, the accumulation of months; on either side were rows of horses and bullocks, whilst huddled up at the farther end lay a group of sheep and lambs. Forty-three animals and six men shared my humble abode. These latter were crowded round a small lamp in one corner of the room, smoking and using not very complimentary language towards the Giaour who had invaded their sanctum. The atmosphere inside the place was stifling, the odour overpowering, so I took up a strong position near the door, determined to have as much fresh air as possible. My zaptieh returned in about a quarter of an hour, and we together made a fire, then ferreting out a saucepan from my hoorjeen (small leather mule trunk), and a cake of "Riz-au-gras" from my holsters, I prepared my dinner. I cannot too strongly recommend these invaluable productions of the "Société General des Potages Economiques" to those travellers to whom expense is an object. They are very cheap, very portable, and, though not quite so tempting as the more costly soups, yet the fact that eight cakes of the "Riz-au-gras" occupy the same space as one tin of soup makes them preferable to those whose means of carriage are limited. A tumbler of very dirty water, the evil effects of which were nullified by a dash of brandy, washed down my meal, and was conducive to a sound sleep. Alas! my fellow-lodgers were averse to fresh air, and no sooner had I rolled myself up in my blanket than one stealthily rose and closed the door. To open it again was the work of an instant, and as there appeared every probability of a second Eastern Question being raised on that same subject, I informed my zaptieh that if it was again closed he should have to stand sentry with his back against it for the remainder of the night. This threat induced him to enter into an alliance, offensive and defensive, with me, and I turned round once more in search of sleep. Vain effort ! I had counted forty-three animals in that den but half an hour previously; I now was turned into a grazing ground for a hundred times that number of those domestic insects which are supposed to haunt English lodging-houses. I learnt a little of the habits of these diminutive creatures when occupying Barra-durrees, on the road to Srinuggur, but a real knowledge of their powers must be reserved for those whose fortune leads them to the khans and odahs of Armenia. I was forced to own that I was profoundly ignorant of their ways : their sole aim and object seem to be to deprive their human enemies of all sleep ; and the ingenuity they display in discovering new methods of assault, their perseverance in overcoming every obstacle that man can contrive to prevent their access to his flesh, the utter disregard they have for all those chemical preparations which are presumed to be "insect destroyers," prove most conclusively to my mind that Armenia is the home and birthplace of the " industrious flea." It was with no small sense of relief that at one a m. I heard footsteps outside, and my fellow-traveller from Constantinople, " Mr. Williams," entered the stable ; fortunately, my soup was still hot, and I was enabled to give him what he stood in great need of—a good meal. Leaving him in undisturbed possession of the khan, I got up at four a.m., and started off once more towards Erzeroum, descending the lower slopes of the Chulat Dagh, and passing through Ardasat, Gumesh Khaneh, and Khadrak, I reached Baiboort about two p.m.

Here I was assailed by two men, who, like most Orientals, seemed persuaded that all English are doctors, and who insisted upon my prescribing for them. From past experience I knew that severe and sudden remedies are much appreciated by all dwellers in the East, who certainly would never believe in homœopathic treatment. My knowledge of the Pharmacopœia is limited, so was my store of medicines; but the never-failing Cockle came to the rescue, and giving each man six pills, to be taken three at a time, I left them and rode on. I presume they still live, but I doubt if they will ever forget the Ingliz hakeem who passed through Baiboort on the 20th May, 1877.

Ascending the Kop Dagh range, which was covered with snow, and on the summit of which I passed a battalion of the 5th army corps, straggling in a manner that showed too plainly that the want of competent regimental officers, and the utter absence of discipline, would be the ruin of the Ottoman cause. It was nearly dark ere I reached the next staging-house ; but as the road was good I determined to push on, and reached Karabooyak at ten p.m., having covered, according to my watch and the milestones, one hundred and twenty-six miles in seventeen hours. I here found a very comfortable room attached to the post-house, stables luxurious as compared with my previous night's lodgings, inasmuch as I was alone, and enjoyed comparative immunity from the visits of nocturnal enemies.

The road the whole way from Trebizond was in excellent order—by far the best hill road I have yet seen, one that throws quite into the shade the Himalayan and Tibet road from Simla to Cheenee, and infinitely superior to that which runs down our Punjab frontier from Kohat to Jacobabad. Every few miles we passed bands of peasants dragging heavy siege guns up the steep inclines, singing merrily to airs played on the zoorna and dhaol, similar instruments, with similar names, to the soornai and dhole of the Affghan tribes; and more than once I passed small bodies of volunteers pushing on to the front; some of them were headed with a small band, and all carried the national standard. They were in their own peasant dress, armed with their own arms, old flint smooth-bores; but these they hoped to exchange in Erzeroum for new Martini-Peabodies.

I had only twenty-one miles to do the following morning, and I rode into the Consulate at Erzeroum at about ten a.m., where the hospitable representative of her Majesty received me with much kindness, and gave me what seemed drink fit for the gods—a bottle of Ind and Coope. From him I learnt that Ardahan had fallen, Mukhtar Pasha's forces were much scattered, and that the Russians were fast making their hold good in the eastern districts of Asia Minor. An American missionary, Rev. J. E. Pierce, very kindly placed a room at my disposal, so now I am resting in clover, waiting for my baggage to arrive before proceeding to the front. Moreover, I wished to spend a day or two at Erzeroum, to look over the defences of the place, and ascertain what means Mukhtar Pasha has of making any stand in this neighbourhood.

During my ride I passed five battalions of Regular

troops and three of the Reserve Mustahfiz, pushing on
to the front; I also saw four batteries of Krupp's field
guns, 34 guns of position, Krupp's pattern, but made
of bronze — I learnt that they had been cast in the
Tophané at Constantinople; they were chiefly 12 and
15 centimeter guns, but I believe there are some of 18
on the road—and nine 8-inch rifled howitzers. The
regiments of regular troops were from Syria, and the
physique of the men, on the whole, was good, though
there was a great deal of falling out, and many men
were left lying sick by the roadside. They were armed
well, four battalions having the Martini-Henry, the
fifth the Snider rifle. The accoutrements were very
bad, one pouch behind containing fifty rounds, belts
and pouches of bad material, bad shape, and ·in very
bad condition. The rifles also were in a shocking
state—evidently inspection of arms does not occupy
company officers many moments at morning parade.
The men all had great-coats, with hoods, some of dark-
blue cloth, some of brown homespun; knapsacks, and
canteens. The shoes were all of different patterns, and
generally in bad condition—a sandal made of strips of
carpet being the favourite. There was a fair supply of
tents to each corps, but no commissariat transport, no
hospital comforts, and no doctors. The officers appeared
perfectly ignorant of the meaning of the word discipline,
and the men sauntered along as they pleased. The
officers were generally mounted on little ponies, which
carried their bedding, clothes, and cooking utensils, and
themselves. Their clothing was in as bad order as that
of the men. I noticed one mule carrying a tent which
had fallen into a muddy quagmire, and was fast being
submerged. The man in charge was doing his best

to extricate the poor beast, and called on comrade after comrade who passed him to lend a hand; but they one and all passed by on the other side. Finally, the officer commanding the rear-guard came up, and, in spite of his appeals, the poor wretch was left struggling with his dying mule and abandoned tent. There seems to be no enthusiasm—no *esprit de corps*—among the officers. To note one thing, I saw just opposite the guard-tent of a regiment in camp a small bridge, which was broken down, making the road quite impassable for guns. The officer commanding the regiment knew that a large convoy of carts and guns was following him, and yet no attempts were made to repair the bridge, although 500 or 600 men were lolling about the camp. Strings of arabas (bullock-carts much resembling the hackery of India) were on the road the whole way from Trebizond to Erzeroum, laden with tents, corn, and ammunition; but the rate of progression was so slow that more than a fortnight must elapse before any of this can reach Mukhtar Pasha.

The following morning, in company with the talented interpreter to the British Consulate, Monsieur Antoine Magack, I visited the various bazaars, hospitals, and other places of interest. Permission to go over the detached works was refused me, and as a similar refusal had been accorded to a request preferred by Colonel Macgregor and Captain Lockwood, of the Quarter-Master General's Department in Bengal, I was not surprised at my rebuff.

Situated on the southern portion of a large plain some thirty miles in length by twelve in breadth, and nestling, as it were, under the crests of the Devi-Dagh range, Erzeroum is fully exposed to the cold blasts which

whistle over the peaks of the Giaour-Dagh. To the
north of the town, at a distance of three miles, flows the
Euphrates, here called the Kara-Su, or Blackwater, and
a small, muddy-looking, insignificant stream it is. The
city possesses few peculiarities. The ancient citadel, a
brick building almost in ruins, consists of a double wall,
with ditch in front; the governor's house and some
barracks are in it, but for defensive purposes it is useless.
An enceinte on Vauban's principle, with a perimeter of
about three miles, surrounds the place. The ditches
cannot be flooded, nor are they deep enough to afford
any serious obstacle to an assaulting army. The escarp
and counterscarp have been allowed to fall into dis-
repair, and can be scaled in many places. Nor are there
any ditch defences, except the fire from the flanks of the
bastions. The main ditch is not extended round the
ravelins, and on the southern face the ground slopes
down into the work. The parapets are all revetted with
sods, laid on vertically, and, as may be imagined, the
revetments are not of much value.

The guns, which are all Krupp's breechloaders, the
majority being 12, 15, or 18 centimeter, are mounted
en barbette. The carriages are painted scarlet, and,
whilst affording a pleasing sight to the eye, they make
an admirable target for an enemy's fire. In addition
to the bastioned enceinte, there is a series of outworks
built on the adjoining hills, as well as I was able to
judge, following the general rule in Turkish fortifications,
all of which were commanded by neighbouring heights.

Erzeroum is by no means a striking-looking place,
even for an Oriental town. It contains about 40,000
inhabitants, the majority being Mahomedans; but there
is a large Christian community; perhaps the finest

public building is the Armenian cathedral. I was informed there were forty-five mosques and nineteen baths. I won't dispute the point. Twice that number would be far too few to cleanse either the minds or bodies of the good people of the place, for a more evil-looking, dirty set of rascals as were daily to be seen grouped at the corners of the streets, I have never met. Persians and Georgians, Circassians and Kurds, Jews, Greeks, Armenians, and Turks, all dwell together, but not in brotherly love. The wrangling and noise going on at every door were never-ceasing; at the same time, the different costumes, composed, as many were, of the bright colours which all Orientals love, lent a pleasing effect to the scene. The cause is beyond me, for a Turkish saddle is no worse than an Indian one, but I certainly saw more sore backs in Erzeroum than I have ever seen before; and whether it is the air of the place, or contact with Turkish rule, I know not, but I never saw so much cruelty to animals. I have seen horses, wounded, sore, and lame, in such a state that to kill them would have been mere charity, driven to the nearest fountain, rather than that their brutal owner should have the trouble of carrying a bucket of water twenty yards to water them.

Situated on the slopes of the Devi-Dagh range, Erzeroum should be a splendidly-drained city, whereas, with the exception of Kars, it is the very dirtiest town I have been in. The streets are badly paved; whilst down the side runs an open channel, into which all the refuse from the houses is thrown. Much of this is devoured by the dogs, who, I think, exceed even their brethren of Constantinople or Cairo in numbers. What is left by them remains to be washed away by the next shower, and in the meantime poisons the air and breeds disease. The houses are for the most part lower than the street, and are built of stones and mud, with flat roofs, and, as a rule, have but one floor. The windows are seldom glazed, but in winter are covered over with greased paper; as summer approaches, this is torn off to admit fresh air, which during the cold months is religiously excluded. Except in the houses of the rich, horses, cattle, sheep, and poultry all share the same roof as their owners, so the atmosphere inside an Armenian house is simply indescribable.

The most striking buildings in the city are the Iki-Chifteh, two exceedingly graceful minarets standing near the citadel. They are fluted, like Byzantine columns, with a light-blue, highly-glazed brick. Originally they formed a portion of a Mahomedan college, but the dome-like roof of the original structure has fallen in, and none have cared to repair the place. I could learn no more about them, nor could I gather any information concerning the numerous circular towers with conical tops, which greet the eye in every direction. I was told they were tombs of holy men who died in the fourteenth century. There must have been a goodly number of holy men in Erzeroum in those days!

One of the most amusing scenes in Erzeroum was the witnessing the operations of the herdsman. Leaving the city in the morning, accompanied by two dogs, he would start from his own home with his own small flock, and perambulate the city. At every turning he would be joined by yet other flocks and herds, brought to the corners by their owners or their owners' servants. These would soberly amalgamate with their former acquaintances, and walk quietly out of the city towards the Euphrates plain. In the evening, on his return, he would simply follow his old route, and as each little flock neared its own home, it would break into a trot, and scurry off to its own door. The intelligence of the dogs here showed itself. There never was the slightest attempt to head them back; though such slack discipline as breaking the ranks at any other time of the day would be promptly checked. Every owner of cattle, or sheep, or goats—and nearly every household in Armenia possesses some live stock—pays the herdsman a small sum annually for the trouble in escorting the beasts to the plain. I never knew which to admire most, the utter *nonchalance* of the man, the sagacity of the dogs, or the bright intelligence of the cattle and sheep, which joined in the whole affair as a matter of course— though I fancy it would take some generations before English beasts would behave likewise.

There are a few shops in Erzeroum where European goods may be bought. These are kept chiefly by Armenians. As in most Oriental towns, each craft keeps to its own quarter—one street being devoted to workers in iron, another to workers in brass, a third to leather workers, a fourth to tailors, to silversmiths, to provision sellers, to butchers, and so on. The bazaar where meat was sold was the one to be avoided—flies abound; and the dogs looking hungrily up at the joints, which appeared to have been torn from the carcase, not cut, as in England, gave me the idea that the canine species aided the butchers in their labours. The "Kassai" bazaar in Indian towns, notably at Kalabagh, on the Indus, is bad enough, but they are simply magnificent markets when compared to the like places in Asiatic Turkey.

The climate of Erzeroum is bad—bitterly cold in winter, during which snow falls to a depth often of four feet; it is oppressively hot in summer. The want of drainage and the filthy habits of the people cause an immense amount of sickness, typhoid and dysentery being the principal scourges.

The manufacture of brass is carried on to a great extent in Erzeroum, some of the brazen vessels and large candlesticks being particularly handsome. There is also a large trade in leather goods—saddles, bridles, and such like; silks and wine from Kharpoot; carpets and tobacco from Persia; cats from Van; furs from Russia; and Manchester goods are also seen in large quantities. The wine is a very fair red wine, not unlike Bordeaux, but decidedly superior to much that we drink in England. I thought it preferable to some Georgian wine given me in Kars. The price was moderate, and assuredly during the hot months it was most refreshing.

D

CHAPTER III.

THE HOSTILE ARMIES.

The Turkish Army, and its Changes during the Present Century—Thirty Years Stagnation—Abdul Azeez's Reforms—Equality of Race as regards Military Service—Nizam, Ichtayat, Redif, and Mustahfiz—Military Districts—Administration Staff—Sappers and Miners—Artillery—Guns—Equipment of Mounted Branch—Horses—Pay of all Grades—Cavalry Equipment—Horses—Men—Pay of all Grades—Infantry Staff—Uniform and Equipment—Arms and Pay—Rations and Quarters—Scarcity of Officers—Mukhtar's Forces—Russian Army—Composition—Artillery—Position of Turkish Army—Position of Russian Army.

ERZEROUM, *27th May.*

BEFORE entering further into the details of the campaign, it may be advisable to describe somewhat fully the organisation of the Turkish army, and in doing so I shall dwell at greater length on the constitution of the Fourth or Armenian Corps, although it is but a sample of the whole.

Until the year 1801 the corps of Janissaries formed the sole standing army of the empire. In that year, however, Sultan Selim III. raised a new corps, styled the " Nizam geded," officered, armed, and clad after the style of European armies. In 1807 he was deposed, and his army massacred. In 1826, on the disbandment of the corps of Janissaries, Mahomed II. determined to organise his forces on the Prussian model. Taking advantage of the peace after the campaign 1828-29, and availing himself of the services of one Captain von Moltke, then travelling in Turkey, he raised an army of 215,000 men, based on the model of the Prussian Landwehr. In

1834 this system was in fair working order, and in 1837 a school for young officers was established in Constantinople. In 1842 Abdul Medjid improved on the work of his predecessor. All able-bodied men between the years of eighteen and twenty-six were liable to serve five years in the active army, after which they were drafted into the Redif, or reserve regiments. The artillery were organised on the Prussian, the other branches on the French, system. The army was divided into six *corps d'armée*, each of two divisions of three brigades, the total strength being about 300,000 men.

Thus the army remained for thirty years. The victory of Sadowa, however, opened Sultan Abdul Azeez's eyes to the fact that his troops were not fit to cope with those of other European powers; and in 1869 a committee, of which the late Hussain Avni Pasha was President, assembled to decide on a new military system that would provide an army large enough to satisfy the requirements of modern warfare. The result of their labours was the Hatti-Houmayoun of the 18th of February, 1869, which, annulling all previous decrees on the subject, drew up a series of regulations to provide for the better defence of the country. Theoretically these are second to none in the world.

Having first satisfied themselves that a force of 150,000 men would be ample for the peace footing of their army, the committee judged that a first reserve of 50,000 would be necessary for the purpose of strengthening the standing army in the event of rebellion or disturbances in the interior of the kingdom. Looking to disquieting causes from without, the conclusion was arrived at that 200,000 men in Roumelia and 150,000 in Anatolia would suffice for all defensive purposes, while an additional 300,000, as a last reserve, should be organised, in order to have at hand an army fully prepared for any eventuality. Having thus laid down the strength of the army, it now became a difficult question to determine the means for providing a healthy flow of young blood through its ranks. Since the abolition of the corps of Janissaries in 1826 the army had undergone many transformations, all being based on the Prussian model; therefore, the population was in some measure accustomed to conscription, and was consequently prepared for the edict that all able-bodied males—Jews, Greeks, and Christians—were alike, with Mahomedans, liable to military service between the ages of twenty and twenty-six. Religion, however, has proved an insuperable bar to military employment, even in this great war, when the resources of the empire have been strained to their uttermost. In the Armenian army corps not a single Christian was to be found; Mahomedans flocked in sufficient numbers to fill the ranks of the standing army; so the services of Jews and Christians not being needed, a poll-tax, varying from sixteen to thirty piastres per annum, is levied on all Jews and Christians, they thus purchasing exemption from service. As this tax is permanent, and clings to the Giaours from birth to death, it falls heavily—too heavily—on the poorer classes. A Mahomedan wishing to escape service pays a fine not exceeding 2,300f. and not less than 1,500f.

The duration of military service was fixed at twenty years for all arms, and this period was apportioned as follows:—Six years in the Nizam, or standing army; six years in the Redif, or reserve army; eight years in the Mustahfiz, or territorial army. The Nizam, or standing army, furnishes the 150,000, or peace-footing organisation. In this every man serves—in the infantry four, in the mounted or ordnance branches five years, after which he is draughted into the Ichtayat, which has a fixed strength of 60,000, and is supposed to serve as that first reserve to be drawn upon in the event of internal complications. The infantry soldier serves two years, other branches one year in this force. Having completed his time with the colours, the Nizam soldier, should there be no need of his services, is permitted to go to his home, when he reports himself to the officer commanding his recruiting district. From him short periods of leave may be obtained, not exceeding a month at a time. Permission to marry is refused, and the Ichtayat soldier is liable at any moment to be recalled to his own regiment or battalion, on the rolls of which he is still borne. Thus it may justly be considered that the Ichtayat consists of Nizam soldiers at home on furlough, for they still draw pay and rations. Having completed his six years with the colours, the soldier is transferred to the Redif, or reserve army. This is again subdivided into two " bans " or classes, in each of which a service of three years is required. These furnish 240 battalions of 800 men, or the 190,000 men requisite to bring the army up to its strength of 400,000 men, deemed the number requisite for the proper defence of Roumelia and Anatolia.

Like the Ichtayat, the Redifs are under the orders of the officers commanding their recruiting district ; but they are only called upon to serve in case of war, and for short periods of training, under the direction of the Minister of War. They obtain pay and rations only when enrolled. The Redif battalions are supposed to be complete in officers, non-commissioned officers, and men. Their arms, uniforms, and equipments are in store at their recruiting depôts, and every man knows, in the event of his services being required, exactly where to go.

Having served six years with the colours and six with the Reserve troops, the Turkish soldier is now draughted into the Mustahfiz, or Territorial Army, the period of service in which is eight years. This force is destined to furnish the 300,000 men necessary to bring the total strength of the Ottoman forces to 700,000. The *cadres* of all these corps are complete; but it must be remembered that a vast army numbering 863 battalions, or 676,200 men, is nominally enrolled in the infantry of the Redif and Mustahfiz. Being without officers, they cannot be considered tactical units of the army, but they practically form inexhaustible reserves from which the gaps formed by war may readily be filled.

The Turkish army is divided into seven army corps, each of which has a territorial as well as a numerical designation; and the empire is apportioned into seven circles, one of which is allotted to each corps. These circles are subdivided into districts, the number varying in each circle, and these districts are once more divided each into four divisions. Each of these divisions forms, as it were, a depôt centre, and is the head-quarters of three reserve battalions—viz., one of each class. A permanent staff is quartered in the depôt barracks, where are stored the arms, equipment, and clothing of the men. Each military district comprising four divisions furnishes, therefore, one complete regiment of each class. The regimental staff are quartered in the chief town of the district, while in the capital of the circle dwells the staff of the army corps. The following is a table showing the name and designation of each corps, with the number of divisions and districts into which it is divided:—

1st, or Constantinople, Corps d'Armée.	Ismidt. Broussa. Koniah. Kali Sultanieh.	Isbarta. Kaisarieh. Kara Hissar.
2nd, or Shumla, Corps.	Shumla. Sofia. Adrianople.	Tchorum. Angora. Boli.
3rd, or Monastir, Corps.	Monastir. Jasina. Uskub. Drama.	Smyrna. Aidin. Seraievo. Travnik.
4th, Armenian Corps.	Erzeroum. Van. Kharpoot.	Diarbekir. Sivas. Kars.
5th, Damascus.	Damascus. Antioch. Jerusalem.	Aleppo. Beyrout. Adana.
6th, Bagdad.	Bagdad. Mossoul. Kherkouk.	Hilla. Solimanie. Bassorah.
7th, Yemmen.	In course of formation.	

The districts of Trebizond, Tireboli, and Samsoon, each furnish four battalions in either ban of Redifs. These troops are not permanently attached to any corps, but are meant for coast defences—during the war they will be employed in Batoum.

Taking the Fourth Army Corps as an example, it will

be seen that it comprises six districts, and is, therefore, composed of six regiments of Nizam, six of Redif of the 1st ban, six of Redif of the 2nd ban, six Mustahfiz— 24 regiments, or 96 battalions of troops in all. The territorial divisions of the corps are as follows :—

1st District, Erzeroum.—1st Division, Erzeroum ; 2nd, Erzingjan ; 3rd, Kara Hissar ; 4th, Arabkir.

2nd District, Kars.—1st Division, Kars ; 2nd, Batoum ; 3rd, Olti ; 4th, Artvin.

3rd District, Kharpoot.—1st Division, Kharpoot ; 2nd, Molahja ; 3rd, Behesni ; 4th, Argans.

4th District, Sivas. — 1st Division, Sivas ; 2nd, Amasya ; 3rd, Tokat ; 4th, Zileh.

5th District, Van.—1st Division, Van ; 2nd, Bitlis ; 3rd, Sert ; 4th, Bashkale.

6th District, Diarbekir.—1st Division, Diarbekir ; 2nd, Hidja ; 3rd, Djezireh ; 4th, Mardin.

Nizam corps are known only numerically as the 3rd battalion of the 2nd regiment of the Fourth Army Corps ; whereas the battalions of reserve or territorial armies are distinguished by their local designation, as the Kharpoot Mustahfiz battalion, or the 2nd ban of the Djezireh Redif. Cavalry and artillery are distinguished in the same manner.

The constitution of an army corps, the command of which is entrusted to a Mushir, or marshal, is as follows :—Two divisions of infantry, each commanded by a Ferik, or lieutenant-general. One brigade of cavalry, commanded by a Liva, or general of brigade. One regiment of artillery, commanded by a Liva ; one company of engineers.

The staff of each corps is divided into two distinct portions—the executive and the administrative. The former consists of the Mushir, aided by a major-general, as a rule, as chief of the staff, one colonel, one lieutenant-colonel, one major, and seven adjutants-major, and is entrusted with all questions relating to the drill, discipline, or movements of troops in their command. The administrative staff is presided over by a lieutenant-general, with the designation of " Reiss ; " he is assisted by two colonels, one lieutenant-colonel, one commissary-general, one surgeon-general, and one first-class War Office clerk. All matters concerning pay, clothing, and provisioning the men, together with questions relating to hospitals, repairs of buildings, ordnance stores, and armament of men and fortresses, are decided by this body.

To touch briefly on the main points connected with the various branches of the army, commencing with the scientific corps, not one sapper could be discovered in that corps.* Nominally there is a corps of engineers in the Turkish army. The First Corps d'Armée boasts of five battalions of eight companies, but the other corps have to rest satisfied with one company each, the strength of which is six officers and one hundred and eighty-one non-commissioned officers and men, the command being vested in an adjutant-major. Of the pay and equipment of this branch I could learn nothing.

As in other armies, the battery forms the tactical unit of the artillery. These are massed into battalions, each of which consists of three batteries, and into regiments, consisting of four battalions. To each regiment, however, a certain number of extra batteries are attached

---

* I asked many officers to give me information concerning the corps of Sappers and Miners, but to every inquiry I learnt that in the 4th Army Corps engineers did not exist; the Chief of the Staff performing the duties of that branch of the service.

—in all cases one or two of mountain guns, in some one or two field or horse. With the exception of the First, or Constantinople Army Corps, which contains three, one regiment of twelve batteries is considered the normal complement of a corps. The first battalion of a regiment is composed of horse, the other three of field batteries. The regiment is commanded by a Liva Pasha, or general of brigade, with a colonel and lieutenant-colonel on his staff, to which is attached a first-class veterinary surgeon and thirteen other sub-officers. The command of an artillery battalion is entrusted to a *chef de bataillon*, or Bin-Bashi, with two adjutants-major, medical officers, a veterinary surgeon, and three sub-officers as a staff.

All batteries have the same number of officers—namely, one captain and two lieutenants. Horse batteries have 164 non-commissioned officers and men; field, 162; mountain and mitrailleuse, 107 and 139 respectively.

The equipment of a horse battery consists of six guns, two ammunition wagons, one baggage wagon, and one forge in the first line, with twelve ammunition wagons in the second line, and eighty-seven and one hundred and fifty draught horses in the first and second lines respectively. A field battery has the same equipment in every particular, except that the number of riding horses is twenty-five. As a rule, the ammunition, relegated to the second line, is carried on arabas or on pack ponies in small mule trunks.

A mountain battery consists of six guns. The complement of ammunition is carried in ninety-six mule trunks, two on each mule. As a rule, the guns, limbers, wheels, and carriages are carried on the backs of mules, though often they are to be seen dragged with one animal in the shafts. During the campaign in Armenia I was much struck with the battery mules in Armenia —strong, fine animals, many fourteen hands. They mostly come from Persia, and command a long price— indeed, a man asked me £35 for a really good animal, and not only refused to take less, but rode away when I offered it.

There were no mitrailleuse batteries in Asia, but the authorised equipment is twenty-six saddle and one hundred and twenty-six draught horses, six guns; the same number of wagons in the first line as field batteries, and eleven in the second line.

The field-guns in use in the Turkish service, as far as I had an opportunity of judging, are all on the Krupp pattern, made of steel, and are either 4-pounder with a calibre of eight centimeters, or 6-pounder with a 9-centimeter calibre. The twelve batteries in a regiment of artillery are equally divided—six being 4-pounder, six being 6-pounder. The smaller gun with limber complete weighs 3,960 lb.; the larger gun weighs 4,208 lb. All guns are drawn by six horses in both horse and field batteries. There are two systems in vogue in the mountain batteries. The first is Whitworth's small 3-pounder rifled gun. In Asia there were a few of these in Kars. Two, early in the campaign, were entrusted to Moussa Pasha and his Circassians, and were lost by them in the affair at Beghli Ahmed on the 29th of May. The second system is Krupp's bronze $5\frac{1}{2}$-centimeter breech-loading gun; its weight is about two hundredweight.

In addition to the field artillery in the Turkish army there is a very strong body of garrison gunners, destined for the charge of the various fortresses. The company is the unit of this branch, and the number of companies varies in each army corps. The strength of the unit is fixed at three officers and 150 non-commissioned officers and men. The 1st Army Corps has 96 companies, 14,400; the 2nd Army Corps has 20 companies, 3,000; the 3rd Army Corps has 21 companies, 3,150; the 4th Army Corps has 12 companies, 1,800; the 5th and 6th Army Corps have each three companies, 450; and the 7th Army Corps has five companies, 750. The twelve companies in the Armenian Corps were distributed among the fortresses of Ardahan, Batoum, Erzeroum, and Kars. In Europe guns of a calibre of 27 centimeters are mounted on the fortifications. In Asia there are a few 18-centimeter guns in Erzeroum; but in Kars and Ardahan the principal pieces were Krupp-pattern bronze 12 and 15 centimeter cannon, cast at the Tophané at Constantinople, and muzzle-loading 12-centimeter shunt guns. Of these latter there were a great number. The artillery undoubtedly are the finest corps in the Turkish army. The drill, discipline, and bearing are far superior to the other branches. Their practice, as a rule, was excellent, and though provided with nothing but percussion fuzes, the losses they inflicted on the enemy in the numerous engagements in Armenia prove that their training had not been thrown away.

The horse furniture and equipment of the artillery consist of a saddle of the same pattern as that used in the Spanish army, a holster on the near, a wallet on the off, side of the pommel, a valise on the cantle containing one vest, one fez, one shirt, one pair of drawers, one pair of shoes, one pair of laced boots, one housewife, and one turnscrew. On the near side of the saddle, attached to it by D's, hangs a nosebag, and on the off side a leathern water-bottle. The uniform of the men consists of a short tunic, with sling sword-belt, cross-belt, and pouch in black leather, a pair of pantaloons, and half-boots, with the national head-dress of the fez. Drivers are armed with a sword and Smith and Wesson's revolver; gunners with sabre and Winchester carbine.

Artillery horses are mostly imported from Hungary, and are, though small, powerful, hardy animals. They are allowed twelve pounds of barley and sixteen pounds of grass per diem. In the month of May they are turned out to graze for fifteen days, when they receive only half rations of grain.

The pay of the various grades in the artillery is as follows:—Captain, per annum, £70 13s. 2d; first lieutenant, £53 18s. 4d.; second lieutenant, £49 7s. 6d.; third lieutenant, £47 10s. 4d. A gunner in the horse artillery receives 6s. 7d. per mensem; in the field or garrison, 5s. 7d.

The cavalry in a corps d'armée consists of two brigades, each commanded by a Liva Pasha, or general of brigade; the brigade is composed of two regiments, each of six squadrons, the effective strength of which is 152 men and 165 horses. The staff of a regiment comprises one colonel, one lieutenant-colonel, two *chefs d'escadron*, two adjutants-major, two paymasters, nine medical officers of various grades, three veterinary surgeons, an armourer, a farrier, and a saddlemaker. Each squadron is commanded by a first captain, with a second captain, two lieutenants, and two sub-lieutenants under him. The total strength of a regiment consists of 131 officers, non-commissioned officers, and staff, and 831 sabres in the ranks. The uniform of the cavalry is similar to that of the horse artillery, except in the matter of buttons and belt-plates, in which there are slight variations. The armament consists of a sabre carried in a sling belt, a revolver carried in the holster, and a Winchester repeating rifle, with either twelve or sixteen cartridges, slung across the shoulder. In certain regiments some squadrons are armed with lances; however, I saw none of these in Armenia. The equipment consists of sling sword-belt, two small cartridge-cases, each containing twenty rounds, worn on the waistbelt, one on either side of the clasp, a valise strapped in rear of the saddle, containing the same kit as the artilleryman's. The saddle is of the same pattern, and all ranks carry the nosebag and water-bottle. The horses generally are country-bred, and their daily rations are nine pounds of barley and twelve pounds of grass. Occasionally, more especially in the 1st and 2nd Army Corps, Hungarian horses are found. They receive the amount stated as the ration for artillery horses. All animals, country-bred as well as those imported, are turned out to grass for fifteen days in the month of May. The manner of shoeing is different to what we practise. A circular plate of iron, with a small round hole the size of a shilling in the centre, is fastened on with seven nails. This certainly protects the frog, and I found myself compelled to adopt it after a very short acquaintance with Armenian roads, although my horse had up to that time in European Turkey worn only the ordinary English shoe.

The pay of subordinate officers and men is as follows, per annum:—First captain receives £73 15s. 2d.; second captain, £66 0s. 10d.; first lieutenant, £55 12s. 10d.; second lieutenant, £51 4s. 2d.; sub-lieutenant, 1st class, £48 10s.; sub-lieutenant, 2nd class, £44 16s. 10d. A sergeant receives 9s., a corporal 8s., and a private dragoon 6s. 7d. a month.

The battalion is the tactical unit of the infantry. It is commanded by a Bin-Bashi, or *chef du bataillon*, and is divided into two half-battalions under adjutant-majors. These again are sub-divided into four companies each, commanded by captains. I believe it is intended that the battalion shall consist of four instead of eight companies. The administrative staff of a battalion is composed of the *chef*, one adjutant-major, one captain, one lieutenant, and one sub-lieutenant, all selected by the officers of their own grades. Each battalion has two medical officers borne on its rolls. A regiment of infantry consists of four battalions, one of *chasseurs-à-pied*, the remaining three of ordinary battalions. The regimental staff, the head of which is the Mir Allai, or colonel, comprises a lieutenant-colonel, a regimental writer, and eighty bandsmen. The effective strength of a battalion is 827 of all ranks; that of a company 102, which includes three subordinate officers —viz., a captain, a first lieutenant, and a second lieutenant; the administrative staff of each regiment consists of an officer of each grade selected by his comrades, the colonel being the president. Nominally the chasseur battalion is accompanied by two small mountain guns of the Whitworth pattern, but this certainly was not the case in Asia during the present campaign.

The uniform of the infantry consists of a blue tunic with red piping, blue pantaloons with red seam. The universal fez, buttons, and piping (except that the first regiment of each *corps d'armée* wears yellow) are the same in every battalion and regiment; there are no distinguishing marks, so that it is impossible to tell one battalion from another—Nizam from Redif, chasseurs from ordinary line corps. All branches wear a blue great-coat with hood; mounted corps carry this rolled up on the cantle of the saddle, dismounted corps on the back. The equipment of the infantry is as follows :—A waist-belt, with bayonet frog—on the belt is carried a pouch containing fifty rounds; a haversack slung over the right shoulder, capable of carrying three days' supply of biscuit, a small tin canteen, and a pack which contains forty cartridges, and the same articles of kit enumerated as in the possession of artillerymen. As a rule, in time of war spare cartridges are carried on the breast in small stitched receptacles, similar to those which Circassians wear, or else in a coarse cloth cartridge-belt of the same pattern that English sportsmen use, only slung over the shoulder, not worn round the waist. The Martini-Henry, manufactured by the Peabody Company in America, is the weapon of the Turkish infantry, but some regiments are still armed with the Snider. The bayonet is a four-sided weapon, except in the case of the Tallia or chasseur battalions, which carry a sword-bayonet.

The pay of the various grades of subordinate officers is as follows :—Per annum, captain receives £70 13s. 2d.; first lieutenant, £53 18s. 4d.; second lieutenant, £49 7s. 6d. Per mensem, sergeant-major, 13s. 2d.; sergeant, 10s.; corporal, 7s.; private soldier, 5s. 7d.

A brigade of infantry consists of two regiments, or eight battalions, and is under the command of a Liva Pasha, or general of brigade. A division consists of two brigades; this is commanded by a Ferik, or lieutenant-general—the junior grade in the Ottoman army permitted to wear a beard.

Rations per day for all arms are the same, and nominally stand thus:—Bread, 2 lb.; meat, 8½ oz.; rice, 3oz.; butter, ⅓ oz.; salt, ⅔ oz.; onions, ⅔ oz.; candles, 1-10 oz.; wood, 23⅓ oz.; charcoal, 9⅔ oz. ; clarified butter, 1-10 oz.; soap, 1-10 oz. On service the Government reserves to itself the right of issuing 23 oz. of biscuit or of flour in lieu of bread, and the soldier on enlistment has to agree that 2 oz. of meat shall be deducted from his daily rations and sold, and with the amount vegetables purchased to provide him with soup. Companies are divided into messes of eight, and the men have, when in barracks, two meals a day—one an hour after sunrise, the second an hour before sunset. In the Ramazan, or month of fasting, the hours are changed to an hour before sunrise and immediately after sunset. The dinner hour, as in our service, is announced by bugle sounds. The barracks vary much, some being fairly comfortable, but the great majority are, it would seem, low, badly ventilated, and indescribably filthy. The men sleep on wooden platforms raised about a foot from the floor of the room, which is rarely or never boarded. Each man is supposed to have a mattress, a pillow, and two blankets. Sergeants, corporals, and the like grades of non-commissioned officers sleep in the men's barracks ; captains, subalterns, and the higher grades of non-commissioned officers dwell apart in separate rooms.

It must be borne in mind that a Bin-Bashi, or *chef du bataillon* or *d'escadron*, is the junior commissioned officer in the Turkish army. Captains and all below him in rank have quarters in barracks. Adjutants-major and all above that grade have to find

E

quarters in the town. They, however, receive money compensation in lieu of rations, which enables them to do this. Commissioned officers of all branches receive the same pay; those of the mounted receive extra rations for horses, which makes a slight difference in the total amounts.

The annual pay of the various commissioned officers is as follows:—Mushir, £5,420; lieutenant-general, £1,300; general of brigade, £725; colonel, £395; lieutenant-colonel, £270; chief of battalion or squadron, £200; adjutant-major of right wing or squadron, £110; of left wing or squadron, £93. This includes rations and lodging allowance.

It should be remembered that for reasons of economy the Porte made an all-round deduction in 1869 of seventeen per cent. of all pay and allowances of civil and military servants. This has never been remitted. Officers and soldiers also have to subscribe two per cent. of their pay towards the "widows and orphans" fund, and twelve per cent. towards their own pension fund. By a decree published in July, 1877, all salaries were reduced by one-half, in order that the Porte might be enabled to prosecute the war with renewed vigour, and, as the regiments in Armenia are in arrears varying from twenty-four to fifty-one months, the scale of pay laid down by the Hatti-Houmayoun of the 18th of February, 1869, scarcely represents the actual amount drawn by the soldier of the present day, although in that document appears the following paragraph :—

"L'État pourvoit à tous les frais de nourriture, d'équipement, et d'entretien du soldat, et lui donne en outre en numeraire un solde mensuelle fixe qui, contrairement à l'usage générale des puissances militaires, n'est susceptible d'aucune diminution ou retenue."

The composition of regiments and battalions of reserve troops is the same as that of the Nizam. They are called out only in time of war, and though presumably not so efficient as the corps of the standing army, yet in this campaign Nizam, Redif, and Mustahfiz battalions have fought side by side, and to the spectator there was no visible difference between them. The corps which on the 25th of June repelled a flank attack of a Russian brigade on the left of the Zewin Dooz position, charging the enemy, who were the grenadiers of the Caucasus, with the bayonet, and driving them headlong down the valley, was the Aleppo Battalion of the 2nd Ban of Redifs. The battalion which held the Great Yagni hill on the 2nd of October, and was literally annihilated, was the Erzingjan 2nd Redif Battalion. Indeed, the reserve troops in Armenia have proved that in releasing all Redif prisoners at Ardahan the Russians far undervalued their foes.

On paper the organisation of the Turkish army is second to none in the world; in the field they have proved themselves to be the same.

In the Appendix I give the authorised establishments of batteries, regiments of cavalry, and battalions of infantry, as well as a tabulated statement of the strength of the Ottoman army in all its branches—Scientific, Ordnance, Cavalry, and Infantry. The total number of troops nominally supposed to be at the disposal of the Porte in case of war, drilled, equipped, and officered, amount to—

Cavalry	... ...	48,819
Engineers	... ...	8,789
Artillery	... ...	90,000
Infantry	... ...	496,694
		644,302

E 2

This organisation, admirable as it appears on paper, broke down hopelessly when called upon to stand the strain of actual war. The Redif battalions were absolutely without officers. Sergeants and corporals were hurriedly transferred from Nizam corps, with the rank of captain and lieutenant, and the battalions, instead of numbering 800 men, rarely mustered 500.

At a moderate computation Mukhtar Pasha ought to have been able to place a force of 5,000 cavalry (regular and irregular), 65,000 infantry, and 180 guns in the field within a week of the declaration of war. Yet so shamefully mismanaged were all matters relating to the Seraskierate that on the 1st of May his available forces numbered but 87 weak battalions, 24 squadrons, and 20 batteries, of which 11 only were horsed. His troops were distributed as follows :—

Place.	Battalion.	Squadron.	Battery.
Erzeroum	13	6	6
Bayazid	2	2	1
Kars	29	6	5
Ardahan	12	3	3
Between Erzeroum and Kars	8	—	—
Olti	8	—	—
Khagisinan	1	—	—
Erzingjan	4	3	1
Gutentab	2	—	—
Van	6	3	2
Toprak-Kali	2	—	1
Delibaba	2	1	1

The composition of the Russian army was as follows :—

Main Column.—The Grenadier Division of the Caucasus, head-quarters at Alexandropol, and consisted of the 13th, 14th, 15th, and 16th Regiments of Grenadiers, with the Grenadier Field Artillery Regiment.

3rd Division.—The 20th Infantry Division, head-quarters, Alexandropol; commandant, Lieut.-General Heimann; the 77th, 78th, 79th, and 80th Regiments of the Line, with the 20th Field Artillery Regiment, formed the corps.

5th Division.—The 39th Division, head-quarters at Akhalzik, under Dewel, with the 153rd, 154th, 155th, and 156th Regiments, with the 39th Field Artillery Division.

Left Column.—The 19th Infantry Division, head-quarters, Erivan. The commander of this was Lieut.-General Swoyeff, and it comprised the 73rd, 74th, 75th, and 76th Regiments of the Line, with the 19th Field Artillery Regiment.

4th Division.—The 38th Infantry Division under Tergukassoff, head-quarters, Erivan, contained the 149th, 150th, 151st, and 152nd Regiments, with the 38th Field Artillery Regiment.

Right Column.—The 41st Division, under Oklobjia, with its head-quarters at Kutais, consisted of the 161st, 162nd, 163rd, and 164th Regiments of the Line, with the 41st Field Artillery Division.

In addition to these there was a brigade of rifles of the Caucasus, a brigade of sappers, four flying parks of field artillery, 1½ parks of horse artillery, four batteries of Cossack horse artillery, three batteries of Kuban horse artillery, one battery Terek horse artillery, and two divisions of cavalry.

Main Army.—14th Caucasian Dragoons, 15th Caucasian Dragoons, two regiments of Kuban and two of Terek Cossacks.

Left Column.—16th Caucasian Dragoons, 17th Caucasian Dragoons, four regiments of Terek Cossacks.

Showing a grand total of 100 battalions of infantry, one brigade of sappers, 12 regiments of cavalry, and 300 guns.*

Bravely as these showed on paper, I believe it is now an acknowledged fact that, leaving the army operating on Batoum out of the question, the Russian army did not exceed 50,000 infantry, 10,000 cavalry (including Karapapak irregulars), and 128 guns.

It was assumed that their men were better equipped, drilled, and disciplined than the Turkish troops; that their officers were more advanced in the knowledge of the art of war; that their organisation was more complete; and that the campaign in Armenia would virtually be a mere "walk over" for the Grand Duke.

On all these points we were lamentably ignorant. Their transport and commissariat failed utterly in the hour of trial, and their officers, in the earlier part of the war more especially, proved absolutely incapable. With the exception of their dragoon regiments, their cavalry certainly were not superior to the Circassians under Mukhtar Pasha's command, their infantry never proved itself when engaged in equal numbers of the same quality as the Turks, their arms were far inferior, and I doubt if their marching qualities or powers of endurance equalled those of the Osmanli.

Their guns were heavier metal, were better served than those of the Osmanli—indeed, the Russian artillery deserve a passing notice. The field-guns were of the

---

* Colonel Stracey, of the Scots Guards, with whom I travelled through Europe on my way to Armenia, assured me that these numbers were greatly exaggerated, and that I should not find 50,000 Russians in the field. I subsequently found that the gallant Colonel was right not only in this, but on many points of information connected with the Russian army, with which he was good enough to furnish me.

Krupp pattern, made of bronze, either 4 or 9 pounders, the horse artillery brigades being armed with the lighter weapon, whilst infantry divisions were supplied with an equal number of each calibre.

The 4-pounder has a calibre of 8·69 centimeter, and weighs, with limber complete, 3,960 lb., the gun itself being 677 lb. The 9-pounder has a calibre of 10·67 centimeter, and weighs close on 5,000 lb., the gun alone weighing 1,350 lb. This piece, however, may almost be classed a siege gun. Indeed, during the siege of Kars very many of them were mounted in the batteries. Each battery has eight guns, the guns are drawn by eight horses.

The complement of a 4-pounder battery is six officers, 256 men, and 109 horses. The heavier batteries having six officers, 317 men, and 223 horses. The Cossack batteries were armed with a small 3-pounder bronze mountain gun, weighing just 2 cwt. These were sometimes carried on the back of a pack animal, but more often drawn by one horse in shafts.

There are three projectiles used with the Russian artillery, the common shell, the shrapnel, and the round-headed shell, and their weights in a 4-pounder gun 9¾, 11¾, and 14 lb. respectively. In a 9-pounder gun, the missiles, which are of the same description, weigh 27, 29, and 32 lb. The charge for the lighter piece is 1½, for the heavier 3 lb.

The supreme military and political administration was vested in the Grand Duke, but preferring the comforts of Tiflis to the hardships of camp life, he handed over command (virtually) to General Loris Melikoff, a scion of an Armenian princely house, who conducted all operations, assisted by General Dutrovskoi as chief of the staff.

Mukhtar Pasha determined on holding on to Kars, and giving the Russians battle in the neighbourhood of that fortress. Finding, however, they were too strong for him, he fell back, hoping to be able to defeat one of the three wings of the Russian army in some more favourable position, and the Turkish army, when I reached Erzeroum, was disposed as follows :—

The extreme right was at Van. It consisted, as I said before, of eight battalions, 4,000 irregulars, and two batteries, under the command of Faik Pasha. It effectually threatened the flank of the Russian wing advancing from Bayazid, and made its progress a matter of some difficulty. At Delibaba, which commanded the pass over the Kose Dagh, and thus barred the road from Bayazid to Erzeroum, there were eight battalions and two batteries in strong entrenchments. On the Hoonkiar Doozi, or Imperial plateau—a level table-land on the Soghanly Mountains, and scattered between it, Bardez, Zewin, and Yenikui—was Mukhtar's main army, which, with the reinforcements lately received from Constantinople and Syria, amounted to about 40 battalions and two batteries. At Pennek, to the north of Bardez, and at Olti, slightly in rear of Pennek, there were six battalions and a battery; these watched the Ardahan road, and the remnants of the late garrison, who escaped after the assault on the 20th, endeavoured to co-operate with them; they amounted, it is said, to about 6,000 men and twelve guns. Thus Mukhtar Pasha's first line extended from Pennek to Van, and comprised sixty-two battalions and seven batteries, scattered over a front of about 120 miles.

Keeping open communications between Erzeroum and Olti were two battalions, and a battery at Ghiurji

Boghas; and at Koprikui, midway between Delibaba and Erzeroum, were six battalions and a couple of batteries in entrenchments. Erzeroum itself is a very strong position, and might be made much stronger; but, leaving everything to the last moment, the Turks delayed until after the Declaration of War to throw up earthworks and to repair the old entrenchments, which were in sad need of much labour and skill to make them fit to stand against modern arms. The road into Erzeroum from Kars passes over a very difficult pass, the Devi Boyun—or "Camel's Neck"—which might be made a most formidable position. To the east of this lies the Passin Plain, where it seems probable a decisive battle will be fought.* Earthworks were hurriedly thrown up on the Devi Boyun, and I believe redoubts will be erected in suitable positions on the Passin Plain; so doubtless if the Russians ever get so far, they will meet with a warm reception, as these earthworks will receive the guns *en route* from Trebizond, and will make any approach from that quarter a matter of great difficulty.

The Russian army, as far as I could gather, was situated as follows :—

The right wing having captured Ardahan, left three battalions behind to hold the place and keep open communications, and threatened an advance down the main road on Pennek. The centre and head-quarters, having left a sufficent force to mask Kars and prevent the garrison issuing forth, moved down the main road on Erzeroum, and left outposts at Tcharpakli, some twenty miles to the east of the Soghanly range, and directly in front of Mukhtar Pasha's forces. The left wing advanced to Kara-Kilissa (black church) on the direct

* I am here speaking of the earlier events of the campaign.

road from Erzeroum to Teheran, about forty miles in front of the Turkish force at Delibaba. The movements of this column were much hampered by the Van Brigade of Turks, and had a combined attack by the Delibaba and Van forces been made on the Russian left wing, a very decided blow would have been struck on their advance, which at this season of the year was necessarily much impeded by the snowy ranges and swollen rivers they had to cross. I hear that the army is well equipped; their commissariat and ordnance supplies being conveyed on strongly-built light carts drawn by horses, while the men are housed in the felt kibitka, or Central Asia tent. In spite of these precautions, I hear that sickness is rife.

General Loris Melikoff has given orders that soldiers found pillaging will be hanged, and that villagers who place themselves under Russian protection will be well taken care of. It is reported that he has 15,000 cavalry; so when the snow melts and the country becomes more practicable, I fear that the districts for miles round will be open to their attacks, for the Turks have nothing worthy of the name to oppose them.

CHAPTER IV.

THE STORY OF ARDAHAN.

Ismail Kurd's Invasion of Russia—Discontent in the City—The Petition to the
British Consul—Mr. Zohrab—Russian Designs on Armenia—Alacrity in
following up the Declaration of War—Capture of Bayazid—City *Canards*
—Ardahan—Captain Mehmed Bey—Sabri Pasha—Gallant Defence of the
Emir Oghlou—Flight of Sabri—Capture of the Town.

ERZEROUM, 31*st May.*

THERE is no doubt that great dissatisfaction exists in
Erzeroum with regard to the conduct of the Turkish
officials. In the spring, Sami Pasha, who was Governor-General and Commander-in-Chief of the District,
was recalled, and Mukhtar Pasha sent over to take
command of the army, while one Ismail Pasha, a
Kurd, assumed the civil government. The former
is with the main army at Barudez, while the latter
has shut himself up in his citadel, and never appears.
The feeling towards the Civil Governor was much
intensified by a telegram appearing in the *Levant
Herald*, in which it appeared that Ismail Pasha reported to the Porte that he was ready to take the
field with 40,000 volunteers. The grey-beards of
Erzeroum are most wrathful, and ask when has he been
seen outside his palace with four men. Indeed, so
high has this disaffection risen that a large deputation
of the principal Moolahs of the district waited on Mr.
Zohrab,* our Consul here, with a petition signed by
all the chief inhabitants, begging him to use his in-

---

* I happened to be in the Consulate when this interview took place, and
can testify to the fact that there were many Mahomedans in the group,
and that they were more vehement in their denunciation of Ismail Pasha
than the Christians.

fluence to save the city from the horrors of a siege
and bombardment. What confidence can we have,
they say, in our leaders? " Ardahan has fallen without defence ; Kars is about to fall ; Mukhtar Pasha
flies whenever the Russians approach him ; Ismail
Pasha has shut himself up in his palace, and is never
seen ; our troops have received no pay for twenty-
eight months ; they are badly clad, have no hospitals,
are dying by hundreds of disease, and only receive
bread every other day ; how can they fight under
such management, and what is the use of attempting
to stay the advance of the Russians ? We know
Ismail Pasha has made up his mind to retire to
Erzingjan directly the enemy gets any closer, and to
abandon his government here. Why should we suffer ?
Can the city hope to hold out against the Russians ?
Why not send out at once and welcome them rather
than expose ourselves, our families, and property to
the calamity of a siege ?" It is extremely gratify-
ing to find our country represented by a man like
Mr. Zohrab, a gentleman in every sense of the word—
well read, thoroughly versed in all Oriental languages,
with an accurate knowledge of the country-people,
their manners, customs, and history. There is no
man, I believe, in Asia Minor more respected by
Turks and Christians alike. It is pleasing to know
that in their distress the people of Erzeroum turn to
Her Majesty's representative for counsel and assistance. It is well to find that such a representative is
able and willing to advise them effectually and deter-
minedly ; that he can soothe their discontent, appeal
to their better feelings, and by his cheerful bearing,
and by the noble disregard of danger displayed by

him in keeping his family at a post of much difficulty, hardship, and trial, show them that things may not be so black as they are painted. No living man knows this part of the country as well as he does. For twenty-two years he has been intimately associated with its history. As interpreter and private secretary to Sir Fenwick Williams he manfully bore his part, though but a boy in years, through the heroic defence of Kars. Associated with Teesdale in preparing for the siege throughout the winter of 1854, he, on the advance of the Russians, dropped the pen, and taking up the sword, proved himself an adept at either profession. Since those days Mr. Zohrab has held various posts in European Turkey with but little gain to himself, but with much advantage to Government.

The Moscow speech never alluded to Asia; she was omitted in the proceedings of the Conference, in the wording of the Protocol, and in the declaration of war. The promise of the Czar is that his armies will recross the Pruth when the sufferings of the Christians in Turkey have been alleviated; it does not bind him to withdraw one man from his newly-acquired territories in Asia Minor. Thus the Russians have hoodwinked Europe, and, without violating a pledge, will secure to themselves the greater portion of the shores of the Black Sea, the important quadrilateral of Trebizond, Erzeroum, Kars, and Batoum, and will hold the key of the Euphrates and Tigris valleys. They will, moreover, have the only good port in the Black Sea now left to the Turks—Batoum, which is capable of being made a most formidable fortress—and Trebizond, a fairly good roadstead, commanding the direct Persian road. It now appears evident that from the first Asia has been the point aimed at by Russia, and that the movements on the Pruth were meant to occupy the attention of Turkey and to induce her to mass her main army on the Danube for the defence of Constantinople, whereas all last year the Czar has been organising three columns for the conquest of this district. The right column formed at Akhalzik, the centre at Goomri, the left at Erivan, were employed all the winter in preparations for the campaign. Baggage-animals were daily exercised, the men taught by Kurds the art of pitching kibitkas, and stores of grain, &c., formed at depôts on the extreme frontier. Moreover, officers who had been travelling in Asiatic Turkey had sent in very full reports of all the Turkish posts, roads, and grain-establishments. Thus prepared, the Russians commenced their advance, and, crossing her frontier on the 24th of April, declared war. Their advanced guard of cavalry captured a squadron of Turkish horse who were quietly reposing under some trees, and who surrendered without firing a shot, and, pushing on, seized the Turkish stores of grain in the village of Khodja Kaleh and the districts of Alashgird, Ghendeh, Shora-gol, Khagazman, and Childer. The right column, moving rapidly down on Ardahan, invested it, and assaulting it on the 16th of May, carried the place, with but slight loss, the Turks losing about 2,000 men. Leaving a garrison in Ardahan, the column moved down on Pennek. The centre column, advancing from Alexandropol, invested Kars before the end of the month. Mukhtar Pasha moved out on the 3rd of May to attack them, but finding them too strong, he rapidly retired on the Soghanly Range, exchanging a few shots with the enemy, but never facing them fairly in fight.

It appears that the Russians intended compelling Kars to surrender by starvation; for, leaving a sufficient force to invest the place, the Russian commander was following up Mukhtar Pasha on to the Soghanly, and was now halted at Tcharpakli. The left column, advancing from Erivan, crossed the frontier simultaneously with the other two, and it seems probable that this division marched through Persian territory, appearing before Bayazid. The Russian general sent a flag of truce into the place, saying he had seven battalions and three batteries, that if the place capitulated the garrison might march out undisturbed, but that if it were not evacuated on the morrow he would assault it, and no quarter would be shown. Hastily availing himself of this permission, the Turkish commandant withdrew his three battalions and joined Faik Pasha at Van. The inactivity of Faik Pasha is unaccountable, and if he cannot co-operate with the Delibaba force, or conjointly with them attack the Russian left column, he will in all probability have to surrender in a few days.

Extravagant rumours, having no foundation whatever in fact, seem to be the order of the day. The last *bonne bouche* duly transmitted to the Porte, and circulated here yesterday, was that, by the grace of God and the assistance of the light reflected from the Sultan's throne, a body of Circassians had attacked Ardahan, recaptured it, and driven the Russians back with much slaughter. It is unnecessary to add that this achievement was the work of some fertile brain in the neighbourhood of the Pasha's Palace, and that no Circassian has ventured to show himself in the vicinity of the Russian army since the war began.

Details of the Ardahan affair came in slowly, more slowly far than the stream of unharmed fugitives who pour into this city daily.

Ardahan is a town containing about 7,000 inhabitants, and is situated in the valley of the Kur Su; it is surrounded by hills on which are built various detached forts, the principal being the Ramazan to the north at a distance of about 5,000 yards, the Senghier Redoubt, about 1,500 yards distant, and the Emir Oghlou, to the west, some five miles from the town. This was considered the key of the position, and was under the command of Colonel Mehmed Bey, an officer of German origin, whose father had taken service with the Turks some thirty years ago. The garrison of the town consisted of 9 battalions of Nizam and Redif troops, 2 of local militia, 3 batteries of field artillery, and 80 guns of position, many of them being Krupp's 15-centimeter pieces. Hassan Sabri Pasha, the commandant of the fortress, was a man possessing much influence, but even this failed to prevent his removal from a command in Montenegro, the previous year, where he had shown gross incompetence, and it was rumoured also a want of courage. During the winter the Ardahan garrison, owing to scarcity of fresh meat and vegetation, suffered much from scurvy; and when the spring broke, fully one-third of the men were suffering from this complaint.

Towards the end of April, the Russians, having crossed the frontier from Alexandropol, detached a column, under General Komaroff, by way of Zarchat and Boskui towards Ardahan. They were enabled, owing to the apathy or treachery of Sabri Pasha, to throw a bridge across the Kur Su, and thus to make their attack on the Emir Oghlou, the fall of which would necessarily reduce the place to submission. On the 14th May, a large Russian division was seen advancing from the direction of Kars, and these, having effected a junction with Komaroff's brigade, on the 15th inst. took possession of a height commanding the key of the position. On seeing these movements, Mehmed Bey, having some knowledge of the art of war, and spite of change of name, nationality, and religion, not being a firm believer in Kismet, sent word to Sabri Pasha begging for reinforcement in order that he might attack the Russians before they had made good their position. His request was declined, and so, unmolested, the Muscovite artillerymen gained the summit of the crest, hastily constructed batteries, and by 5 p.m. that evening opened fire on the doomed Emir Oghlou. All night the bombardment continued, Mehmed Bey making what defence he could, when in the morning, being very severely wounded, his garrison, who as long as he was able to direct seemed instilled with something like courage, lost heart, and fled into Ardahan. The Russians then, advancing their artillery, moved on to the destruction of the Ramazan Tabia, and by sunset had commenced its bombardment. During the night Sabri Pasha victoriously retired (as a Turkish official informed us), on Ardanutsch with two battalions.

On the morning of the 16th, having seized and strongly held the Emir Oghlou, Loris Melikoff, who it appears was in command of the forces, moved the main body of his troops round to the heights on the south of the town. In this operation the Russians were vigorously attacked by five battalions moved out from the Senghier Redoubt, and suffered some loss from the heavy guns in

F

the Ramazan Tabia, under whose fire they were compelled to pass ; but they succeeded in establishing themselves on a height some 4,000 yards to the south of the
town, which they entrenched during the night, and at
break of day commenced a vigorous bombardment, which
continued for seven hours ; in the afternoon a *parlementaire* was despatched by the Russian general to summon
the garrison to surrender ; the proposal was rejected.
At dawn on the morning of the 17th May, three strong
Russian columns advanced to the assault ; these were met
by troops from the town and from the Senghier Redoubt,
and a sharp engagement ensued. The two armies were
engaged at such close quarters that neither party could
use their artillery, and for upwards of three hours a ceaseless rattle of musketry continued. At noon, the Turks
—having lost enormously, their entrenchments being absolutely piled up with dead and wounded—all their
senior officers having abandoned them, broke and took
to flight, and the main Russian column pushed forward
and entered the town from the south. They were here
met by a well-directed rifle fire from the Pasha's house,
in which a detachment of the Van Redifs had posted
themselves. This act was fraught with much annoyance
to those in the main hospital, which was crowded with
a great number of unwounded men, who gladly availed
themselves of the protection afforded by the ' Red Crescent' waving over the building. In returning the fire
on the Pasha's house, several rifle-bullets struck the
walls and windows of the hospital. Fortunately no one
was hurt, and as the Russians made a rush on the
Pasha's house and carried it, all danger to sick and
wounded ceased. About this time a second Russian
column, mainly composed of Cossack cavalry, entered

the city from the north, and as they advanced on the bridge in the middle of the town, barred the passage of the fugitive Turks, numbers of whom in despair threw themselves into the stream already dyed crimson with the blood of their dead comrades. By 2 p.m. all firing had ceased, but the work of pursuit was vigorously carried on; large numbers of prisoners were brought in before nightfall. For the three succeeding days the place was handed over to pillage, and the Karapapak Irregulars were not slow to avail themselves of this licence. Prior to the assault, Loris Melikoff had announced his intention of shooting any man found guilty of offering violence to man, woman, or child, and I could learn of no case where any outrage had been committed.

From a Turkish medical officer who was made prisoner and subsequently released, I learnt that the Russians had buried 1,930 bodies of their enemies after the fight.

It is now reported that 800 have reached Artvin, and about 500, mostly unarmed, have arrived at Olti and Erzeroum.

Such is the story of Ardahan, as gathered from the lips of men who were there. The Turks lost everything —munitions of war, commissariat stores, magazines of arms, and, including mountain pieces, 112 guns in all. The Russians are now reported busy dismantling the place, and sending the captured cannon over the border to Alexandropol; and Sabri Pasha is still, with his two battalions and a few hundred fugitives, at Ardanutsch, forming a nucleus, as he reports, of a force with which he means to recapture the place.

On the 28th May I paid a visit to the Viceroy at the

F 2

Palace of Erzeroum — a straggling building, in very bad repair, situated in the ancient citadel, which is of Byzantine construction, and stands on a hill in the centre of the city. As I passed through the archway a body of about 200 irregular horsemen were issuing forth—I presume being mustered, for a Turkish officer was sitting down on a chair apparently entering their numbers in a note-book. The men were armed diversely, mostly with a very curved sword and lance. Some had pistols, and there were a few matchlocks among them. They were mounted on small ponies, few of which would have been accepted as grass-cutters' "tats" by any cavalry commandant in India. The swords were carried in sling-belts, but to prevent the nuisance of banging about they were tucked between the saddle and the leg, in such a manner that the drawing of them would be a matter of some difficulty. The lances were short, unwieldy, and heavy; and the men appeared to be indifferent horsemen, and quite valueless as cavalry.

Leaving my horse in a large courtyard, I passed the usual unwashed crowd collected about the feet of all Pasha footstools, up a very rickety pair of stairs, to a small, meanly-furnished room—the office of the interpreter, an Armenian. I had a long conversation with this gentleman, and after about a quarter of an hour's delay, was conducted to the presence of Ismail Pasha.

Although forewarned, I certainly was not prepared to meet a man of Ismail Pasha's stamp in such a position. Entering his audience-chamber, I saw him seated on the usual Turkish sofa, at the head of the room, smoking the everlasting pipe. Two aides-de-camp were in the room, and a menial; one of the aides-de-camp was an aged gentleman, who certainly would have come under the 55-year rule in India some ten or fifteen years ago. The other was a smart, active-looking young man, decorated with the Medjidie and three war-medals, whom I afterwards learnt to know and respect as Colonel Riza Bey. Rising, and shaking me by the hand, with but small show of cordiality, Ismail begged me to be seated. Our conversation was somewhat restricted.

On my asking for news, he told me that he thought it would be far better if the English, instead of sending for news, were to come and fight for the Turks. I endeavoured to explain that it was useless fighting for people who would not help themselves, and that a vast section of my countrymen failed to see why we should fight at all for Turkey. I learnt from him that the rumours of Armenians having volunteered to join the army were all false, for there was not a single Christian in the army. He seemed extremely jealous of Ahmed Mukhtar Pasha, the Commander-in-Chief, and used language concerning him which a British General would certainly never use in the presence of junior officers.

I left him, impressed with the idea that the Porte could not have found a more bigoted, fanatical, or worthless man for the post of Vali of Erzeroum. A short time ago, as I have already mentioned, he telegraphed to Pera that he was preparing to proceed himself to invade Russia with 40,000 Kurds. The Constantinople authorities were so delighted with this news that they sent him by return mail the first-class of the Order of the Medjidie. It is needless to add that Ismail has not collected his 40,000 men, nor is there the smallest hope of his ever doing so. This telegram, being published in the *Levant Herald*, in due time found its way to Erzeroum. Ismail Pasha made many inquiries after

Captain Burnaby, so I take this opportunity of conveying his compliments, as I know of no other means of bringing them to the notice of that adventurous traveller, whose reports on the condition of the Armenians of this district are read with some indignation and much astonishment by the gentry here. It appears that both here and at Erzingjan, Captain Burnaby stayed with the Pasha, and that the accounts of the good feeling existing between the Christian and the Turk must have been culled in conversation with the rulers, not with the ruled. I have had an opportunity of talking with many gentlemen of this neighbourhood, as well as with some of the American missionaries, who devote their whole lives to the task of preaching among the Armenians, and they one and all testify to the manner in which the Christian is oppressed and tyrannised over. Since I have been here I have seen a petition addressed to the Consul by the inhabitants of a Christian village about thirty miles off, complaining that their cattle and corn have been seized by Government officials, their wives and daughters ravished by soldiers, and that no notice having been taken by the Pasha of their complaints, they implore him to protect them. Again, only this morning, two Armenian merchants returning to their homes were set upon within sight of this town, and in the presence of a Turkish caravan robbed of 13,000 piastres. Such acts as these remain unredressed. A Christian has no chance of bringing his complaints before a Court of Justice, so can there be contentment and happiness? There certainly has been no such open persecution as in Bulgaria, but tyranny and oppression are the normal condition here, and after centuries of such misrule the Armenian has become as bad as, if not worse in many points than the Turk. Their mean cringing spirit cannot inspire one with much desire to help them, yet at the same time it would be wrong to allow Captain Burnaby's account to go uncontradicted.

The position of the troops remains practically unchanged since my last. Mukhtar Pasha follows the plan adopted by all Turkish Generals in the defence of Asia Minor, viz., of frittering away his army in small detachments; so that at no one point except Van has he more than 6,000 men. His head-quarters are on the Tchakir Baba plateau, near Bardez; and I am assured, on the authority of an officer who returned from camp yesterday, that he has only 5,000 men and one battery with him. His left is at Olti, and consists of eight battalions; his right is at Delibaba, and there are four battalions and one battery entrenched with advanced posts at Gulentab, two battalions and two guns, and at Toprak Kale two battalions and four guns. At Kuipri Kui, keeping up communication between his main army and Erzeroum, he has 3,000 men and one battery; these men are being employed in throwing up earthworks; and on the Devi-Boyun, near this, he has four battalions of reserve troops, with one battery. There are earthworks there capable of holding four batteries.

Connecting the Olti troops with Erzeroum, he has 3,000 men and a battery at Ghiurji Boghaz, where entrenchments are being constructed. The idea is that no stand will be made until the troops have fallen back on Ghiurji Boghaz and the Devi-Boyun; but I doubt these men under these officers making a stand anywhere. I am assured, on the authority of an English officer who was in Servia, that these troops cannot be compared to

the corps of the Danube, which consists of the flower of
the Turkish army; and I am willing to believe that
the 1st, 2nd, and 3rd Corps are better than the 4th.

Mukhtar Pasha finds much difficulty in providing
food for his men.   On Monday night two urgent messages came from the front, imploring that more food
should be sent him, but there seem very scanty supplies
to draw on in Erzeroum.   Ismail Pasha has telegraphed
to Constantinople for 1,000 horses to be sent here in
order that he may organise a transport train ; but it is
rather late in the day to adopt such an obviously necessary plan.

Sickness and desertion are diminishing the strength
of the army very rapidly. Upwards of 1,200 men have deserted from the centre and right columns of the Turkish
forces during the past week, including runaways from
Kars.   More than 700 have been recaptured, and these
were marched out this morning, under a strong escort—
300, I should say—being handcuffed, to work on the
defences of the Devi-Boyun.   A very miserable-looking
body of men they were, without shoes or great-coats,
and many of them so sick that they could hardly drag
themselves along.

The Russian movements are, I fancy, better known
to you at home than to us here.   The right column is
advancing from Ardahan, and is in the neighbourhood of
Pennek, thus seriously threatening Mukhtar Pasha's left
flank.   The centre column seems delaying for some unaccountable reason near Kars, though its advanced posts
are as far advanced to the Soghanly Dagh as Tcharpakli.
The left column seems to have made a *détour* in the direction of Van with the object of preventing Faik Pasha
effecting a junction with the troops at Delibaba.   Strict,

and in my humble opinion somewhat unnecessary, orders
have been received from Constantinople expressly for-
bidding the Turkish Generals to undertake any offensive
movements, desiring them to act purely on the defensive. There seems some difficulty about their complying
even with that. On Sunday there was a small affair
of outposts. It appears that a reconnoitring party of
Cossacks pushed close up to Toprak Kale, when the
commander of that position deemed it advisable to attack them; so, moving out his whole force, he threw
himself on their left flank and drove them back some
distance, killing five, wounding several more, and suffering the loss of one man himself. What the real truth
of the affair is, of course, one cannot tell. I, however,
repeat it as told to me.

Sir Arnold Kemball, with one A.D.C., Lieutenant
Maitland Dougall, R.N., is in here at present; and he
was joined yesterday by Captain H. Trotter, R.E., who
was attached to Sir Douglas Forsyth's Kashgar Mission in 1874. By this officer's appointment, as extra
Military Attaché to the Embassy in Constantinople, the
Royal Geographical Society lost the opportunity of
hearing an account of Central Asian geography from
the lips of one of the few thoroughly scientific as well
as practical men who have travelled in those regions.
Sir Arnold starts to-morrow for Olti, and thence proceeds round the Turkish position. He has been good
enough to permit me to accompany him; so next week
I trust I shall be able to give you a more detailed
account of the strength of Mukhtar Pasha's army,
which I fear is under 30,000 strong, all told. It is
a great pity that the well-organised expedition we read
of as having been detached to Soukoum Kaleh was not

sent to reinforce Erzeroum. Ten thousand picked troops on the Soghanly would probably make a great difference in the result of the campaign, although at present it seems as if nothing short of a miracle could save the whole country from Erzeroum to Trebizond. The works around Erzeroum, which are in a very bad state of repair, seem not to have been touched for years. Those on the Devi-Boyun are scarcely commenced, and no stores of provisions have been collected for transmission to the front. The town itself is filled with able-bodied men who should be labouring on the defences. It is too late, however, now to think of defending Erzeroum, that is if the Russians push on with anything like vigour, and any reinforcements that might arrive would merely be swept away in the general destruction of Turkish men and material that must ensue when once the enemy drive Mukhtar Pasha back from Kuipri Kui. The slowness of the advance of the Russian General appears quite inexplicable. It is true that the rivers are swollen and the mountains covered with snow; but still there is no army to oppose him, and a steady movement of even 20,000 men would be sufficient to drive the Turks back into the fortress.

It appears from the home papers received by the last mail that the Russian Government has again assured the Powers that she does not intend to annex any territory, and will retire from all conquered provinces on Turkey giving satisfactory guarantees for the efficient carrying out of reforms. Our recollection of Russian promises savours more of their non-fulfilment than otherwise, and looking at the systematic way in which Asia Minor has been ignored throughout the whole correspondence on Eastern affairs, one can scarcely help coming to the conclusion that Russia's promise does not apply to Asiatic Turkey.

I notice in the English daily papers of the 5th of May, under the heading of Military Intelligence, appears a list of seven regiments of cavalry, four brigades of artillery, and forty-three battalions of infantry, ordered to hold themselves in readiness for active service, and the same paper also describes the activity in the various dockyards. All this gives the Turks the idea that at the end we will come and fight for them, and that consequently there is no necessity for them to hurry themselves in the matter. Not a single Turkish officer have I met who has not asked me the question, " When is the English army coming to help us ? " and I invariably give the same answer, " I do not think England will send an army to help you."

CHAPTER V.

ON THE WAY TO THE FRONT.

Fugitives from Ardahan—Sabri Pasha again—Conduct of Russians—Retreat
from Olti—The Herman Dooz—Kuipri Kui and its Defences—Suspicious
Death of a Christian—Khorassan—The Fight at Beghli Ahmed—First
Impressions of Circassians—Ahmed Mukhtar Pasha—The Zewin Dooz—
Disposition of Turkish Troops—Apathy of Ismail Pasha—The Kurds—
Discontent among Troops at Erzeroum—Appeal for Help from England—
Visit to the Camp at Delibaba—The Pass—Turkish Officers—Re-occupation
of Olti—Our Kurdish Escort—Sortie from Kars—Faizi Pasha's Opinions—
Other Versions of Beghli Ahmed—The Head-Quarter Camp—Talked-of
Court-Martial on Sabri Pasha—Want of Cavalry—Position of Russian
Forces—Position of Turkish Forces.

KHORASSAN, *June* 6.

IMMEDIATELY after posting my last, on the 31st ult., Sir
Arnold Kemball, who had most kindly given me permission to accompany him on his visit to the Turkish
camp, left Erzeroum with the intention of proceeding
to Olti to acquaint himself with the disposition of troops
in that neighbourhood, as well as to examine the defensive works reported to be in progress in the Ghiurji
Boghaz Pass (Georgian defile). Captain H. Trotter,
R.E., Additional Military Attaché, and Lieutenant
Dougall, R.N., A.D.C., also accompanied the General.
Leaving Erzeroum at noon we skirted the western
slopes of the Devi-Boyun range, keeping well on high
ground in order to avoid the swamps and bogs which
abound in the valley and make travelling at this season
both difficult and dangerous. Proceeding only at a

foot's pace, in order that our baggage, which was on pack-horses, might not lag behind, we reached Hindsk at six p.m. There we found fairly comfortable quarters in the guest-chamber of the house belonging to the head man of the village, and so made ourselves snug for the night.

We passed a great number of men armed and unarmed, hale and wounded, fugitives from Ardahan. Their accounts of the fall of that place, on the 16th, corroborated my previous news. One and all spoke loudly in praise of Mehmed Bey, the gallant commandant of the Emir Oghlou, whose behaviour seems to have been beyond all praise, while the conduct of Hassan Sabri Pasha, the commander of the forces, seems to have been quite the reverse. It appears that the day before the attack he shot two men, a gunner and a linesman, for desertion; and that on the first symptom of assault he himself abandoned his command. The general idea I received was that the garrison of the Emir Oghlou fought well, but that the troops in Ardahan itself did not show much valour. The losses in the outwork were most severe. Out of four companies of the Angora regiment who were present only sixteen men escaped. This corps, together with the Van, Moosh, and Sivas battalions, seems to have particularly distinguished itself. As a rule, the regimental officers appear to have shown much courage; 112 are reported as killed. The fugitives spoke in the highest terms of the Russians, who treated the sick and wounded with the greatest consideration and kindness, sending the worst cases to their own hospitals for treatment, and distributing the others among the neighbouring villages. All soldiers of the Nizam, or regular troops, taken prisoners are to be sent across the border to Russia; but all prisoners of the Redif, or reserve troops, after being disarmed, were supplied with five days' rations, and allowed to proceed where they pleased, not even being put on their parole to refrain from serving again. Grain also has been distributed among the frontier villagers to sow in their fields. This treatment, so foreign to what soldiers and villagers receive at the hands of their own Government, has produced a most favourable impression. If prompted by political motives, it is a most sagacious step; if by a nobler feeling, it is worthy of the highest praise.

A great number of men perished in the flight owing to the destruction of the bridge over the Kur Su by the Russian guns when it was crowded with fugitives. The cavalry, however, who conducted the pursuit, appeared to have behaved with more forbearance than pursuing cavalry usually do, for they contented themselves with heading the flying masses and driving them back to camp, where, as I have before remarked, they were received with kindness and attention, the sick being well cared for, and the reserve troops being furnished with rations. I am afraid this shows that the Russians, in spite of the reported bravery of the Van, Moosh, Sivas, and Angora corps, do not value the Redif regiments as antagonists, but, despising them as soldiers, do not consider them worth an expense which their detention as prisoners would naturally entail on the Czar's Government.

Early on the morning of the 1st of June we again proceeded on our way, Sir Arnold, accompanied by Captain Trotter, going *viâ* Bar to Kutamar, while Lieutenant Dougall and myself made a *détour* by

Lisgaf, passing through the Ghiurji Boghaz defile. We
saw three battalions encamped at a spot about three
miles north of Hindsk, and in rear of them were two
small earthworks which the men had been upwards of
a fortnight in constructing. They were of weak profile
and in very bad position, being commanded on both
flanks as well as by a hill some 500 yards in front.
What their object in erecting them was I am at a loss
to conjecture; for the purpose of defending the defile
they were utterly worthless.

A few miles farther on we came across the head of
a column of four battalions, with two mountain guns,
accompanied by a string of about 400 pack-horses carrying ammunition, in full retreat from Olti on Hindsk.
There were very few officers with this force, and the
way in which the march was conducted was most discreditable, straggling along in no formation at all.
The men covered fully ten miles of ground, so at least
I reckon from the fact that it was three hours from the
time we met the head of the column until we entered
Lisgaf, where some men were still dawdling behind.
There were no advanced guard and no rear guard. The
ammunition pack-horses were certainly accompanied by
soldiers, who for the most part had slid their rifles
through the slings of the cases, and were strolling along
as they pleased; but, instead of the baggage being kept
well together, it was scattered throughout the string of
the column. The few officers we met were usually in
groups of twos and threes, often entirely unaccompanied
by men. It is no exaggeration to say that we often
covered a mile of ground without seeing one. This was
a retreat caused by the advance of the Russians on
Olti, a movement conducted almost in the face of

the enemy, certainly within striking distance of his cavalry !

Pushing on through Lisgaf, we reached Kutamar at 7 p.m., having been twelve hours in the saddle, and on the same horses; there meeting Sir Arnold, we reported what we had seen. As there were no Turkish troops at Olti—indeed, none between us and the Russians—we abandoned our intention of visiting that place, and deeming a retrograde movement desirable, started at 6 a.m. on the following morning, and, taking a south-westerly course, struck over the Kharga Bazaar range, across the Herman plateau, which stands 9,000 feet above the level of the sea, and reached Killa Varend about 7 p.m. There was still snow remaining on the Herman Dooz. The parts where it had recently melted were covered with wild flowers of every hue and kind. A delicate blue-bell, such as I have never before seen, drooped gracefully at the very edge of the snow, while within a few yards a more homely-looking bell and a delicately tinted pink anemone were to be seen. A large and very handsome orchid, with tulips of every colour, were found on the lower slopes of the mountain, and sweet-briar, mint, thyme, fennel, and wild rhubarb were in great profusion. Killa Varend was a wild, desolate-looking village, situated on a rocky ridge at the foot of the Herman Dooz. We, however, found a most magnificent apartment placed at our disposal, and revelled in the luxury of being free from the odours of stables and from the proximity of fleas and cattle, which at our previous halting-place had shared our humble lodging.

At 8 a.m. on the 3rd of June we moved on to Kuipri Kui, a village on the left bank of the Araxes.

The Araxes, which here takes a bend towards the north, receives an affluent called the Passin Su. This stream gives its name to the fertile valley which lies between it and the main river. A solid masonry bridge with seven piers is situated just below the junction of the waters; it is stated to have been built in the time of Darius Hystaspes. This bridge, which is called the Tcheban-Kerpi, or bridge of grazing grounds, forms the junction of the two main roads, one from Kars, the other from Persia to Erzeroum.

To the west of the bridge are the remains of a few earthworks thrown up in 1854, by order of Sir Fenwick Williams; they are now being strengthened, but in the usual dilatory manner of the Turks; a depôt of commissariat stores has also been established here, and evidently Mukhtar looks upon it as a point which he may have to fall back upon, and which he ought, therefore, to defend. The position he has selected, however good it may have been in 1854, when smooth-bores were in vogue, is quite unsuitable for defence now. The earthworks are commanded by hills running to within 800 or 900 yards. These once in the possession of the enemy, the abandonment of the entrenchments becomes imperative, and a retreat across the plain to the next defensive position, Devi-Boyun, would be a most dangerous affair in presence of the vast cavalry force with which the Russians are accredited. The bridge is barely commanded by these works, which are badly situated, and although only meant for temporary occupation, have closed gorges. Kuipri Kui is a Christian village, and as such suffers more or less from the conduct of the battalion quartered in its vicinity. Indeed, while we were at breakfast we were

G

disturbed by much howling and shouting, several Christians running up towards us. On inquiry we found that a Turkish soldier had, just at that moment, shot an Armenian (in whose house he had been living for a month) through the head with his revolver, killing him on the spot. Our zaptiehs, of course, said the affair was an accident; but our Christian servants, who were close by when it occurred, said that there was a dispute about a bridle, when the zaptieh drew his revolver and shot the poor fellow through the head, killing him instantly. I believe the lieutenant-colonel commanding at Kuipri Kui will hold an inquiry into the occurrence. After breakfast we pushed on along the left bank of the Araxes to Khorassan, reaching it at five p.m. Here we found excellent quarters in the telegraph office, and Sir Arnold determined on making it his head-quarters for some short time.

Encamped in the plain, just in front of our window, are the two battalions and the two mountain guns which have just fallen back from Gulentab, an outpost on the Araxes, whence a road branches off to Kars, and where there is a wooden bridge. Here we heard that Ahmed Mukhtar Pasha had fallen back from the Tchakir Baba position to one near Zewin, and that the Russians had pushed forward their outpost as far as Sara Kamysh, on the Soghanly Dagh. We met a number of Circassian horsemen escorting sick and wounded to Erzeroum. They gave us details of the fight at Beghli Ahmed, a village situated about eighteen miles south-west of Kars. According to their accounts, 2,000 Circassians, commanded by Moussa Pacha, moved out to attack the Russian cavalry, who numbered sixteen regiments. After a sharp skirmish, owing to ammunition running out (these men are all armed by the Turkish Government with Winchester repeating rifles), they were forced to retire, having about thirty killed. They complain of the want of leaders, and boast that if they only had six good battalions and a good commander they would drive the Russians back to Goomri. According to some accounts the enemy, prior to the fight, brought up 6,000 infantry, mounted behind the dragoons, and, having posted them in a very good position, sent the cavalry forward. These fell back before the Circassians, and thus drew them into the ambuscade so cleverly prepared, when, being exposed to the infantry fire, they were forced to retire. These men say that all the Circassians on the Russian side are most disaffected, and that many are coming into Turkish head-quarters daily. They remind me much of the better class of Pathans, on the north-west frontier of India—simple and unaffected in their manner, gallant in their bearing, talking with perfect freedom and openness, they easily win the hearts of all Englishmen with whom they come in contact. They make excellent irregular cavalry, though I fancy that the hand which held them in would require a strong steel glove under the kid covering. They are well armed with their own native sword and pistol, and the Winchester carbine supplied by the Turkish Government. Mukhtar Pasha has altogether about 1,500 of these men, but only about 1,200 were engaged in the Beghli Ahmed affair on the 28th ult. In common with all Turkish cavalry, they are mounted on small, under-sized ponies—wiry, hardy animals, but dreadfully over-weighted; and though possessing great endurance, without any speed whatever. Their saddlery is of the rudest description—cord reins, tape bridles, huge wooden

G 2

saddles, like howdahs, with a sheepskin coat strapped on
the cantle, two large holsters on the pommels, and rough
leather saddle-bags complete their equipment.   Each
man, however, carries in addition a whip, and many lead
a spare pony, generally the property of some Christian
in a far-off village.   There are no men in the world
equal to the Tcherkess for looting.

On the 4th, finding myself so close to Mukhtar
Pasha, I determined to pay him a visit.   Lieutenant
Dougall and myself left Khorassan after breakfast,
and, escorted by a zaptieh—who was stupid even for
his class—tried to find our way by a cross-country and
short cut to Zewin.   Of course our escort professed
to know the road perfectly well, and of course he
was as ignorant of the geography of the district as
he was of the binomial theorem; so although we rode
pretty fast, it was not until 4 p.m. that we found ourselves opposite the General's tent.   His chief of the
staff, Faizi Pasha (General Kohlman), a Hungarian
by birth and an old defender of Kars under Sir
Fenwick Williams, welcomed us most kindly, and of
course produced cigarettes and coffee.   I had a letter
of introduction to General Kohlman from an old
Hungarian friend, and armed with this I found myself a welcome guest.   After a conversation of about
half an hour we went to pay our respects to the Commander-in-Chief, who is a short, square-built man,
with a determined face surrounded by close-cut black
moustachios and beard.   Ahmed Mukhtar Pasha is
an exceedingly good specimen of a Turkish General;
having spent the greater part of his career in the
Palace, his manners are more those of the courtier
than of the soldier; but although his influence is due

to the fact that he was for many years an aide-de-
camp and trusted friend of the late Sultan Abdul
Azeez, yet amongst the men he is better known for
his conduct when on the head-quarter staff in the
Yemmen and Cretan Expeditions, for which he earned
his promotion to Major-General and subsequently to
that of Mushir or Field-Marshal. He was appointed
in 1873 to the Viceroyalty of Erzeroum. In 1875 he
was transferred to the command in Montenegro, where
his conduct as Commander-in-Chief brought down
upon him severe criticism from the outside world.
How far this was deserved I know not. On the announcement of the armistice in the autumn of 1876
Mukhtar Pasha was transferred to Crete ; but the
Porte, feeling convinced that a collision with Russia
was inevitable, availed themselves of his knowledge
of the Armenian theatre of war, and appointed him
Marshal of the 4th Turkish Army Corps, which he
joined in March, and straightway busied himself in
all arrangements for the supply of the troops in the
field, for the organisation of the reserve forces, and
for the concentration of the reinforcements from the
Syrian and Arabian Army Corps. With an empty
treasury, with an antagonistic civil coadjutor, and
with the worst staff a General ever took the field with,
Mukhtar occupied a very unenviable position. However, he set to work with an energy rarely seen in a
Turkish official, and although he could not command
success he certainly deserved it. He was quite simply
dressed in the undress blue pea-jacket, trimmed with
red cord, so much affected by the Turkish officer, without order or decoration of any sort. He seemed perfectly open and free in his conversation, and dilated

with some enthusiasm on the strength of his position, which certainly is a most excellent one for defence. It is situated on a plateau to the west of Zewin, and is about 2,000 feet above the Chan Su, from which the ground rises gradually for about a mile, after which the ascent is more difficult and in many parts almost scarped. The plateau extends for about two miles, with a knoll some 150 feet high in the centre; and to the south, at the distance of another mile, but separated from the main position by a deep and difficult ravine, is a lofty ridge dominating the Zewin Dooz, which, jutting forward to the Chan Su, completely flanks the whole position. To the rear, again, is a still higher ridge which commands the whole. The plateau is at the junction of three roads from Kars, and is about equi-distant from Delibaba, the right of the Turkish line of defence, and Olti, the left of the line.

The front of the Zewin Dooz is protected by shelter trenches which run completely from north to south, and there are earthworks for four batteries, one of which is on the commanding spur south of the ravine, one on the knoll in the centre of the position, the other two nearly about the centre. The force actually with Mukhtar Pasha available for the defence of the Zewin Dooz consists of eighteen battalions of infantry, 500 regular cavalry, including zaptiehs, two field batteries, and two mountain batteries. The Commander-in-Chief told us that he had counter-ordered the march of the troops from Olti, and that to-day the disposition of his troops was as follows:—

	Battalions.	Cavalry.	Field Guns.	Mountain Guns.
Olti	8	—	—	6
Zewin Dooz	18	500	12	12
Delibaba	6	200	6	—
Moola Suliman ...	6	200	6	8
Toprak Kale	2	200	—	4
Khorassan	2	—	—	2
Kuipri Kui	1	—	—	—
Ardish	6	500	6	6
Devi-Boyun	4	—	—	—
Erzeroum	4	—	18	12
Total	57	1,600	48	50

There are besides 4,000 irregulars also at Ardish.
This is the force I reported in my last at Van. The
Russian troops pushed forward from Bayazid to operate against them fell back, so Faik Pasha moved up
to Ardish, where he certainly threatens the flank of
any force moving along the Persian road.

The Russian advanced posts are reported at Pennek on the right, Tcharpakli, Sara Kamysh, and
Kaghisman in the centre, and Kara Kilissa on the
south, the right column being still at Ardahan, the
centre in the neighbourhood of Kars, and the south at
Bayazid. What their intentions are it is difficult to say;
their delay in advancing, and their conduct with regard
to the incomplete investment of Kars, is perfectly inexplicable. Yesterday an officer, Lieutenant-Colonel
Ibrahim Bey,* arrived in camp only two hours before
we did, and he reported the road to Kars perfectly
clear and open. The Commander-in-Chief himself informed me that there was telegraphic communication with
the beleaguered (?) fortress, which was well provisioned,

---

* He is a brother of Djameel Pasha, and I therefore had an early opportunity of delivering the letters entrusted to me, and of making the
acquaintance of one of the most modest and most gallant officers in the
Turkish army. He speedily earned his promotion to Colonel for gallantry
in the field.

the health and spirits of the troops being excellent. Mukhliss Pasha has recently come into head-quarters, and Hassan Hami Pasha now has the chief command there.

Just before I left Erzeroum the Governor of Bayazid came in, and his account of the capitulation of that place does not reflect much credit on the officers concerned; 1,700 men with six guns moved out of the place without firing a shot, and the Governor, though he saved his harem and all his private property, had no time to bring away either treasure or Government records! There seems to be but little cordiality between the civil governors and the military commanders. The former accuse the latter of ignorance and cowardice, while the latter retaliate by calling the civilians apathetic idlers, who hamper the movements of the military by neglecting all commissariat arrangements, and who delay wilfully the forwarding of supplies and *matériel*, thus endangering the safety of the army. There is no doubt that if any disaster befall this army the blame will rest chiefly on Ismail Pasha, the Governor-General at Erzeroum. He shows no energy whatever in sending supplies to the Commander-in-Chief, and as for endeavouring to hasten onward the guns now *en route* from Trebizond, and which were despatched from that place with such expedition and in such excellent condition by that energetic officer, Djameel Pasha, such a thought has never entered his head. Fifty-four of those guns a fortnight ago were within 100 miles of Erzeroum, and as yet not one has arrived. More guns, more food, more doctors, is the cry daily coming from the Commander-in-Chief, and though the road from Trebizond is literally covered with guns, and though the district is full of food and stores of grain in villages within a few miles of Erzeroum, Ismail Pasha fails to collect it; the consequence is that the soldiers are on short rations, and the Christian villagers are robbed and plundered by them in order to satisfy the cravings of hunger.

The complaints on all sides of the conduct of the Kurds are constant and most bitter. After their subjugation by the Turks their custom of levying black mail was summarily stopped, and they themselves compelled to pay revenue. Now, when their services are required by the Government, and they are sent away from their homes to fight the common foe, they have recommenced their predatory habits, and levy contributions from every village they pass through. Numerous petitions setting forth their misdeeds have been laid before the Governor, who (himself a Kurd from Shoragel, near Kars) pays no heed whatever to the prayer of the Christian villagers, who seem more favoured by the attention of these gentry than their Mahomedan neighbours. In despair, the Christians have appealed to Mr. Zohrab, our consul, and it is to be hoped now that the constant reports of ravishing women, highway robberies, plundering villagers, and murders will cease. As soldiers they are worse than useless—as the chief of the staff informed me—so, for the sake of all, it would be preferable that they should be sent back to their homes and allowed to plunder the Russian camps, if they are so minded, rather than left to ravage territory as yet untouched by the horrors of war. As long as Ismail Pasha reigns in Erzeroum, it is much to be feared that nothing will be done to check the Kurds or to place the Christians on a better footing. His conduct towards the troops now in garrison at Erzeroum very nearly led to an *émeute;* indeed, the men of one battalion were in a state of open mutiny for some hours, and were only pacified by the conduct of the major, who insisted on some pay being disbursed among them, and on their receiving proper food. It is scarcely to be wondered at that the feeling among the men should be somewhat mutinous when they are nineteen months in arrears, and when they only receive rations every other day, and then merely the allowance of flour, all other articles, from motives of economy, being carefully withheld.

Were the Commander-in-Chief only provided with men, provisions, and money, I feel satisfied affairs would shortly assume a very different complexion; but, with a total of about 40,000 men, and with 48 field-pieces, in place of the recognised complement of 120, it is impossible that he can make much show of resistance against the vastly superior force the Russians are bringing against him. Had the expedition despatched to Soukoum Kaleh—which, after all, can effect no real good—been sent to reinforce him, those 10,000 men and those 24 guns would have enabled him completely to check the enemy in any attempt at an advance. As it is, his small force now is necessarily spread over a vast extent of territory, and is liable to defeat in detail, the blame of which would, of course, be thrown on the general, and not on the Minister of War, who is really responsible for the paucity of troops in Anatolia, or on Ismail Pasha, who is responsible for the scarcity of supplies and consequent deterioration of the *morale* of the army.

I hope the society for the relief of sick and wounded Turkish soldiers will remember the troops in Anatolia when they are distributing their comforts and coin to the army. In the army of the Danube the men are in a good climate, near home, with large towns and cities near at hand to which their sick and wounded can be sent. Moreover, nearly every battalion has two Italian, French, or German doctors. Here the men are in a climate which will shortly bring on them tropical heat, to supersede the almost Arctic cold to which they have been exposed; they are badly clothed, ill-supplied with food, there are very few doctors, and nearly all these are in Erzeroum attending the hospitals, which are filled with typhoid patients; there are no ambulances, and very few litters, to carry sick and wounded, who are consequently transported on arabas, the jolting of which on those hilly roads must be almost death to an invalid; the supply of medicines is very limited, and I shudder to think of the misery which will ensue should any great battles be fought. Hundreds of our countrymen, ay, and countrywomen, nobly volunteered in the Franco-German War, numbers gave their services in the Servian and Montenegrin campaigns last year, but as yet not one Red Cross man has appeared in Anatolia, where there is more need a thousand times for them than there was in 1870. I trust it may not be said that the climate has frightened them away, but it is the fact that no wars in tropical or semi-barbarous countries have been accompanied by the Red Cross train. In Ashantee our medical arrangements were never supplemented by voluntary assistance, and here in Asia Minor the faulty hospital requirements and scanty medical comforts of the Turkish service are left to satisfy the wants of the vast army of sick and wounded which must necessarily be the results of this campaign. Surely the Mahomedan troops in Anatolia are deserving of the same attention and comforts as their more fortunate brethren waging war in more favourable circumstances on the banks of the Danube, and I trust that my feeble efforts to bring their sufferings and their wants to the notice of the Stafford House and Red Cross committees may be the means of diverting some of the good things from the broad channel of the Danube to the mountainous regions of Armenia.

On the morning of the 6th of June, I rode out to the Delibaba Pass to look at the position on the right of the Turkish army. The Araxes, which flows about one mile south of Khorassan, was very full for this season of the year, and the small raft by which foot-passengers cross was too frail a craft to carry a horse, so I was fain to swim the stream, and got thoroughly wet in consequence. A hot sun soon dried my clothes, but my saddle suffered somewhat from my imprudence. Following the right bank of the Taikhojeh stream, I reached the village (whence the rivulet takes its name) at about 7 a.m. There I found encamped two battalions of infantry, the finest I have yet seen, men of good physique, and well set up, arms clean and in good order, tents regularly pitched, and a general air of smartness and discipline about the whole detachment, very different from the style generally adopted in the 4th Army Corps. They were Redif battalions of the 2nd Ban from Erzeroum and Erzingjan. Leaving Taikhojeh, I continued along the valley of the stream until I hit off the road from Erzeroum to Bayazid, when I turned to the left, and following a nearly easterly course, in an hour crossed a ridge, on the crest of which was encamped another battalion.

Dropping down the eastern slopes of this branch of

the Kose Dagh, I reached the Delibaba camp at 11 a.m., and found four battalions encamped in the plain at the mouth of the Pass; and a couple more, having piled arms, were resting on the ground. A staff-officer rode up to me, and very civilly asked me into his tent, where, during the inevitable coffee and cigarettes, I learnt that Lieutenant-General Mahomed Pasha, commanding the Division, was expected in every moment with the force recently occupying Moola Suliman, which had been ordered by the Commander-in-Chief to fall back on Delibaba. Major Issit Bey very kindly offered to accompany me through the Pass until we should meet the Pasha, so moving on we entered the defile, which at its western extremity presents a very formidable appearance, but after proceeding about a mile the hills get broken up; all the eastern slopes, being gentle, present no difficulty whatever to an attacking force. Indeed, there is no reason why field-artillery should not avoid the defile altogether and advance over the hills themselves. In about half an hour we met the General, who was accompanied by five battalions of infantry, two field and one mountain battery, and a weak regiment of Dragoons. The men were all in good condition, and though naturally dusty and weather-stained from their long sojourn in camp, as well as from the effects of their long march, looked thoroughly up to work. Their arms were in capital order, clean, and evidently well taken care of. The field batteries were well horsed with small hardy animals, reminding one of the stamp of cattle used in the Punjab frontier batteries, rather than those with which our own horse artillery troops are drawn. The mountain guns, instead of being carried on mules, as in our service, and in other batteries of this arm I have seen

in this country, were each drawn by one mule.*   All the
artillery were Krupp's, and seemed in thoroughly ser-
viceable condition.   The cavalry, though far superior
to any I have yet seen, were very bad in every respect
except their armament; and I am inclined to think the
repeating rifle is an admirable weapon for cavalry, especially in hilly country, where their value is necessarily
much impaired, and where long-range shooting is not
absolutely necessary.

Returning to camp with Mahomed Pasha, I was introduced to Mustafa Pasha, a very stout little gentleman, who bustled about everywhere, and seemed the
mainspring of the division.   From him I learnt that
a small cavalry detachment of the Russians was at
Toprak Kale, but that there was no force of any strength
nearer than Dijadin, and that this retrograde movement
had caused much dissatisfaction among the men, who
were most anxious to be led against the enemy.   After
a stay of about an hour I took my leave of the
General, and going to Major Issit Bey's tent, was
introduced to several officers, among others the Colonel
commanding the artillery, and the Lieutenant-Colonels
of the Erzeroum and Kharpoot battalions.   They all
seemed strangely ignorant of the movements of the other
portions of their army, and though cognisant of the
fall of Ardahan had heard no particulars, for the few
I could furnish them with were most thankfully received.   They appeared anxious to be led forward, and
certainly expressed no very favourable opinions of their
leaders.   They were very anxious to know if England
was going to declare war, and a telegram in Turkish
was shown to me stating that six regiments of cavalry,

* As in France.

four brigades of artillery, and fifty-nine battalions of infantry were under orders for active service; also that provisions for 80,000 men had been ordered to be collected at Alexandria. This information has been printed on small slips of paper and freely distributed in the army.

Bidding adieu to my new-found friends, I turned my horse's head homewards, and after once more swimming the Araxes, reached Khorassan at about 5 p.m., where I found Captain Macalmont, an extra military attaché, who had just arrived from England to join Sir Arthur Kemball's staff. About half an hour afterwards the General, accompanied by Captain Trotter, R.E., and Lieutenant Dougall, R.N., rode in, having been on a visit to the Commander-in-Chief's camp, and brought back the welcome news that the Russian reconnoitring party of three battalions of infantry, one regiment of cavalry, and one battery of mountain guns, had evacuated Olti, and that Ahmed Mukhtar Pasha was going to re-occupy it with eight battalions, two regiments of cavalry, and six mountain guns. So, early in the morning of the 7th, Captains Trotter and Macalmont rode out to Zewin and accompanied this force with orders to report on its movements, and the large room in the telegraph station at Khorassan was left to the General, Dougall, and myself.

On the 8th Sir Arnold Kemball, wishing to see for himself the nature of the country round Delibaba, and to ascertain from personal observation whether the position could be turned or not, proposed a visit to Mahomed Pasha's camp. I asked permission to accompany him, so setting out at 6 a.m. we reached the camp at 8 a.m., and after a short stay with the Lieutenant-General, rode on through the Pass towards Moola Suliman, accompanied by an escort of mounted Kurds, dressed fantastically, armed extravagantly, and having the appearance of men more calculated to fly than to fight. They one and all reminded me of the guard who escorted Mark Twain to Jerusalem, and whose appearance is so graphically described in the "New Pilgrim's Progress." Following the Pass for about an hour, and having seen more than one road diverging from it towards Erzeroum, we retraced our steps, and when within about three miles of Delibaba, dismissed our Bashi Bazouk escort, and, turning up a path, took a southerly course for a mile or more, when, seeing a village to our right, we proceeded to it, and hitting off a track quite practicable for guns, crossed the Kose Dagh at a height of about 7,200 feet, by a road lying midway between the Delibaba and Khara Darband Passes; and, after passing the village of Audak, situated at the source of the Taikhojeh stream, we followed the water until we reached the Araxes. Sending our horses over with our grooms, we crossed by the boat and reached our quarters at 6 p.m. The 9th we spent at home, and on the 10th, Lieutenant Dougall being still on the sick list, I accompanied Sir Arnold Kemball to head-quarters, distant about fifteen miles. We breakfasted with the Commander-in-Chief, and afterwards went over the position, which, in my humble opinion, though well chosen, is too extended for the small force at Mukhtar Pasha's disposal.

While in his Excellency's tent three Circassians came in with letters from Kars, giving an account of the affair on the 8th of June, which appears to have been of very little importance; the Russians, changing their position from the southern to the northern side of the

fortress, were attacked in flank by a sortie from the garrison. The action lasted some hours, and its severity
may be judged by the fact that the Turks lost seven
and the Russians about twenty wounded. As Faizi
Pasha, the chief of the staff, naïvely remarked to me,
"It was not a brilliant victory, but it is very encouraging." Poor fellows, they need some encouragement, opposed as they are to an army superior to them
in numbers, equipment, in cavalry, artillery, in the
military knowledge of their leaders, and in pecuniary
resources. I had an opportunity during my visit to the
head-quarter camp of conversing with some men who
were present at the affair near Beghli Ahmed on the
29th ult., and I also was present when Mukhtar Pasha
himself was discussing the business. It appears that
his Excellency despatched Moussa Pasha, the Circassian
chief, with about 1,500 men, accompanied by a squadron
of regular cavalry with two small Whitworth Galloper
guns, to attack the enemy. When within about thirty
miles of Kars they came upon the Russian outposts,
who fell back before them, and presently found themselves opposed to about 6,000 horse. Among them
there were six regiments of Circassians, who, refusing to
operate against their Mahomedan brethren, may be put
out of the fray.

According to the Turkish accounts, infantry were sent
out from the Russian camp, posted in broken ground,
and then the Cossacks fell back until the Turkish horse
came under the fire of the ambuscade, when, finding themselves outnumbered and outmanœuvred, they retired. I
am inclined to think that the Russians, dismounting some
of their men, employed them as skirmishers against the
Circassians. Be this as it may, the accounts agree that,

H

having suffered a loss of 13 killed and 37 wounded, the Turks retired in some disorder. Many, escaping round the enemy's flank, got into Kars, and being returned as missing, swelled the casualty roll. Recent returns from the fortress, however, have reduced the list, and I feel sure you may safely accept the above statement as substantially correct. The Turks say that the Russians suffered severely from the fire of their Galloper guns, but I am inclined to doubt this, and as no details of the Russian loss can be obtained, it is difficult even to make an estimate of it.

Mukhtar Pasha's force is at present encamped on the spur which runs down from the Kargha Bazar range towards Zewin. It is in two lines, the front occupying a ridge about a mile and a quarter in length, with a deep, almost scarped, ravine in front. In the centre of this ridge is a knoll 300 feet above the main camp, on which is placed an earthwork holding four guns, and on the extreme right of the ridge, which here takes a sweep forward, is another knoll, on which is placed a battery of two field-guns; five battalions are encamped on the reverse slope, and the whole front is covered by shelter-trenches of a novel construction, for the earth from the trench, instead of forming a parapet in front, is carefully spread about the ground, thus giving the defenders a *minimum* amount of cover with a *maximum* of labour. Immediately in rear of this ridge is a deep ravine, the descent to which is very steep and precipitous; the ascent, however, is gradual, forming a natural glacis, about 1,000 yards in length, to the crest of the second position, which consists of a semicircular ridge with its convex side to the enemy. On it are placed six field and eight mountain guns in earthworks; two of the latter, being on the right flank and slightly thrown forward, sweep the whole front. The defence of this is entrusted to 11 battalions, while on a steep hill two miles to the front, and on another nearly as far to the rear, are posted two battalions with four guns. A deep ravine runs entirely round the right flank and front of Mukhtar's position, up which advance would be difficult, and as the fire from the hill on the right completely searches this, it may be considered a source of strength rather than weakness. The left flank is more open, and is approached through rocky, undulating ground, affording cover to the enemy, and much facilities for an attack. This is the weak point of the defence, and, strangely enough, is left comparatively undefended. As I said before, the position is naturally a strong one, and, looking at it with the eye of an inexperienced man, I should venture an opinion that although his Excellency has made the very best dispositions possible, yet it is too extended a one to hold with his small force. Could he put 30 more guns and 10,000 more men on it, he might defy the Russians for weeks. The situation is high (6,500 ft. above the sea), the air clear and bracing, water plentiful and good, grass sweet and abundant, and firewood obtainable in the neighbourhood. There is every natural advantage; only the means are wanting to make a stubborn resistance.

I have been informed on the highest authority that orders have been received from Constantinople for the trial at Erzeroum of Hassan Sabri Pasha, the commander of the troops at Ardahan. He reached that place on the 7th inst., accompanied by Mahomed Bey, the gallant defender of the Emir Oghlou, whose wound does not appear to be so severe as was reported. They brought with them 1,300 men. This makes up the total now re-assembled out of the nine battalions to about 3,500 men, but a very large proportion of these are unarmed. Some are wounded and many are sickly. The reason for Sabri's delay on the road remains to be known. He evidently is afraid to account for his weak resistance and hasty flight, and so delayed three weeks on a march which, taking into consideration the fact that he was unopposed, and in very light marching order, should not have occupied more than ten days at the extreme limit. It certainly is advisable that a very stern example should be made of him, especially at this juncture, when Kars is besieged and in danger of daily assault. Thus, hampered by incompetent lieutenants, thwarted at every step by an uneducated and apathetic civil superior, left with an empty treasure-chest, utterly unprovided with commissariat or means of transport, and with an army mainly composed of raw levies, it is not to be wondered at that Mukhtar Pasha is unable to undertake any offensive operations. The conduct of Ismail Pasha, the Governor-General of Erzeroum, is little short of criminal. It is now seven weeks since war was declared, and yet no preparations have been made for the defence of that city. Although situated in the midst of a most fertile district, a land literally flowing with milk and honey, and filled with corn and wine—for here we see large herds of oxen grazing on all sides, goats and sheep cover the hills, the valleys are bright with young green corn-fields, and the vine-yards of Kharpoot supply a large stock of drinkable claret—yet, with all these means at hand, there posi-tively is not grain enough in the city of Erzeroum to furnish 20,000 men with a week's rations, nor live stock for a day's food. The guns which, owing to the untiring energy of Lieutenant-General Djameel Pasha, were pushed on from Trebizond in such haste, have been lying at Baiboort, 50 miles from Erzeroum, for more than a week, awaiting the transport to bring them in. Five batteries of field-guns lie unhorsed in the citadel yard, within 100 yards of Ismail Pasha's house, and yet, in spite of Mukhtar Pasha's repeated entreaties for more guns, more guns, more guns, no attempts are made to fit out and forward these 30 pieces of cannon to the front. Again, the earthworks ordered to be constructed on the Devi-Boyun to the east, and in Ghiurji Boghaz defile to the north of Erzeroum, present much the same appearance that they did a month ago. Instead of employing all the able-bodied men of the district to throw up works which would detain the Russians, he sends out some weak battalions, who for the first few days scratch up a few scarcely bullet-proof trenches, and then sit down in their tents and wait orders. By his apathy in all matters relating to the defence of his capital, and his neglect in not punishing his own tribesmen the Kurds, who are harassing the whole district, he has exasperated the population to such a pitch of excitement, that his recall becomes a matter of imperative necessity. More than a month ago, as will be remembered, he telegraphed to the Porte that he was setting out to invade Russian territory with 40,000 Kurds. This telegram was, I presume, firmly believed in Stamboul, for he was immediately decorated with the 1st Class of the Medjidie. Yet he has not only never set out, but has never collected his 40,000 men. The idea of 40,000 Kurds venturing to invade Russia is sufficient to raise a smile, but the sight of Ismail at the head of them is past ridicule. An able, energetic man at Erzeroum would have put a different complexion on the campaign. Its disastrous results will be entirely owing to the carelessness of the Porte in not selecting the best men for important and responsible posts.

The actual position of the Russians is difficult to ascertain, solely for the reason that, owing to his paucity in cavalry, Mukhtar Pasha is quite unable to reconnoitre properly. Even had he plenty of horsemen, I doubt if he has an officer in his army to whom he could intrust a reconnaissance. Absurd as it may appear, he asked me—one of the pests of modern warfare, as I believe a young and distinguished general officer stigmatised the profession to which I belong—if I would furnish him with a sketch of the Delibaba Pass and the roads thereto. I am glad I was enabled to gratify His Excellency. It seems that the right column of the Russians, numbering three battalions, one regiment of cavalry, and six mountain-guns, are close by Pennek, having fallen back from Olti on the 5th inst. The centre and main column, leaving outposts at Tcharpakli, Sara Kamysh, and Kotanli, are concentrated round Kars, while the left wing, in three detachments, are at Bayazid, Utch Kilissa, and Kara Kilissa. This latter force numbers in all twelve battalions, forty-eight field and four mountain-guns, with 1,500 Cossacks.

The Turkish forces occupy much the same ground they did a fortnight ago. Eight battalions, six mountain-guns, with two regiments of Bashi-Bazouk cavalry, and 1,200 Circassians, are at Olti, under Hadji Raschid Pasha. Mukhtar Pasha, at Zewin, has 18 battalions,

two field and two mountain batteries, with one squadron
of regular and 800 Circassian horsemen. A battalion
with two mountain-guns is at Khorassan, and Mahomed
Pasha, leaving four battalions at Delibaba, has to-day
moved forward to Moola Suliman with ten battalions,
one field and one mountain battery, one weak regiment
of regular and 400 irregular horsemen. Detachments
of varying strength occupy Kuipri-Kui, Hassan Kale,
the Devi-Boyun, and the Ghiurji Boghaz defiles, while
Erzeroum has three field-batteries horsed, five unhorsed,
and about six battalions of infantry. The strength of
the posts in rear is so constantly changing that I am
unable with any degree of exactness to report them.

The Van column, under Lieutenant-General Faik
Pasha, is in the Abagha district, between the Van lake
and Persia, with its head-quarters at the Bagir Fort
(Beigir Kale in Kiepert), and consists of four to six
battalions, six mountain-guns, and, it is now said, nearly
5,000 Kurdish horsemen.

The movements of the Russians point to an early
assault on Kars. Should it be successful, a rapid advance on Erzeroum will be its immediate consequence.
Mukhtar Pasha, however, is very confident it will hold
out; his best troops are there, and the place is provisioned for a year. If the Turks repel the attack,
there is hope that the Russians may be checked for
some weeks, by which time reinforcements of men,
money, and guns will have reached him, and a fairer
contest be waged on the Zewin Dooz.

CHAPTER VI.

THE BATTLE OF TAGHIR.

A Fatal Omen!—With Sir Arnold in Search of a "Scrim"—Mahomed Pasha
wishes to Fight—Our Breakfast Interrupted—View the Ground—Kurds
and Circassians—A Rough Time of it—Russian Intentions—Disposition of
our Troops—Description of the Ground—Wild Firing of the Turks—
Gallantry of their Gunners—Pluck of the Tcherkess—Excellence of Russian
Infantry—Waste of Ammunition—Our Flank Turned—Yahvash! Yahvash!—A Run from the Cossacks—Hospital Arrangements—Reflection on
the Fight—The Energetic Djameel Pasha—Turkish Losses.

LATE last night Sir Arnold Kemball was good enough
to inform me that the Russian force, under Tergukassoff,
was pushing a reconnaissance towards the Delibaba
Pass, and that there was every chance of a collision.
So, obtaining the General's permission to accompany
him, I started from Khorassan at 6 a.m. We had
been disturbed during the night by three very sharp
shocks of earthquake, which caused the telegraph house
to shake to its very foundations, and certainly gave me
the idea that the whole building was coming down,
and subsequently had been kept awake by the persis-
tent tapping of a raven at our window—*absit omen!*
Crossing the Aras by raft, we passed Taikhojeh, where
we met two battalions and nine guns, all under orders
to move up to reinforce Mahomed Pasha, who we heard
was at a place unnoticed in the chart, about five miles

AFFAIR AT TAGHIR

June 16th 1877.

to Zeitkau

to Zeitkau

Zeitkau Stream

Russians {
1st Position { Infy
Cav.
2nd Position { Cav.
Infy
}

Turks { Cav.
Infy

from Erzeroum

From Bulakbassi

ENGLISH MILES

London, Cassell, Petter, & Galpin.

short of Moola Suliman. On reaching Delibaba, the
late head-quarters of the left wing, we found it entirely
deserted. Breakfasting by the side of the stream at
eleven, we pressed on, and passed stray men going to
the rear in charge of regimental baggage. From them
we learnt that the division had struck camp, and was
moving forward to meet the Russians, who were
advancing from Zaidikan, where there had been a considerable encampment for some days. Passing large
quantities of baggage and commissariat stores, we
traversed the Eshek Khalias Valley, and, crossing the
watershed of the Delibaba and Zaidikan streams by a
ridge 8,200 feet high, descended the eastern slopes, and
reached Taghir at 2 p.m. Here we found Lieutenant-
General Mahomed Pasha, with one battalion—the Ohf
Corps of Lazitan—and, dismounting, heard from him
that the Russians in the morning had struck camp, and
advanced westwards ; but that being entirely destitute
of cavalry—he had only two troops in his division,
barely 70 sabres—he was unable to watch their movements, especially as they were very strong in that arm.
He pointed out that there were three roads from
Zaidikan, and that he had despatched a force consisting of three battalions, two mountain and one field
gun, to the crest of the hills commanding each road,
thus disposing of nine battalions and all his guns, and
meant to oppose them should they continue their
advance during the day ; if, however, they stood fast,
in the morning, when he would be reinforced by four
more battalions, 1,000 cavalry, and nine guns, he would
move down and attack them.

The enemy advanced along the centre road, but,
seeing the crest held, moved off to the right, hoping

to turn the position by a hill road quite impracticable for guns ; but on finding the heights commanding it crowned by a strong force of infantry, they withdrew into Zaidikan. Their force consisted of one regiment of dragoons, two of Cossacks, about 1,200 irregular cavalry, six battalions of infantry, and at least twelve mountain guns. I could see no field artillery. Shots were exchanged between the cavalry, without any loss on our side. One Cossack was seen to fall, but I doubt if there were any other casualties, as the range was far, and the firing wild. The reports brought in by scouts and spies point to the fact, that the small body of Russians seen by the Turkish outposts had fallen back to the main body encamped at Zaidikan. Statements as to their strength varied, though all agreed in the detail of the cavalry force.

At six p.m. Lieutenant-General Mahomed Pasha sent word that he would send his dinner to our tent, and do us the honour of sharing it with us. Sir Arnold Kemball, whose *aide-de-camp* had been compelled to return to Erzeroum owing to sickness, was alone, and very kindly permitted me to accompany him, had suggested, that for the sake of " travelling light," we should only take one tent between us, and divide the services of our attendants, so, at hearing of the change in our entertainment, he brought his Oriental experience to bear on the subject. Beds were stowed away, carpets produced—very old and dirty they were, having been used to save our waterproof sheeting from fraying against pack saddles—and at eight p.m. the General's Turkish orderly announced the Pasha. Mahomed Pasha was accompanied by Major-General Mustafa Pasha, his second in command, and by Toghra Werdi

Bey, a deserter from the Russians, who until lately had held the post of Adjutant-Major of one of their Circassian regiments; but shortly after the outbreak of war had joined the Turks with five men of his regiment, and now is the right-hand man of Mahomed Pasha, who asks his opinion on every subject, and, what is worse, takes it, too. All correspondence passes through his hands, and he is treated with much more deference than any colonel in the division.

After dinner the Lieutenant-General became very lively, assured us of his intention to attack the Russians in the morning, and told us that he had certain information they were in very small numbers, and had only five field-guns. Mine differed from his; however, as his sources of information were presumably more trustworthy, I bowed to his superior knowledge. Subsequent events proved him wrong, however.

On the morning of the 15th we rode out to visit the position, and saw that the Russians had crowned the heights occupied by our advanced posts yesterday. We employed our time in going over the whole line, which certainly is very strong, and were the Lieutenant-General to push on to a ridge about 1,200 yards in front, I believe he would be able to hold his own against three times his force. Going slightly in front of the ridge now held by our men towards a stream, where Sir Arnold Kemball suggested breakfast, we found ourselves drawing down the Russian fire. Their shells fell short, but still too close to the stream to make breakfast desirable, so we abandoned our enterprise, and on our retiring, the Russians ceased firing. At noon it was quite evident that Mahomed Pasha did not mean to attack, so we climbed to the top of the peak to the left of the Turkish position and surveyed the ground. From that spot we could see the Russians moving up in considerable force to the ridge on the extreme east of my plan, and by 4 p.m. they had sixteen field-pieces in battery there, with two battalions and a very heavy cavalry force.

At about 2 p.m. we noticed a great gathering of the Kurdish horsemen, numbering about 300, in the vicinity of Mahomed Pasha's bivouac, so descending from our vantage-ground we joined the Turkish General, who informed Sir Arnold he was going to meet a large body of Circassian horse, sent to his aid by Mukhtar Pasha. The conduct of the Kurds who accompanied us augured badly for any Russian cavalry that might stand in their way on the morrow. Every now and then a solitary horseman, his feelings overpowering him, would dash out from the crowd, spur his horse vigorously down the slope, shivering his lance, gnashing his teeth, and uttering anathemas against the Giaour. His example would be speedily followed by yet other men, who, dashing forward, would make as if they were about to attack each other, and soon the whole body of these fantastically dressed creatures, with their embroidered muslin burnooses flying behind them, were to be seen circling round in the plain, brandishing their lances, and hurling curses of defiance at their invisible foe. In less than a quarter of an hour we saw emerging from the Taghir defile the head of the column of Circassians. They moved slowly forward until their rear was clear of the Pass, and then advanced in line across the plain. Mahomed Pasha halted them, and addressing a few words of encouragement to their officers, promised them a fight on the morrow, where he hoped they would sus-

tain the honour of the Ottoman Empire, and make the
Russians feel the power of those swords they had discarded in days gone by. There was an air of business
about the Circassians sadly lacking in the Kurds, and
I fully hoped to see them distinguish themselves should
occasion arise in the coming fight.

Having seen the Circassians " dismissed," we once
more rode round the position, which now was in many
parts fairly entrenched. No positive orders had been
given on the subject, but the commandants of those
battalions situated in the immediate vicinity of the
Zaidikan road had thrown up shelter trenches from the
ridge dominating the stream to the right of our position as far as the foot of the knoll on our extreme left.
Much was left undone that might have been done —
little done that ought to have been done.

A ridge some 1,200 yards in front of us, running
parallel to our line, and which completely commanded
us, was left unoccupied. The possession of this was
cf vital importance, and if seized by the Russians
nothing could prevent their turning us out of our
position. We were excessively weak in artillery owing
to some unaccountable delay. The battery and two
battalions at Taikhojeh had failed to join us, although
Mahomed Pasha had sent orders the previous day for
them to be moved up with all despatch. In spite of
all this the General was confident of success, and promised me that I should see the Giaours running before
the Moslems ere I was twenty-four hours older.

Unfortunately, some mistakes had occurred in the
orders given as to our baggage, and we saw night coming
on with every prospect of our having to sleep on the
hill-side in our cloaks and without a chance of any food.

Our bivouac was over 8,000 feet above sea level, the range to the south was still covered with snow, and the wind passing over it most bitterly cold. Firewood there was none, and though occasionally Circassians would pass us carrying beams of wood from some dismantled house, no pecuniary consideration would induce them to part with a single stick. At about 10 p.m., when tired of stumping up and down the ridge, in the endeavour to keep our feet warm, we huddled together in a cleft of the ground. Sir Arnold's faithful body servant produced from his saddle-bag a piece of tongue. Fortunately it was dark, and we could not see the state it most assuredly must have been in, so we ate it contentedly enough, and lay down, hoping that the morrow would bring up our servants and supplies of meat and drink.

At 4 a.m. we rose from a very uncomfortable night's rest on the hill-side. Washing was out of the question; no water was to be had, and breakfast seemed very problematical. The business of the day, however, put all such thoughts out of our heads, for passing our glasses over the Russian position, some three miles distant, we saw indications of a coming attack, and straightway mounting our horses, which seemed none the worse for no corn and no shelter, rode in search of Mahomed Pasha, whose dispositions we now learnt. The Russians held a very strong position about 4,000 yards—perhaps rather less—to the east of the Turkish front, which was stretched along a ridge running from the high knoll to the north of their line. Between the two lay a third ridge, completely commanding us. Between this and the Turks was a deep ravine, which ran down to a stream with precipitous banks. This flowed to the south of the ridge forming the right flank of the Turks, and round the unoccupied ridge. So convinced was Mahomed Pasha that the Russians were not in strong force that he neglected to occupy this vantage ground, the possession of which was the turning point of the day. The Turkish force consisted in all of fourteen battalions of infantry, one battery of field and one of mountain guns, three troops of regular cavalry, 600 Circassians, 300 Kurdish horse—the latter a great deal worse than useless. This force was disposed as follows:—One battalion, with one mountain gun, on the knoll to the right of the front, and commanding, not only the road by which the Russian artillery would be forced to advance, but also the ravine, which skirted the whole flank, and which gave cover to any turning force the Russians might send. One battalion, with three guns, was on the neck of the ground connecting the right knoll with the road; and then running along the front of the whole position up to the very high peak on the left were stretched five more battalions, with two guns in a battery, about half a mile north of the road; one mountain gun the same distance further on, and one more on the peak to the extreme left. In reserve were two mountain guns and six battalions. The cavalry was massed to the right of the road, behind a ridge; and of the reserve battalions three were quite close up, and about 400 yards in rear of the reverse slope of the position, which was succeeded by a series of ridges, all springing from the same peak, which was 1,500 feet above our ground, and at a height of 7,700 feet above sea level. The remaining three were drawn up in line about a mile and a half in rear of the first line, on the road leading to Delibaba.

To the front of the centre of the Turkish line the

ground sloped gently away for a distance of about 800 yards, where there was a very deep, stiff ravine, which, as I said before, ran along the front of the unoccupied ridge. To this was sent a body of about 200 Circassian horse, armed with Winchester rifles. As they were perfectly powerless to act as cavalry in that position, for the ravine was completely commanded from the Russian side, and as they were perfectly untrained men, it is difficult to conceive why they were sent forward at all. The gentle declivity, however, in front of the centre, completely swept by our fire for more than 700 yards without a vestige of cover for a man to avail himself of, made an assault in that quarter a matter of much danger and difficulty; and the deep, precipitous ravine on the right flank, while affording cover to an attacking force and concealing them from sight until close to our position, quite prevented any artillery fire being brought to bear on them during their advance, owing to its tortuous character.

At 5 a.m. four battalions of Russians moved down the road in column of companies, with one battalion about half a mile in rear. Their guns, of which 16 were distinctly visible on the sky-line of their position, opened fire, but their shells fell far short of our front line. I had accompanied Sir Arnold Kemball to a point about two-thirds of the way up the peak, when, sending our horses behind the ridge, we sat down to watch the proceedings. At 6.10 some Russian skirmishers, whose advance we must have overlooked, appeared on the central ridge, quietly lining it, while a small body, in admirable order, crossed it, our shells doing them no harm (although the range could not have been more than 1,500 yards), and descended to their left, evidently with a view of turning our right flank, and at this moment their guns opened fire, their shells falling over the ridge. As yet only a few men had appeared here, but they were gradually strengthened. Now our artillery fire on their line became hotter, some few men even opening with their Henry-Martinis at a distance of about 1,500 yards. I particularly noticed the men, who evidently looked upon sights as a useless appendage, and fired wildly in the air, giving what elevation they considered necessary. Some officers exerted themselves to restrain their men from thus throwing away their ammunition; but the men objected strongly to obey these orders, and so this random firing continued all along the line. The Russian skirmishers behaved admirably, a few men now and again showing themselves, evidently with the intention of drawing our fire and distracting attention from the main attach on the right.

At a quarter to 7 the Russians, who up to this had only been firing an occasional shot, now got the range of our position, and the shells came in quick and with consummate accuracy. I must bear witness to the extreme gallantry with which the Turkish gunners stood to their pieces, and the steadiness with which they served them under the rain of shells from the 16 Russian guns, which ploughed up the ground round our two-gun battery in every direction, many falling into the earthwork itself. Owing to the softness of the ground, the plunging fire, and the badness of the fuses, many of these shells did not burst; still, the gunners suffered considerably, and most nobly stood to their guns. About a quarter past 6 Mahomed Pasha sent forward some 200 Circassians to line the ravine immediately beneath the

I

central ridge. From the nature of the ground this movement could not be seen by the enemy.

At 7 o'clock two Russian battalions, moving to the front in column of fours at company distance, appeared above the further crest of the central ridge, and our guns immediately opened fire on them. The men then extending, crossed the level ground in loose order, and formed up, lining the nearer crest, one battalion on the right, one on the left of the road. They at once commenced plying the Circassian horse with rifle fire, who answered with their Winchesters, whilst our guns plied the crest with shell. In a very short time it was evident that the cavalry must fall back, which they did in small groups, leaving a few killed in the ravine, and some horses. On crossing the natural glacis to the Turkish position they came in full view of the Russian guns, who had the range to a yard, and pitched their shells one after another into the retiring horsemen with great accuracy. Owing, however, to the aforementioned cause, the casualties were small— a large proportion of the missiles failing to burst. The gallantry of the Circassians was most marked. In spite of the heavy rifle fire on the ravine, in spite of the accurate artillery fire on the ground to be crossed before reaching it, many men were to be seen crossing, leisurely leading horses on which to carry back their dead, wounded, or dismounted comrades. It was 8 p.m. before these two battalions had established a strong position on this ridge; but no sooner had they done so than four field-pieces, of far heavier calibre than our own, were brought into action on the western crest of the same ridge, and firing over the heads of their own skirmishers, made beautiful practice on our line and on the retreating Circassians. At the same time Mahomed Pasha moved two battalions which, until now, had been in reserve to the left of his position, to strengthen his centre, which he apparently conceived would be the main point of attack. These, moving across the brow of the hill in column, were warmly welcomed by the Russian guns, and as they passed in rear of our own position, we, in turn, for a few seconds, were under an unpleasantly heavy artillery fire. As they passed on we were once more left unmolested, and from our vantage ground could see both forces below us—the Russians advancing in splendid order—men moving rapidly from point to point, taking advantage of every cover they could find, and working in a style that proves them not only to be admirably drilled, but well disciplined and skilfully and gallantly led. At a quarter past 8 two more Russian battalions appeared on the central ridge, and crossing over the plateau at the double, extended to reinforce the front line, which now consisted of two strong battalions on either flank of the road. With them came up six guns to the right, making a complete battery of eight guns (it must be borne in mind that the Russian field-batteries consist of this number) on that side of the road, with two only on the left. These eight guns, being only 1,500 yards from our line, made excellent practice—shell after shell bursting right among our men, many even in the shelter-trenches. Up to this time only percussion-fuses had been used; but now they commenced with the time-fuses, which were fired with remarkable accuracy.

It was now that the gallantry of the Turks showed itself—not a man moved or flinched from his post, and the two solitary field-guns which were able to reply to this overwhelming fire nobly did their duty. No troops could have shown more valour. Alas! it was of no avail. At half-past 8, for some unknown reason, the Turkish General withdrew his three guns from the right of his position, leaving in the front line one mountain-gun on the extreme right, and the two field-pieces so constantly mentioned, in the centre. At five minutes to 9 small parties of Russian skirmishers appeared, advancing up the ravine skirting the extreme right dank of the Turkish position, and a very heavy fire was opened on them from the two battalions and the one mountain-gun holding that knoll, which had been strengthened by weak stone breastworks. The Russians now pushed up the remaining six guns to the battery already in position on the left of the road, and the sixteen pieces commenced pounding the Turkish line. At ten minutes past nine the fire was so hot, shell after shell falling into the gun-pits—I counted thirty-seven shells pitch into one gun-pit in four minutes, and yet the gunners never showed a sign of abandoning their position, never quailed before the death-storm rained upon them—that the general gave orders for the withdrawal of the only two pieces left in the front line, the defence of which was now left to the infantry, eight battalions of which lined the position, three of them only being in shelter-trenches. The fire from these battalions was very rapid, and altogether ineffectual. Very few of the enemy showed themselves, and those only at a distance of 800 yards. Yet a ceaseless rattle from the Henry-Martini told the tale that ammunition would soon run out, unless the officers could restrain their men from such reckless waste of what later on would be priceless material; but instead of this, the officers seemed to encourage them, and the game went on brisker than ever.

The skirmishers, now advancing up the ravine, appeared in large numbers, and commenced ascending the knoll. They were supported by four regiments of cavalry, who came down the hill-side in column of troops, with the evident intention of moving round the right rear. Our guns having been removed, this large force was enabled to advance unmolested, and at the same time three more cavalry regiments in column of troops moved down the main road in support of the central attacking force. At half-past 9 Sir Arnold Kemball expressed a wish to join the Lieutenant-General, and we consequently abandoned our position under the peak to the left of the Turkish line, and passed along the line to the extreme right, running the gauntlet of the Russian fire, which was unpleasantly heavy—shell after shell passing close by us, plunged into the opposite bank of the ravine, and bursting, sent their hurtling fragments around us. I was glad when we got on the knoll to the extreme right; but very soon shells began bursting there also, and after hunting about for the General for about half an hour, we determined on pushing up to our old spot, which we did, again having to pass straight across the line of fire. On reaching the height we saw that the skirmishers of the central attack had pushed down to the ravine in front of their position, and were drawing the fire of the Turks by an occasional shot, while the Turks were firing wildly in their direction, although not a man could be seen. The waste of ammunition was terrible, officers encouraging their men to fire when the enemy were under excellent cover, whilst the men, needing no encouragement, were raising their pieces in the air and discharging round after round at an angle of 45°. I spoke to one man of the Amassia regiment, who I noticed had not been wasting his ammunition, and he told me that his regiment had gone into action with only fifteen rounds per man, and that he had but seven left, which he was keeping for close-quarter business.

At a quarter to 12 there was a lull in the Russian fire, during which their turning movement was being prosecuted with much vigour, men having ascended the front of the knoll on the right, and, under a sharp fire from a battalion not 200 yards off, had thrown up a rough shelter-trench, from which they speedily commenced a very effective return fire. Seeing the cavalry moving up the ravine, I went round to the rear of the peak to reconnoitre for a safe line of retreat, and while away, an officer came to Sir Arnold to report the death of Mahomed Pasha, who had been shot through the head, and to announce that Major-General Mustafa Pasha had succeeded to the command. While this message was being delivered by the *aide-de-camp*, I noticed that the right of the position was completely turned, that the Russian cavalry were driving back the infantry skirmishers from the entrenchments on our right, and seriously threatened the line of retreat to Delibaba. We accordingly pushed down the hill quickly, to find the infantry falling back off the ridge in a confused crowd, with the Russian horse among them. The reserve battalions were too far off for reach, and not caring to date my next to you from Moscow, I counselled a retreat, which was speedily put into execution.

It was 11.45 when we left the ground, and then we

became aware that the affair had assumed very much the appearance of a rout; that the Cossacks were getting round the rear, and that if we did escape it would be merely by a short neck. Our horses were not in very good condition for a twenty-five mile gallop after all the hard work they had gone through the last three days; however, there was no help for it, and so we pushed on, pressing up over the watershed of the Taghir and Delibaba streams, through the Eshek-Khaliass valley, where we met two battalions leisurely proceeding to the front. On Wednesday they received orders to move on to join the left wing of the Turkish army, and to press on, as fighting was imminent. They were then forty-seven miles off, and true to the watch-word of the country, "Yahvash, Yahvash" (slowly, slowly), they proceeded by ordinary marches. Having put them between us and the Cossacks, we thought we were safe, and, pulling up, were proceeding to the village of Delibaba to telegraph the result of the day's work to the Commander-in-Chief, Mukhtar Pasha. Some providential inspiration induced us to turn off when within a mile and a half of the village, and, striking across the hills, we cut into the Khorassan route. We had not changed our plans half an hour, when a friendly sergeant of zaptiehs dashed up breath-less, saying the Cossacks had passed through Delibaba, reaching it by another road, and were now close behind. Fortunately, we knew that there was a battalion with six guns about two miles farther on, and I can assure you we did not spare our horses in that gallop. Having reached Taikhojeh, the village in which the troops were encamped, we warned the colonel, who could not find a bugler, and not knowing the strength of the pursuing force, and not caring to see a fight between a surprised Turkish detachment, who evidently could not be got under arms for the next half hour, we pushed on, forded the Araxes, and reached Khorassan at three p.m. We at first thought of moving back on Kuipri-Kui; but abandoned that intention on hearing that a regiment of cavalry and three of infantry were moving into Khorassan to hold the ford across the river.

Of the bravery of the Turkish troops it is impossible to speak too highly; of the utter incompetence of their leaders it is equally impossible to speak in terms of sufficient disparagement. On the Thursday evening the Turkish General held the position from which the Russians commenced their attack — one almost impregnable, and certainly commanding all ground within four miles. That evening he abandoned it, and on Friday morning found a Russian field-battery and a strong body of cavalry holding it. Even then it would not have been too late to recapture it, with the force at his disposal, for the Russian main force we knew was at Zaidikan, five miles off; but Mahomed Pasha was under the belief that the Russians dared not attack him. All men could see with the naked eye sixteen cannon cutting the sky-line, but his spies said the Russians had only five field and five mountain guns; so he abstained from bringing up six guns, which were about twenty miles off—the timely arrival of which might have saved the day. Then, instead of employing his time on Friday in throwing up really good entrenchments, he contented himself with a few short shelter-trenches and two gun-pits, without any screens in front of them. These were placed on the sky-line, and served as admirable marks for the very efficient Russian artillery. The arrangements, too, concerning ammunition were simply disgraceful. Each regiment has attached to it thirty-two ponies, carrying each two boxes of 1,000 rounds; but these were by some fatality ordered to the rear in the morning, and to my knowledge more than one battalion went into action with a very short supply in the men's pouches.

A brief *résumé* of events leading up to this disaster may be of value here, and, at the risk of appearing tedious, I give it.

The Russians, crossing the frontier on the 23rd of April, the day prior to the declaration of war, advanced, as you are aware, by three roads on Erzeroum. Each was defended by a fortress, and consequently until these barriers had been removed the movements of the separate columns were somewhat hampered. Bayazid, on the southern road, capitulated without firing a shot, on the 26th of April, the garrison escaping to Van. Ardahan, on the northern road, fell after an assault on May 17th; but Kars, the strongest of the three places, kept the main central column employed, and still does so. It seems that the Russian plan is, not to advance on Erzeroum until Kars has fallen. Reconnaissances, however, were pushed on, and in such considerable force that the Turkish army (also in three columns) at Olti, on the Hoonkiar Dooz, and at Toprak Kale, fell back on the Ghiurji Boghaz, Zewin, and Delibaba. Subsequently the Russian advanced brigades occupied Olti on the 28th of May, and Zaidikan on the 9th of June. Ahmed Mukhtar Pasha learning they were not in any strength in these places, determined to advance his two wings. So reinforcing his left to a strength of eleven battalions, three regiments of irregular cavalry and six mountain-guns, he pushed it forward. The Russians retired, avoiding a collision, to beyond Pennek, and Olti was reoccupied on the 7th of June. Delighted with this success, he now ordered up three more battalions and 600 cavalry to strengthen Mahomed Pasha at Deli-baba, and ordered him with seventeen battalions, two field and one mountain battery, with about 800 cavalry, to drive the Russians out of Zaidikan. On whom the blame rests no one ever will know, but the fact remains that one field-battery, which I was assured by Mahomed Pasha on the 15th had been ordered up to Taghir from Taikhojeh, never left their quarters at all, and on passing through that place on the afternoon of the 15th, after our narrow escape from the Cossacks, not only were the guns parked along with commissariat stores, but the horses were all grazing on the neighbouring hills. Either Lieutenant-General Mahomed Pasha had never ordered these guns up—guns which might have saved the day—or else the officer commanding the battery had deliberately disobeyed orders. An officer high on the staff of the army informed me that two battalions at Kuipri-Kui had been directed to march forthwith from Deli-baba. This was on the 12th. On the 16th, after the fight, I met them quietly straggling through the pass, moving to the front, truly, but having taken four clear days to cover thirty-two miles. The officer commanding was informed of the fight, rout, and flight of the force in his front; but instead of taking measures to occupy a strong position and endeavour to cover the *débandade*, he allowed his men, already in the usual state of disorder that a Turkish regiment exhibits on the line of march, to continue their straggling advance, and on meeting the baggage of the retiring army a block occurred in the narrow pass near Eshek Khaliass. This was increased as the fugitive troops passed through, and these being quickly followed by the pursuing Cossacks, a scene ensued that can only be imagined by those who have seen cavalry acting on a disorganised, and for the most part unarmed, body of troops. Thus it happens that instead of attacking a Russian brigade at Zaidikan with seventeen battalions, two field and one mountain battery, the Turks were themselves attacked, when they actually had only fourteen battalions and five guns to oppose the Russian forces. Taghir, or Tahar, is in the main caravan road from Erzeroum through Delibaba to Bayazid, but the hills being particularly steep just there, the road branches off into three, one being practicable for carts all the year round, the southernmost one; the centre being practicable for wheeled vehicles only in summer; while the third, or northern road, is only available for horse-traffic. On the 14th, Mahomed Pasha having advanced from Delibaba with ten battalions, one mountain and one field-battery—he had most unaccountably left one field-battery and two battalions at Taikhojeh—was informed by his outposts that the Russians were in force at Zaidikan. He accordingly sent forward three battalions, with two mountain and two field-guns, along each of the roads to the west immediately above Zaidikan, and stayed at the village with one battalion, contenting himself with the stories of the Kurdish spies as to the Russian position and strength, never dreaming of proceeding to the front to verify their reports himself. In the evening more Kurds came in, saying that they had had an engagement with the Russian cavalry outposts, whom they had driven in, killing 40. This report also was believed, and Mahomed Pasha avowed his determination of attacking in the morning. However, late at night fearing a sudden surprise, he withdrew his men from the advanced ridge, which commanded everything within range, and, hearing that the Russians were advancing on the southern road, massed his troops on the westernmost and lowest of the three spurs south of Taghir. At dawn the Russian horse had appeared on the late Turkish ground, by 9 a.m. a field-battery was in support, and by noon a mixed force, with two field and one mountain battery, had entrenched themselves on the ridge unnoticed in any way. The road once secured, their work was easy. In the evening we could distinguish four regiments of cavalry, seven battalions, besides artillery, within three miles of us; and, in spite of the evidence of his own eyes, the Turkish commander assured me that he knew positively they had only five field-guns. He, however, told me he had ordered up the battery from Taikhojeh, which should, according to the original instructions, have moved with him.

At 5 a.m. on the 16th the Russians advanced to the assault. At 9.15 they had, owing to their overwhelming force of artillery, driven the Turkish guns out of action, and by noon were in possession of the ridge held by the Ottoman troops, and of nearly every gun they possessed; following up the infantry, who were out of ammunition, they drove them through the pass to Delibaba, capturing about 1,000 prisoners, while a second body of cavalry, with horse-artillery, moved rapidly by another road to Dodi, and appearing on the hill above Taikhojeh on the morning of the 17th, very effectually prevented all communication between Mukhtar Pasha and the remnants of the right wing, and, as I hear, easily captured a number of prisoners from the battalion and battery encamped on the Taikhojeh stream. The whole arrangements of the Turkish army are faulty in the extreme. On the 15th of June there was but one ration of bread served out to every four men. Wood to cook with or meat to eat there was none, and yet the country is not only fertile, but the surrounding hills were covered with flocks and herds grazing; money, and common sense, and energy only were wanting, and these three commodities Turkish officials do not indulge in.

Doctors and hospital arrangements there were none —absolutely none. I saw wounded officers being carried to the rear, thrown bodily across baggage-mules, and thus being driven, wounds undressed, across stony, mountainous roads to a place of safety—not to field hospitals, for the nearest was 46 miles off, and such a thing as a regimental hospital did not exist. There was not a doctor with the division. Far different were the Russian arrangements, for in the rear of the skirmishers were litters with awnings to protect wounded men from the sun, and the men, instead of presenting the ragged, forlorn, miserable appearance of the Turkish troops, were neatly dressed, and all provided with white cap-covers, which they wisely discarded during action. The regimental commanders in the Ottoman army showed as much carelessness as their superiors; no precautions were taken to fill up men's pouches prior to the fight, or, indeed, to keep the 32 ponies carrying spare ammunition within easy distance. Considering the nature of the ground, it would not have been difficult to have kept them under cover behind some friendly ridge. One corps, the Amassia battalion, went into action with one full packet of ten, and a few (rarely more than five) loose rounds per man. It seemed optional whether shelter-trenches were thrown up in front of regiments or not; and although the position was held on the 15th, and battalions posted in the very spots they occupied on the day of the engagement, very few commanders took the trouble to entrench their men, and even then a little earth scratched up or a few stones piled in front of a man were considered sufficient. The Russians, on the contrary, on reaching the eastern ridge, which they did in very small numbers on the morning of the 15th, immediately deployed a regiment of cavalry; and thus screened from view threw up what appeared from the distance to be very formidable works. The training, too, of the Turks was such that they should never have been suffered to contend with a disciplined foe. Men ignorant of the rudiments of drill, and perfectly innocent as to the meaning and use of sights on their rifles, were to be seen standing upright on a sky-line, or collected in groups drawing down artillery fire, and discharging their weapons wildly in the air; some truly taking aim, but many more merely letting off their pieces at an angle of 45° when the enemy was fully 2,000 yards away. The Turkish cavalry, too, were not worthy of the name. A body of some 500 Circassians, armed with Winchester 16-shot repeating carbines, behaved with some gallantry. Indeed, there were many cases of individual heroism; but, undrilled and undisciplined, they had no chance of standing against the Russian horse, whose movements over the broken and mountainous ground, over country where our horsemen would never dream of working, were steady in the extreme. I shall never forget the sight they presented as four very strong regiments moved down the mountain in column of troops to support the flanking movement on our right; and the way they operated on the Turkish infantry after their steep descent and hard gallop up a stony ravine was a beautiful and yet a ghastly scene. The Kurdish cavalry, some 300 in number, who were supposed to face the well-trained Russian troops, were a mere bundle of fantastically-dressed and ridiculously and badly armed rubbish. As I have before written, on the evening of the 15th of June they amused themselves by dashing about the plain, shaking their spears, gnashing their teeth, hurling curses of defiance at their Christian foe, and chanting pæans of the victory that was to be. On the morrow they contented themselves—the few that remained, for early in the day their numbers diminished wofully—with keeping well behind a ridge, ever and anon firing a flint pistol in the air to the extreme danger of their braver Circassian comrades, who were in front. One more fault—ay, crime—requires to be pointed out. All through the winter and spring numerous guns were despatched from Constantinople to Trebizond, with which to arm Erzeroum. On the 3rd of May there were 86 of these lying on the beach, just as they were disembarked. On the 23rd of May these pieces—thanks to the untiring energy of that indefatigable officer Lieutenant-General Djameel Pasha —had reached Baiboort, 66 miles from this, and to-day, 28 days after—thanks to the apathy, listlessness, and criminal neglect of the Erzeroum officials—they are still lying at Baiboort, and the earth-works on the Devi-Boyun are yet unarmed.

As a set-off to the conduct of those in authority it is more than a pleasure to bring to notice the great gallantry of the rank and file of the Turkish army. Untrained men, ignorant of the use of their weapons, and for the most part agriculturists fresh from the plough, they were yet unused to the hard school of war. Cold and hungry, badly clad and badly shod, uncared for and unnoticed, they stood their ground right nobly under a murderous fire from the sixteen 16-pounder Russian guns playing on their front, under a hailstorm of rifle bullets from the battalions that had turned their flank, and it was not until their ammunition had failed and the Cossacks were riding them down, that they turned and broke. A squad of the Erzingjan battalion of the 2nd ban of Redif went quietly forward and dragged the field-guns out of action when shell after shell from the Russian battery burst among them, doing terrible damage, and yet these untrained raw militia never hesitated a moment, but performed their task in a manner that her Majesty's Guards could not have surpassed. The rank and file of the Turkish army are men of whom any nation might be proud. The real Turkish loss we never shall know. The nearest computation to the truth, I opine, is that which can be given by the only two Englishmen on the ground, and that is that not a single gun has been saved, and not a battalion preserving its formation reached Delibaba. About 800 fugitives of various corps arrived at Kuipri-Kui. Many of these, however, left before the action was in full swing; the Circassians and Kurds, finding the day going against them, and assuming that discretion was the better part of valour, retired, suiting their own convenience, at about 10 a.m.

Having had many opportunities of conversing with officers and men of battalions present in this engagement, and with the doctors quartered at the field hospital at Hassan-Kale and the general hospital at Erzeroum, I have ascertained that the losses of the Turks on the 16th were 1,426 killed and missing, with 963 wounded. The Zileh and Amassia regiments suffered most heavily, two subalterns of the former corps being the only officers who escaped. The Erzeroum Redif battalion lost 60 killed and 200 missing, while eleven pieces of artillery were abandoned in the headlong flight.

J

CHAPTER VII.

A LULL IN THE STORM.

Ismail's Canards—Halit Bey—Disorganised state of Turkish Right Wing—A Russian Scare—A Fish Dinner—Position of the Hostile Armies—Re-occupation of Bayazid by Faik Pasha—Mukhtar Pasha reinforces and assumes Command of Right Wing—Ismail the Kurd joins Central Column—Moussa Pasha—News of a Turkish Success at Eshek Khaliass—Awkward Position of Tergukassoff—Faik Pasha's Division.

ERZEROUM, *June* 21.

I AM afraid that this letter will be dull and uninteresting, after the stirring events of the past few days which I endeavoured to describe in my last. Since my arrival on Sunday the place has been filled with rumours, those current among the Christian population tending to magnify the Russian advantages, and placing Tergukassoff far nearer this than even he possibly can be; those, on the other hand, concocted in the governor's palace, and disseminated by the Mahomedans, make little of the affair on the 16th, and prophesy the early destruction of the Russian forces. With these contradictory reports flying about, it is simply impossible to give you any accurate statement of the present position; but as far as I can judge the Turks seem to be disposed thus:—The Olti forces, numbering nine battalions, six mountain guns, and a regiment of cavalry (Bashi-Bazouks), have joined Mukhtar Pasha at Zewin Dooz, bringing up his force to twenty-six battalions, about 3,000 cavalry (mostly irregulars, and worthless), and two field batteries with eighteen mountain guns. At Khorassan and Kuipri Kui are five battalions, 800 Circassians, and one horse artillery battery. At Deli-baba are the remains of the right wing; but it is impossible to estimate their strength, and I certainly do not think they have a gun with them. The Governor of this place, Vali Ismail Pasha, has at last gone to take command of the central brigade, situated at Khorassan and Kuipri Kui. He telegraphs word this morning that Tergukassoff is surrounded, as Mukhtar Pasha is advancing from Zewin Dooz *via* Mezingerd to Gulentab, and so cutting off his rear, while Mustafa Pasha, with the right wing of the Turkish army, will attack him on the flank at the same time as he does so in front.

I give you these telegrams; but long before this letter reaches you the wire will have apprised you of the true state of affairs. I do not think I am over-stating the case, and my opinion was concurred in by others present on the 16th, when I say that in the right wing of the Turkish army there was but one officer who showed himself fit to command a corporal's guard, and it is only just that he who proved himself the very mainspring of the division, who posted every picket, who conducted every reconnais-sance, and who warmly and urgently pressed the neces-sity of holding the advanced ridge, the abandonment of which gave the Russians an enormous advantage, should be brought to public notice. If anything had to be done, the call was for Halit Bey; if any doubt was expressed as to the strength or position of the enemy, Halit Bey was sent to reconnoitre; if a regi-

mental officer ventured to ask where he was to obtain
bread for his half-starved men, he was referred to Halit
Bey ; if a battalion had to be moved, Halit Bey had to
give the necessary orders ; if the miserable Kurds came
in with a story of a victorious skirmish in which they,
unaided, had overthrown the Cossack outposts, Halit
Bey at once dispelled the Lieutenant-General's joy by
doubting the whole story, and ordering the Kurds to
bring in the dead bodies and thus show proof of their
prowess ; and, finally, on the death of Mahomed Pasha,
officers were to be seen galloping over the field looking
for Halit Bey, whose advice now was sought by Mustafa
Pasha, on whom the dead General's cloak of irresolution
had fallen.

On the morning of the 17th, whilst engaged in
making a fair sketch-plan of the preceding day's operations, we were disturbed by the advent of two staff officers
whom Mukhtar Pasha had despatched, the one to bring
him accurate information as to the state of his right
wing, the other to order up all troops from Kuipri Kui,
and to stop and send back to the front all fugitives from
the late Mahomed Pasha's army. From these officers
we learnt that the losses had been quite as serious as we
had imagined, that not three battalions had reached
the Delibaba Pass, and that the whole road between
Taghir and Erzeroum was crowded with men flying from
the scene of combat. It was barely noon when firing
was once more to be heard in the direction of Taikhojeh.
Our horses were too done up to risk another gallop, and
as a strong body of Russians, horse and foot, were distinctly visible on the hills just across the Araxes, we
packed our scanty kit, and hurried off towards Erzeroum.
Midway between Khorassan and Kuipri Kui we passed

two battalions of infantry, moving up to the front. These were the men that Mukhtar Pasha on the 13th had informed me had been ordered up to support Mahomed Pasha, and now, four days after the receipt of the Commander-in-Chief's orders, they had condescended to leave their camping ground. Passing through Kuipri Kui, crowded with fugitives, who were being collected by an A.D.C. of the Mushir, we passed a brigade of five battalions of infantry, one horse battery, and 800 cavalry, under the command of Reiss Ahmed Fazil Pasha. That night we slept at Hassan-Kale in a khan filled with soldiers. Our servants and kit were all behind, but a tin of sardines had found its way into my holsters, and this, opened with the point of Sir Arnold's sword, furnished us with an excellent meal. At dawn we rose, and reached Erzeroum in time to partake of Mr. Zohrab's excellent breakfast, and to receive the warm congratulations of all at our escape, for the first rumours of the fight that reached the city had magnified exceedingly the risks we had run; indeed, if I had led Sir Arnold in headless, it would not have surprised the terror-stricken inhabitants of the capital of Armenia.

As matters stand now, Mukhtar is at Zewin, with 20 battalions, two field and two mountain batteries; two battalions at Khorassan guard the ford of the Araxes; at Delibaba is the remnant of his right wing; at Kuipri Kui is Ahmed Fazil Pasha with the brigade above mentioned; whilst at Olti, Rasched Pasha has 11 battalions. Tergukassoff (with his cavalry at Taikhojeh and Karatchurga) is at Taghir. Melikoff, with 17,000 men, is advancing from Kars, whilst Komaroff, with a weak brigade, is falling back from Pennek to Ardahan.

Ismail Pasha, Vali of Erzeroum, has, I have already

stated, at last, in consequence of peremptory orders from Constantinople, set out for the army. He has, ever since the declaration of war, been ridiculing Mukhtar Pasha, and accusing him of cowardice in not assuming the offensive. These accusations, freely transmitted to Stamboul, have led the Ottoman Government to believe that the Commander-in-Chief was not making the best of his means, and consequently an order arrived on the 19th directing the Vali himself to proceed to the front. What his position will be I do not know. Mukhtar Pasha is a Mushir of some standing, while the Vali has but recently been promoted to that grade ; but it is rumoured that he will take command of the recent reinforcement despatched to the front, amounting to about five battalions, 1,000 cavalry, and one horse battery. These troops are at Khorassan and Kuipri Kui. If, as is reported, Tergukassoff has fallen back on the Khaliass Plain, and abandoned Taikhojeh, Ismail may effect a junction with Mustafa Pasha, who still must have some 3,000 or 4,000 men with him, and with these his present intention is to attack Tergukassoff in front, while Mukhtar Pasha, reinforced as before stated, cuts off his retreat. There is no doubt that the Russian General has fallen back, but the reason of this retrograde movement is evident. After the fight of the 16th he pursued the beaten Turks in two columns. One, passing by the Delibaba Pass, pushed them hard, while the other, advancing *via* Dodi, on Taikhojeh, cut Mustafa Pasha off from communication with the main army. The right column was commanded, I believe, by Emiliffkassoff, a Georgian Prince, and a major-general of cavalry. This officer pushed on a strong advanced guard as far as Kara-tchurga ; but the stubborn defence of Kars prevented the Grand Duke Michael from supporting Tergu-kassoff by a move of the central army, and he being too weak to hold such an advanced position himself, and moreover, Ferik Faik Pasha, with the Van Division, being reported as advancing in his rear, he recalled the cavalry brigade, and retired to a very strong position in the Khaliass Plain, whence the Turks will find it hard to dislodge him.

In conversation with Sir Arnold Kemball, that officer came to the conclusion, owing to Tergukassoff's forward movement subsequent to the action of the 16th, that Kars must have fallen, and that the advance of the left wing was but a prelude to the general move on Erzeroum of the whole Russian army. The halt on the 18th renewed hopes that Kars still held out, and the retrograde movement yesterday from Taikhojeh to Khaliass confirmed that view. Late last night the Commander-in-Chief telegraphed that there had been a heavy artillery duel going on for more than a week at Kars, and that the Turks had made one or two very successful sorties. This would fully account for peremptory instructions being sent to Tergukassoff not to compromise himself by a too rapid advance. This morning news, which I ought to have no reason to doubt, has reached me that Faik Pasha, with the Van division, numbering six battalions, six mountain guns, and 5,000 Kurdish irregulars, has re-occupied Bayazid ; the Russian garrison, numbering only 300 men, retiring without provoking a conflict. It seems extraordinary that there should have been such a small garrison left in so important a position, for Bayazid commands the road from Erivan, one of the three lines of communication that the Russians possess. That it should have changed hands twice in such a short space of time possibly points to the fact, that its possession is not deemed of much importance by either Turk or Russian. However, its capture will be made much of by the Ottoman journals, and will give colour to the rumours that the Muscovite is not having it all his own way in Armenia. Still, I cannot quite believe that the Russians should have abandoned Bayazid without a conflict.

June 22nd.

Shortly after despatching my letter yesterday, I received authentic information that Mukhtar Pasha had crossed over from Zewin to Delibaba to assume command of the right wing of the Turkish army, which for the future will be known as the head-quarters of the Fourth Army Corps. The command of the central division has been taken over by Ismail Pasha.

The right wing and head-quarters now consist of the remains of Mahomed Pasha's troops, strength quite uncertain; five battalions and a battery which have been moved down from Zewin, one battalion from Gulentab; one battalion and a battery from Taikhojeh; three battalions, 1,000 horse, and two batteries from Erzeroum; and two battalions from Khorassan, together with two battalions not engaged on the 16th—total, fourteen fresh battalions, with four batteries. I presume he has, then, a total of about twenty battalions, all told, at Delibaba. At Zewin he has twenty-one battalions, with one field and two mountain batteries; and at Olti two battalions and six mountain guns. There are in the various camps about 4,000 irregular horse, all well armed, but not organised, and for the most part very badly mounted. There are also nearly 1,500 Circassians *en route* from Trebizond; but these men will not face the Russian cavalry, are under no sort of discipline whatever, and when they see affairs turning against them leave the field without waiting for orders, and entirely at their own discretion. It is true the Circassians will advance against infantry, but they never continue to do so when once they find casualties occurring. The Kurds, of whom there are a great number, are worse than useless. Scarcely an Armenian village in the country has escaped their heavy hands. They do not content themselves with stealing, plundering, and murdering their weaker and unarmed fellow subjects, but they outrage and violate every girl on whom they can lay their hands. The stories that reach us—stories from too authentic a source to admit of doubt—are perfectly unfit for publication. The Ottoman Government are showing great want of policy in encouraging, arming, and feeding these men, who, useless in action, are causing all the Christians of Armenia to turn with thankfulness to the Russians as their deliverers, instead of aiding the Government with all the means in their power to repel the Muscovite aggressor.

Moussa Pasha, too, the Circassian chief, a fanatical Mahomedan, left head-quarters' camp a few weeks ago, ostensibly to proceed to Constantinople, but he remained here, proceeding from mosque to mosque preaching a Jehad, or religious war, against all Christians. Fortunately, the Vali is a man of a very timid disposition, and foreseeing that the massacres of Christians would only bring them retaliation when the city fell into Russian hands, he called Moussa up, pointed out the danger he was running, and summarily ordered him out of the city. Now he is returning to head-quarters, where I trust he may find some opportunity of earning fame at the head of his Circassians.

This man was for many years in the Russian service, and finally rose to the command of a cavalry regiment, and was by them known as Colonel Kondukoff. For some fancied slight he abandoned the Muscovite and entered the Turkish army, where he was received with open arms, given the grade of lieutenant-general, and on the outbreak of war was despatched to Asia Minor to assume command of the irregular cavalry of the Fourth Army Corps. For some unknown cause he is eminently unpopular amongst both his countrymen the Circassians and the Turks. His conduct at the action of Beghli Ahmed on the 29th May cannot have raised him in the opinion of the authorities; indeed it is pretty generally rumoured that Mukhtar Pasha wishes to be rid of him, and gladly gave him permission to proceed to Constantinople, hoping that once in Europe some other command might be found for him.

Yesterday the public criers were going round the city calling on all good subjects of the Porte, Maho-medan or Christian, to arm themselves and go out to repel the common foe; those that owned horses to go mounted, those too poor to do that to go on foot. I have not heard that the order was largely responded to; indeed it seems to me that the advent of the Russians is hailed with unbounded pleasure by both Mussulman and Christian alike.

Mukhtar Pasha evidently is not satisfied with the behaviour either of officers or men in the affair of the 16th, for on the 19th he had a general parade of the troops, and an order of the day was read to them, stating that some officers and men of certain regiments had misbehaved themselves on the field of battle and had deserted their post. He exhorted all present to vindicate the traditions of Turkish gallantry when called upon to meet the foe, and announced his determination of shooting all those concerned in the " *débandade* " of last Saturday. True to his word, he has caused inquiries to be made into the subject, and this morning two regimental officers were degraded and flogged in the citadel of Erzeroum—somewhat a summary proceeding, surely, and one not calculated to encourage the others, for from what I saw of the action junior regimental officers and the rank and file behaved with consummate gallantry, and only gave way when, by the negligence and incompetence of their leaders, they ran short of ammunition, and were surrounded by the enemy. No troops could have behaved better under the very disadvantageous circumstances in which they were placed, and when I remember that these men had not seen pay for eighteen months, and received but one ration of bread among four soldiers for three days prior to the fight, my wonder is that they fought at all.

While I write, news has just come in that Mukhtar Pasha, reaching Delibaba early in the morning of the 3rd, at once pushed on through the pass to attack the Russians in the valley of Eshek Khaliass. He took with him nineteen battalions infantry, twelve field, ten mountain guns, and about 2,500 cavalry. That afternoon there was slight skirmishing between the outposts, in which the Turks lost three killed; the troops bivouacked on high ground overlooking the Russian camp, and at dawn moved on to a stronger position on very commanding ground. At noon the Russians under Ter-

gukassoff advanced to attack, numbering ten battalions,
eight field guns, some mountain guns, and some say
one rocket troop. The Russians fell back to their camp,
leaving one mountain gun in the hands of the Turks, who
may claim a decided success, although their losses were
most severe—400 killed and the same number wounded
being the official report. The Turkish troops bivouacked
on ground slightly in advance of their previous night's
position, and were prepared in the morning to follow
up their advantage; but the Russians, according to my
news, broke their camp and retired. The news has only
just come in, in a short note from one of Her Majesty's
extra military attachés on the field. Captain M'Calmont, 7th Hussars, who was present, says the Turkish
infantry behaved with consummate gallantry, but that
their supports were not pushed up quickly enough, or
else the result might have been a signal victory. The
Turkish horse behaved badly, and this, coming from a
cavalry officer, I am glad to say, confirms the opinion I
have so frequently expressed as to the worthlessness of
these irregulars against the highly disciplined Russian
cavalry. The same officer reports that the artillery
practice was bad, and this was the case on the 16th,
when the Russian gunners drove the Turkish pieces
out of action very quickly. Tergukassoff is wise to
fall back; his force is not very strong, and he appears
to have pushed on too far from the main army before
Kars, endangering his communications; for Faik Pasha,
having left sufficient force to besiege the small garrison
at Bayazid—which I learn did not abandon the place,
but fell back into the Citadel, a masonry building ill-
adapted to withstand a siege—is marching on his rear
to join Mukhtar Pasha, and unless reinforcements

are sent down from Kars, and can reach the Russian left wing *viâ* Kagisman prior to the arrival of the Van column, the Armenian general Tergukassoff may find himself seriously compromised. On seeing his rapid advance after the fight on the 16th, I could not avoid coming to the conclusion that Kars had fallen, and that the move on the left was but a part of a general advance on Erzeroum. On hearing positively yesterday that Kars still held out, I was not surprised to learn that Tergukassoff had fallen back on Eshek Khaliass, and entrenched himself. There he is in an admirable position (were he not hampered in rear by the Van force, under Faik Pasha), having three roads by which he can advance into the Passin Plain, and three roads by which he can communicate with the central army, viz., one by Kagisman, Alamad, Toprak Kale, and Zaidikan; a second by Zerbkhana, Toprak Kale, and Zaidikan; and a third by Gulentab.

The Van division, under Ferik Faik Pasha, which has just re-occupied Bayazid, now consists of six battalions of infantry, the late garrisons of Moosh, Bitliss, Bayazid, and Van; of a field battery and a half, two mountain guns, 7,911 irregular infantry, of whom 6,000 are equipped with the Henry-Martini rifle; 1,640 irregular cavalry, of whom 800 are armed with the Winchester rifle. These irregulars, led as they are by fanatical priests, may possibly be of some use should Tergukassoff be driven back by Mukhtar Pasha; but I cannot venture to hope that they will ever face the enemy in fair fight, though they doubtless would harass the Russians in retreat very severely, and will be very useful, if he maintains his position on the Alishgird plain, in cutting off the convoys of provisions, which must necessarily be forwarded to him now from Kars, as his communications with Bayazid are completely cut off — in fact, if Mukhtar Pasha and Faik Pasha now only behave with common prudence, they ought utterly to destroy Tergukassoff's force; but the greatest promptitude is necessary in order to overwhelm him before reinforcements can arrive from Loris Melikoff.

CHAPTER VIII.

THE MOSLEM AT BAY.

Leave Erzeroum once more for the Front—The Battle of Eshek Khaliass—
Conduct of Turkish Cavalry—No Ammunition!—Wounded Men—German
Doctors—Hand Wounds—True Missionaries—Sir Arnold Kemball—Fresh
Men of Eshek Khaliass—Turkish Losses—Fate of Skirmishers against
Shelter Trenches—More Fighting—Another Stampede—Tcherkess Heroes
—A Christian Village—Reinforcements for Zewin—Rumours of a Fight
—"*Perish India*"—Outrages on Christians—Faizi Pasha's Victory—Enthu-
siasm of the Turks—Ismail and the Koran—Russian and Turkish Losses—
Value of Turkish Cavalry—Value of Turkish Casualty Returns—Melikoff's
Returns.

CAMP, KUIPRI KUI, *June* 24.

I LEFT Erzeroum this morning at 6 a.m. with Sir Arnold
Kemball and his aide-de-camp, Lieutenant Dougall,
en route to rejoin Mukhtar Pasha's head-quarters
at Eshek Khaliass. Reports received from Captains
Trotter and M'Calmont yesterday, giving brief details
of the engagement on the 21st, certainly gave me the
impression that the Turks had achieved a decided success, and that with comparatively slight loss. I own I
was at a loss to account for the difference in form between the contending forces. On the 16th the Russians
moved in excellent order, men kept well in hand,
fired very steadily, were supported by an admirable
artillery fire, and finally carried everything before them;
the Turks showing but little enthusiasm, no discipline,
and not the remotest knowledge of hill warfare. According to the accounts received of the action of the

21st, the Turkish skirmishers moved in "beautiful order," showed great enthusiasm, and at the close of the day bivouacked in advance of their morning's position.

On the road between this and Erzeroum we met numbers of officers and men coming in wounded, and the account they gave of the affair gives a very different description from that we first heard. It appears that Mukhtar Pasha advanced from Delibaba on the 20th with nineteen battalions, two field batteries, ten mountain guns, and about 2,500 cavalry, to attack Tergukassoff, who, after the fight on the 16th, had taken up a strong position, which he entrenched, in the hills near Eshek Khaliass. That afternoon the cavalry of the two forces came in contact, and desultory skirmishing ensued. The following morning (21st), leaving all his field guns and five battalions in reserve under Mustafa Pasha (who succeeded to the command on the 16th, on the death of Mahomed Pasha) at Haidar Kui, about five miles in rear, Mukhtar Pasha advanced to attack the Russian position, consisting of eight battalions, eight field guns, one rocket troop, and some—number not stated—mountain guns. The enemy threw out skirmishers, who were pushed back on the left to their own entrenchments, when a severe fight ensued. I have conversed with numerous officers and men of the Amassia battalion, who were in the assaulting column on that flank, and they complain bitterly of their ammunition running out, no fresh supplies being sent them, and that they were never supported. A British officer present on the occasion told me that had this attack been properly supported the Russians must have given way. I saw this battalion in action on the 16th, and know for a fact that they entered the fight with only one complete packet of ten rounds and what few loose cartridges they had in their pouches. As they commenced firing when the Russians were upwards of a mile distant and in skirmishing order, it naturally came to pass that in the final attack they were without ammunition, and so the Russians advanced up the glacis to the crest of the position at Taghir in unbroken order and unchecked. This I saw on the 16th, and from all I can gather the same mismanagement occurred on the 21st. Troops advanced to the attack with unfilled pouches, and were shot down like dogs when gallantly trying to carry the Russian entrenchments.

Reports are many, and from the many it is difficult to extract even one grain of truth. It is evident that there was a heavy engagement on the 21st, lasting from noon till dark; that the Turks attacked the Russian position, but failed to carry it. They claim a success, as Tergukassoff fell back the following morning from Eshek Khaliass to the ridge he entrenched on the 15th above Zaidikan, and Mukhtar Pasha reports that Schamyl's son captured three guns with his Circassian horse. This does not tally with the accounts given by the British officers on the ground, who say all behaved well except the cavalry.

The loss, considering the number of troops engaged, has been awful. The Commander-in-Chief himself telegraphs 400 killed, and to-day, on the road between Erzeroum and this place, which is nearly fifty miles from the battle-field, I have seen from 800 to 1,000 wounded being carried in to the hospitals—some walking, some on mules, and the remainder in country carts; doubtless many more, and those the most serious cases,

K

are yet behind, for one doctor assured me the total could not be less than 3,000 casualties. The sights I have witnessed to-day must be seen to be believed. Half-starved, half-naked men tottering along, vainly striving to reach some place where their wounds should be attended to; hundreds sitting by the roadside, near pools of water, endeavouring to moisten their clotted bandages or cool their fevered limbs. At Hassan Kale, twenty miles from Erzeroum, a small field-hospital of fifty beds has been formed. There are already in the village 270 serious cases from last Saturday's fight, and the two German doctors there have their hands full; but in the midst of a group of 400 wounded men I saw these two men nobly upholding the honour of their profession, standing bareheaded in the broiling sun, and working with a speed and vigour that boded fairly to clear off the ghastly group by which they were surrounded before the arrival of the next train of carts. I saw Turkish soldiers standing up while their wounds were being probed, and not flinching a muscle; and I saw others, unable even to crawl, lying on the ground, waiting their turn to at least have their hurts bandaged. A very large proportion of the men were hit on the hands and arms—indeed, of the group of men we saw entering Erzeroum, nine out of every ten were wounded there; and I began to look with suspicion on them. However, it has been represented to me that men fighting behind breastworks show only their heads, arms, and shoulders. Those struck in the head rarely figure among the wounded. Hence the apparently large proportion of slight hand-wounds. However, as we increased our distance from Erzeroum and came upon the more seriously wounded men, I am forced to confess that there were as many body and leg-wounds among the later arrivals as there were hand-wounds among the earlier batches. The doctors, as you may guess, were terribly overworked, and their stock of bandages and lint was soon exhausted, so all they could do was to apply fresh dressing, thoroughly wash the wounds (this was done by the men suffering from slight wounds), and replace the old stiff and clotted rags which the unfortunate fellows had themselves applied.

The American missionaries, the Reverend Messrs. Pierce and Cole, in Erzeroum, have nobly volunteered to proceed to the front and assist the doctors all in their power; but as the supply of bandages and lint is very small, until more arrive their services without material would be useless. I trust that my many appeals in former letters have produced some effect, and that a moiety of the vast stores despatched to the Danube may be forwarded to Armenia, where the Turks have to contend with a far worse climate than their more fortunate comrades in Europe, and where there is no regular hospital organisation as in the other army corps.

I hope to reach head-quarters to-morrow, when I will send you what more particulars I can gather with reference to the fight, which seems to have been continued, but without much vigour, on the 23rd. It is also rumoured that a force of 16,000 men has been despatched from Kars towards Zewin Dooz, where Ismail Pasha is commanding but fifteen battalions, with one field-battery.

Here we have five battalions guarding the bridge over the Araxes. The old earthworks thrown up in 1854, under the direction of Sir Fenwick Williams, are still

K 2

here untouched in any way; the small redoubt that has been thrown up during the last month, and the slight shelter-trenches now in course of construction, will afford but slight opposition to the Russian advance.

Captains Trotter and M'Calmont have this moment arrived from head-quarters. They assure me that the fighting was most severe on the 21st. In one brigade there were upwards of 200 killed, but they think the Russian loss was heavier. As far as I can now ascertain, the Turkish loss was 400 killed and 2,000 wounded. I must now close to catch this mail, and will send you further reports by next steamer. The Russian published official loss amounted to 54 killed and 375 wounded.

Information has reached me from a very high source, that the Russians have offered a reward of 2,000 roubles for the head of any English officer. It seems scarcely credible, and I shall be glad to learn that this rumour is untrue; but I have had it from many sources. The position occupied by Sir Arnold Kemball is one of great importance, requiring much tact and discretion, a thorough knowledge of Oriental character, coupled with a keen appreciation of military difficulties. I doubt if there is another officer in Her Majesty's army qualified to hold the post. A soldier by training and profession, yet a diplomatist from a thirteen years' experience as Consul-General at Bagdad, Sir Arnold possesses all the qualifications for his present responsible appointment. He possesses a thorough knowledge of Persian, Arabic, and Turkish, and can converse or correspond with equal fluency in any of these languages. From his intimate knowledge of the customs of the people, learnt during a lengthened sojourn in Turkey,

he is able to gain their confidence, and so to advise
them in delicate and difficult matters, when a less
experienced man would have to stand aloof, or when
his advice would be neglected. Not that General
Kemball ever advises during the present crisis, for his
functions are to watch and report to Government upon
the affairs in Armenia, not to mix himself up with
actual military operations. Sir Arnold earned his
"jacket" for conduct in Afghanistan nearly forty years
ago, and had the "Bath" conferred upon him for
gallantry in Persia, and yet he is well content to sleep
on the hill-side wrapped in a Turkish officer's coat, to
share the greasy and innutritious food found in
Turkish camps, to stand by the side of Turkish troops
under a fire that our younger soldiers of Abyssinia and
Ashantee do not dream of; and for what cause? Not
for the honour and glory that would naturally fall to
a Major-General of artillery standing with British
troops exposed to the same danger and privations, but
merely because he has been selected by the Foreign
Office to represent Her Majesty's Ambassador at Constantinople with the Turkish army in Asia Minor. It
needs the constitution of a strong man to stand a
ride of 259 miles in five consecutive days, with changes
of temperature from snow-clad hills 9,000 ft. above sea-
level to the dry and dusty plains of the Passin river.
It needs a man with manly vigour to ride all day and
write all night; it needs a General with something
more than his country's reputation at heart to travel
about, occupying the position Sir Arnold Kemball
does occupy here, unattended by an aide-de-camp,
often accompanied only by a single Mahomedan horse-
keeper, trusting to luck for his food, and to the cold

hill-side for his bed. By all this, by his simple, un-affected manner, his unostentatious style of living, his warm sympathy for the Turkish soldiers, his severe condemnation of the conduct of many of their officials, his indomitable energy and perseverance, his cheery spirits, and his gallant bearing on the field of battle, Sir Arnold has knitted to himself all with whom he has been thrown into contact, and while upholding in a pre-eminent degree the character of the British soldier, has never, to the slightest extent, given the Turkish officers reason to believe that his mission was to help them, or in any way to compromise the neutral position of our Government.

I have been much annoyed by the announcement just received from the chief of the telegraph-office here that my telegram, despatched on the 17th, giving you a full description of the action at Taghir, has been de-tained by order of the Ottoman Government, and the amount paid for it will be returned to me. I suppose I ought not to complain, as I happen to know that all cipher despatches from our Consul here are refused; but still it seems an absurdity that the Porte should endeavour to hide from its own subjects news which in a few days must be known all over the world, and should encourage the dissemination of false reports, to the detriment of the public good.

CAMP, KUIPRI KUI, *June 26th.*

There are few things more difficult, none more dis-heartening, than the attempt to extract trustworthy information from the Turkish officials. I forwarded you a short note on the 24th, giving you the few par-ticulars I could gather concerning the battles that were fought on the 21st at Eshek Khaliass. Since then I have had an opportunity of conversing with Captains Trotter and M'Calmont, additional military attachés, the only English present on the field; but as they were on the right of the position, where the fighting was confined merely to an artillery duel, it is impossible for me to give you any very accurate account of the engagement, and I much fear that until the Russian official and detailed reports are published, we shall be ignorant of the particulars of one of the bloodiest battles, considering the number of men engaged, of this century.

I reported to you in my last that on the 19th inst. Mukhtar Pasha, hearing that General Tergukassoff had established himself in a very strong position at Eshek Khaliass, moved across from Zewin Dooz to Delibaba, the head-quarters of the right wing of the Turkish army, taking with him five battalions, with six field and six mountain guns. He had previously ordered up one battery from Hassan Kale, and one from Taikhojeh, three battalions and 1,000 horse from Kuipri Kui, two battalions from Khorassan, one from Gutenlab, one from Taikhojeh, and two joined the force a few hours subsequent to the engagement on the 16th. What his total force was on the morning of the 20th I am unable to ascertain with any degree of accuracy. As I said before, it was perfectly impossible to estimate the losses at the battle of Taghir; but from what I saw, and what I could learn, only three battalions reached Delibaba that night, whilst two were sent back from Kuipri Kui, whither they had fled. This opinion is strengthened by the report given by the officers above-mentioned, who state that Mukhtar advanced from

Delibaba on the morning of the 20th with all his forces, leaving but one battalion at Taikhojeh to keep up his communication with his centre at Zewin Dooz, and that his force consisted of nineteen battalions,* twelve field and ten mountain guns. Advancing through the pass, he left a reserve of five battalions and all his field guns under Major-General Mustafa Pasha, at Haidar Kui, about six miles from Delibaba, and pushed on with the remainder towards the Russian position. That evening there was slight skirmishing between the cavalry outposts, the Turkish division bivouacking on a ridge about three miles from the Russian camp. At dawn on the 21st the Turks once more advanced, and at 8 a.m. had taken up a position overlooking the Russians, their camp being distinctly visible about two miles distant, immediately below the Turks. Captain M'Calmot assures me that he could see the Russian troops parading, and that had Mukhtar Pasha brought up a field-battery to play on them, he would probably have driven them off before they could have formed; but, although thus surprised, no attack was made on the Russians, who quietly paraded, struck camp within sight of their enemy, and then moved off to commanding ground in the immediate vicinity, which they had previously entrenched.

It was not until noon that the fight commenced, when the Russians, having taken up position on this

---

* As reinforcements to the extent of fourteen battalions and two batteries had reached Delibaba between the 16th and 19th, and as the forces engaged at Taghir, to my certain knowledge, amounted to twelve battalions, one field and one mountain battery, with one battery at Taikhojeh, the obvious conclusion is that the Turks lost seven battalions and twelve guns in the action of the 16th, and from what I saw I see no reason to doubt this estimate.

ridge, opened an artillery fire on the group of horsemen composing the head-quarter staff, and sent forward a body of infantry to turn the right flank of the Turkish position. This attack was checked, and apparently not persisted in, the contending forces on this part of the battle-field contenting themselves with long-range firing. On the left of the Turkish position, however, very severe fighting occurred ; but to get at any accurate report is beyond the bounds of possibility. The Turks evidently advanced in some force, with the view of carrying the Russian entrenchments. They pushed quite close up to them, and were repulsed only to renew the attack over and over again. The regiments composing this brigade complain bitterly that they were not properly supported, and they also complain that they were sent into action with a very limited supply of ammunition, their pouches not having been filled up prior to the engagement. It is reported that on one occasion the infantry were supported by a body of Circassians under Moussa Pasha; but that the Russians immediately let loose two regiments of dragoons on the irregular horse, who were crumpled up like a pocket-handkerchief, with a loss, so Moussa Pasha says, of thirty killed and sixty wounded. This I doubt, for reasons I will dilate upon later.

The Turks failed to capture the position which the Russians still occupied at nightfall. The Turks claim a success, however, as they bivouacked on ground that night in advance of the spot they were on in the morning; and the following day, early, the Russians moved off to a ridge about three miles in rear, which they at once entrenched. Prior to their march, they removed their dead from the battle-field, and in the afternoon the Turks moved down to collect theirs,

amounting to over 400. Mukhtar Pasha did not follow
them up, and although in his report he claims a victory,
and announces the capture of two guns, yet, at the
most, it was a drawn fight, and his loss was enormous.
Turkish officers have, in conversation with me, estimated
it at 2,000 men, and I am inclined to think this is not
an exaggeration. I myself saw fully 1,000 wounded
men on the road between Erzeroum and this; those
able to walk were forced to struggle on as best they
could, those able to bear removal were placed on mules
or country carts, while the more dangerous cases were
left in villages by the roadside. The Commander-in-
Chief estimates the Russian strength at ten battalions,
with thirty guns, and their loss at a figure much heavier
than his own, while he announces the capture of
two field-pieces. This latter statement is unfounded.
Attempts were made by the infantry on the left to
capture a redoubt which contained that number of
guns, but they were unsuccessful; and as Captains
M'Calmont and Trotter were on the ground the whole
time, and went over the battle-field the subsequent day
with Mukhtar Pasha, and assure me that no guns
were taken, I must own to a belief that the Turkish
Commander-in-Chief has been misinformed on this
point. The whole Turkish force engaged amounted
to seventeen battalions and nine field and ten mountain
guns, for, as the fight waxed hotter, large calls were
made on the reserve, so that the Russians were over-
matched in men; and the British officers present also
assure me that they certainly had only eight field and
a few mountain guns and one rocket-troop in action, so
that in point of artillery fire the opposing forces were
pretty equally matched. I am inclined to doubt, from

what I have seen of the Turks, if the Russian loss were so heavy as it is supposed to have been—firstly, because I know how wildly the Ottoman soldier fires away his ammunition ; secondly, because I have seen how utterly regardless he is of cover; thirdly, I have watched the Russians skirmishing on the hill-side, and have been struck with admiration at the manner in which they conceal themselves while advancing, husband their ammunition, and never waste a shot. In addition to all this, those present state that the Russians scarcely showed themselves at all; indeed, Captain M'Calmont informed me that he never saw a single battalion, and very seldom a skirmisher. Taking all these things into consideration, it appears patent to me that the Turks, with their usual dauntless courage, recklessly exposed themselves in storming the entrenchments, and, while unable to touch the Russians, were shot down by them in hundreds from the perfectly secure position they enjoyed behind their breastworks. I am afraid this is a very meagre account of the battle; but, in spite of all my endeavours, I have as yet been unable to get any more details, so I must content myself with sending you what I have, in hope that I may shortly be in possession of fuller particulars.

Yesterday morning, early, Sir Arnold Kemball was informed that the Russians were advancing in two columns, and that severe fighting might be expected at both Zewin and Delibaba. We accordingly moved on to Khorassan, it being a very central position on the road. However, we met numbers of Circassians tailing off to the rear, certainly between 200 and 300 men. From these we learnt that a strong force of Russians had attacked Ismail Pasha on the Zewin Dooz, and that

Moussa Pasha, who with 1,000 Circassians had been detailed by Mukhtar Pasha to proceed to support Ismail, had been unable to force his way through them, and was at present encamped at Khorassan, while on the right bank of the stream Mustafa Pasha was posted with five battalions. We accordingly sent back our baggage-animals, and moved on. We constantly ascended the hills on our left to see if any signs of the enemy were visible; but beyond Mustafa Pasha's battalions posted on the crest of a ridge about three miles to our right front, and large parties of Circassians hastening to the rear, not a sign of war was noticeable. We reached Khorassan at 6 p.m., but were not allowed even to give our horses a feed of corn. The Circassians had reported a large body of Cossacks advancing on the village, and their leader, Moussa Pasha, judged it expedient to beat a hasty retreat. He insisted on our leaving immediately, and even waited to see us mount. So, bowing to necessity, we once more set off, and, in company with Moussa Pasha's horsemen, forded the Araxes, and proceeded by the right bank to Kuipri Kui, pushing on so as to avoid the Circassians who we knew would occupy every nook and corner of every village we might reach. The first place we came to, Yuz Vairan, where we had hoped to find a rough night's lodging, was in flames, having been fired by the Circassians and Kurds, and was, of course, quite deserted. The fact that it was a Christian village was quite sufficient excuse for these gentry to destroy it. As Sir Arnold, accompanied by his two orderlies, and Dougall and myself, passed through at about 9 p.m., we came across a party of Ghazi Mahomed's (Sheik Schamyl's son) men, returning from Delibaba, with that officer's belongings. Seeing our English costumes, these men raised a cry of "Russ! Russ!" and dashing off, left baggage, grooms, and horses to their fate. One of Sir Arnold's orderlies followed and calmed them, and together we moved on, finding fairly comfortable quarters in the "odah" of a stable at Komadsor, where we passed the night. Such a sight as the march of this body of cavalry, said to be 1,000 strong, I never saw, and, for the sake of Turkey, I hope never to see again. When we mounted at Khorassan I fancy there must have been about 400 men; but, instead of marching in one compact body with their chief, they moved off as it pleased them, in twos and threes, by whichever road suited their convenience. Scarcely 200 men crossed the river with their leader and these soon dwindled down to a small troop of about 40 men. As I write I see the tent of Moussa Pasha pitched within a quarter of a mile of mine, surrounded by about 100 other bell-tents, all occupied by the horsemen whose dashing gallantry and fanatical hatred of the Russians were announced as certain to bring the war to a speedy conclusion. So far from these men showing any dashing gallantry, when in bodies they display a remarkable tendency to keep out of the way of the enemy, and spend their time in ravaging villages, pillaging the inhabitants, living in clover, and never paying a sou for anything they appropriate. The fattest lamb in the flock, the best horse in the stable, the largest cooking-vessel in the "khan" are all considered fair prize: it is not to be wondered at, then, that Armenian and Mahomedan alike should look forward with feelings of welcome to the coming of the Russians. It is exasperating to see the Circassians all round one lying down in comfortable tents, living on

the fat of the land, and declining to join in the conflict,
while the Turkish soldiers are without cover, without
food, and fighting gallantly for their country.   For two
days now heavy fighting has been reported as going on
at Zewin Dooz, where Ismail Pasha, aided by the
gallant Hungarian General, Faizi Pasha, with a force
of barely 10,000 men, has kept at bay a Russian force
which is reported to be half as strong again.   Instead
of proceeding to the assistance of the beleaguered Turks,
who are much harassed by the Russian cavalry, Moussa
Pasha and his Circassians take it easy at Kuipri Kui,
25 miles to the rear.

Yesterday five battalions and three guns forced
their way up to Zewin from this place; but they
moved off before I learnt their intentions, and, as it is
quite impossible to join the camp except in company
with a large body of infantry—for strong bodies of
Cossacks are prowling about the road, have cut the
telegraph-wire, and captured small parties endeavouring
to join Ismail—and as I have no wish to date my
next letter from Tiflis, having had one narrow escape
from an unforeseen journey in company with a Russian escort, I am naturally rather careful where I go.
So when Moussa Pasha informed us at Khorassan that
the Cossacks were within half an hour of the village,
I gladly joined in the evacuation of the place.

Naturally, since I have been here I have had many,
very many, opportunities of conversing with Turkish
officers and men on the so-called Eastern Question; and
the consequence is that, arriving in the country a strong
philo-Turk, deeply impressed with the necessity of
preserving the " integrity of the Empire " in order to
uphold " British interests," I now fain would cry with

Mr. Freeman, "Perish India rather than one English soldier should fall fighting for Turkey." * I am fully aware that partisans of the Ottoman Empire maintain that we should not be fighting for the Porte, but to keep open our communications with India, which would be seriously imperilled by the contiguity of such an aggressive Power as Russia. What did we fight for in 1854, and what was the result, at a sacrifice of life almost unprecedented in our annals of warfare? At a sacrifice of 100 millions of English money we bolstered

---

* In deference to Mr. Freeman's injured feelings, betrayed in a somewhat lengthy letter to the *Times*, on the 25th of July, 1877, I here give the exact words he made use of in the St. James's Hall speech of December, 1876, and apologise for my mis-quotation:—"Perish British interests, perish our dominion in India, rather than that we should strike a blow on behalf of the wrong ' against the right!'" On reading the lucid explanation of the true meaning of this sentence, I find I am quite of the same opinion as its originator. My experience of India and the East, I humbly submit, is equal to that possessed by Mr. Freeman. I have many, very many, warm friends there, native as well as English, and am the last man to wish a deluge to submerge the peninsula of Hindostan, as the Somersetshire historian would seem to imply is the translation of the words "Perish India!" As regards the objection to the phrase "fighting for Turkey," by Turkey I mean the government of that country. Mr. Freeman, whose knowledge of the Turk surely must be very limited, wishes blows to be struck "against the Turk." There is no finer race in the world than the Turk proper. Brave, honest, industrious, truthful, frugal, kind-hearted, and hospitable, all who *know* the Osmanli speak well of him. He is as much oppressed by the curse of misgovernment as his Christian fellow-subject; and had the members of the Eastern Question Association as keen a sense of justice as they have love of writing, they would long ago have obliterated the word "Christian" from their lengthy documents, and striven to ameliorate the condition of the lower orders of the subjects of the Porte, down-trodden as they are by an effete section of the Mahomedan race, who have degenerated in mind, body, and estate, since coming in contact with Western civilisation. The fanatical hatred towards the Moslem shown by a large section of the Christian community in England has done more to bring about the present crisis than we dream of.

up an effete Power, and for twenty-five years allowed it to labour under the impression that we should always prop it up by our stalwart aid when assailed. What has been the consequence? The upper classes have enriched themselves by sucking the life-blood of the lower; the country is in a state of bankruptcy owing to its maladministration; the officials buy their promotion with money extorted by threats and compulsion from the poorer community, and continue in office by the same means; trade is at a standstill, and no man durst embark in a new venture, on account of the heavy fees demanded by every Government official as his own private perquisite; and, although the actual Imperial taxation is small and falls lightly even on the poorer classes, yet the power placed in the hands of all Government servants is so enormous, and usually is so arbitrarily wielded, that the inhabitants groan under a yoke almost too hard to be borne.

The constant reports by our energetic Consul of the gross outrages committed on Christian villagers, and his inability to obtain adequate compensation; the burning houses of Yuz Vairan, which we ourselves saw on the 26th; and the deserted Armenian hamlets all over these hills, point to the fact that oppression, however much it may be denied by the Constantinople officials, is openly practised and connived at, at any rate by those in authority in Asia Minor. Several glaring cases have come under my own personal observation, and many more have been reported to me by the American missionaries and our own consular officials in Erzeroum. I do not for one moment mean to deny that there are honest, energetic Turks, capable of exercising their talents for their country's good; but these men are powerless. The vital powers of the nation are so sapped by centuries of misrule, the minds of the majority are so imbued with the belief that all ideas not born of Moslem brains and sanctified by Moslem usage are false and to be scorned, that were any honest-minded gentleman to rise to power, and endeavour to check the present system of misgovernment, he would not remain in office one week.* After accompanying a Turkish army in the field, after witnessing the privations of the men owing to the criminally faulty commissariat arrangements, after seeing the miseries of the wounded, untended and uncared for, after hearing of, as well as seeing, the oppression habitually exercised on Christians by all Mahomedans, after reading the history of the Ottoman nation, and after learning from the lips even of Turkey's staunchest supporters of the vacillation and weakness of her Ministers, I cannot help feeling that she is past redemption, and that any encouragement given to her will only prolong the present struggle, afford Russia a pretext for further aggression, and make the blow when it does come fall the harder upon the misguided nation.

On the 27th we made one more attempt to make our way to the head-quarter camp, but were strongly recommended by an officer commanding a battalion we met on the road, to turn back, as he was unable to force his way through the Cossacks, who were in large numbers near Ala-Kilissa. Fearing our attempts would be useless, we determined to abandon them, and to join the Commander-in-Chief at Delibaba. With this in

---

* Captain Gambier's able article on the " Life of Midhat Pasha," in the January (1878) number of the *Nineteenth Century,* bears me out in this idea.

view we once more forded the Araxes, found our way into our old lodgings at Komadsor, and revelled in the luxury of home news, for here we found a missing mail. At night we learnt from a Turkish captain that Mukhtar Pasha had pushed across from Delibaba to Zewin, that Mustafa Pasha was holding the ford at Khorassan, and, astounding assertion, that Tergukassoff, with all his forces, had surrendered to the Commander-in-Chief on the preceding day.

CAMP, ZEWIN DOOZ, *June* 28.

Leaving Komadsor at 3 a.m., we forded the Araxes. Fearing Cossack patrols, who had been reported as scouring the country, we passed over the hills *viâ* Ardost, in rear of the Zewin Hills, reaching the camp at 10 a.m. We proceeded at once to Mushir Ahmed Mukhtar Pasha's tent, where we found him and his gallant old chief of the staff, Faizi Pasha, in a great state of exultation. It appears that the fight on the 25th here was a complete success. The Russians attacked the position very heavily on the right front. Unfortunately, however, for the Muscovites, this front, owing to the open nature of the valley running up it, defied attack.

The battle lasted until 8 p.m., when the Russians drew off, leaving 265 dead bodies on the ground. From reports of officers on the ground, it appears that the Russians, who, as I have already informed you, had detached a force of 16,000 men with 1,500 cavalry from Kars, were reported at Mellidooz on the 24th inst. A reconnaissance showed that their General had detached a force of five battalions, a battery, and some cavalry, towards Khorassan, with the view of cutting off the right

ENGAGEMENT ON THE ZEWIN PLATEAU
25th June, 1877.

Chan Su

to Kars Ghom

to Meringhen

Zewin

to Yenikoi & Bardiz

to Khorassan

From Kuzerl Kul.

Turks

Russians

0   1   ENGLISH MILES   2   3 Miles

London, Cassell, Petter, & Galpin.

E.Weller, lith.

wing from the centre, and probably also of seizing the Kuipri Kui position (at present almost undefended) by a *coup-de-main*, and thus forcing the centre of the Turks to fall back on Erzeroum without effecting a junction with the Delibaba division. At 11 a.m. the Russian column, consisting (as now could be distinctly seen) of fifteen battalions, three batteries, and from 1,500 to 2,000 cavalry, was visible, moving over the hills from Mellidooz to Zewin. Without waiting even to halt and rest his men, the Russian General (by some said to be Loris Melikoff himself, by others General Heimann) pushed on heavy columns to the right front of the Turkish position, where the ground is split up into numerous rocky ravines, terminating under the Turkish entrenchments, in almost precipitous walls, enfiladed for a distance of about 800 yards, and in many places exposed to cross-fire from three entrenchments held by infantry, as well as to a sweeping fire from the six Krupp guns. The Russian guns, owing to the nature of the ground, could not come into action at a nearer range than 5,000 yards, and the Turks being about 1,500 feet above their batteries, shots not actually striking the entrenchments either buried themselves in the ground, on the face of the slope, or passing over, fell harmless a long distance in rear of the ridge. The infantry fire, too, owing to their low position, was to a great extent nullified, while the Ottoman troops, safe behind their shelter-trenches, rained in a tempest of bullets from their Martini-Henry rifles that no troops could have lived under. Ten times were the Russians driven back, and ten separate times did they, with the gallant obstinacy characteristic of the nation, assail this almost impregnable position—certainly impregnable from the face they attacked it from. Seven-

L 2

teen Turkish battalions, armed with the best-shooting weapon in the world, poured down an almost incessant fire on the Russian column; and when they, shaken and broken by their heavy losses, endeavoured to move off to their right up the valley, and attack the more open ground in that direction, they were met by two fresh battalions, accompanied by two field-guns, very fortunately sent down by Faizi Pasha, and although these suffered very heavily (one having no less than 150 men put *hors de combat*) they effectually checked the enemy. Again and again did the Russians press their attack, sometimes to within 200 yards of the Turkish trenches. Again and again were they forced back, unable to face the furious storm hurled against them. The sun went down on this scene of carnage, and yet the fight went on, the midsummer moon lending her bright light to enable aggressor and oppressor to carry on their dread slaughter. In spite of their enormous losses, in spite of the death of two of their most gallant and determined leaders, in spite of their being unable to inflict any loss on their opponents, the Muscovites pressed on their attack; but at half-past eight in the evening, having lost nearly one-fourth of his force, Melikoff drew off to Zewin. Had the Turkish commander possessed any confidence that his men would face their foe in the open, the Russians would have been followed up, and probably not a man would have escaped to tell the tale to the Grand Duke Michael at Kars; but, knowing that the strong point of his men was in fighting behind entrenchments, and being destitute of cavalry (for Moussa Pasha had been idly lying at Khorassan all day instead of moving up to support his bravely-fighting compatriots), Faizi Pasha wisely determined to abandon all hope of pursuit, and allowed the Russians to draw off unmolested to a position near Zewin, on the left bank of the Chan Su.

The following morning, on the 26th, a smart cannonade was commenced by the Russians at a very long range, and under cover of it they retired to Mellidooz, where they now are, waiting for reinforcements from Kars. On the arrival of these they, doubtless, will once more try conclusions on the spot. The Turks now are inspired with confidence in themselves and their leaders. Dispirited by the surrender of Bayazid, the capture of Ardahan, and the defeat of Taghir, they were somewhat encouraged by the slight success gained at Khaliass, when the Russians certainly fell back before Mukhtar Pasha; and although the very heavy loss sustained that day somewhat damped their ardour, the complete victory on the 25th here has inspired them with the greatest enthusiasm, and will probably put a very different complexion on the issue of the next few weeks' campaign.

As I have already told you, Mukhtar Pasha, on the 19th, crossed over to Delibaba, and Kurd Ismail Pasha on that day assumed command here. On the 25th he satisfied himself with sitting on the ground reading his Koran, and praying in a rapid and audible tone. In my humble opinion, and in the opinion of every Turkish officer with whom I have conversed, the whole credit of the day is due to Faizi Pasha, the chief of the staff, whom Ahmed Mukhtar had wisely left here to assist Ismail. Not only did this gallant old officer superintend all arrangements, personally visiting every battalion and shelter-trench, but once or twice early in the day, when the Russians, pressing close up to the entrenchments, caused the Turks to waver—in one instance, indeed, to retire somewhat rapidly—he himself led them forward, revived their drooping spirits, inspired them with fresh courage, and so won the day for his adopted Government.

A Hungarian refugee after 1848, Captain Kohlman, as he was then called, sought employment in the Turkish army under Kmety. He gained some renown, and was rapidly promoted to the rank of Major-General; but, with their usual obstinacy and pride of race, the Turks look with jealousy on the man who fought and bled at Kars, who executed the fortifications at Batoum, who reorganised the Fourth Army Corps; and although he has changed his faith, and is now as orthodox a Mussulman as the most conscientious Turk, Faizi Pasha has the mortification of seeing men who were boys when he won his spurs in the Ottoman army pass over his head, and gain the coveted rank of Mushir, while he still grows grey in the grade of Ferik. It is to be hoped that the Porte will show signs of some gratitude, and as his just reward give him the rank of Marshal. With seventeen weak battalions and twelve guns he completely defeated fifteen very strong Russian battalions with twenty-four guns, inflicting on them enormous losses, while his own casualties did not amount to 500 men. The division of General Heimann, on the contrary, is reported by prisoners taken subsequent to the battle, and by deserters, to have lost 2,000 killed and upwards of 3,000 wounded. An Austrian officer present on the field, one who graduated in the '57 and '66 campaigns, and held high rank on the staff of the cavalry division at Sadowa, informed me that their losses were fully 3,000 men. The villagers of Zewin informed us that upwards of 1,000 men with seventeen superior officers

were buried on their hills, and the Turkish soldiers state
they buried 265 in front of their own position. All
these reports must be received with caution, but I think
the Russian losses may certainly be put down at from
1,500 to 2,000 men. The Turks suffered heavily in
officers, fifty-seven out of the 500 being of the commissioned grade. Lieutenant-General Mukhliss Pasha
received two severe wounds in gallantly encouraging
his men, and many officers commanding battalions fell
at the head of their regiments.

I must mention one incident in the action, showing
the value of the Turkish cavalry and their leaders.
When the Russians, shaken by the fire in front,
endeavoured to move off to their right, they were met,
as I told you, by a couple of battalions and two guns,
who checked and drove them back. The scene of this
affair was an open valley well adapted for cavalry
manœuvres. Faizi Pasha ordered his horse, some 500
Kurds, Circassians, and zaptiehs, down the hill, to
charge the broken infantry. Instead of proceeding down
the watercourse which opened into the valley, and where
they would have been completely covered, these dauntless horsemen moved boldly across the sky-line of the
ridge, fully exposed to the Russian fire, and before
any attempt to descend had been made they suffered
casualties to the extent of about seventy horses, when,
considering they had sufficiently vindicated their cha-
racters, they retired, and declined to fight again that
day.

I have endeavoured since my arrival here to report
fairly and conscientiously all that has come under my
personal observation. I have never hesitated to expose
the vices, follies, and shortcomings of the Turks, but I trust

at the same time that I have fully given them their due for their gallantry in the field, or their noble conduct in bearing privations which no other nation in the world would submit to. It is no pleasure to harp always on one string, and it has been a source of sincere gratification to me that I have at last been enabled to change my note, and chant my feeble lay of praise to the honour of the officers and men engaged in the battle-field of Zewin Dooz on Monday last. It is more than a pleasure to be able to recount the energy, good judgment, and gallantry shown by the Commander-in-Chief, Ahmed Mukhtar, in the operations of the last few days. His conduct at Kars, subsequent retreat from that place at the end of April, and the apathy he evinced at the commencement of the campaign, led to his bravery being freely questioned, officers and men inveighing in no measured terms against a leader who was rarely seen out of his tent, never visited the regimental camps, invariably retired on the advance of the Russians, apparently took no pains to insure his commissariat being regularly supplied, and allowed his men to suffer cold, hunger, and want without raising a finger to assist them. I am inclined to think that Mukhtar Pasha was hampered by the Constantinople officials, who permitted him to open a campaign with an empty treasure-chest, and then with a flourish of trumpets sent him £35,000, and bade him go in and win, and also by the jealousy of Kurd Ismail Pasha at Erzeroum, who took no pains to feed the army in his district, or to horse and push on the numerous guns lying useless at that city to the Fourth Army Corps. However much the Commander-in-Chief's conduct may be open to criticism prior to the 16th, there is no doubt that, subsequent to that date, he has shown an energy and capacity rarely seen in a Turkish official. Immediately on learning of the defeat at Taghir, and consequent depression and loss of *morale* of the Delibaba Division, he himself proceeded to the spot, led the men forward against the Russians, and gained a decided success. Although achieved at a frightful sacrifice of life, it showed the Turks that they could hold their own against their foe ; and thus having inspired them with fresh courage, and seen personally to the faulty commissariat arrangements, which the unfortunate Mahomed Pasha entirely neglected, he crossed back to Zewin—too late, however, to participate in the gallant fight of the 25th, the success of which must be attributed to the arrangements and gallant bearing of the chief of the staff, Faizi Pasha.

As I close this letter, Osman Bey, aide-de-camp to the Commander-in-Chief, and as gallant an officer as ever drew sword, has just come into our tent and reported that the Russians have retired both from Mellidooz and from Zaidikan, leaving the front both of the headquarters and Delibaba Division free from threatened attack. It seems that the Russians lost heavily in the fight at Khaliass, and that Faik Pasha, moving up from Bayazid with his force (the details of which I have previously given you) amounting to about 11,000 infantry and 1,600 cavalry, with nine guns, has placed Tergukassoff between two fires, and forced him to fall back. From the same source I learn that, having detached this division to attack Zewin, the Grand Duke Michael has but twenty-eight battalions at Kars ; and that Mukhtar Pasha, feeling the *morale* of his troops so much improved, has determined on making a forward movement. I trust, however, that this may not be true, for his weakness in artillery will bring ruin on the Turks if they attempt to act on the offensive. It has been ascertained beyond doubt that Loris Melikoff commanded in person on the 25th here. If so, he deserves to be removed from his command; and the Russian General, whoever he may be, who led his men against the position* without a reconnaissance, and sacrificed thousands of valuable lives in driving them against precipitous cliffs, deserves to be tried by court-martial. Very different was his conduct from that of Tergukassoff on the 16th, who handled his men in the most perfect style, and gave as pretty an illustration of hill warfare as could well be desired.

CAMP, ZEWIN DOOZ, *June* 30.

I find it quite impossible to obtain any accurate information as to the Turkish losses at the battle of Taghir. All reports, even assurances from officers on the personal staff of the Commander-in-Chief, and Ahmed Mukhtar Pasha's despatches themselves, are directly contradictory to the opinion formed by Sir Arnold Kemball and myself on the battle-field. I am almost tempted to disbelieve the evidence of my own senses, and to accept as a fact the statement, now officially put forward, that the Turks did not lose a single prisoner or a single gun. Yet I can hardly reconcile this with

---

* There can be no excuse urged by the partisans of the Russian General. The Russian maps give an excellent representation of the ground; and as Paskiewitch defeated Salegh Pasha on the same spot on the 19th of June, 1829, and as admirable plans of that battle were published by the Russian Topographical Department, showing the impracticable nature of the hills in front of the old Château of Zewin, the easy gradients to the north, it seems incredible that, casting aside the experience gained in the war of 1828—29, Melikoff should have run the risk of incurring such a crushing defeat as he did on the 25th of June, 1877.

the sight I saw on the 16th of June, when the Russian
cavalry, charging up the slope, were mingled in one
confused mass with the disordered Ottoman troops;
nor with the accounts of various regimental officers
with whom I have conversed, who admitted that their
own regiments lost many prisoners—one, indeed (the
Erzeroum battalion), having as many as 200 captured.
The number was given to me by two men of the corps
on two different occasions, as well as by a wounded
officer. I cannot reconcile, then, the official reports
with what I actually saw; and I am the more tempted
to place faith in my own report when I read the Russian
account of the affair at Beghli Ahmed, and compare it
with the statement made by the Commander-in-Chief,
who distinctly said in my presence that the total casualties of the Circassians were 13 killed and 37 wounded,
omitting all mention of the loss of the two Whitworth
guns with which Hussein Hami Pasha, the commandant
of Kars, had provided them, although he owned that
they were in action. Now, after the publication of the
Russian account, Mukhtar Pasha confesses that they
did lose upwards of 100 killed, many prisoners, and not
only the two guns, but also 70 tents, which they abandoned in their flight. After these discrepancies I must
confess I cannot place much faith in the Turkish official
reports, and utterly disbelieve their statements of the
losses at Taghir, which they aver amounted to only 25
killed and 119 wounded. If this is a fact it reflects
the greater discredit on the Turkish army, for I saw
hundreds of men in small groups moving over the hills
in rapid flight, many of them being unarmed fugitives;
and an officer of the Commander-in-Chief's staff, whom
I met at Khorassan the day after the flight, informed

me that he had been ordered to Kuipri Kui to turn
back any fugitives he might meet. I again encountered
this officer on his road back from Kuipri Kui, when he
assured me he had turned back two battalions who had
precipitately fled from the field, and while I was conversing with him he pointed out various bodies of men
belonging to different corps, whom he had met on the
road and ordered back to join the force at Delibaba.
Viewing the battle of Taghir from my own standpoint,
and from that of the Turks, I find such vast differences
that I am again forced to disbelieve their version of the
battle of Khaliass, when they confess to have lost 368
killed and 1,020 wounded; and later on, the battle of
Zewin Dooz, on the 25th, which they claim as a complete victory, in which they assert that the Russians
lost 2,000 killed and 3,000 wounded, and they themselves but seven officers and 131 men killed, 15 officers
and 313 men wounded, seems to me a complete mystery.
I have gone over the ground, and can quite believe that
any troops in the world attacking such a position held
by steadily disciplined men would have suffered enormously; but then, again, I was informed by officers on
the staff of the Turkish army that they had buried 265
men in front of their position, and that the villagers
of Zewin had seen 1,080 buried in the bed of the Chan
Su. I myself went to the village, questioned the few
remaining inhabitants, and could not find a single trace
of a grave beyond some half-dozen on the hill-side. I
saw the bodies of a few horses, and also of two Turkish
villagers, evidently spies, whom the Russians shot in
punishment for having led them into such a trap as
they found the Zewin Dooz position. I have traversed
the road for seventeen miles taken by the Russians in

their retreat, and passed through their first bivouac, fifteen miles east of Zewin, on the Mellidooz, but could see no traces of burying-places. Any soldier will know that a retiring army numbering but sixteen battalions would not carry 2,000 dead with them, but would inter them near where they fell, especially as they remained within two miles of the battle-field for two days.

So the glorious victory of Zewin remains to me a mystery. That there was an action I cannot doubt, for the Turkish position is fairly ploughed up with shell; that the Russians were driven back, too, is clear, and that they left some dead and many stand of arms on the hill-side is also clear. But I venture to throw discredit on the greatness of the victory, brief details of which I telegraphed to you on the faith of the Commander-in-Chief's own statement. Until we get General Loris Melikoff's report we shall never know the truth. His accounts of the capture of Ardahan and the minor engagements at the commencement of the campaign have been marked with such fairness and moderation, that I think they can be implicitly accepted.

CHAPTER IX.

IN PURSUIT OF THE RUSSIANS.

Visit from the Mushir—Complications in Daghestan—An Advance on the Enemy—A Cold Night—Inefficient Quartermaster-General's Department—The Bivouac on the Mellidooz—Treatment of Sir Arnold Kemball—March to Sara Kamysh—A Turkish Camp—Turkish Hospitals—Rations of the Turkish Soldier—Discipline on the Line of March—Peabody-Martini Rifle—Russian Letters—The Opinion expressed in them of the Conduct of the War—Russian Retreat from Zaidikan—Desecration of the Graves of Russian Dead—Stripping the Dead—Disposition of the Army—Rumour of Russian Retreat—Turkish Reverse near Ardanutsch—Kurdish Atrocities—Lawlessness of the Circassians—Russian Wounded killed on the Field—Murder of Two Karapapak Irregulars—A new Mushir with Reinforcements—Detail of our Army—Officers of Redif Battalions on the Line of March—Stories of Russian Cruelty—Not borne out by Facts—Plunder of Christian Villages by Circassians—Vairan Kale—A Late Dinner.

CAMP, MELLIDOOZ, *July 1st.*

YESTERDAY morning I was compelled to stop writing, as his Excellency came to our tent to pay a visit to Sir Arnold. He seemed full of exultation at the result of the battle of the 25th, and the subsequent retreat of the Russians. In the course of conversation he informed me that he had certain information that the enemy had fallen back behind Toprak-Kali and Sara Kamysh (*i.e.*, that both wings had retired), and that he was thinking of advancing to relieve Kars. He had heard rumours from villagers, obtained in conversation with Russians, that there was a rising in the Caucasus; that the Georgians had seized Tiflis, and that the Grand Duke Michael was falling back on to the Russian frontier. Of all this he assured me with the utmost gravity, and seemed to consider the campaign

at an end, with the exception of the trifling finishing
touch of driving the Russians over the Caucasus. Although he said he had thoughts of advancing, it was
with no small surprise that we learnt at 4 p.m. that
the Commander-in-Chief had actually left camp, taking
with him twelve battalions, six field and six mountain
guns, and all the cavalry; also that Faizi Pasha was
to follow early in the morning with the remainder of
the head-quarter division, amounting to an equal
number of battalions and guns. We speedily had our
horses round, and with cloaks only, and three days'
grain for our animals, followed the Mushir's track,
making a *détour* by the village of Zewin to see the
Russian graves, without success.

At 8 p.m. we overtook the straggling column, which
was halted on a crest 8,600 feet above sea-level, without water or wood, and with a bitterly cold wind
blowing. We ourselves moved on below the ridge to
a spot some three-quarters of a mile in advance, when
we found a beautiful clear stream and a soft bit of
grass. Then, hobbling our horses, we bivouacked for
the night, with our syces for our only attendants, hard-
boiled eggs and soldiers' biscuits for our dinner. It was
a bitterly cold night, and I do not think any of us got
much sleep; for there was no wood with which to make
a fire, and we were 8,200 feet above sea-level, and with
a heavy dew falling, the temperature was not conducive
to sweet slumbers. At half-past one we awoke, perish-
ing with cold; and as the Commander-in-Chief had
given orders that he would march at 3 a.m., we sent
one of the syces to forage for wood, in order to get a
cup of tea before our start. Our haste was needless,
for it was five before the first bugle sounded, and 6.20

before we got off. You may imagine our disgust after riding for less than half an hour to arrive at a beautiful grassy plain, studded over with groves of fir-trees, and covered with the huts made by the Russian army, who three days before had bivouacked on the spot. The Turkish cavalry had passed over the ground two days previous to our advance, staff officers had ridden over it that same afternoon, and yet the Turkish General preferred allowing his men to sleep on a bare mountain crest, where they were unable even to light a fire, or get water to wash down their unpalatable biscuit, rather than accept the reports of his staff officers, and move on a mile to an equally strong and in every respect far more advantageous position.

I am now writing on a ridge east of the bivouac of the Russian army, the Turkish troops having drawn up on it, piled arms, and there is some show of entrenching the place. Whether Mukhtar Pasha will remain here or not it is difficult to say. His intention yesterday was to move on and relieve Kars ; but as I look around me and see the undrilled, undisciplined battalions that constitute his army, I cannot think he will be rash enough to face Loris Melikoff in the open field ; and yet to hold this would be sheer madness. Thick fir forests surround it on all sides but the rear, approaching on the southern face to within 200 yards, and on the eastern to about 400 yards, affording admirable cover to an enemy who, I know from personal experience, avail themselves of shelter when advancing under fire in a manner that I have never seen equalled by our troops. There is a ridge also on the eastern front, about 1,400 yards distant, well covered with pines, along which an enemy could easily plant their batteries undetected, while three miles off, sloping down to our right flank, is a conical hill, the lower spurs of which dominate and enfilade our position. This is the very spot where, on the 20th June, 1829, Marshal Paskie-witch defeated Hakki Pasha; and the remains of the old Turkish breastworks may yet be seen around us.

I think I mentioned in my last the fact that the Russian field artillery was of much heavier metal than the Turkish, and that on examining the fragments of a shell at Taghir I gathered it must have been fired from a gun resembling our 16-pound field-gun. At Zewin it appeared that they had still heavier metal; an unex-ploded shell was brought to the Commander-in-Chief's tent, which Sir Arnold saw and pronounced to weigh about 30 lbs. It was thickly coated with lead, through which the scoring of the groove was plainly visible. An Austrian officer present at the fight informed me that they had two of these heavy guns with the six 16-pounders composing their batteries, and that they never came within 400 yards' range, when the practice was excellent. I was much struck with the neatness of the Russian bivouac, each battalion having halted them-selves under the boughs of fir-trees, the company lines being quite distinct. Fireplaces made of stones, with forked sticks at either side, were left standing, and the well-dressed lines of horse leavings and unused hay showed that they paid as much attention to the appear-ance of their encampments as we ourselves do.

It is but a duty I owe to the English public that they should be informed of the very scant courtesy our mili-tary *attaché* receives at the hands of the Turkish officers. Sir Arnold Kemball is too old a soldier, too tried a poli-tician, and too deeply imbued with a sense of the

M

extremely delicate nature of his mission, ever to let fall
even a hint that he is dissatisfied with the treatment he
receives ; but it must, nevertheless, be galling to an
officer of his position to be left without attendants,
allowed to bivouac on the open ground, when even
regimental officers carry tents, and to be not only kept in
the dark as to the intentions of the Commander-in-Chief,
but constantly misinformed as to the actual state of
affairs.   Attended only by his *aide-de-camp* and one
Turkish orderly officer, Sir Arnold may be seen riding
through the camp, making himself thoroughly acquainted
with the real state of affairs ; and although attired in the
uniform of a British general officer, he is rarely received
with any marks of respect, and is still more rarely
saluted by either officers or men ; all day long in the
saddle, at night sleeping on the bare ground, wrapped
only in his cloak, sharing the rations of the Turkish
soldier, and cheerfully putting up with privations that
few of our generals would stand.   It is but just to add
that there was a marked change in the treatment of
Sir Arnold after the relief of Kars, when all superior
officers received him with every mark of respect.   Yet
throughout the campaign it grated on my sense of the
fitness of things, that the Turkish subaltern, his orderly
officer, was saluted by every man who passed, whilst
the British general rarely received the honour due to
his rank, even from the private soldiers.

Camp, Sara Kamysh, July 3rd.

The night before last we succeeded, after some
difficulty, in procuring a soldier's bell tent, for the cold
on the Mellidooz plateau, which is about 8,600 feet
above sea level, was intense, and the great variation in

temperature between the extreme heat of the sun in daytime and the bitter coldness of the nights was beginning to affect some of our party. We were aroused at five a.m. yesterday by a squad of men striking the tent about our heads, and at nine a.m. the column advanced through the Mellidooz Pass. The road was most picturesque—high cliffs on either side, well covered with thick clumps of fir-trees, and further on soft grassy slopes, thickly wooded with pine and beech, and carpeted with flowers of every hue, while a clear stream bubbled down the centre of the valley. It was a great treat to get a wash—for two days we had been restricted to less than a quart a day for all purposes, as the well from which the camp was supplied was more than three miles from our halting place. The state of the road over which we advanced was very different from that left behind Zewin ; every stream was well bridged with the trunks of fir-trees, the numerous bogs which abound wherever streams crossed the path were filled in with boughs of trees, fascines, &c., gradients eased off ; in fact, our progress was far more rapid over the improved Russo-Turkish frontier road than over any other cross-road that I have seen in the country. At last, after a march of twelve miles, we reached the two villages of Sara Kamysh, situated at the eastern end of the pass, and ascending a ridge to the left we saw the plain of Kars. The troops bivouacked on the slopes on either side of the pass, in dense groves of fir-trees, at an elevation of 8,200 feet above sea level. Firewood there was in abundance, but the water-supply was bad and at a great distance. The arrangements of a Turkish army in this are perhaps more disgraceful than in any other respect. There are no such things as water pickets, and the consequence is

M 2

that men bathe, wash linen, and water horses where they please. Those acquainted with Oriental customs will know how fatal they are to all hopes of a pure supply of water, and no soldier will wonder that in an army where no attention is paid to this most essential point, dysentery and sickness should be rife.

I have had an opportunity of conversing with some of the German doctors attached to the army, and from them have had the most harrowing accounts of the sufferings of the sick and wounded. The hospitals at Erzeroum can accommodate about 1,000 men; prior to any engagements every ward was filled with patients suffering from typhoid fever, dysentery, and pneumonia, the average death-rate being thirty to forty a day. The three actions of the 16th, 21st, and 25th of June furnished their quota of invalids in increasing the number by upwards of 2,000 wounded men, giving more than enough work to the eleven doctors already overworked in Erzeroum. There being insufficient accommodation for these wounded, they were distributed amongst the khans and native houses in the vicinity of the hospital; but, as the supply of medicines, bandages, and instruments was more limited even than that of doctors, the suffering and privation of these poor fellows can hardly be imagined. I do not know why some of the money collected in England for the relief of Turkish soldiers has not been diverted from the capacious maw of the European-Turkish army to the far worse equipped Fourth Army Corps. Here the men have received no pay for two years, their rations are distributed with gross irregularity, and it is a very rare occurrence for the men ever to see meat. Thus on short commons, unable to purchase even the commonest necessaries of life, it is not to be wondered that the unfortunate soldiers suffer terribly from sickness, and when once struck down it is still less surprising that the death-rate is so high. The American missionaries, the Rev. Messrs. Pierce and Cole, have, as I have already mentioned, nobly volunteered to come out to the front, when occasion requires, to assist the few overworked doctors in their distressing labours; and now these two gentlemen, regardless of creed or race, are doing true missionary work by daily visiting the various hospitals in Erzeroum, and spending hours in endeavouring to alleviate the sufferings of the unfortunate men, aiding the surgeons in replacing bandages, washing wounds, reducing fractures, and, by distributing unknown luxuries, such as fowls, meat, eggs, tobacco, &c., among the men, enabling them to bear up better under their dreadful privations than if they were living on the meagre war rations issued with the same irregularity in the hospital as in the camp. Want of money is the great stumbling-block. I have succeeded in collecting a small sum, so small, indeed, that it seems but a drop in the ocean compared to the amount we really need. This sum I have intrusted to the Rev. Mr. Pierce, to be spent in such necessaries as he may be able to purchase; but lint, bandages, clean linen, &c., are simply unprocurable. For these we must depend entirely on the exertions of the committees at home, and I can only trust that should the good people of England forward any sums of money to Erzeroum to be expended on behalf of the wounded Turkish soldiers, they will annex as a condition that it is on no account to pass through Turkish hands, but to be placed solely at the disposal of the American missionaries and German doctors in Asia Minor.

With regard to the fund for wounded soldiers, I
have been at some pains to ascertain, from various
sources, the real state of the hospital arrangements in
this camp, and the means taken for the comfort and
transport of the sick. The total strength of the corps
is about 16,000 fighting men, and possibly another
1,000 followers. To attend upon this force there are
two Prussian and three Turkish doctors; there is one
case of amputating instruments. Each surgeon has
his own small pocket case. There are twenty tents, but
without beds, for the accommodation of the sick, two
cases of lint, bandages, &c., and two cases of medicine,
and this is all that the Turkish Government has provided
for the poor fellows with the head-quarters of the Fourth
Turkish Army Corps! There are no ambulance carts or
litters with the army. In Erzeroum there are many
lightly constructed litters, with wheels, by means of
which it would be easy to convey wounded over these
hills. But, as with their guns, so with their litters,
the Turkish officials strongly object to bringing them
to the front, and the wounded accordingly suffer. Sick
men get no stated rations, but occasionally a sheep
is served out to the hospitals. Fortunately for the
men themselves, this army is mainly composed of
battalions of the Redif, men who, having served their
time in the army, have returned to civil life, been
draughted into the reserve, and now in time of war are
called out for the defence of their country. These men,
consequently, have small sums of money of their own,
and so are not dependent on their rations for subsistence.
The men of the Nizam, or regular army—men solely
dependent on their pay and their rations—are very
poorly off for food. I believe no army in the world

is better fed than the Turkish in time of peace, or
rather, than they would be if their regulations were
strictly carried out. It may interest some of my
military readers, if I give the scale of rations as laid
down, and also the amount they now are allowed in
the field.

Scale of Rations for Turkish Soldiers :—

					Ounces.
Bread	...	...	...	...	... $34\frac{1}{4}$
Meat	...	...	...	...	... 9
Rice	...	...	...	...	... 3
Butter	...	...	...	...	... $\frac{1}{3}$
Salt	...	...	...	...	... $\frac{2}{3}$
Onions	...	...	...	...	... $\frac{2}{3}$
Oil	...	...	...	...	... $\frac{1}{10}$
Wood	...	...	...	..	... 25
Charcoal	...	...	...	..	... 11
Soap	...	...	...	...	... $\frac{1}{10}$

Thirty of these rations are computed at 16 francs.
In time of war bread is replaced by 25 ounces of
biscuit or of uncooked flour; and the fresh meat by $4\frac{1}{4}$
ounces of preserved meat.

The above is the daily scale of food ; now, however, in
consequence of the emptiness of the treasure-chest, the
soldier gets but 200 drams of bread, and a sheep is
occasionally given for distribution among the men
of a company, which numbers little more than fifty
to sixty men. The extra luxuries are never given, but
as I said before, the men of the Redif are able, now
and then, to provide themselves with butter, eggs, &c.,
which enable them to eat the very unpalatable ration
bread with a little gusto.

The march of the division yesterday, through the
Sara Kamysh Pass, was not one that reflected any
credit on the staff or regimental officers. The men

straggled disgracefully; baggage animals moving on
in the midst of a battalion column; whilst Circassian
horsemen, Kurds, and zaptiehs, marched in twos and
threes, as it pleased them. Men never ask permission
to fall out, but leave the ranks with their arms and
accoutrements, as occasion arises, and either rejoin their
company at the next halt or straggle on in the rear.
At one spot on the road, near a stream, where there
was a sharp descent, with a stiff pull-up on the far
side, a block occurred, I dismounted, and, sitting on
the grass, watched the mass of guns, cavalry,
infantry, and baggage train disentangle itself from
the apparently overwhelming confusion that reigned;
the men, as usual, showed great cheerfulness, running
forward with a shout to man the drag-ropes and get the
guns over the crest, which they did in a very creditable
manner; but the officers looked on with their usual
stolid indifference, smoking their everlasting cigarettes,
and offering no assistance whatever. Coming down the
incline—which was very steep—the officer commanding
the battery never attempted to lock his wheels, or ease
the strain for his horses. How the wheelers stood it
I do not know. I fully expected to see one down and
run over every moment. I was very thankful when
the guns reached the bottom, and I saw the gallant
little beasts, all safe and sound, panting and quiver-
ing in every nerve, after their exertions.

The field-guns with this force are of two descrip-
tions, Krupp's four and six-pfünders. The former are
issued to the horse, the latter to the field batteries.
They are all manned with eight horses, the forge and
wagons only having six. It is a matter of some surprise
to me that the batteries have only two wagons each, the

remainder of the ammunition being carried in country carts or on ponies, in the same manner as the spare ammunition of the infantry corps is carried. I have also been struck with the armament of the infantry. The rifle, which is a very close imitation of our Henry-Martini, is called the Peabody-Martini, presumably because the barrel is of the Peabody pattern. The lever for opening the breech is of a slightly different pattern to ours, and the bayonet (except in the Tallia or Chasseur battalion of each regiment, which is armed with the sword-bayonet) is a four-sided weapon, deeply fluted, and capable of producing a particularly nasty wound. I had heard from Americans that the arms were very roughly turned out, and would prove as destructive to friends as to foes. I, however, saw them very hardly used at Taghir, when one or two regiments fired away upwards of 100 rounds, and I can gather no complaints reflecting on their strength and durability. An English officer, who was present at Khaliass, informed me that he saw 120 empty cartridge-cases in one heap by the side of a soldier, so I think the Providence Company may be congratulated on the success of their contract, more especially when the treatment to which the arms are daily exposed is taken into consideration; rarely cleaned, thrown down on rocks, piled carelessly, and unpiled violently; it, to me, is a simple marvel how the weapons stand it at all. I have constantly taken the rifles out of men's hands and examined them, finding them in a condition that would drive the captain of a line regiment into an early grave.

I must not omit to mention that last night a party of Circassians captured a Russian post proceeding from their position at Beghli Ahmed to Tiflis. The bag contained some eighty letters, seven only of which were brought in. These were private (no official letters, apparently, being in the mail) from officers present at the battle of Zewin, which they describe as being disastrous. The fire from the shelter-trenches is styled "*un feu infernel*," and their losses are stated at 790 killed and wounded. As I said before, until we receive the Russian official reports it will be impossible to obtain anything like a truthful report. There is a great difference between the 5,000 killed and wounded of the Turkish despatch and the 790 of the Russian officers' letters. The letters go on to speak of the hardships endured during the campaign, one man complaining bitterly of the price of sugar, which, he says, is most difficult to procure. I trust that Ahmed Mukhtar Pasha will have the good taste, now that he has read the letters, to forward them to their destination, for I doubt not that those eighty poor fellows have many hundred friends and loved relatives at home looking out anxiously for news from Asia Minor; many dim eyes are tearfully scanning the accounts of the battles of Taghir, Khaliass, and Zewin, hoping against hope that the loved name may not appear in the fatal list, so coldly recorded in the public press. " As cold water to a thirsty soul, so is good news from a far country." Would that the Turkish general would remember this, for I feel sure that no act would go further towards healing the deadly breach between Turk and Russian than the simple act of kindly courtesy in sealing up and forwarding to their destination these eighty private letters, and in sending an intimation to the Russian general that this has been done.

Some of the letters speak of the action itself, and give the names of the various officers killed and wounded.

One in particular, a Prussian, Schrœder by name, seems to have behaved with the greatest gallantry. All speak in very strong terms of the conduct of Loris Melikoff, who accompanied the forces, but permitted General Heimann to plan and carry out the scheme of attack, which ended so disastrously for the Russian arms. This latter officer was very anxious, indeed, to press the assault on the following morning, but in consequence of the very serious losses sustained on the 25th Melikoff refused to entertain the project, and, finally, on the 27th, determined to fall back on the main army at Kars, as the force at his disposal was quite inadequate to the task of forcing the Zewin position and pushing on to Erzeroum. There seems no doubt that the Grand Duke Michael detached the two forces under Tergukassoff and Loris Melikoff to force the Delibaba and Zewin roads, and effect a junction at Kuipri Kui, march straight on Erzeroum and seize that place. Had these two Russian divisions been successful in their attempts to drive back the Turks from Delibaba and Zewin, the capture of Erzeroum might easily have been effected, for its garrison was nominal, its armament most defective, and the works in a most dilapidated condition. Fortunately for the Turks, the Russian corps were far too weak for the purpose assigned, and by the timely aid of reinforcements pushed up after Taghir, Mukhtar Pasha was enabled to check the advance of Tergukassoff at Delibaba, while Faizi Pasha effectively defeated Loris Melikoff himself. Checked on both flanks, and threatened in rear of his left wing by the Van force, the Grand Duke had no alternative but to recall his two advanced columns, endeavour to entice the Turks into the plain, and there defeat them in detail with his combined forces.

HEAD QUARTERS, 4th TURKISH ARMY CORPS.

CAMP SARA KAMYSH, *July 4th.*

By the courtesy of an English gentleman present I am enabled to give you an account of the Russian retreat from Eshek Khaliass, an account totally at variance with the exaggerated reports brought in by Major-General Mustafa Safvet Pasha. On the afternoon of Wednesday, the 27th ult., cavalry reconnoitring parties brought in word to Reiss Ahmed Pasha, the Lieutenant-General commanding the Turkish right wing, that the Russians were retiring from their position on the ridge above Eshek Khaliass. Moving forward his whole force, the Turkish general prepared to attack their rearguard, but the bold stand made by the two Russian battalions, aided by two batteries, with some dragoon regiments, effectually checked the efforts of the Ottoman troops, who apparently were not very eager for the fray. The enemy retired by alternate half-batteries, screening the movements of the rearmost one by a mass of cavalry, which was withdrawn directly the guns were well off. The Turks never approached within a mile and a half or two miles of the enemy, who retired in the most orderly manner, moving as steadily as if on parade.

All night through this retrograde movement continued, but the Turks abandoned all pursuit on Thursday afternoon, failing even to follow up the enemy sufficiently to ascertain by what road they moved after passing Zaidikan. It is conjectured, however, that hearing of the defeat of Loris Melikoff, at Zewin, and of the approach of Faik Pasha in his rear, Tergukassoff judged it expedient to fall back on the Araxes and endeavour to join the Grand Duke at Kars, or else that he will return towards the Russian frontier at Parnawut. The Russian column apparently kept their pursuers at a very respectable distance, and succeeded in carrying off everything except two or three carts which had broken down, but had previously been cleared of all contents except a few pounds of sugar and some cigarettes. At Zaidikan they abandoned a considerable supply of wheat, of which about 800 sacks were recovered unhurt, the remainder having been burnt. The Turkish official account states that the Russians abandoned stores, wine, tents, rifles, large quantities of ammunition, also many bullocks and horses, and that the Kurds and Circassians hovering about the columns cut off stragglers, in one case a whole company of fifty men being cut down to a man. Mr. Williams, who accompanied the staff of Reiss Ahmed Pasha throughout the operations, assures me that he did not see a single tent or cart captured, nor a single rifle or dead or wounded Russian on the road, that the whole of the stores captured consisted of 800 sacks of wheat, and that any other statements are deliberate fabrications. As for Kurds and Circassians venturing to face the Russian infantry, that is an absurdity, and on this occasion, Mr. Williams assures me that they showed anything but an anxiety to meet the foe. One thing he saw, however, which he very properly brought to the notice of the Commander-in-Chief and of Sir Arnold, and that is, on passing through Zaidikan, where the Russians interred their dead after the battle of Khaliass, he saw the Kurds busy opening the graves and despoiling the corpses of their clothes. Such barbarity deserves universal reprobation. A grave

containing some Turkish bodies, which evidently had
been left on the field after the flight from Taghir, had
been opened and the bodies disinterred. These were
all clothed in uniform, showing that the Russians respect
the bodies of their slain, and bury them with decency.
On our side, however, I regret to say that both officers
and men roam over the field, stripping all the corpses,
which are invariably buried naked. The clothes are
appropriated by the finders, and there are numbers of
officers present here, whose battalions were in Servia,
clad in the brown jacket of the Servian uniform—the
commandant of Mukhtar Pasha's own personal escort
is thus attired! Although I believe the custom of
violating the graves of the dead is not practised by
the Turkish soldiers themselves, yet the custom of despoiling the slain is openly sanctioned by authority.

Head-quarters of the army moved on this morning
from this place in the direction of Beghli Ahmed, where
Mukhtar Pasha proposes to encamp, and now at this
present moment the disposition of his army corps is as
follows:—Head-quarters, consisting of fifteen field and
six mountain guns, twenty-five battalions, 500 regular,
and 3,000 irregular cavalry, at Beghli Ahmed; left
wing, consisting of twenty-four battalions, twelve field
and ten mountain guns, and 1,000 irregular cavalry,
with about 200 regular Nizam horse, at Kara Kilissa;
one battalion, with fifteen field-guns, at Kuipri Kui (of
these nine guns are under orders for this force); in the
Ghiurji Boghaz, three battalions, with six field-guns;
at Erzeroum, thirteen battalions. All the regiments
there are very weak, few numbering more than 500
men, while the majority are under that strength; and
as they all belong either to the 3rd Ban of the reserve

or to the Mustahfiz (old soldiers who have passed through the line and all three grades of the reserve) they cannot be considered very formidable troops.

Both Reiss Ahmed Pasha and the Commander-in-Chief have committed the error of pushing forward their troops without taking means to keep open their line of communication; and as they are entirely dependent for their supplies on the stores collected at Kuipri-Kui, they would be very awkwardly situated if the Russians moved their numerous body of cavalry round, and operated on the many mountain roads left unguarded in the rear of the two Turkish divisions. Here especially a few men passing round by Tscharpakli and Kara Orghan might in half an hour, with the aid of a few ounces of gun-cotton, completely block up the Sara Kamysh Pass, through which we advanced, by levelling trees and blasting a few rocks. Between Kuipri-Kui and this place, a distance of sixty-six miles over a mountainous road, Mukhtar Pasha has not left a man or a gun to cover his retreat, while there are on either flank of him three or more roads leading to his base, by which the Russians can send a force to cut off his communication.

HEAD-QUARTERS, 4TH TURKISH ARMY CORPS,

CAMP KIRK PUNAR, *July 6th.*

Here we are at last within easy distance of Kars, which lies about twenty miles north-east of our encampment. Men ride in and out daily, and this morning a large party, including Captains M‘Calmont, 7th Hussars, and Trotter, R.E., have ridden in to spend a few days in the beleaguered fortress. The problem appears to me without solution. One short fortnight ago the Russians seemed about to make a military promenade to Erze-

roum; their right and left columns were face to face
with weak divisions of Turkish troops, which, though
equal in numbers, were far inferior to their enemies in
guns, in discipline, and in organisation. The check at
Khaliass and the defeat at Zewin, so far as we on the
spot, judging from appearances only, can determine,
seem to have completely overthrown the Russian plans,
and of the army of 100,000 well equipped men with
which they are said to have invaded Armenia, only forty
battalions are in the field; at least, the strength of the
Russian army before Kars, I am assured by the highest
authority in the camp, amounts to forty battalions of
infantry, three regiments of dragoons, fifteen regiments
of Cossacks, and eighty field guns. Their head-quarters
are at Zaim, a spot some seven miles north-east of Kars
on the Kars Tchai, and their line stretches from Ainali
to Mazra. Mukhtar Pasha states that they are in full retreat, and have removed their heavy artillery to Kharrak
Darrah, an excessively strong position on the Alexandropol
road. From Kara Kilissa we hear that Tergukassoff very
cleverly effected a retreat from before the vastly superior
forces of Reiss Ahmed Pasha, and that, without losing
a gun, he has so far eluded the vigilance of the Turkish
cavalry, that they do not know by which road he has
moved off, but believe he has succeeded in following
cross-roads towards Parnawut, on the Russian frontier.

The Russians at Ardahan may claim a slight success.
Some few weeks ago Lieutenant-Colonel Dedi Bey was
detached from Batoum with two regular battalions, and
directed to raise an irregular corps in the Livana district. He succeeded in organising five volunteer battalions, which he placed under the command of Major Ali
Nihad Effendi, and left in Ardanutsch while he himself

moved about the district endeavouring to collect more men. The Russian general at Ardahan, profiting by his absence, detached a brigade, consisting of one field-battery, one regiment of Cossacks, and three infantry battalions, to attack Nihad Effendi, and on the 27th ult. a small skirmish occurred, in which the Turkish irregulars were completely dispersed. The Russians, having destroyed Ardanutsch, fell back on Ardahan.*

Of course Turkish official accounts tell of the atrocities committed by the Russians; pillaging of villages, outrages on women, and slaying of children being freely attributed to the foe. I believe none of these things. I have now for the last week been following in the wake of the retiring Russian army, and can see no traces nor hear any reports of any such misdeeds. On the contrary, they appear to have behaved with the greatest moderation, and paid for everything they consumed. It is true that there is a great scarcity of grain in the villages through which they passed, but this is accounted for by their large force of cavalry requiring enormous supplies of this commodity. Fowls, sheep, goats, and cattle are as plentiful in the district recently occupied by the Russians as in that in rear of the late Turkish positions. And while all over the Passin Plain there were signs of misrule and piratical violence, and loud complaints of outrages perpetrated on the Christian populations, outrages of which it is not well to speak, here all is peace and plenty; no smoking villages to speak of Kurdish atrocities; no wailing women crying for their murdered husbands; no ruined husbandmen seeking redress from Circassian pillagers. We have here in camp a force of

* Ardanutsch was again captured on 17th December by a Brigade under Komaroff, detached from Ardahan.

N

4,000 Irregular Cavalry—Kurds and Circassians—men without any organisation, under no discipline, and obedient to no chief—men who go and come as they please; rarely receiving pay, they are dependent for subsistence on their own exertions, and the loud complaints of their conduct, which reach us from all sides, and which have constantly been reported to the Commander-in-Chief, show that there is a thorough understanding between the Turkish Government and its levies as to the method of drawing their rations. It was only the day after Zewin that the Circassians deliberately refused to follow the Russians unless Ahmed Mukhtar Pasha gave them 60,000 piastres. Instead of treating these mutineers as any other general would have done, their demands were complied with. Again, after the battle of Khaliass, Moussa Pasha declined to advance, as his men had no tents, and finally, on hearing of a Cossack detachment in his front, fell back on Kuipri Kui. Once more, a body of 1,100 Circassians, on arrival at Erzeroum, proceeded *en masse* to the palace and demanded revolvers in addition to their Winchester rifles, declaring that they would go no farther until these were distributed. I do not know which reflects more discredit on the army—the insolence of these men, or the weakness of the leader who complied with their demands.

I mentioned in my last the fact that a Russian post had been captured, with many private letters from officers speaking very openly of the battle of Zewin. It appears that in more than one of them mention was made of the fact that the Turks killed all the wounded men left on the ground. I am afraid that the accusation is too true, for I can learn of not a single wounded man having been saved, although 265 dead were found

close up to the Turkish entrenchments. I am aware
that in Servia no quarter was given or expected; but
after the treatment of the prisoners taken at Ardahan it
speaks badly for the spirit actuating the Mahomedan
troops if they refuse quarter to wounded Russians. It
is not to be wondered at that a spirit of vengeance pervades the latter, or that more than one writer should
declare that henceforth no Turk shall be taken alive.

I regret that now I have to place on record an act
which reflects the greatest discredit on the Turkish
commander. On the 3rd inst. two Karakapaks were
seized by a Circassian patrol. They owned that they
were the bearers of letters from one Russian division
to another, and without any attempt at concealment,
produced them, candidly declaring that they were to
receive seventy piastres for their safe delivery. They
were not spies, they were not disguised in any way,
they were not in the vicinity of our camp, but, while
conveying a post from Kars to Tergukassoff's army,
were apprehended by Circassians, taken up before the
Mushir, quietly led to a secluded spot, and then, by
his orders, shot, and left to lie unburied on the bare
hill-side. Their corpses, riddled with bullets, were seen
by more than one Englishman, and I trust that all who
did see the ghastly sight will place on record their
detestation of the cowardly deed, so utterly opposed to
all sense of justice, and so opposed to all military law.
Although spies are employed by all armies, their fate,
if caught, is too well known to need comment; but
that the bearer of a letter should be subjected to the
same dog-like death is an event unparalleled in my
knowledge of military history.

This morning, Mushir Mustafa Memenli Pasha
N 2

marched into camp with five battalions of infantry, three field-guns, and 300 Circassian horsemen. The battalions were in excellent order, of more than average strength, and moved exceedingly well; the guns, too, moved by in line as well as any Woolwich commandant would care to see. This makes our force now thirty battalions, eighteen field and six mountain guns, one regiment of regular and 3,500 irregular cavalry. The garrison of Kars, a moiety of which could always be pushed forward to join in any fight that might now occur, amounts to twenty-nine battalions of infantry, five field-batteries, one regiment of regular cavalry, and 280 siege-guns. To-morrow, Major-General Mustafa Djavid Pasha is expected from Gulentab, with three more battalions, so that if the siege of Kars is raised, Mukhtar Pasha would be able to follow up the Russians, who are said to contemplate falling back on Goomri, with forty-eight battalions, at least, forty-eight field-guns, and 4,500 cavalry. At Kara Kilissa, Reiss Ahmed Pasha, now reduced by the three battalions which Mustafa Djavid Pasha is bringing up here, has twenty-six battalions, twenty-one field and sixteen mountain guns, with about 3,000 irregular cavalry and 8,000 irregular infantry. This includes the force with which Faik Pasha was attacking Bayazid, as it was supposed it would effect a junction with the Turkish right on the 4th inst. The troops which Mushir Mustafa Pasha brought in to-day, are two battalions of regular Nizam troops, and three of Redifs, organised from the remnants of the Ardahan force. The Mushir himself has just arrived from Constantinople, and is under orders to proceed to Kars, to relieve Hussein Hami Pasha in command. The last-named officer will remain there, holding his own position of Ferik.

This force is divided into two divisions, each division into two brigades; but I fancy the new arrangement will be upset, owing to the arrival of the five battalions which reinforced us to-day, and the three expected to-morrow. The 1st division is commanded by Lieutenant - General Hadji Raschid Pasha; 1st brigade, Colonel Osman Bey; 2nd brigade, Colonel Mehemet Bey. The 2nd division is commanded by Major-General Shefket Pasha; 1st brigade, Colonel Suleiman Bey; 2nd brigade, Colonel Ibrahim Bey. The artillery is commanded by Lieutenant - Colonel Tefik Bey, and the cavalry by Major-General Mustafa Safvet Pasha, thus making three generals of that name in camp. The battalions are made up as follows:—Four battalions, 1st army corps; twenty-one battalions, 4th army corps; five battalions, 5th army corps. Of these thirty battalions, only four are regulars or Nizams. The remainder all belong to reserve troops only called out in time of war, men almost entirely ignorant of drill, and officers equally so; in fact, so under-officered were these Redif battalions that dozens of non-commissioned officers in the Nizam regiments have been promoted to superior grades, and a sergeant of last month is to-day a captain. Thus it is not to be wondered that the discipline or drill of these men should be defective; it only reflects the more credit on them that they should be able to defeat the Russians, and, to my mind, proves that if the Turk was well led and well trained he would be second to no soldier in the world.

The army has been detained here two days owing to heavy rain. To-morrow, if the weather holds up, we hope to move to Beghli Ahmed, only twelve miles from Kars; and then, I hear, that Mukhtar Pasha means to attack the Russians and try to raise the siege. Their preponderance in artillery and cavalry makes the issue appear very problematical; but, as I said in the commencement of this letter, so I now say at the close, that the conduct of the Russians in permitting us to advance so far from our base, without severing our communications, and thus starving us into submission, is to me perfectly inexplicable.

To-day, our servants and kit rejoined us, much to our delight; having been without a change of clothes for a fortnight, a clean shirt was a luxury: and the meal with which the faithful " Mr. Vincent" regaled us, after the sun went down, tasted to us, who had been revelling in soldiers' biscuits, worthy of Bignons or Vefours. This little Maltese, albeit somewhat nervous of the Muscovite, was a treasure in his way, and a bit of a humourist, as well as of a tactician. His droll sayings often raised a smile on our faces, and the air with which he would lay a tin plate containing stewed kidneys on the ground at our feet, as he announced " Rognons sautés," was worthy of more polished scenes.

Mr. Vincent, fearing a Russian surprise, had made a system of night signals with the grooms, who generally bivouacked some short distance from our own sleeping-ground, and before going to sleep, for at this time he shared a tent with Sir Arnold Kemball, Mr. Dougall, and myself, he would assure us that all arrangements were made in the event of a " combination," which being interpreted meant a night surprise. When we got into a standing camp on the Aladja Dagh, he endeavoured to make us comfortable, improvised a table out of a one-dozen case, a table-cloth out of the advertisement sheet of the *Times*, and fed us on the fat of the land.

HEAD QUARTERS, 4TH TURKISH ARMY CORPS.

CAMP VAIRAN KALE, FRIDAY, *July 6th.*

At eight a.m. this morning the army left their camping ground on the Kirk Punar Hill, and moved across the Kars plain to Vairan Kale, distant about thirteen miles. The two divisions formed up to the north of the ridge in column of brigades, which marched in line of quarter-columns. The artillery was massed in line of batteries between the two divisions, and as the men moved off in fair order with bayonets fixed and bands playing, the sight was pretty enough; but the whole idea was marred by the childish manner in which flank guards were thrown out, a long line of skirmishers in single rank, men at intervals of six paces, moving parallel to the column, at a distance of 100 yards on either flank. As this line extended from the front of the advance guard to the rear of the long string of carts and ammunition animals, the number of men wasted in this absurd manner can be easily conceived. With the exception of about 300 regular cavalry, who, with swords drawn, moved in the immediate front and rear of the guns, the whole of this branch of the army was away some miles in front reconnoitring. There are supposed to be about 3,500 irregular cavalry with this force, but as the men are not formed in regiments, and move hither and thither at their own sweet will, I do not think Ahmed Mukhtar Pasha could collect 1,500 men in the event of occasion requiring their services, and of these I much doubt if 500 could be induced to face the enemy. In marching across the valley, we passed the villages of Kara Hamza, Ali Sofa, and Beghli Ahmed, the first two Mahomedan, the last a Christian hamlet. I saw numerous signs of plenty in the abodes of the followers of the Prophet, while the unfortunate Armenians had been forced, owing to the oppression and tyranny exercised by their own fellow-countrymen, to abandon their houses, leaving large stores of grain, grass, fowls, cattle, &c., to the prey of the marauding Circassians.

On all sides, from the Marshal and his staff down to the poorest villager, we hear tales of the cruelties practised by the Russians, how cattle have been stolen, grain carried off, corn trampled down, women and children killed ; but as far as we can see, and we have moved directly in the route taken by the Russians on their march to and return from Zewin, facts point exactly to the contrary. The Mahomedan villages teem with men, women, and children, all following their usual avocations ; fowls, turkeys, geese—all in great numbers—are seen feeding in the immediate vicinity of the plain ; large herds of cattle and flocks of sheep are grazing on the neighbouring hills. The corn is now full in ear, and shows plainly that the Russian troops carefully avoided trampling down the crops, while the abundance of rouble notes, for which the villagers refuse to take less than their full value, is satisfactory evidence that Loris Melikoff's army possesses sufficient discipline to respect the property of harmless villagers, and that his men pay for all they take. Very different is the sight when we approach Christian villages. These are considered fair field for pillage by the irregular horsemen of the Turkish army, and I regret to say that

these disgraceful proceedings are not checked in any
way by the officers of the army. Yesterday, as I have
just informed you, we passed through the village of
Beghli Ahmed, the scene of the cavalry action on the
29th of May, when the Russian horse surprised the
Circassians, defeated them with heavy loss, and captured
their two guns. These brave warriors, who by their
own accounts abandoned their camp and artillery after
suffering only fifty casualties, returned when the coast
was clear, accused the unfortunate Christians of having
given information to the enemy, straightway massacred
thirty-one men in cold blood, and proceeded to pillage
the village. When we passed through, the place was
completely deserted, doors of granaries burst open, the
contents spilt over the road, eager groups of soldiery
being busy filling bags with grain, a commodity never
supplied to horsemen by the Turkish commissariat.
Stacks of straw were being pulled down, and large
bundles carried off by all who chose to lay hands on
the same; while infantry soldiers were busy filling
their various vessels with the flour strewn in front of
the houses. Others were cutting the half-ripe corn,
and driving off ponies and donkeys laden with huge
sheaves of the same. I regret to say that I encouraged
this system of pillage by purchasing from a Circassian
a large wooden water-bucket, for, owing to the scarcity
of vessels to contain this precious fluid, we have often
been put to the greatest inconvenience a man can suffer
on service; and this bucket was almost priceless to us.

At 6 p.m. we crossed the Kars stream just below
this village, selected a nice green spot to the south of
the group of houses for our camping-ground, and proceeded in a very heavy thunderstorm to pitch our tents,

getting thoroughly wet through in the operation. Only those who have travelled in Asia Minor and been burdened with Turkish servants can understand the difficulties we experienced in obtaining food, or only those whose travels have been in company with a large force can thoroughly appreciate our situation. It was half-past 7 before our tent was pitched, and then we discovered that our zaptiehs had quietly gained the shelter of a friendly house, leaving us to obtain our own food, firewood, water, and stabling for our horses. As a last resource, I proceeded myself to the village, which was crowded with Circassians, Kurds, and regular soldiers, loudly hammering at every door, demanding food and house-room. Every house was shut, the inhabitants knowing full well that food and shelter given to the men entailed a heavy pecuniary loss, for the irregular horseman of Turkey having obtained what he requires, which is invariably the best that a village can afford, mounts and rides away. Money compensation never enters into his head. Is not he fighting for his country, and so entitled to all he can lay his rapacious hands upon? It was another hour before my persuasions, backed by the silent eloquence of a 100-piastre note, induced the mukhtar of the village to produce eggs, milk, water, fowls, and sheep for our men; but attaching myself to this worthy's sleeve, I followed him from house to house, and found that an Englishman with Turkish paper money in his hand could rush in where even Circassians feared to tread. I returned to the tent laden with my spoil, and at 11 p.m. we sat down to a sumptuous repast of omelettes, and lamb chops, washed down by sherry and water, an unexpected luxury produced by my faithful Maltese servant, a treasure of his kind, who triumphantly entered the tent with a bottle in his hand. As we none of us possessed such a beverage, we were anxious to know whence it came, and learnt that the ever-thoughtful wife of our Consul at Erzeroum (a truer specimen of the kind-hearted English lady never drew breath) had, unknown to us, sent him some few bottles to produce when our own stores should fail. Any tribute of mine to the care and kindness shown by Mr. and Mrs. Zohrab to all wanderers in the desert would be superfluous. It is but fair to own that all our comforts, and not a few of our necessaries, are due to the goodness and hospitality of this English couple, who, exiled in Erzeroum, are ever ready to welcome warmly all Englishmen, provide them with the best their house can afford, and fit them out for the longest journeys, content to earn their reward in the kindly remembrances in which they are held by all who have had the pleasure of meeting them.

Our camp here is situated most picturesquely on a grassy knoll, a few yards to the south of the village of Vairan Kale, which nestles in a deep ravine bounded on both sides by rugged basaltic rocks. Between these flows a clear, rippling steam, with cherry-orchards on either bank. Smaller ravines run down from the higher mountains to the Vairan stream; in each of these are encamped the various battalions of our force, their snow-white tents on the emerald carpet, with the rough grey crags as a background, and in the far distance the dark hill of Kars, from which ever and anon a 15-centimeter Krupp belches forth its volume of smoke and flame, the whole forming a picture rarely to be equalled in any country.

CHAPTER X.

THE RELIEF OF KARS.

We enter the Fortress—The old familiar Names—Turkish Forts and Turkish
"Obstacles"—Losses during Bombardment—Round-headed Shell—Russian
Siege Batteries—Changes in our Staff—The Town well supplied with
Provisions—Fortress with Ammunition—Description of the place from
the *Moskovskiya Vêdomosti.*

KARS, *July 9th.*

LITTLE did I think one short week ago that I should be
able to date my letters from this place. I am almost
tempted to haul down my colours, forswear all my
forebodings, count the Turks superior in numbers, in
discipline, and aptitude for warfare to the Russians,
and prophesy a triumphant entry into Tiflis. Indeed,
judging from present appearances and the events of the
past few days, it seems as if the Muscovites were beaten
out of the field, and that nothing remains but to
advance on Loris Melikoff, and push him back on
Goomri. Situated as we now are, 100 miles from the
nearest telegraph-office, our latest English dates being
the 31st of May, we are necessarily dependent on the
Turks for all our European news. So we are ignorant
of the march of events on the continent, where complications may have arisen to account for the quietude
of the Grand Duke's force, and for our unmolested
advance from the Zewin position. To attribute the
inactivity of the enemy to their two adverses at

Khaliass and Zewin is an absurdity, for their losses in these two actions certainly did not exceed those of the Turks. Impeded as we are by faulty commissariat arrangements, an absence of transport, and the very worst system for moving an army that I have ever seen or read of, we have contrived to move this force forward, and take up a decidedly strong position for the support of Kars. To call it a relief is an absurdity. We have not brought up one pound of grain or one round of ammunition to the place; but we have placed within striking distance a force equal in strength to the garrison, and one that, combined with it and supported by the fire of the batteries, might venture with some hope of success to drive the enemy from the ridge they now occupy.

And now for Kars. Yesterday morning, after an early breakfast, I started, in company with Sir Arnold Kemball and his aide-de-camp, Lieutenant Dougall, R.N., to visit the beleaguered fortress—the place that has been haunting our dreams day and night—rumours of the fall of which have reached us ever and anon with such a minuteness of detail as to lead us to doubt the stories of its impregnability, and to fancy that, sooner or later, it must fall. It was not without some small feeling of pride that I rode through the open *chevaux de frise* in the outer entrenched line to the south of the town, and, looking at the frowning heights above, thundering forth their notes of defiance to the Russian batteries, I thought of that gallant band of our own countrymen, under whose heroic guidance, twenty-two years ago, the Turkish army withstood one of the most memorable sieges of modern times, finally surrendering —when starvation stared them in the face, and all hope of succour, owing to the supineness of the Ottoman Government, had passed away—to a foe as chivalrous as they themselves had proved to be.

It is hard for an inexperienced pen like mine to attempt to give an idea of this fortress, which two decades ago was familiar to all Englishmen, and which has been so ably, so minutely, and so often described by men whose names are household words in all military circles. In these times, however, of blind faith in the all-powerful wisdom of the rising generation, of scornful scepticism as to the gallantry or skill of the giants that lived in those days, there may be many who have never read of the difficulties experienced by Sir Fenwick Williams, and of the indomitable valour and perseverance with which they were surmounted. There may be many to whom the names of Fenwick Williams of Kars, of Kmety, of Lake, of Teesdale, convey no meaning whatever, although little more than twenty years ago all England was ringing with the sound of their gallant deeds, and all Russia paying a noble meed of tribute to their bravery and endurance.

Kars is situated at the extreme end of one of the easternmost slopes of the Soghanly range. This spur is pierced by the Kars Tchai stream, which flows between precipitous banks, rising some 950 feet above the level of the water. On the eastern side of this river the ridge constitutes a flat plateau, about one mile in length by 800 yards in breadth, with steep rocky slopes to the north and south, and a gentle grassy glacis towards the Russian frontier. On this eastern spur are built the Karadagh and Kara Paltak forts (the latter known as the Arab Tabia in the days of 1855). Five miles off on a spur some 300 feet below the Turkish crest, lies the

army of the Czar, their siege-batteries being placed in a
ravine some 4,000 yards from our works. The hills on
the western side of the Kars Tchai extend on commanding heights for about a mile, when a second stream cuts
the Soghanly spur, and beyond it the range is lower,
and, consequently, valueless for all military purposes to
friend or foe. On this western hill are built the largest
forts—I believe it is generally conceded that when
the Karadagh falls the place cannot hold out, for it commands the town, situated as it is on both banks of the
Kars Tchai, on the southern slopes of the hill; and in the
town are the magazines, commissariat stores, hospital, &c.,
the possession of which by the enemy would necessitate
the capitulation of the fortress. At some distance from
the town, in the plain on the southern side, three
very substantial permanent redoubts have been built
since the campaign of 1855; these are connected with
each other by a breastwork of strong profile, which is
carried on over the hills, and runs from fort to fort. I
was not enabled to ascertain exactly the profile of any
of the works, but I judged the trench running round
the works to have a parapet four and a half feet in
height and six feet in thickness. It was revetted with
stones (!), and had a trench two feet deep and about six
feet in width in rear. The whole front was defended by
various obstacles—*troup de loup*—smaller military pits,
and wire entanglements being freely made use of. At
irregular intervals small batteries for two or more field-
guns were placed. These were neatly constructed, but
I am afraid the School of Military Engineering at
Brompton Barracks would not approve the Turkish
works. The *troups de loup* were about four feet deep,
and about five feet in circumference; in fact, they were

excellent rifle-pits for an enterprising enemy. The sod revetments, which were few and far between, were built up with the turf being laid, not horizontally but vertically; they were not even pegged in; while the splinters from the stone revetments caused the casualties from the enemy's shell-fire to be largely increased. The works on the plain and on the western hills are very substantial, the parapets being from twenty-four feet to thirty-six feet in thickness, with a command varying from fifteen feet to twenty-four feet; but the batteries, four in number, on the Karadagh hill are very weak, with only from six feet to ten feet of thickness. These are not revetted, and, consequently, are in a very dilapidated condition. The shots fired by the enemy show that they have some sixteen and a half centimeter guns, and altogether thirty-five heavy siege-cannon in their advanced batteries. It may appear absurd, but I was assured by an officer of the Royal Engineers, on the authority, I believe, of the Turkish Commandant of Artillery, that the garrison commenced firing at the enemy's camp at a range of upwards of 10,000 yards, and at that distance did considerable execution!!

The day I went over the batteries was the twenty-first of the bombardment, and during that time the Turks had fired 17,558 shell at the enemy, who in their turn had replied with an average of 2,000 a day, their largest number being 3,200. It was amazing to see the ground round about the Kara Paltak and Karadagh batteries, which had been the principal objects of the Russian fire. The place was literally covered with fragments of shell, and in many places with unburst sixteen-centimeter projectiles. It was marvellous to see the wreck that the ridge appeared, and then to learn that the total damage done by this frightful cannonade had been eighty-five men killed, 155 wounded, three women and one child killed, one field 6-pounder completely disabled, one fifteen-centimeter Krupp partially disabled, one nine-centimeter shunt gun partially disabled, three carriages totally disabled, and eight expense magazines blown up.

It is impossible to estimate the Russian loss, but twelve magazines have been seen to explode. They have not as yet attempted to advance by regular approaches, but threw up, at what I should judge a distance of 6,000 yards, two batteries, each containing two 16½-centimeter guns, and then they constructed, under cover of their fire, six batteries at 4,000 yards' distance; these each contain five fifteen-centimeter guns, but whenever a bombardment is contemplated, forty field-guns are brought up before dawn,* placed in the trenches which connect the siege-batteries, and with these the fire is considerably strengthened. The projectile fired from some of these field-pieces excites considerable curiosity, and is as unfamiliar to the British officers present as it is to the Turk. The diameter was 3 inches, the extreme length 9½ inches. A hollow cylinder of ½-inch iron, surrounded by four belts, is surmounted by a solid iron shot, through which the percussion-fuse is screwed, connecting it with the charge of powder in the lower cylinder. On striking, the fuse explodes the bursting-charge; the shell scatters its splinters in every direction, and the solid round shot is propelled for a further distance—sometimes as much as 2,000 yards. So I am assured on the authority of the Turkish commandant of artillery, Colonel Hassain Bey, an officer who studied

* These were 9-Pfünder field Krupps, with a shell equal in weight to the 12-centimeter siege guns of the Turks.

for seven years at Woolwich, and who would be a credit to the ordnance branch of any nation. I saw a great number of these projectiles; some were perfect, the fuse having failed to explode; the cylindrical shot was still unseparated from its spherical head, while in others the round shot was only found intact, the cylinder having burst into innumerable fragments. I do not know whether I am attaching undue importance to a well-known invention, but never having seen such a shell in any of my numerous visits to Woolwich, I cannot help thinking that as complete a description as my unprofessional pen can give may be of interest to some.

The Russian batteries were very well constructed. The Turks have an idea that they have Moncrieff carriages, as they never see the gun, only the puff of smoke; but my glasses, which are an excellent pair, showed me screens at a distance of about thirty yards in front of each battery, which would fully account for the guns being invisible. The whole line was covered with rifle-pits about fifty yards in advance of the batteries, and in these all day long were seen the white cap-covers of the Russian infantry.

The Turkish garrison at this time consisted of twenty-nine battalions of infantry, averaging about 400 rank and file, 1,700 garrison artillery, 1,500 armed citizens, and about 300 cavalry.

The Turkish forts, as I said before, are all connected by a trench of strong profile. This is manned day and night by one-half of the garrison, so that the duties of the men are exceedingly heavy, and they suffer in health accordingly. The gunners never leave the batteries, so they may be said to be continually on duty, and under fire too. There has been a slight change in the staff of the two forces since we arrived. Mushir Mustafa Pasha, who arrived on the 6th instant with five battalions of infantry, assumed command of the fortress on the 8th, and took Faizi Pasha (General Kohlmann) as his chief of the staff; the late commandant, Hussein Hami Pasha, remains in Kars as second in command, and Hassan Kiazini Pasha, chief of the staff in Kars, joins this force in the same capacity. We were reinforced yesterday by three battalions from the right wing of the Turkish army under Major-General Mustafa Djavid Pasha, who succeeded to the command on the death of Mahomed Pasha, at Taghir; so that now, including the Kars garrison, we have here sixty-three battalions, six field-batteries, two regiments regular and 3,500 irregular cavalry, a force with which Mukhtar Pasha ought to be able to raise the siege. But I doubt if he will face the Russians in the open field, although I am assured on the highest Turkish authority that the enemy have only forty-eight battalions, three regiments of dragoons, fifteen of Cossacks, and eighty field-guns in front of Kars.

The stories as to the want of provisions here are all false. Stores of all kinds can be obtained in great quantities, even luxuries, such as sugar, tea, brandy, and wine, being easily procurable. Indeed, prices of many things are lower than in Erzeroum. Ammunition also is abundant, there being 62,500 rounds for the siege-guns, enabling them to fire 500 shells a day for 125 days, while the supply for field-guns and small arms is comparatively inexhaustible. Now the Commander-in-Chief has made up his mind to remain encamped at Vairan Kale, and to bring up victuals and ammunition enough to last the garrison a whole year. Whether the Russians will allow him to remain unmolested is another matter. The following description of the fortress, taken from the *Moskovskiya Vedomosti*, gives a far better description of the works than I can; so I produce it, merely adding, that advanced batteries have been constructed in front of the Mukhliss, the Karapatlak, and the Karadagh redoubts, and that these contain fifteen-centimeter Krupp guns, of which there are a considerable number on the works. The artillery for the defence consists of 327 siege-guns (not 100), all rifled; I did not see a smooth-bore on the works. A very large number of traverses have recently been thrown up; their utility has been demonstrated by the marvellously small loss sustained by the garrison, during the late siege.

From the right wing we hear that Reiss Ahmed Pasha has been leisurely following up Tergukassoff, who, moving by Kara Kilissa and Dijadin, has effected a retreat across the Alasgird Plain, to the mountains in the immediate vicinity of Balykly lake, where he is apparently waiting for reinforcements, and whence Ahmed Pasha means to drive him, following him up, if necessary, to Tiflis—at least, those are the orders he has received; but as Reiss Ahmed during the Russian retreat from Zaidikan never attempted to attack Tergukassoff, I cannot think that he will be so rash as to beard the lion in his den.

THE FORTRESS OF KARS.

The *Moskovskiya Vedomosti* gives the following description of Kars :—

" The fortress of Kars lies at a distance of 57 versts (30 English miles) from the Russian district-town Alexandropol, and 200 versts (130 English miles) from Erzeroum, in the fertile valley of the Kars Tchai, on the principal transit route from Erzeroum to

Tiflis. The situation is very picturesque. The town and its three faubourgs are crowded into a kind of amphitheatre in the western, southern, and eastern slopes of a pretty high hill, cut through from the south-west to the north-east by the River Kars Tchai. That river flows through the town in a course of about 2,500 yards, and makes three decided bends. Entering the town from the south, it flows first for a distance of about 1,000 yards in a northerly direction, during which it is broken up into several arms by two large and several small islands. Then it makes a curve, and leaves the city in an easterly direction. To the south and east of this curve, on a high hill, stands the town, properly so called, and the citadel. Further south lies the faubourg of Orta Kapi ; to the east is that of Bairam pasha ; and to the west, along the left bank of the river, stretches the narrow faubourg of Temur-pasha.

" Kars is surrounded by a continuous wall. The citadel, called by the Turks Itch Kaleh, extends for about 300 yards along the highest ridge of the hill on which the town is built. It is composed of a high brick wall, with stone foundation, of which the largest side faces the town in the form of a re-entering obtuse angle. The opposite side, crowning the steep descent to the river, is built almost in a straight line. On each face of the re-entering angle is a small tower, and within the walls are two large towers. Behind the north-eastern tower is the powder-magazine. The walls of the citadel are constructed for defence by artillery. There is but one gate, and it is to the south. The easiest approach is from the east. To the west and north there is a high precipice. From the side of the town the slope is steep ; but along it runs the most convenient road by which the citadel is provided with supplies. The fortifications are too weak to bear a long siege. As the walls could not resist the destructive force of the artillery now in use, the Ottoman Government has constructed forts all round the place according to the plans and under the directions of foreign engineers, chiefly English. These forts, of various strength and construction, have converted Kars into a strongly fortified camp, which could not be taken by sudden open attack. The exterior fortifications crown the ridge of hills which approach the town from the north-east and the west ; but the three principal forts are on the plain, on the east and south of the town. All the surrounding heights compose three groups, under the names of the Karadagh, the Shorakh, and the Tchakhmak Hills. The highest of these, commanding all the others, are the Karadagh Heights, forming the continuation of the ridge on the western extremity of which stands the citadel, and extending along the right bank of the Kars Tchai. The Shorakh and Tchakhmak Heights lie on the other side of the river, and form the extreme eastern offshoots of the Tchalgaour Hills, which lie to the north-west of Kars. They are separated from each other by the Tchakhmak Ravine, which runs from the village of Tchakhmak in the direction of the citadel. The Shorakh Plateau begins near the left bank of the Kars Tchai, about two miles above the town, and extends to the village of Tchakhmak. The highest point of it is called by the Russians Bashi-Bazouk Hill. The Tchakhmak Hills stretch from the Tchakhmak Ravine towards the north-east till they reach the Kars Tchai, about a mile and a half below the town. They cover the town on the north and north-west ; but they are less elevated and more liable to be attacked than the others.

" Let us now turn to the description of the exterior fortifications, beginning with those on the right bank of the river. These may be divided into three groups—those on the Karadagh Hills, those on the plain, and those on the left bank of the river.

"I. On the Karadagh Heights.

" 1. Arab Tabia, or Karapatlak, presents an irregular figure, the gorge of which is closed by stone barracks. The left face is built on the top of the high precipitous bank of the Kars Tchai, commanding the opposite bank, on which are the forts Williams Pasha and Teesdale Tabia. It serves to protect the approaches from the valley. The front and right face are strengthened by a supplementary parapet, constructed in advance of and parallel to them. The fort is composed of earthworks, and surrounded by a glacis arranged for defence by artillery and musketry. The following are the proportions of the profile :—Height of the principal parapet, 14 feet ; thickness of the parapets, the principal one, 40 feet, and the supplementary 37 feet ; breadth of the *terre-plein,* 22 feet. There are no ditches or traverses. The powder-magazine is constructed under the extremity of the right face of the chief parapet. The line of fire of the chief parapet is 606, and of the supplementary 312 paces.

" 2. Karadagh Tabia lies at a distance of 560 paces to the south-east. Its form is an acute salient angle cut off at the point. It has an elevated battery called Ziaret, defensive barracks, and a glacis for defence by artillery and musketry. Like the former, it has no ditch, because it is built on rock. The height of the parapet is from 9 to 12 feet, and the thickness from 21 to 24 feet. The battery Ziaret is placed behind the chief parapet, on a square stone foundation 21 feet high. Each side of the square is 65 paces in length. There is one small powder-magazine. The fort defends the approaches on the side of Melik-Kui and Mazra, and serves for the cross defence of the forts Arab and Hafiz. The length of the whole line of fire is 1,518 paces. In the principal fort there are two powder-magazines, one in the advanced gorge and the other at the end of the right face of the chief rampart, under the parapet.

"II. On the Plain.

"3. Hafiz Pasha Tabia is on the plain at a distance of 1,890 paces from Fort Karadagh. It has the form of a bastioned fort, having traverses for the chief parapet and for the covered passage. The length of the exterior side is 266 paces; the parapet is 9 feet high and 21 feet thick. Depth of the ditch not known. The entrance faces the town, and is defended. At 230 paces in front of the south-eastern bastion is a *flèche* (called by the Turks Ekhali), having faces of 77 paces in length. Inside of the fort is a stone barracks and a small powder-magazine. The length of the line of fire of the chief parapet and the *flèche* 1,782 paces.

"4. Kanli Tabia lies at a distance of 3,103 paces from Fort Hafiz, and is composed of three separate fortifications, two redoubts and a *réduit*, having the form of a lunette, closed at the gorge by barracks, with supplementary constructions of a bastion form, with *ravelins* or *demilunes*. All the fortifications are surrounded by a common ditch. The covered passage has traverses. Small powder-magazines are arranged in the lunette. In the chief lunette the parapet is 21 feet high. The breadth of the *terre-plein* with *banquette* is 42 feet. The ditch is 12 feet broad, and 6 feet deep. The length of the whole line of fire is 2,163 paces.

"5. Suvari Tabia, at a distance of 1,690 yards from the preceding, has just been constructed, and is said to be one of the strongest forts around Kars, but we have no details concerning it. Another new fort, it is said, has been recently built in this part of the defences, and armed with Krupp guns; but of this likewise we have no information.

"III. ON THE LEFT BANK OF THE RIVER.

" 6. Yassif Pasha Tabia, called also Fort Tchim or Ted-Kharab, has the form of a lunette. It is intended to defend the defile through which the river flows, and the back of Fort Suwarri. It is composed of earthworks, and being built on rock has no ditch. At 57 paces in front of the parapet there is a glacis. Under the parapet of the left flank is the powder-magazine. The parapet is from 9½ feet to 12 feet high, and 18 feet thick. The line of fire extends to 415 paces.

" 7. Fort Lake, called also Fort Veli Pasha, at 1,200 paces from Yassif Pasha Tabia, and 960 from the citadel, is an inclosed fort, three sides of which are bastioned. The fourth side—facing the citadel—is protected by stone barracks and a defensive wall. The exterior side of the bastion-faces is 107 paces. The parapet is 28 feet thick, and 24 feet high. The ditch is 21 feet wide, and 7 feet deep. The length of the line of fire is 335 paces. There are two entrances, one through the barracks, another through the curtain from the ditch. The left flank of the fort has no ditch. The glacis is constructed for defence with musketry. The fort is intended to cover the back of the Forts Takmash, and Laz-Tabia, and to defend the approaches to the northern side of the faubourg of Temu Pasha from the direction of the Tchakhmak Defile.

" 8. Fort Takmash, 2,100 yards distant from Fort Lake, and 2,650 from Yassif Pasha Tabia, consists of two bastioned forts connected together. Inside the fort there are barracks and a small powder-magazine. The entrance is from the side of Fort Lake. The parapet is 12 feet high, and 12 feet thick. The ditch is 9 feet wide, and 7 feet deep. The length of the line of fire is 520 paces. Fort Takmash is intended to bar the approach to the Shorakh Heights from the side of Shorakh, Kumbet, and Tchiftlik.

" 9. Fort Yarimai Tabia, situated about 580 paces to the north-west of Fort No. 8, is a bastioned fort without glacis. The parapet is 12 feet in height, and the same in thickness. The ditch is 9 feet broad, and 7 feet deep. The length of the line of fire is 520 paces. The aim of the fort is to defend the approaches from the villages Shorakh and Tchiftlik. According to the description of the taking of Kars in 1828, this fort stands on the spot where General Moura-vieff placed his battery, and from which Count Paskiewitch watched the movements of the attacking columns.

" 10. Yaksek Tabia lies to the north of the preceding fort. The length of the line of fire is 261 paces.

" 11. Laz-Tabia, or Fort Tchakhmak, crowns the Bashi-Bazouk Hill—or, more strictly speaking, a rocky position with precipitous sides near the top of that hill—commanding the left bank of the Kars Tchai. It is composed of three distinct batteries, surrounded by one glacis, constructed for defence with musketry. The parapet is 12 feet high, and 24 feet thick. The length of the line of fire is 806 paces. The fort protects the approaches from the villages of Tchiftlik, Djavra, and Mazra.

" 12. Fort Bluhm-pasha lies to the east of Laz-Tabia. The proportions and profile of that fort are unknown to us.

" 13. Williams Pasha Tabia is situated at a distance of 1,860 paces from No. 12, and 1,420 paces from No. 1. It is an irregularly-traced inclosed fort, with an entrance from the south-east, and constructed merely for musketry defence. The parapet is 14 feet thick, and 9 feet high. The ditch is 21 feet broad, and 7 feet deep. Length of the line of fire, 262 paces.

" 14. Teesdale Tabia, the most northerly of the forts, about 815 paces from Fort No. 13, and 1,210 paces to the west of Arab Tabia. It has been recently constructed, and is of an irregular form, with open gorge. It is constructed on the brink of the precipice, in order to cover the approaches from the defile of the Kars Tchai to the Tchakhmak Plateau. Though the trace of the parapet is irregular and broken in several places, there are situations in front not exposed to its fire. The parapet has a *banquette;* and it is intended to dig a ditch for the westward faces. The height of the parapet is $9\frac{1}{2}$ feet, and the thickness 21 feet. Length of the line of fire, 429 paces.

" From this description of the Kars fortifications, we see that the entire length of the line of defence exceeds 15 versts (about 10 English miles), and the inclosed space about 17 square versts. The artillery for the defence of the works, now that all necessity for secrecy has passed away, may be given. It may interest some of my readers. It, at any rate, will show that the Turks failed to make the most of the many months' leisure during which it was patent to all the world that Russia meant war.

" There were in the works 157 siege-guns of 9, 12, and 15-centimeter calibre, with 60 4 and 5-pounder Krupp field-guns ; and there were 48 field Krupp guns in field-batteries. Many of the siege-guns were muzzle-loaders, some being M.L. bronze guns, rifled, with a calibre of 9, 12, and 15 centimeters; others were the old 6 and 9-pounders, smooth bore. The breech-loading siege-guns were all of Krupp's pattern, bronze, 9, 12, and 15 centimeters, made in the Tophané at Constantinople. Of the largest size there were but 18.

"The normal garrison, according to the length of the lines, should consist of 23,000 men; but the actual number of troops in the place at present is unknown. The *Cologne Gazette* gives the number as 32,000; but according to the data obtained by the Russian army from deserters there are not more than 15,000. Looking at the position from the point of view of attack and defence, we may draw the following conclusions:—

"The advantages for the defenders are—

"(1) The favourable arrangements of the heights commanding the surrounding country; (2) the strong mutual defence of the forts by artillery; (3) the rocky subsoil, which prevents siege operations.

"The disadvantages of the position are—

"(1) Its great extent; (2) the absence of ditches in many of the forts; (3) difficulty of repairing the parapets, in consequence of the scarcity of earth; (4) the absence in some forts of flank ditches; (5) insufficiency of strong buildings for sheltering the garrison and storing the supplies; (6) absence of water in almost all the forts, and difficulty of obtaining it; (7) absence of covered traverses, and the small number of ordinary traverses; (8) the exposed position of some powder-magazines; (9)—and this is the chief weakness—the differences which have arisen between the garrison and the inhabitants, who, according to the latest accounts, obstinately demand the surrender of the place."

The old citadel, called now Itch Kaleh, was built by Sultan Amarath III. in 1578, when it played an important part in the Turko-Persian war, then raging; in 1732 Sheik Nadir besieged it, after having defeated the Turkish army, but was forced to raise the siege in the following year, owing to the advance of Topal Osman, who signally defeated him near Bagdad; in 1807, the fortress then only consisting of the old citadel and some batteries on the Karadagh, successfully resisted

the Russian attack, but on the 24th June, 1828, owing
to the treachery of Emin Pasha, it surrendered to Paskiewitch, after a bombardment of two days.   In 1854,
after a most gallant defence, it was starved into surrendering to Mouravieff on the 28th November,
since which time, the fortifications, then much improved
by the British officers under Sir Fenwick Williams,
have been strengthened, the number of outworks increased, and heavy guns of Krupp pattern mounted
under the able direction of Faizi Pasha.

CHAPTER XI.

CAMP LIFE IN FRONT OF KARS.

Massacre at Bayazid—Kurdish Atrocities—Conduct of Faik Pasha—Murder of a Russian Doctor near Kars—His Diary—Russian Opinion of Battle of Khaliass—Strictures on Heimann—The Siege raised—Yet one more instance of the value of Turkish Cavalry—Siege Batteries—Move our Camp to Vezinkui—Beggars on Horseback—Success of the Turks deemed only Temporary—Conduct of the Officer in charge of Hospitals—An Interruption to our Breakfast—An Interchange of Civilities on the Slopes of the Yagni—Kindness of the Consul at Erzeroum—Energy displayed by the new Governor there—News from Van—Treatment of Christians throughout Armenia—Russians change their Camp—Their Kindness to Turkish Prisoners at Ardahan—A Flag of Truce fired on, and Bearer killed, by the Russians—The Polish Legion—Cavalry Skirmish near Sarbatan—Turkish Opinion of Kurds.

HEAD QUARTERS IV. TURKISH ARMY CORPS.

KARS, *July* 10*th.*

FROM Bayazid we learn of an act of atrocity that will do more to harm the Turkish cause than half a dozen defeats. It appears that on the 13th of June Faik Pasha, advancing on that fortress, encountered the Russian forces, consisting of two battalions and 1,200 Cossacks. As the Turkish division numbered six battalions, two batteries, and about 8,000 Kurds, a fight in the open was hopeless, so the Russian commander retired to the citadel, leaving the Cossacks in the town; then seeing that resistance was out of the question, offered to surrender, and this offer being accepted, they laid down their arms. A flag of truce was sent to the citadel calling upon the commandant to capitulate.

While their messenger was away the irregular Kurds
came up and commenced vilifying some Mahomedans
who were among the prisoners. One of these answered
somewhat sharply, and was immediately cut down. The
sight of blood and of unarmed and defenceless men was
sufficient for these scoundrels, who immediately fell on
their hapless prisoners, and deliberately massacred three-
fourths of them in cold blood; the number of those killed
varies, some saying 970; others, among these being the
Commander-in-Chief, put down the slain at 170. Some
regulars coming on the scene, the work of slaughter
was stopped, and Faik Pasha coming up, despatched the
survivors under escort to Van. On the road the detachment was set upon by a second body of Kurds, who
murdered some more men, stripped the remainder perfectly naked, and left them to pursue their journey
unmolested. It is but fair to add that Mukhtar Pasha
has sent orders that a certain number of these scoundrels
shall be hung, that the prisoners shall be furnished with
clothes, money, food, and all that they require, and sent
on immediately to Constantinople. Whether the execution of these villains will have the desired effect of
restraining them I much doubt, and I refrain from
passing any comments on the above facts, which admit
of no contradiction, as the Commander-in-Chief himself
owned to them, but what I do comment upon is that in
spite of the known atrocities committed by Kurds and
Circassians alike—in spite of the continual complaints
made of their conduct to the Mushir—in spite of his
oft-expressed opinion as to their utter uselessness in the
field—Mukhtar Pasha still retains a body of 4,000 of
them in his own camp, every village in the vicinity of
which has been pillaged under the very eyes of the

general himself, and by keeping them in its pay the Turkish Government silently approves their acts. Were these villains disbanded, disarmed, and sent to their homes, Europe would believe that Turkey meant reform; but as long as bands of undisciplined barbarians are provided with the best weapons that America can produce, as long as these men are kept in the pay of the Ottoman Government, so long must the support of every right-minded nation be withheld from the Porte.

I regret to have to report another circumstance which goes far to prove that the Russians had some authority for stating their wounded were never cared for by the Turks, and rarely escaped alive. It appears that after their last fight on the 4th the Russians left their wounded men in the village of Tchiflik-Kui, about three miles from Kars, in charge of a doctor, that they put up a white flag over it, and were making arrangements to send in a flag of truce to ask permission to remove them, when a body of Kurds swooped down on the village, and massacred and stripped every man in it. This is the story given by the Commander-in-Chief himself, and I must own that it is disgraceful enough. A German doctor, however, in this service, gives the following version—viz., that on the fight of the 4th being over, the Russians sent in a flag of truce with a doctor to ask permission to see the wounded prisoners, and ascertain the treatment they were receiving. The flag was fired upon by the Turkish infantry, every man slain, stripped, and left naked on the field. I do not know which is the true story; but I glean that a doctor, attending the wounded, was shot with the Geneva Cross flying over his head, that his body was stripped. His diary is now in the tent of the Turkish Commander-in-Chief, and in it he states that the total strength of the army which invaded Armenia was 50,000 men, of whom only 25,000 were operating on the Kars frontier.

If these numbers be true, I do not know which nation deserves the palm for military incapacity—the one that invaded a country and undertook the siege of a place like Kars with but 50,000 men, all told, or the one which has allowed a small force to besiege a first-class fortress with a garrison of 20,000 men, and to keep a second 20,000 fully employed for two-and-a-half months. This unfortunate man had, from all I can hear, kept a complete and very interesting diary of the proceedings since the 24th of April. He wrote somewhat strongly of General Heimann's conduct at Zewin, and the supersession of that officer leads me to believe that there must be some foundation for the numerous strictures passed on him so freely. He puts down the Russian losses at Khaliass as 500 killed and wounded, and at Zewin as 800, all told. The former affair he considers a success for the Russians, as their ten battalions withstood Mukhtar Pasha's attack of twenty-three battalions, held their ground all day, and retired unmolested on the following morning to Zaidikan, where they remained for a whole week. I think a Russian may well be pardoned for considering Khaliass a success, for they certainly held their own against a vastly superior force, and drew off unpursued twenty-four hours after the fight. The battle of Zewin he owns to have been most disastrous. This, in common with all his countrymen, he ascribes to the wanton conduct of Heimann, who, without reconnoitring, led his men up by deep precipitous ravines to a perpendicular wall, where they were shot down by hundreds without any hope of success.

I am in hopes that the few lines I am now sending will reach Trebizond in time for the same steamer that carries mine of the 9th to you. It was at noon on that day that messengers were sent out to Mukhtar Pasha, encamped at Vairan Kale, to inform him that the Russians had raised the siege and moved off bodily from Kars. I could scarcely believe my ears when I heard the news, but that it was true was evident. Not a sign of a tent was visible. How the Russians contrived to slip away unobserved is a mystery, and one that reflects but little credit on the vigilance either of the garrison or of the Circassian horsemen, 4,000 of whom are encamped within four miles of this place. On the 8th instant the bombardment had slackened considerably, but large bodies of foot and horse were seen constantly moving about. Spies accounted for this by saying that a considerable force had received four days' provisions, and had moved off to the south. The trenches, moreover, presented an unusually lively appearance, teams of horses being sent down every now and again to the batteries. This agitation seems to have excited no comment, and at night the blaze of several bonfires in the Russian lines, though noticed by the Turkish sentries, aroused no attention. It was not until 9 a.m., apparently, that some of the garrison, struck by the unusual quietness reigning in the trenches, thought of turning their eyes further northward to the spot where the long row of Russian tents usually glistened in the morning sun. To their surprise none were there. On reports

being made to the new commandant, Mushir Mustafa
Pasha, he sent out parties of irregular horse to reconnoitre. These soon returned with the news that not
only were batteries, trenches, and encampments deserted,
but that the Russians had gained the pass of Kharrak-
Darrah, where, on the 8th August, 1854, Mouravieff inflicted such a signal defeat on Zarif Mustafa Pasha, and
had established two other camps at Yeni-kui and Gadikler, where they had strongly entrenched themselves.
On proceeding to the late siege works, the reason of the
last night's bonfires was apparent; not a gun platform,
gabion, or fascine was left in the batteries, their charred
and smoking remains showing that Loris Melikoff, judging retreat desirable in the face of the superior forces
now in front of him, had determined that no material
should fall into the enemy's hands. So quietly and so
expeditiously had he set to work, that without exciting
the suspicion of the garrison, he succeeded in removing
all his stores, tents, and guns safe to the entrenched position at Kharrak-Darrah without any molestation. The
siege works appear to have been constructed with much
care and skill, and with all the improvements that late
experiments, both in England and on the Continent,
show to be necessary, owing to the increased range and
accuracy of rifled cannon. The batteries were half
sunken; owing to the soil being of a peaty nature,
crumbling up readily when once broken, the parapets
were shored up with large beams. The traverses between the gun portions contained bombproof recesses for
the detachments, thus doubtless affording perfect immunity from all shells bursting in rear of the battery. I
believe the batteries did not seem to have suffered much
from the Turkish fire, though the screens, thrown up in

P

front at a distance of about twenty-five yards, were much knocked about. These were about four feet in height, and about ten feet in thickness, while the parapets were about eighteen feet in thickness; they had been revetted with sand-bags, the majority of which had been removed, but a fair number were left on the ground. The whole of the trenches, bombproof recesses, and rifle-pits were well lined with grass, showing that the comfort of their men was studied by the Czar's officers. The timbers used in the construction of the magazine, &c., were heavy beams, from nine inches to twelve inches in diameter. Most of these were destroyed in the bonfires of the preceding night, but some few were necessarily left. It is surprising that the Russians contrived to move off, not only their men and guns, but all the material, without exciting remark and provoking a conflict, for at this time, in and around Kars, Mukhtar had 64 battalions, 48 field-guns, 1,000 regular and 4,000 irregular cavalry.

It is useless speculating on the future or dreaming on the past of this campaign, pregnant as it has been with the most glaring errors on both sides. When I arrived in this country I was assured that the invading force consisted of 100,000 men, of whom 16,000 were cavalry, with 300 field-guns. The week before last I was informed by an officer high on the staff that they had only sixty-four battalions at Kars and with Tergukassoff's column. Last week Mukhtar Pasha himself said they had forty-eight battalions, three regiments of dragoons, fifteen of Cossacks, and eighty field-guns before Kars alone, and now he maintains that his information has proved correct, that the Russians invaded Armenia with 50,000 men all told, and that the force in front of Kars never exceeded

25,000 men. To extract the truth from these conflicting statements is obviously impossible. Should the larger number of men be correct, it goes far to prove that Russia has degenerated as a military power, that the lessons the campaigns of the past ten years have taught the world have been wasted on her, and that she need no longer be feared as a foe. Should the smaller number be accurate, it shows that she has far under-estimated the value of her enemy, and, by despising the improvements effected in the armament and equipment of the Turkish forces, has drawn upon herself well-merited defeat. Being ignorant of any outside cause that may have tended to bring about the abandonment of the occupation of Armenia, and assuming that Loris Melikoff commenced the war with the six divisions for which he has been given credit, I can only stand aghast at the innumerable errors he has committed, the many chances he has lost, and the total failure of a campaign the success of which would have been assured had ordinary forethought and care been exercised by the Russian general.

Yesterday Mukhtar Pasha moved his force from Vairan Kale to a ridge east of Vezinkui, about ten miles south-east of Kars; but on hearing of a more favourable position he shifted camp this afternoon to a plateau under the Sevri Tepe possessing very strong natural defence, some five miles further east. There he has entrenched his men, and probably means to provoke a conflict with the Russians, who are said to be twelve miles north of him. I have ridden out to the camp, which to my mind is very extended, and which in the eyes of an Englishman possesses the extreme disadvantages of having a scanty supply of bad water and being totally destitute of firewood. These are drawbacks which never

P 2

enter into the calculations of Turkish generals, who, in
my short experience, rarely, if ever, study the comfort of
their men, the endurance, willingness, and gallantry of
whom cannot but excite the warmest admiration of all
who may be thrown into contact with them.   Flushed
with success, the Turks are not pleasant companions.
In their distress a month ago, when all seemed going
against them, an Englishman was treated with courtesy
and deference.   Now, when appearances seem favourable, they are filled with pride, openly talk of the
selfishness of our Government—one that only consults
her own interests, as they complain—and loudly pro-
claim their ability to defeat the Russians single-handed,
and their intention in a few weeks of carrying the war
into the enemy's territory.   Although the Turks have
gained successes in the past three weeks which I deemed
perfectly impossible, yet when I look round me and see
the material with which these successes have been gained,
see the absence of all commissariat arrangements, and
hear the cries on all sides from both officers and men of
want of money, shoes, and clothing, I cannot but cling
to my opinions previously expressed — look upon this
phase of the campaign as but a temporary check for the
enemy, and prophesy the ultimate success of the Russians.

I may mention one trivial circumstance here, which
goes far to prove how utterly the Turkish regimental
officers disregard the feelings of their men.   I stayed
behind in Vairan Kale for a few hours after the camp
had moved on to Vezinkui.   The hospital, which was
the last to go, was under the charge of a captain, who
struck his tents and moved off.   A foreign doctor, in
medical charge, begged for a working party to bury two
men who had died that morning.   This request was

refused ; nor was the doctor granted leave to remain behind to see the corpses interred. Some short time after the party had moved off, my servant came to me and reported the circumstances, when I obtained some villagers, who, for a small pecuniary consideration, buried the poor fellows. There was no excuse for the conduct of this officer; the army was only shifting camp a few miles, so that the few moments' delay to enable their co-religionists to receive a decent burial would not have been a grave military error; indeed, the incident was only on a par with the general behaviour of the company officers to the rank and file in the Turkish army.

HEAD-QUARTERS, FOURTH TURKISH ARMY CORPS,
CAMP NEAR VEZINKUI, *July* 14*th.*

This morning we were informed by an officer on the staff of the Commander-in-Chief that a Russian deserter had come into camp at dawn, reporting that the whole of the Loris Melikoff forces had struck camp at Yeni-kui, and marched during the night to Kharrak-Darrah—where previously only one division had been entrenched—and that this move was only prior to a general retreat on Alexandropol. Owing to the thick haze over the plains we were unable to see the Russian tents which yesterday had been distinctly visible to the north, and so were unable to verify this man's statement. As the Mushir himself believed it, we saw no reason to doubt the truth of the story, and consequently prepared ourselves for a quiet day. Our breakfast, however, was rudely disturbed by the sound of artillery ; so, hastily swallowing a meal, which certainly was not worth dallying over, we mounted our horses, and set out in the

direction of the firing, which from the sound we judged
to be about three miles distant. Descending the ridge
on which the head-quarters camp was pitched, at an altitude of 8,400 feet above sea level, we rode along the
most fertile table-land it has been my lot to traverse;
for miles and miles it stretched to the east and south-
ward, until lofty snow-clad peaks, rising grandly from
its undulating surface, brought the luxuriant vegetation
to a standstill. Not a yard was under cultivation, and
with the exception of a few kibitkas, or Kurdish black
blanket tents, not a sign of habitation was visible, and
yet the soil was rich enough to please a Kent farmer,
and the vast expanse of clover through which our horses
literally waded would give a handsome competence to
any one energetic enough to cut and transport it.

As the sun rose the mist cleared off, and there in
the plain some 2,000 feet below us, we saw glistening
to the north the Russian camp at Yeni-kui, and farther
eastward their entrenchments at Kharrak-Darrah, thus
proving the story of the deserter to have been false,
and showing without doubt that Armenia was not yet
rid of the Muscovite invader. All firing had ceased, but
small parties of Kurdish and Circassian horsemen were
hastening to the left to join a large body of irregular
horsemen, who were drawn up in columns — if the
irregular crowd they formed may be so designated—at
the north-western edge of the plateau. As we advanced
we saw coming down on our left two Turkish horse
artillery guns, while in rear of them, with standards
flying, bugle sounding, and men cheering, were two
battalions moving to the front in columns of double
companies. We joined the artillery, who came into
action a few moments before noon at a distance of some

5,000 yards from the enemy. The Russian force consisted of three regiments of dragoons and eight of Cossacks, as well as I could judge, and were accompanied by a half battery of Galloper guns. They were all dismounted, but had taken up a position on the southern slopes of the Yagni Tepe, a lofty tor (as we should call it in the west country), or conical hill, from the summit of which a good view of our whole position was distinctly visible.

At noon precisely our guns opened fire, the shells all bursting fully 2,000 yards short. After a few rounds they were pushed forward about 500 yards, and at the same time bodies of irregular cavalry were advanced on either flank. On this, at 12.45, the Russian guns leisurely came into action, but finding the range too great, ceased firing after four rounds, and leisurely moved off, the cavalry accompanying them. No attempts at following the enemy were made by Mukhtar, and in this he was wise, for his badly-mounted, undisciplined irregular horsemen are no match for the well-organised cavalry Loris Melikoff that day showed us. While this little diversion was occurring we saw a large convoy of carts, &c., moving from Yeni-kui to the eastward towards Goomri, this cavalry demonstration evidently being made with a double object of protecting it during its flank march straight across the front of our position and of ascertaining the strength of our force. Although the enemy's troops consisted entirely of cavalry, and never approached within five miles of our camp, Mukhtar Pasha took the opportunity of manning all his entrenchments, thus displaying to the Russian general all the troops at his command, and at the same time a body of twenty battalions, with three field batteries, moved out from Kars under the command of Faizi Pasha, with the intention of intercepting the retreat to Yeni-kui of the Russian cavalry. They were, however, discovered long before they could effect their purpose, and retired again about sunset, when they pitched on the banks of the Kars Tchai stream, about five miles to the north-east of the fortress. At three p.m., the enemy having effected their retreat to camp, and there being no intention of following them up, we returned to camp, where we found awaiting us a box of provisions, sent out by the ever-thoughtful consul at Erzeroum, who, mindful of the tastes of Britons, had enclosed what were, indeed, pearls of great price, some bottles of beer. To us, whose sole beverage for the past six weeks has been water, tempered, when its quality was more offensive than usual, with a dash of brandy, this consignment was a perfect godsend.

We had been so constantly on the move during the past month, and our means of communicating with Erzeroum are so precarious, that I have been unable to give you more than the news immediately concerning the head-quarters of this army corps. It appears that since the departure of the governor, Ismail Pasha, to join the left wing of the army in the Alashgird Plain, the authorities have awoke to the fact that prayer and the constant reading of the Koran were not sufficient to supply the army with food and reinforcements. The new governor, Hassan Pasha, seems to be a man of energy and determination, and to have infused some of his spirit into the palace officials. To the Olti road, whence all troops had been most unwisely withdrawn on reinforcements being needed at Delibaba, he has despatched eight battalions, 1,200

irregular cavalry, two field and one mountain battery.
These are in an entrenched position in the Ghiurji
Boghaz defile, a short distance to the north of Hindsk.
He also has called up twelve more battalions from
Angora, Konieh, Kharpoot, Diarbekir, and Bagdad,
with 600 cavalry from Angora, and about 3,000 irregulars from Syria. These men will be forwarded, half to
this and half to the left wing of the Turkish army.
He also has obtained permission from Constantinople
to make a forced levy of all males in Armenia between
the ages of sixteen and sixty. By this means he hopes
to raise 50,000 men; and towards their equipment he has
already received 25,000 Martini-Peabody rifles, 25,000
sets of accoutrements, and the same number of infantry
uniforms. To provide transport for these men he
himself has issued an order that every one hundred
houses in his vilayet shall furnish one horse, either
for pack or cavalry purposes. Thus he has already
collected some 1,500 ponies and horses. The need of
provisions which was being severely felt in Erzeroum
has passed away, and there now is sufficient to feed the
army for the remainder of the year. Last week 1,000
camels and 2,560 horses and mules arrived laden with
wheat, barley, and flour from Bagdad, Moussaul, Mardin,
and Diarbekir; 680 camels also arrived from Sivas, and
1,800 horse-loads of biscuit from Trebizond. It will be
seen that at last the civil administration are awakening
to the urgency of the situation, and seconding with
promptitude the energy displayed by Ahmed Mukhtar
Pasha and his brave soldiers. The latter have shown
throughout the campaign the greatest patience, endurance, and gallantry.

The news from Van daily becomes more revolting.

Faik Pasha seems quite unable to restrain the Kurds, who commit every description of atrocity unopposed and unchecked. The American missionaries have been forced, for fear of their lives, to take refuge in a boat on the lake, where they enjoy comparative immunity, although they have to be careful, when in need of provisions, to land at night and move off again before dawn. Their Christian charges have been subjected to the grossest treatment—crops cut and carried away, cattle killed, villages burnt, men murdered, and worst of all, women and even children violated. Churches afford no refuge for these wretched mortals. Ten who fled for safety into the church at Utch-Kilissa were there foully murdered, and at Tsitawankh, near Erzeroum, the Armenian superior of the monastery has been threatened with death if he ventures to preach again. Hundreds of Christian villages in Armenia, having been gutted and fired by these miscreants, are completely abandoned, and their inhabitants have fled for refuge into the Russian camps. Hordes of fanatics, led by Moolahs, have joined the Turkish army; their fury, daily fed by the exhortations and addresses of the priests, who have denounced the war as a menace to the Ottoman religion, leads them to commit every conceivable excess against the defenceless Christians, whom they accuse of furnishing information to the enemy. Facts prove the reverse, for as yet not a single Armenian spy has been discovered by the authorities, while several Kurds and Circassians, preferring money to faith, have paid for their treachery with their lives; in short, every spy hanged during this war has been a Mahomedan.

In spite of the gallant manner in which she has repelled the Russian invasion of Armenia—a feat which no one can but admire—Turkey has irretrievably alienated the good wishes of even her best supporters by the cowardly and cruel excesses committed by her irregular soldiers—excesses which, if not connived at by the authorities, are invariably excused, and seldom punished. Outrages on Mahomedans, being against the Koran, are visited with great severity; outrages against Christians, who are considered beyond the pale of the law, are left unnoticed. The massacre at Bayazid, the desecration of Russian graves, mutilation of corpses, violation of a flag of truce, and the recent cruelties towards the Christians at Van, all furnish excuses, and valid excuses too, for a continuance of the war. We cannot hope that a great power like Russia will sit quietly down under the reverses her arms have sustained during the past month, and will permit the Christians, on whose behalf she has ostensibly made war, to be treated in Armenia as they were last year in Bulgaria. She must compel the Porte, by force of arms, to respect the rights of all her Christian subjects, and afford to them equal protection and privilege as to Mahomedans. At present this is far from being the case, Mussulman officials literally treating them worse than the dogs which act as scavengers in their streets. I mean this as no mere figure of speech, but as an actual fact, borne out not only by what I myself have witnessed, but also by reports of occurrences which have come under the notice of many of the American missionaries in Armenia, who daily receive complaints from their Christian congregations of the cruelties and acts of oppression they endure at the hands of the Kurds, whom the Ottoman Government have now let loose in Anatolia.

July 16th.

Last night we were disturbed by rumours that the Russians had struck camp at Yeni-kui, and were advancing in force to attack us. However, these turned out, as most camp rumours usually do, to be false, for on riding out in the morning to our advanced posts, I saw that the first half of the rumour certainly had some foundation, for not a single Russian tent was to be seen on the Yeni-kui ridge; but, instead of coming forward to attack us, Loris Melikoff had concentrated his forces round Kharrak-Darrah and Parget, a village on the Kars Tchai stream, about four miles north of the Goomri road. It is impossible to estimate his forces; but, from the number of tents, I am of opinion that he cannot have less than 40,000 with him.

It is rumoured that the Russians are preparing to evacuate Ardahan, where they have mined all the barracks, and completely levelled the earthworks. How far this is true I cannot say; but this I know, that they have upwards of 240 wounded Turkish prisoners in the hospital there, whom they have been treating with the greatest kindness. Among those taken on the 17th of May were four Turkish and two German doctors. As I told you in a previous letter, they released all prisoners belonging to the Redif, or reserve force, and with them the four Turkish doctors, who proceeded to Erzeroum; the two German doctors, Ardler and Weiss, were retained, and placed in charge of the wounded Turks, receiving the same pay guaranteed by the Porte. I hear from all sides of the consideration shown to the sick and wounded, who receive far better nourishment and far more attention in the Russian hospitals than they do in their own. While recounting their generosity, it pains me to be compelled to place on record an act of savagery committed by the Russians before Kars on the 5th instant, which, if true, admits of no excuse. Unfortunately, I have it on such good authority—authority independent from any Turkish source—that I cannot but believe it to be true. It appears that Hussein Hami Pasha, the commandant of Kars, wished to send a flag of truce to the enemy respecting their shells, which were doing considerable damage to the main hospital. Above this the white flag was certainly flying, but owing to the Karadagh hill being between it and the Russian siege works, it was not possible for the enemy to see the hospital flag; and, moreover, it was so situated that all shells passing over the Karadagh redoubt must necessarily fall in the vicinity of the hospital. I therefore am of opinion that the damage done to the building, which was very trifling, was purely unintentional. However, the Turks thought, and still think, otherwise; and Hussein Hami Pasha, accordingly, despatched a Kol-Aghassiz with a flag of truce to the Russian camp. This man proceeded alone, unaccompanied even by the traditional bugler. He was fired on and killed, whether intentionally, and in revenge for the murder of the doctor killed, with the Geneva Cross above his head and the white badge on his arm, the day previously, as the Turks maintain, or whether accidentally, I cannot say. I give the story as I have learnt it from lips which ascribe the deed to revenge. The same officer who informed me of the above also told me that a "chaous," or sergeant of regulars, went about Kars boasting that he had killed the Russian doctor by cutting off his head as he would that of a sheep!

It seems that there is a certain amount of discontent rife among the small band constituting the Polish Legion in this army. From what I can learn, it appears that, after volunteering for service, they were detained in Stamboul for some weeks, and then despatched to Trebizond to escort back 400 Polish prisoners captured in sorties from Kars, or rather deserters from the Russian army before that place. These men they were to organise, drill, and instruct in Turkish, and with them they were to form the nucleus of a Polish regiment, which was to be sent to the Danube. On arrival at Trebizond they were told that the prisoners were in Erzeroum, and these misguided men were conveyed there in arabas, receiving no pay and no meat on the road. At Erzeroum they, of course, learnt that not a single Polish deserter or prisoner had been seen. Having come so far, the thirty-six men determined to join the army, and so were forwarded on to Mukhtar Pasha. Now I hear that their wrath against the Russians has somewhat subsided, and that no pay, short rations of bread and meat, and total abstinence from all spirits do not tend to increase their admiration for the Ottoman rule. They have been provided with a large standard with the Polish national colours emblazoned on it. The idea is that on the occasion of the first great fight they will proceed to the front, holding this aloft, when the numerous Poles serving in the ranks of hated Russia will throw down their arms and at once espouse the cause of the Porte and—Liberty!

This afternoon the force here was reinforced by six battalions and one field battery, under the command of

Mustafa Nihadji Pasha, who has been detached from
Kars. This brings up our strength to forty battalions,
four field batteries, one mountain battery, two weak
regiments of regulars, and about 4,000 irregular cavalry.
When I think of the days when I joined the Mushir's
army on the Hoonkiar Doozi, and found a marshal of
the Ottoman Empire in command of eight battalions
and a battery, and then look round me on this army, I
am overwhelmed with astonishment at the energy displayed by the Turkish authorities. To-day Mukhtar
Pasha has been making a reconnaissance, but I doubt if
it will lead to any decisive movement, though it is
extremely probable that the head-quarters will be
advanced some three miles in the direction of Kharrak-
Darrah—to a hill higher, more barren, and further from
water than its neighbours, and, therefore, for this reason,
I suppose, possessing inestimable advantages in the eyes
of our Commander-in-Chief.

July 18*th.*

The signal-gun denoting that the Russians were
moving boomed out at 10 a.m. My servants by this
time are as well drilled as an outpost of Punjab frontier
cavalry, and in six minutes from the sound of the gun
my horse and orderly were in front of my tent.
" Yahvash " being the watchword of the camp as of the
empire, I had to wait some ten minutes before the
Commander-in-Chief's pony was ready, and then we
ambled—for our chief is no horseman—towards the
advanced battery, which had given us notice of the
enemy's movements. On reaching it I saw two bodies
of Russian cavalry in the plain below, at a distance of
about five miles. They had dismounted, and were

quietly feeding their horses on the luxuriant crops of grass which bound the banks of the Kars stream. Beyond them, shining brightly in the morning sun, lay the two Russian camps, at Parget and Kharrak-Darrah; but as for any movements betokening an advance of the enemy, the most powerful glasses could not discover anything approaching them. At about noon, however, the cause of this demonstration was apparent, for a long column of men, horses, and guns were visible winding along the road to the foot of the Karajal hill, toward the Kizil Tepe hill, which was shortly afterwards crowned by a strong party of infantry, supported by a battery of field-guns. In the meantime the remainder of the column, passing round the rear of the hill, commenced pitching their camp on the left bank of the Mazra stream, in the immediate vicinity of the village of Bash and Onka-Gadikler. It was a very formidable defensive position, protected in front by the deep, precipitous ravines of the Mazra, whilst the Kizil Tepe hill dominated the whole plain by which an attacking foe would advance. Our right was seriously threatened, too, by the new camp of the enemy, who, under cover of the broken ground on the western slopes of the Aladja Dagh, would find it an easy matter to move forward by Hadjiveli and Bolanik to the Olya Tepe, and thus turn our flank.

The Russian Commander-in-Chief being idle was no excuse for our gallant Marshal to abstain from employing his men, and, consequently, the brigades of Ibrahim Bey and Captain Mahomed Bey were moved off some five miles to the right to cover a valley up which it was just possible the enemy might advance, while the remainder of our troops, with fixed bayonets, lined the shelter-trenches surrounding our camp. For six hours did the poor fellows remain in this cramped position, although at no time was a single Russian infantry soldier in sight, and the cavalry never approached within five miles. It is such acts as these, the unnecessary worrying of these men, which, to my untutored mind, show the imbecility of the Turkish commanders. I noticed Moussa Pasha, the whilom commandant of the Circassians, on the staff of the Mushir. He has at last been removed from the command of the Circassians, who are much incensed, and justly so, at his conduct throughout the campaign.

Edhem Pasha, who has assumed command of the cavalry, gave the Circassians a chance of showing their mettle this afternoon. It appears that after the Russian demonstration in the forenoon, which was evidently made with the view of covering the movement of their division from Parget to Kizil-Tepe, a regiment of dragoons was left to cover the retirement of the cavalry corps making the demonstration. At 4 p.m. this regiment began to fall back, when the Circassians, to the number of some 2,000, who with Edhem Pasha had been thrown forward in advance of our position, asked permission to attack and endeavour to cut them off. He accordingly sent forward a couple of regiments, with one more in support, at the same time drily remarking to a British officer at his side, " See how these Tcherkess will split up into small bodies and be kept at bay by that handful!" The Circassians dashed forward at a gallop, and in a quarter of an hour were within 400 yards of the Russian dragoon regiment, who, merely dropping a squadron to cover their retreat, continued falling back at a walk. The officer commanding this squadron dismounted his

Q

men, and they, acting as infantry skirmishers, kept
their pursuers at bay. Directly these were checked,
Edhem Pasha's estimate of them proved correct, for
they at once broke into small groups. All three
regiments became intermingled, other bodies came
galloping out from the reserve, and in swarms of tens
and twenties they harassed the Russians on all sides.
As far as sound was concerned, the fight now re-
sembled an infantry skirmish, for the constant crack-
ing of the Winchester rifles from one side, and the
steady fire from the dismounted Russian dragoons, did
away with all one's ideas of a cavalry encounter.
Slowly falling back, the Muscovites came abreast of the
small village of Sarbatan, from behind the friendly
shelter of which swooped down, on the Circassian left
flank, a fresh squadron of dragoons. Though barely
numbering 120 sabres, their dashing leader never hesitated a moment, but charged clean across the front of his
dismounted comrades, clearing the ground in a moment.
The sight of the gallant Tcherkess, to the number of some
1,500, tailing off to the rear as hard as their ponies could
carry them, was one scarcely calculated to increase
Edhem Pasha's opinion of the value of his troops.
When they were well beyond the reach of Russian
sabres, the bolder spirits rallied, and continued harassing the retiring enemy with a harmless long-range
fire from their Winchesters. Every now and again
the colonel of dragoons would leave a troop hidden
in some ravine, which by a dashing charge would
drive the Circassians still farther back, and finally, at
6 p.m., they drew off on the appearance of a second
regiment of Russian cavalry moving up to support
their comrades. The Russian loss, though unknown,

is reported as immense. I have it on the best authority, however, that they certainly did not lose half-a-dozen men, and considering that the only attempt the Circassians made to get at them was with their repeating rifles, and knowing the value of mounted fire, I am inclined to think the above estimate correct. It is very difficult to get at the truth of the Circassian losses, but I hear they had twenty-two men and forty-seven horses killed, and twenty-seven men wounded. The flank charge of the Russian squadron certainly did some execution; the Chef d'Escadron himself was seen to cut down four men, and from the fact that the above numbers come from a Turkish source, I am of opinion they are entitled to some weight. I must not omit all mention of the Kurds, a body of whom were sent out with the Circassian supports. These men, cheering loudly, galloped forward, firing their pieces as they advanced. Unfortunately, their gallant intentions were frustrated by the conduct of some of the fainter spirits in their midst, who commenced to lag behind as the distance between themselves and the enemy was lessened. On the sudden appearance of the Russian supporting squadron from behind the village, an irresistible impulse to strengthen the reserve seems to have seized them, and they accordingly rode back as defiantly as they had advanced. I have conversed with many officers on the staff of the Turkish army, and they are unanimous in their denunciation of the employment of these men, who are simply useless as soldiers, untrustworthy for purposes of reconnaissance, and faithless as spies, and who by their dastardly cruelty bring discredit on the name of the Ottoman army.

Q 2

CHAPTER XII.

ON THE WATCH.

Shift our Camp once more—Strength of our Forces—Stoppage of Telegrams—
Hospitals in Erzeroum—Relief of Bayazid by Tergukassoff—That General's
Operations during the War—The Kurds once more—Court Martials on Faik
and Sabri Pasha—Turkish Accounts of Relief of Bayazid—Circassian Account
of same Affair—Losses in the Engagement—Russian Punishment of Kurds—
Pleasures of Camp Life—Expectations of a 'Scrim' disappointed—Turkish
Reconnaissance into Russian Territory—The Enemy's Attempts to cut it
off—Peace and War—Russian Reinforcements at Tashkale—Hailstones and
Pigeons' Eggs—Spies' Tales of Bayazid—British Officers' Accounts of Scenes
in Bayazid—Sir Arnold Kemball's Endeavours to stop the Kurdish Atrocities—Mukhtar Pasha's little Affair with the Circassian—His stern Ideas
of Discipline—Russian Atrocities in Armenia—Utterly False—Disposition
of Russian Troops.

HEAD QUARTERS IV. TURKISH CORPS.

CAMP ABOVE SARBATAN, *July* 19*th.*

THIS morning we followed Mukhtar Pasha, who had
struck his camp, and moved the majority of his army
to this spot, which is situated on the same table-land as
our late encampment, but about nine miles to the north-
east. Immediately below us to the north, distant about
five miles, lies the Russian camp at Kizil-Tepe; while
four miles farther to the north is their entrenched position
at Kharrak-Darrah. It is quite impossible to estimate
their strength, but I judge it to be greater than ours.
We have been further reinforced to-day by a division
of twelve battalions, under Hussein Hami Pasha, from
Kars. These are holding our old ground, and connect

us, in some measure, with the fortress. A body of 600 Circassians, under the command of Mahomed Schamyl Pasha, son of Schamyl, the old Circassian chief, also marched in here. This now brings up our force to fifty-two battalions infantry, five field batteries and one mountain battery, two regiments of regular and about 4,600 irregular cavalry. The force is very much extended, and, lining as we do the edge of the northern slopes of the Aladja Dagh, we must present a very formidable appearance to our foes who are on the plain some 2,500 feet below us. Although the mountain positions present many advantages to a general who prefers to act on the defensive, they are extremely distasteful to the men. Many regiments have to send three miles for water, and the supply of firewood is absolutely *nil*. The health of the men suffers from the extreme changes of temperature. At midday the sun is overpoweringly hot, while at night the cold wind whistling over the snowy slopes of Ararat pierces our bones. With good English blankets we are enabled, to some extent, to defy the elements; but the poor soldiers, with but a thin greatcoat made of contractor's cloth as their only covering, must feel the chilly nights terribly.

My telegrams denouncing the arrangements for the wounded have, I learn, been stopped in Constantinople. I regret this for two reasons—first, because I was in hope that by calling the attention of the British public to the destitute condition of these men, I might touch that chord of sympathy which never fails to raise in breasts of our fellow-countrymen a desire to aid in the relief of pain and distress; and, secondly, I regret the circumstance, because by their folly in hiding the defects of their system, the Ottoman Government allowed the wounded men to lie comparatively uncared for and untended for more than a month.

When I tell you that in the company of a very distinguished British officer I passed upwards of 1,000 wounded men, many hundreds obliged to walk seventy miles to the nearest hospital ; when I tell that with my own hands I distributed money, and, what was even more welcome, tobacco, to as many as my limited means would allow on riding from Erzeroum to Kuipri Kui ; when I tell you that I collected among our small English community here the sum of £55, which I was enabled, through the unselfish exertions of the American missionaries, to distribute in meat and suchlike luxuries among the wounded Turks, I think you will agree with me that however strong my telegrams may have been, they were actuated by no ill-feeling to the men with whom I am now daily thrown in contact.   Would that the Ottoman authorities had awoke to the necessity of aiding these sick and wounded, for here we are in the immediate presence of a large hostile force, in expectation of a great battle, and there is not a single litter or ambulance with the 4th Turkish Army Corps !

From Bayazid we have just received the news that Tergukassoff, who had succeeded in eluding Kurd Ismail Pasha, and who had effected a retreat to Igdyr to the east of the Balykly Lake, moved suddenly to the south, and threw himself on Faik Pasha, who, with six battalions, one field and one mountain battery—together some 8,000 irregulars—was besieging the two Russian battalions in the citadel.   After a sharp encounter, Faik was driven back with the loss of three guns ; and knowing that Ahmed Pasha was moving down from Moussin, Tergukassoff, collecting all the sick and wounded of the late garrison, abandoned the place, and crossed the frontier with the whole of his charge. Throughout this campaign the only Russian who has shown any pretension to generalship has been the man Tergukassoff. The manner in which he handled his men at Taghir on the 16th of June, when, with eight battalions, he thoroughly defeated the twelve which Mahomed Pasha opposed to him: the stubborn resistance with which he checked Mukhtar Pasha's onslaught on the 21st at Eshek Khaliass; the gallant retreat which his half-division effected in front of Ahmed Pasha's twenty-three battalions; and, finally, his dashing flank march from Igdyr to Bayazid, and the relief of that place in front of two Turkish corps, both superior to him in numbers, stamp him a general of division of the first class. Had the Czar many more like him, this war would have been completed a month ago.

Continued reports of Kurdish outrages reach me from Van and Bayazid, where these outrages on Christians are now beginning to bear fruit in the literal starvation of the Turkish armies; all the stores of grain, herds of cattle, and flocks of sheep belonging to Armenians were considered fair pillage by these gentry. Now that the troops are more than 100 miles from Erzeroum, and the difficulties of transport are being severely felt, Ahmed Pasha turned to the Christian villages for commissariat supplies. Alas! all the stores have been gutted and burnt by his auxiliaries, and the result is that his men are suffering the greatest privations.

The conduct of Faik Pasha in permitting the escape of the Bayazid garrison is very severely criticised here, and it is rumoured (with what truth I do not know) that Mukhtar Pasha has applied for a court-martial on

him. While, however, Sabri Pasha, the commandant of
Ardahan, and Moussa Pasha, the late Circassian chief, are
permitted to go unpunished, it is absurd to suppose that
any serious notice will be taken of the misdeeds of Faik.

We hear rumours of a revolution in Daghestan, and
that the Grand Duke has been forced to withdraw men
from Loris Melikoff to support authority in these regions; if this is the case, the inactivity of the Russian
commanders is accounted for.   At the same time it reflects little credit on the Czar's Government that such
a complication was not taken into consideration and due
allowance made for it when the plan of campaign was
laid out.   Had the most ordinary forethought entered
into the minds of the Russian authorities, a first-rate
Power would scarcely have been driven back by the
undisciplined, semi-organised reserves of the Ottoman
Empire.

CAMP ABOVE SARBATAN, *July 25th.*

The news from Bayazid is, of course, most conflicting,
and it seems quite impossible to obtain a true statement
of what actually occurred.   The story in vogue at head-
quarters is that Ismail Pasha, although warned by spies
of Tergukassoff's movements, never attempted to succour
Faik Pasha, but remained at Moussin with his twenty
battalions, and that after a short fight, in which the
Haideranly Kurds, who form no insignificant portion
of Faik Pasha's force, did not distinguish themselves,
Tergukassoff drove the Turkish commander back on Teperiskui with heavy slaughter, capturing three mountain-
guns.   My experience of Orientals leads me not to place
too implicit trust on head-quarter rumours, and when I
scan Mukhtar Pasha's official telegrams in your columns

and compare them with the events that occurred under my own eyes, I am not tempted to change my want of faith. Ismail Pasha's official despatch ran as follows:—

"A Russian division, consisting of 12 battalions, eight regiments of cavalry, and 30 guns, coming from Erivan, arrived before Bayazid, evidently with the intention of surprising Munib Pasha, who was occupying the hills commanding the town. The enemy being in very superior numbers, Munib Pasha was forced to fall back under a heavy musketry fire. On hearing of the Russian advance, I immediately detached a brigade of six battalions, one battery, and 400 cavalry, under Hakif Bey, who attacked the enemy with much spirit. After a sanguinary contest of some hours, the Russians were put to flight, leaving on the field, besides a large number of dead, many thousand stand of arms, several *fourgons*, and a large train of provision wagons. I now am myself marching down to effect a junction with Faik Pasha's corps, and intend to make a combined attack on the enemy. Send immediately large quantities of provisions and ammunition, as we are in need of both."

This story differs considerably from the Commander-in-Chief's report, which acknowledges the success of the Russians, who captured three guns, and succeeded in carrying off all their sick and wounded and blowing up the citadel when they evacuated it.

From an intelligent unofficial source I obtained the following information, and as I have had an opportunity of hearing what Ghazi Mahomed Pasha (Schamyl's son) —who, with his Circassians, was present at the fight— says on the subject, and as it agrees in the main with my informant's story, I give it without any hesitation as the really true account of the battle of Bayazid. On Friday, the 13th of July, a Russian division, consisting of twelve battalions of infantry, thirty-two field-guns, two regiments of dragoons, and five of Cossacks, arrived at dawn in front of Bayazid from Erivan. Munib Pasha,

who, with four battalions, five field-pieces, and 1,200
cavalry, held two hills to the east of the citadel, completely commanding the ground, on the approach of the
enemy, seeing their superior strength, evacuated his position, and endeavoured to fall back on Faik Pasha's force
at Teperiskui. Rapidly moving forward his cavalry, Tergukassoff cut off Munib Pasha's retreat, and compelled
him to accept battle. In the meantime the Russian
artillery and infantry came up, and a sharp encounter
ensued. Munib Pasha being unable to retire on Teperiskui, owing to the Russian cavalry being on the road, fell
back towards Moussin, and at about 2 p.m. was reinforced
by Hakif Bey's brigade, consisting of eight battalions,
one battery, and 1,200 cavalry, which Ismail Pasha had
detached to his support. The fight then continued
until 5 o'clock, when the Turks fled in disorder to Kizil
Diza, about ten miles N.W. of Bayazid. Tergukassoff
then fell back to the town, where he remained the night,
making arrangements for the transport of the sick and
wounded of the beleaguered garrison to Erivan. On the
15th he moved off unattacked, blowing up the citadel
and partially destroying the town. Thus, in face of a
force at least double his own strength, and which was
fully aware, not only of his movements, but of their
object, Tergukassoff, by a rapid march and brilliant victory, succeeded in relieving the garrison of Bayazid, who
for twenty-three days had been closely besieged by the
faint-hearted Faik, who, though his forces numbered
13,000 men, feared to assault the citadel, with its gallant
garrison of 1,270 men. The battle of Taghir, the retreat
from Zaidikan, and the relief of Bayazid, stamp the commander of the thirty-eighth Russian division a general of
no mean order. Were the other divisional leaders or the

Commander-in-Chief of the same calibre as Tergukassoff, I much doubt if our advance from Zewin would have been unopposed, or if we should have relieved Kars without a struggle.

It is simply impossible to estimate the losses of the Turks in the engagement on the 13th inst. Mukhtar Pasha acknowledges to 500 killed, besides wounded and prisoners, as well as three mountain guns which fell into the hands of the Russians; and this tallies in the main with my own information, which gives three guns (not mentioning whether field or mountain), 800 prisoners, and 900 killed and wounded. The Commander-in-Chief has sent down instructions for Faik Pasha to be placed under arrest, and tried for failing to afford support to his advanced brigade under Munib Pasha.

From all sides we hear complaints as to the scarcity of provisions in the Bayazid, Van, Dijadin, and Kara Kilissa districts—a scarcity amounting to a famine. The Turkish commanders telegraph daily to Erzeroum for corn, grain, flour, and meat to be sent out immediately and in the largest possible quantities, as every village store has been clean swept by the Kurds. It appears that these worthies, of whom there are some 10,000 with the Turkish right wing, have been roaming over the country, taking whatever they pleased, and murdering any one who said them nay. Such cattle as they could not drive away they slaughtered and left to rot in the sun. Grain that they could not carry away was either burnt or thrown into rivers. It appears that thirty Kurds were captured by the Russians after the affair of Bayazid. These were immediately brought before a court-martial, and twenty of them sentenced to death. Of these many were inhabi-

tants of Russian territory, one Ayub Aga, the son of
Jaffir Agha, chief of the Zilan Kurds, who dwell on
the left bank of the Araxes.   This man held the rank
of honorary colonel in the Russian army, and was
decorated by the Emperor Alexander on his visit to
Alexandropol some years ago.   Having been convicted
of atrocities on Russian prisoners in Bayazid as well as
of faithlessness to his salt, he well merited the punishment he received.

The past week has been so devoid of incident that it
seems hardly worth while to attempt to chronicle the
doings of the camp for the benefit of your readers.
Incessant rain, with vivid lightning, varied the dull
monotony of our existence both yesterday and on Monday.   Two miserable days indeed; when to write was
impossible, for my paper was reduced to the consistency
of pulp if I removed it from my sabretache for a
moment, and my brain so sodden with the atmosphere
that all ideas were as vapid as the air around me.
Night was a relief indeed, and in spite of the damp
surroundings, in spite of the prognostications that damp
blankets foreboded rheumatism, fever, ague, any and all
the ills that Oriental travellers are exposed to, I slept
as soundly as man could wish.   At six a.m. I was
rudely awakened by Sir Arnold Kemball's orderly informing him that the Russians were advancing in force,
and our troops moving off to meet them.   Damp boots,
damp saddles, and damp coats were quickly rubbed
down, and in a very few minutes our horses were at the
door, and we ready to accompany the Commander-in-
Chief; but, in spite of the agitated assurances of the
excited Moolazim (Sir Arnold's Turkish orderly officer),
there seemed to be an air of peacefulness over the

Mushir's camp that boded of anything rather than an impending attack; so, leaving our horses by the tents, we moved on to the edge of the ridge about a couple of hundred yards from us, and sat down to watch the progress of events.

There was no doubt as to a movement on the part of the enemy, for half way between Kizil-Tepe and Sarbatan were three regiments of cavalry, five battalions of infantry, and two field batteries, while between Tainalik and Jelanly were a couple of cavalry regiments. Our 1st cavalry brigade, under Mustafa Pasha, was moved down to Chela, and our second, under Edhem Pasha, from Bolanik to Hadji-veli, and at one time I certainly thought an engagement was imminent. The Russian horsemen, however, dismounted, and commenced feeding their animals on the rich green grass with which the plain below us is covered, and our Circassians, mindful of the losses they sustained almost on the very spot now occupied by Russian dragoons only one short week ago, never ventured beyond the range of our guns on the ridge below Kharkana. As the enemy certainly was not likely to run under the fire of their Krupps, my expectations were disappointed, for at 11 a.m. the Russians mounted and retired to their camp in rear of the Kizil-Tepe hill, the infantry preceding the cavalry by about half an hour. I cannot imagine what was the object of this demonstration, unless it was to give the men a marching-out parade to warm them after the damp chilliness of the past two days.

THURSDAY, *July 26th.*

This morning I learnt that the Commander-in-Chief had yesterday detached 1,200 cavalry, under Major-

General Mustafa Pasha, on a reconnaissance across the Arpa Chai to Mastara, in Russian territory, and that, fearing their retreat might be threatened, he meditated moving out with a strong force to support them at 9 a.m. Previous to that hour an unusual stir was seen in the Russian camp at Gadikler, and presently two battalions of infantry, twenty squadrons of cavalry, and two horse batteries were seen moving out in the direction of Aras-Oghlu, evidently with the intention of cutting off Mustafa Safvet Pasha's retreat. Marching down the banks of the Arpa Tchai, this brigade drew down upon it the fire of the troops posted in the Nakharji-Tepe, and as they debouched into the plain between Utch Tepe and Aras-Oghlu, Edhem Pasha, at the head of a body of Circassians, moved out to oppose them, the Mushir supporting him by a heavy fire from two batteries, which on the first announcement of the Russian advance had been ordered out to Chela.

This was replied to with much spirit by the Russians. The Commander-in-Chief, however, at 11 a.m., advanced three brigades of infantry to support the Circassians, who were contenting themselves with firing at the enemy's skirmishers, never attempting to come to close quarters. On this the enemy retired to Aras-Oghlu, and occupied a ridge to the east of the village, whence it would have been difficult to dislodge him. Desultory firing between the Circassians and the infantry skirmishers of the Russian force now was the order of the day, and it was not until 2 p.m. that Loris Melikoff advanced a division from the Gadikler camp to support his detachment. It was a pretty sight to see the men parade in front of their snowy tents, and, as the sun shone on their white caps and glistened on

their bayonets, they presented a fair enough spectacle
for any artist to delineate. The column was headed by
four regiments of dragoons, moving in column of troops,
and in splendid order; in rear of them were two horse
batteries, followed by two more cavalry corps. As they
were without the white head-dress, I concluded they
were Cossacks. Immediately behind these men was a
battery, and then, in half-battalion columns, came two
infantry brigades, numbering twelve battalions—fine,
strong corps, too, numbering fully 800 bayonets. As
these moved out to the eastward, another force advanced
straight to the front on Sarbatan, consisting of four
battalions, one battery, and five squadrons of horse.
The scene now witnessed would have been an admirable
study for a picture of "peace and war." The opposing
armies, in all the pomp and circumstance of war, moved
in compact order over the ground, already dotted with
the gathered sheaves of corn, whilst the husbandmen,
regardless of the roar of cannon in their vicinity, continued their reaping with the stoicism and nonchalance
of which only a Mahomedan is capable, whilst here
and there was to be seen a herdsman quietly watching his flocks browsing on the stubbly fields. In the
low ground between Tainalik and Kharkana, lay one
of these; for a long time his goats were a subject of
discussion amongst us, one thinking they were a Russian
column well in advance of the main body, the other
maintaining they were animals. The first shell whistling
over their heads served to strengthen the delusion, for,
frightened by the noise, and awakening to the sense
of danger, the goatherd commenced driving his herds
towards our camp, and they in turn, startled by the
fire, which now became hotter, spread out into irregular

order, and running forward some fifty or sixty paces, stopped, and gazed round in bewilderment. The anxiety of the villager to get safe away was natural, though ludicrous, and we could not help indulging in a hearty laugh as a few Circassians galloped forward, and soon covered the retreat of their future meals.

Being thus threatened, Mukhtar, by a heavy attack on his front, withdrew his force from the attack on Aras-Oghlu, moved to his left, and opposed the Russian division, who, covering their front with a long cloud of skirmishers, supported on either flank by a battery, moved on until they came within range of the Nakharji-Tepe. On our left another column advanced, covered with cavalry and guns, but on nearing Sarbatan it was halted, and opened a desultory fire, freely responded to by our guns.

In the meantime, the Russian general detached five squadrons of Cossacks, who threatened the left flank of our troops near Bolanik. Ghazi Mahomed at once went out to repel this attack, and though in doing so his Circassians came under the fire of a field-battery, posted on the lower slopes of the Kizil-Tepe Hill, they charged the Cossacks most gallantly, driving them back on to their guns.

Neither party seemed willing to advance; the Russians not caring to come under the fire from our entrenched position, and the Turks not venturing to face an overwhelming force of cavalry in the plain; so at sunset both armies retired to their own camp, a frightful hailstorm considerably hastening their movements. Taking advantage of the diversion on their right, Meli-koff pushed forward a couple of regiments of cavalry, two batteries, and two battalions to Ani—which they occupied unopposed, and held for a couple of hours, but unaccountably evacuated about sunset.

One thing I learnt, which up to that time had escaped the notice of the Commander-in-Chief, namely, that a strong cavalry camp had been formed at Tash-kale, about twelve miles to the north-east, and that the Gadikler camp contained one complete division of infantry. This had been a moot point in camp, the Turks maintaining that there were only cavalry there, while the English officers were equally certain that infantry formed the front line of the encampment.

I trust you will excuse the shortness of this letter. It has rained heavily the last three days. Everything in my tent is thoroughly saturated. I myself am wet through, and, though I fain would write more, I feel that the effects of quinine and the aching in my bones are but too sure indications that even damp blankets are preferable to wringing clothes.

CAMP ABOVE SARBATAN, FIFTEEN MILES EAST
OF KARS, *July 26th.*

The past week has not been marked by any stirring incident. Continual rain, violent hailstorms, and the absence of all military movements have made the monotony of camp-life almost insupportable. Our days are spent in watching the two Russian camps at Kharrak-Darrah and Gadikler, and vainly endeavouring to discover the symptoms of advance; our nights in futile attempts to make our tents waterproof. Our efforts in these directions were not attended with success till noon yesterday, when a long string of cavalry, *fourgons* and guns moving from Alexandropol to Gadikler told us that the long-expected reinforcements had arrived, and that our

R

eyesight had not been strained in vain. Alas! the endeavour to keep a whole tent over our heads was less successful, for the most violent hailstorm I ever witnessed broke over the camp, and raged with frightful violence for two hours. The hail, breaking the outer covering of our tents, drenched everything inside, and caused us a night of misery.

Until now, I had been wont to regard the stories of hailstones as large as pigeons' eggs as travellers' tales, but now I awoke to the fact that they were indeed a reality. Much damage was caused not only to the tents, which, originally made of weak material, had from exposure become quite rotten, but also to the sheep and cattle in the commissariat camp, many of which were killed by the violence of the storm. The crops in the neighbourhood of Sarbatan and Kharkana also suffered greatly.

The reports I have received of the relief of Bayazid reflect the greatest credit on General Tergukassoff, the commandant of the 38th division of Infantry. It appears that after the battle of Eshek Khaliass, on the 21st of June, where, with eight battalions he successfully resisted the continued assaults of Mukhtar Pasha with nineteen battalions, he retired on Zaidikan, where he remained until the 27th, when, being threatened in the rear, he fell back through Kara Kilissa and Djiadin, across the frontier to Igdyr. In this retreat he was cautiously followed by Ismail Pasha, who, however, never ventured to attack him, but contented himself with encamping at Moussin, on the western shore of the Balykly Lake. Ismail Pasha did not attempt to cut off his retreat, but remained satisfied with closely investing the citadel of Bayazid, the garrison of which on the 13th had suffered a severe repulse at the hands of Faik Pasha near Teperiskui, whither they had advanced to attack him, falling back into the citadel in some confusion. They lost many horses and some prisoners, and the Turks pressing them closely, invested the place. As might have been expected, the most strenuous efforts were made by the Grand Duke to effect the relief of the beleaguered garrison; and on the 10th of July General Tergukassoff, having been reinforced by four battalions, bringing up his strength to thirty-two field guns, three regiments of dragoons, four of Cossacks, and twelve infantry battalions, moved rapidly down on Bayazid. Although it seems that Ismail Pasha had warning of this movement—indeed, there is no doubt that he was aware of it, for on the morning of the 9th he rode over to Teperiskui, where Faik Pasha was encamped, and spent the day with him—it was not until that morn ing that he detached a brigade, under Hakif Bey, to reinforce the six battalions, two batteries, and about 10,000 irregulars who were besieging the town. At dawn on the 13th General Tergukassoff appeared on the north-east front of the place, where Major-General Munib Pasha, with three mountain guns, four battalions, and 1,200 cavalry, was holding a commanding position. Finding himself opposed to such a superior force, Munib evacuated his position and endeavoured to fall back on Teperiskui. A rapid movement of Russian cavalry cut off his retreat. Munib was forced to fight his way to the north, where Hakif Bey's brigade, consisting of eight battalions, a battery, and some 600 horse, was seen advancing. A junction was effected; but General Tergukassoff's onslaught was so vigorous, that the whole force was driven back on Kizil Diza, with the loss of three guns, 500 killed, and 800 pri-

R 2

soners.   Upwards of 1,500 wounded are reported to
have been sent into Van. Faik Pasha never attempted
to support Munib Pasha, and well merits the court-
martial which Mukhtar Pasha threatens to bring him
before.

From the accounts of two British officers who have
visited Bayazid since the relief, it appears that the
whole town is in ruins and filled with the bodies of
Christians whom the Kurds ruthlessly slaughtered.
The Turkish soldiers for six days were employed in
burying the dead citizens.   In this crisis Mukhtar
Pasha has not only shown himself a gallant and able
officer, but also a firm disciplinarian and a humane,
courteous gentleman. He openly spoke of this massacre to Sir Arnold Kemball, and not only assured him
that he had given orders for the ringleaders to be shot,
but that he had also sent instructions for the Haideranly Kurds, numbering more than 8,000 men, to be
disarmed and sent home. He complained of the extreme difficulty of apprehending the delinquents, as they
were always warned of their danger by their chiefs, and
got out of the way.   I may give two instances to show
his determination to conduct the war on principles that
cannot fail to merit the approval of European nations.
On the 10th inst. a report was made to him by the
head man of the village of Tchiflik Kaiah, near Kars,
that two Circassians the preceding evening had ridden
into the place and stolen a lamb, and that, on being
remonstrated with by the owner, one of them raised
his Winchester rifle and shot the villager dead. As
the man was easily identified, the Mushir summoned a
court-martial, who found the Circassian guilty, whereupon the Commander-in-Chief gave orders that he

should be hanged. All the chiefs begged his life, and one went so far as to threaten that if the man was hanged he would retire to his home with his whole tribe. Undeterred by this, Mukhtar carried the sentence into execution, and, to the dishonour of the irregular cavalry, I grieve to say that 1,100 men deserted the following day. The second instance is as follows:— Yesterday 500 irregular cavalry arrived from Diarbekir. Reports had preceded them as to their vague notions of *meum* and *tuum*, and, consequently, on their arrival in camp the Commander-in-Chief paraded them, and informed them that if any man was brought up for the theft of a single egg he would hang him, and if the culprit could not be found, he would cause the whole detachment to draw lots in his presence, and that he on whom the lot fell would suffer.

I must now, in the most emphatic manner, deny all reports of Russian atrocities in Armenia. I have had the privilege of accompanying Sir Arnold Kemball throughout this campaign, and, should any atrocities have been committed, I should assuredly have seen or heard of them. On the 31st of May, in company with Sir Arnold Kemball, I proceeded towards Olti, and on the way met hundreds of the Ardahan fugitives. So far from their accusing the Russians of cruelties, they were loud in praise of their kindness, and assured us that they had received free passes to their homes, which they showed us, and also five days' provisions. They told us that several German doctors had been retained to look after the Turkish sick and wounded, and that all those who wished and were able to travel to their homes were permitted to depart. In addition to the testimony of those men, I may mention that I have marched with the

Turkish army in the wake of the retiring Russian
forces from Zewin to this place, and that so far from
there being any signs of oppression, it is impossible to
believe that we were in a country forming the seat of
war.   All Mahomedan villages are left untouched, cattle
feeding on the pasture-land, the crops ripe for the sickle,
and all seems as if smiling peace, not grim war, was
around us.   To-day a village happened to be between
the Turkish cavalry and the Russian guns, and as shells
screamed overhead we saw the phlegmatic Turk coolly
driving his goats under cover.   Does this look as if the
Russians really committed the atrocities of which they
are accused?   One instance, and one only, has come
under my notice, which happened in this wise :—The
villagers of Tchiflik, to the north of Kars, were warned
by the Russians that as their hamlet lay between the
fortress and the siege-batteries, they must either move
into the fortress or into the Russian lines.   They not
only refused to do either, but were strongly suspected of
giving information to the Commandant of Kars which
enabled him to surprise the besiegers.   Consequently,
the villagers were driven into the fortress at the point
of the bayonet.   There are stories of women being violated, and of men who refused to embrace Christianity
being sent to Siberia.   These are all false.   I heard the
story of Tchiflik from the lips of one of the sufferers, a
man who, having held the post of personal orderly to
Sir Fenwick Williams in the siege of 1855, would not
have hesitated to tell the truth to an Englishman.   He
denied all the statements except that they were forcibly
driven out of their homes, and I feel sure that any
English general in similar circumstances would have done
the same.   Were I to harp on the atrocities committed

by Kurds and Circassians on the Christian inhabitants
of Armenia I should be dubbed a "Russophile," and
probably disbelieved. All I can say is that between
Kuipri-Kui and this I have not seen one Christian village
which has not been abandoned in consequence of the
cruelties committed on the inhabitants. All have been
ransacked, many burnt, upwards of 5,000 Christians
in the Van district have fled to Russian territory, and
women and children are wandering about naked, bereft
of their honour, and despoiled of all they possess. If
Turkey had more men like Mukhtar Pasha, her future
might yet be one of prosperity; but when her rulers
are of the stamp of the men who at Bayazid were
powerless to stop the massacre, it is no wonder that
many look on her as doomed.

The Russians now are in three divisions in front of
us, the main and strongest being at Kharrak-Darrah, the
second at Gadikler, the third at Tashkale, in Russian
territory. General Tergukassoff, with his left wing, is
at Igdyr, and Komaroff, with a small brigade, is holding
Ardahan. When they advance they will find a powerful
army opposed to them, who have been raised to the
highest state of enthusiasm by recent events, whose
equipment and organisation have been vastly improved
by the energy of the Commander-in-Chief, and who,
thanks to the zeal of Djameel and Hassan Pashas at
Trebizond and Erzeroum, are now well supplied with
commissariat and ordnance stores; indeed, until very
strong reinforcements arrive, a forward movement on
the part of the enemy is impossible.

CHAPTER XIII.

HEAD-QUARTERS, FOURTH TURKISH ARMY CORPS.

The Russian Retreat—Machinery of Turkish Staff—Medical Department—
An Amateur Opinion on Russian Reconnaissances—A Skirmish on the
28th—Cossacks left to bear the brunt of the Fight—Dash of the Circas-
sians—More Russian Reinforcements—Story of a Deserter —Strength of the
Invading Army—Demoralisation after Defeat at Zewin—Russian Casual-
ties—Projected Assault at Kars—Value of our Cavalry—Russians occupy
Ani unobserved—Mukhtar attacks them—Fresh Details from Bayazid—
The Instigation of the Massacre—Sir Arnold Kemball demands their
Punishment—Positions of Ismail Pasha and Tergukassoff—Turkish official
Telegrams—Their close Adherence to Truth—Interchange of Civilities
between Melikoff and Mukhtar—Ahmed Vefyk Pasha and the Stafford
House Surgeons.

CAMP, HEIGHTS ABOVE SARBATAN, *Aug. 2nd.*

THROUGHOUT the afternoon of Friday, the 27th July,
groups of officers might be seen congregated in front of
the head-quarters tents, anxiously scanning the Russian
camp at Gadikler. Their excited looks and vehement
gestures betokened some move on the part of the
enemy; so, inspired by curiosity, I strolled down about
sunset from the English camp and joined the party. I
certainly was not prepared to see the stolid Turk betray
so much eagerness and pleasure, nor was I prepared for
the news which was vehemently imparted by some of
them—namely, that the Russians were in full retreat,
that tents had been struck, and that cavalry, artillery,
and infantry were moving in long strings towards
Goomri. This has been reported to me so often during

the past fortnight that I must own that I received it with some incredulity, which was not lessened by the fact that my field-glasses, on which I most particularly pride myself, failed to show any movement of troops, except that the left of the enemy's position had been strengthened by four battalions, and that their artillery and cavalry encampments had considerably increased.

I mentioned my doubts as to the retirement, and my certainty as to reinforcements, to my friends on the staff; but my announcement was received with scorn, and not caring to argue the point, I, after again satisfying myself as to the actual position of affairs, returned to my own tent, struck with wonder at the absence of all trustworthy intelligence in camp, and marvelling greatly at the smooth way in which the machinery, rude and primitive as it is, of the Turkish staff worked. Untrained men, who had never handled a rifle in their lives, have in a few short weeks been converted into obedient, enthusiastic, and workman-like troops; and this, too, has been achieved by officers notoriously inefficient, and who, in this instance, are no exception to the rule. The various departments which are deemed in European armies so absolutely necessary for the harmonious working of the whole, are here wanting —adjutant-general, quartermaster-general, commissary-general, paymaster-general, advocate-general—are not to be found here. A chief of the staff, aided by two young officers from the military school at Constantinople, and one civilian secretary, comprise the staff at head-quarters. Divisional generals are provided with one staff-officer; officers commanding brigades with none. There is not an officer on the staff capable of making a military sketch. It was only last week that a supply of maps was received, and these are copies of the Russian ordnance survey. The men have received no pay for upwards of two years; they are poorly clad and badly shod; their rations are limited in quantity, and of bad quality; our hospitals are destitute of the commonest medicines, and there are but four doctors among 40,000 men. In fact, the administration has left no stone unturned to insure the discontent of their men and the defeat of their armies; and yet, in spite of all, in spite of the lack of officers, in spite of their faulty organisation, the Turks have checked and held at bay an army far their superior in numbers and equipment, and one which confidently expected to conquer Armenia in six weeks.

In fact, looking at the Russian troops as I have now seen them in some half-dozen encounters, there seems nothing to prevent them doing what they please with the Turks, and yet they hold back. Their troops, in appearance, in manœuvring, in organisation, in marching power, leave nothing to be desired; and yet, with the one exception of General Tergukassoff, their leaders appear to be men of little intelligence and no dash. The numerous reconnaissances they have conducted the last few days have been marked by the grossest incapacity. Although large bodies of troops, generally numbering from 10,000 to 15,000 men, have been employed in the course of these operations, detached troops have been pushed forward unsupported, and often sacrificed uselessly.

On the morning of the 28th one of these reconnaissances was made. At dawn two battalions of infantry, four regiments of cavalry, and three field-batteries were detached from Gadikler, and, marching by Aras-Oglu and Ani, passed down the Arpa to our right

rear. At the same time five regiments of cavalry, two
field-batteries, and twelve infantry battalions, advanced
from the Kharrak-Darrah camp, by Chalif Oghlu, towards
Vezinkui. This place is held by Hassan Hami Pasha,
late commandant of Kars, with twelve battalions, two
batteries, and a few hundred irregular horse. Fearing
for this position, Mukhtar Pasha detached Major
General Edhem Pasha with his cavalry brigade, numbering nearly 3,000 sabres, to the Yagni Tepe, a lofty
conical hill some four miles north of Vezinkui to operate on the Russian flank. By the time Edhem Pasha
had reached this position the lower slopes were held by
a body of Cossacks, while the main Russian column,
passing round the western slopes, had come under fire
of the guns on the Vezinkui position. They replied
vigorously to this, and, rapidly moving forward his
cavalry, the Russian general was enabled to capture a
small convoy of provisions *en route* from Kars to the
head-quarter camp. In the meantime, a very dashing
cavalry combat was going on on the eastern slopes of the
Great Yagni Tepe, where a regiment of Cossacks—some
say Lesghians—were endeavouring to ward off the flank
attack of Edhem Pasha. Why this regiment was not
supported by guns it is difficult to say ; and why it was
not drawn off when the main column retired is inexplicable. After most gallantly holding his own, entirely
unsupported for more than an hour, the Cossack commander, seeing that the main body were clear out of
action, endeavoured to draw off his men ; but being left
entirely unsupported, the Circassians, who all day had
behaved with the greatest gallantry, closed in on them
and pursued them round the hill with great vigour.
On emerging on the north side, however, a few rockets,

judiciously planted in the midst of the Circassians, sensibly cooled their ardour, and they wisely drew off on seeing two infantry battalions of the line manœuvring in support of the rocket-troop. The Russian commander now drew up his men in the plain to the east of the Yagni Tepe, and endeavoured to entice the Turkish troops away from the hills ; but Raschid Pasha, who had taken out an infantry brigade and a battery to support the Circassians, refused to expose his men ; so, after waiting for more than two hours, and seeing there was no chance of provoking a conflict, the Russian commander retired unmolested to Kharrak-Darrah. In the meantime, four infantry battalions, two regiments of cavalry, and a battery had moved out from Gadikler towards Sarbatan, with the endeavour to entice Mukhtar Pasha from his entrenchments, but without success, and after remaining on the ground until 4 p.m., this brigade also retired.

It is impossible to estimate the Russian loss. That they carried off some dead I am confident, yet I am not prepared to receive the Turkish official reports, which say they left 300 dead on the ground, for I went over the field immediately after the engagement with Sir Arnold Kemball and his indefatigable aide-de-camp, Lieutenant Maitland Dougall, R.N., and we could only discover three Russian bodies, which, in conformity with Turkish usage, had been stripped; and two, I regret to say, were grievously mutilated. Eight Russian prisoners, Mahomedan irregular cavalry soldiers, fell into our hands. Our published loss amounted to 30 killed and 161 wounded.

From the prisoners we learnt that up to the 27th four regiments of cavalry, four battalions of infantry,

and three field-batteries, had marched into camp from
Goomri; and that rumours were prevalent at that place
that peace or an armistice would be concluded in the
course of the next few days. I am forgetting the
Russian brigade which marched round Ani on Saturday
morning: it returned about sunset; but I am unable to
report its movements, except that it never came into
collision with our troops.

From a deserter of a Russian dragoon regiment, who
gave himself up to our outposts on the 29th, I have
learnt some details of the enemy's forces, which may
account for the want of success achieved by General
Loris Melikoff in the campaign, as well as for his inactivity at the present moment. It appears from this
man's statement that at the outbreak of the war the
Russian army of the Caucasus consisted of seven complete infantry divisions—namely, the Grenadier, the
19th, 20th, 21st, 38th, 39th, and 41st divisions; two
divisions of cavalry, five brigades of horse-artillery, and
eight batteries of Cossack horse-artillery. Each infantry
division consisted of four regiments of four battalions and
a brigade of field-artillery, consisting of two 4-pounder
batteries and two 9-pounders. I now speak of German
"pfünde." The field-batteries have eight guns, the
horse-artillery brigades have four batteries of six guns,
Krupp's 4-pounders, and the Cossack batteries have
four Krupp 3-pounder mountain guns. There were
also three rocket batteries attached to the cavalry
divisions. General Melikoff's army consisted of the
Grenadier and 39th divisions complete, one brigade
from the 19th and one from the 20th division. The
Batoum forces consisted of the 41st division complete
and a second division composed of brigades of other

corps. General Tergukassoff, operating on Bayazid and the line of the Araxes, has the 38th division complete. The distribution of the cavalry and artillery I cannot give you with any accuracy, except that I know the 2nd division of cavalry, with a rocket troop, was with Tergukassoff, who had the artillery of his own division complete. Loris Melikoff had eighty field-guns, one rocket troop, and a cavalry division, consisting of three dragoon and four Cossack regiments; but his force has been considerably strengthened since the commencement of operations. The 39th division was detached to aid in the capture of Ardahan, and subsequently rejoined head-quarters at Kars; and the Grenadier division proceeded, under General Heimann, to force Mukhtar Pasha back from Zevin. According to my informant's story, it appears that this division suffered so heavily in the battle of the 25th of June that on its return march it was moved round by Vezinkui and Ani into Russian territory, and never rejoined the head-quarters at all. Where it has been sent he is unable to say; but it would be either to Erivan or Tiflis, as it has never even passed through Goomri. The story of another deserter, a Pole, who was servant to the commandant of artillery, confirms this, and says the Grenadier division had to fall back owing to failure of ammunition, and that for three days after the fight the men had no rations. It must be borne in mind, however, that deserters, in order to insure good treatment, are very likely to exaggerate the difficulties of the army they leave, and that not only do the Russian official accounts put down the casualties at under 1,000, but that the numerous letters from officers found in the intercepted letter-bag on the 29th of June, while freely criticising Heimann's dispositions,

never put the loss at more than from 900 to 1,000 men.
The Polish gunner gave some interesting details regarding his own corps during the siege of Kars. He stated
the number of casualties to have been seventy killed
and 156 wounded, and he added that four guns had
been disabled, one from a Turkish shot and three from
the rapidity of their own fire. He also said that during
the twelfth night of the siege all arrangements were
made for assaulting the fortress, and that at 10 p.m.
the columns were all drawn up, and an extra ration of
liquor served out to the men, when the accidental discharge of a gun in one of the Russian batteries alarmed
the Turks, who at once opened a very heavy fire from
the Mukhliss and Karadagh redoubts, and the attempt
had to be abandoned. This account was confirmed by
Hassan Bey, colonel of the Turkish artillery, who states
that on that night a gun was fired from the siege batteries, which he vigorously replied to on the supposition
that an assault was intended.

On Sunday, the 29th of July, no movements were
made; but on Monday, the 30th, at noon, we were
somewhat surprised at seeing a hurried stir in the head-
quarters camp. We learnt that the Russians had suddenly moved down from Tashkale and occupied Ani in
force. To mount our horses and canter through the
tents of the first division to the extreme right of our
position was, perhaps, the work of half an hour, and I
could scarcely credit my senses when I saw encamped
on the plains of Ani a division of infantry, four field-
batteries, and two regiments of cavalry. The whole
road from Tashkale was covered with strings of waggons
and detachments of cavalry. The fact that this move
was carried out in broad daylight, within full view of

the troops on the Nakharji-Tepe, within two miles of our right cavalry brigade, and within five miles of our main camp, shows of what miserable material our horse are composed, and what enormous difficulties Mukhtar Pasha has to contend against. It was not until the greater portion of this division was encamped, and their outposts, consisting of two battalions, twelve field-guns, and two regiments of cavalry, had been pushed forwards to the vicinity of Chela, that the Commander-in-Chief learnt the news, when he at once detached Lieutenant-General Raschid Pasha with fourteen battalions and three mountain guns to attack from the south, while he, with both cavalry brigades, moved down towards Chela to engage the enemy's outposts. As he advanced across the open between Kozludja and Chela, the Russian guns opened fire, and after a round or two succeeded in getting the range of the Circassians, who immediately commenced tailing away in such numbers that Mukhtar deemed it advisable to order them to retire at once, when Edhem Pasha moved them round to the northern slopes of the Nakharji-Tepe, where, under cover of its guns, and also protected by the extremely rugged nature of the ground, they were presumably safe from attack.

In order to divert attention from Raschid Pasha's movement, Mukhtar engaged the Russian artillery in a duel with his horse batteries, and threatened them with an infantry attack, but all was of no avail, for owing to the deep precipitous ravines to the south of Ani, which is a ruined fortified town, in a very commanding position, and possessing great capabilities of defence, Raschid Pasha was forced to draw off his men without even threatening the place; and, finding all opposition withdrawn, the Russian general called in his outposts, and continued the pitching of his camp.

I have received fresh details concerning the lamentable occurrences at Bayazid, and as they come from an official source, I am justified in claiming some attention for them. I gather that after the engagement at Teperiskui on the 13th of June, between Faik Pasha's division and the Russian garrison, the latter, being overpowered, fell back on the citadel. The infantry succeeded in reaching it in safety; but the cavalry were surrounded by some 6,000 Kurdish cavalry, under a Moolah, named Sheik Jelaludeen, and called upon to surrender. Their fate I have previously related, and to dwell upon it can do no good. After deliberately murdering the Cossacks, the Kurds, under their fanatical leaders, Sheik Jelaludeen, Obeidullah of Nari, Sheik Pekar of Vastan, Fahim Effendi, Mahomed Beg of Julamerik, Sheik Tell, and his nephew Osman, both of Sert, and Takhir Beg of Van, entered Bayazid. The scene that ensued was one of unparalleled horror. The town contained 165 Christian families, and all of the men, women, and children were ruthlessly put to the sword. A Turkish officer who visited the town a few days subsequently states that there was not a single inhabitant left; all had fled, and, including Russian prisoners, upwards of 2,400 people had been killed. In every house he entered small groups of dead were lying shockingly mutilated and in the most revolting and indecent positions. Captain M'Calmont, who visited the place shortly after the Russian relief, states that it is entirely deserted, and a mere heap of ruins; also, that soldiers were employed for six days in burying the dead, the number of whom it was impossible to estimate. On

s

hearing of this massacre, Mukhtar Pasha at once sent
down orders to have the Kurds disbanded and disarmed, and their ringleaders shot. They, however,
anticipated the first of these instructions by throwing
down their arms and deserting *en masse* on the approach
of Tergukassoff's column on the 10th of July. Safe in
their mountain fastnesses, these miscreants will defy the
Commander-in-Chief's orders, and unless Europe sternly
demands their execution, and deputes officials to see the
sentences carried into effect, they will escape. We are
very fortunate in possessing an officer of Sir Arnold
Kemball's calibre with the Turkish head-quarters. He
has strongly impressed on Mukhtar Pasha the necessity of
inflicting summary punishment on these vile scoundrels.
Immediately communications were opened between
Mukhtar Pasha's forces and the Van column, he
detached Captain M'Calmont to Ismail Pasha's camp,
with instructions to point out to that officer the horror
with which these atrocities would be regarded by the
whole civilised world, and the injury that would accrue
to Turkey owing to their perpetration. He requested
that he might be furnished with a list of the authors
and the punishments meted out to them, and directed
that in the event of any further atrocities being committed Captain M'Calmont was to leave the Turkish
camp immediately, and to report to Ismail Pasha his
reasons for doing so. I fear that the ringleaders will
not be apprehended, and I am aware that Mukhtar
Pasha holds out but small hopes of his ability to put his
hands upon them. The employment of this irregular
soldiery, the savage mode of warfare they practise, the
cruelties and outrages they have committed, and the
failure to bring them to punishment, must surely

alienate from Turkey the support of the few who yet
hold to her. While on the subject of these atrocities,
it is but just that I should state that Ahmed Mukhtar
Pasha has received Sir Arnold Kemball's representations
in a friendly spirit, that he has exerted himself, and, as
far as his own immediate command is concerned, has
fairly well succeeded in keeping his irregular troops in
hand. He has cordially concurred in General Kemball's
demands for the punishment of the Bayazid criminals;
and, adjudging Lieutenant-General Faik Pasha to be
in blame, inasmuch as he was in command of the force
and was unable to stop the massacre, he has suspended
him, and directed that he shall be brought before a
court-martial. This latter statement, though received
from the highest authority, must be accepted with the
reservation due to all Turkish official reports, as I hear
from a British officer now at Bayazid that Faik Pasha
still commands a division there.

Mushir Ismail Hakki Pasha, governor of Erzeroum,
is in command of the army corps which is now encamped
at Narriman, some four miles west of the town of
Bayazid. It consists of five batteries of artillery, 4,000
cavalry, of which all but 500 are irregulars and Kurds,
twenty-six battalions of infantry, and 3,000 irregular
infantry. The force is divided into two divisions of
thirteen battalions each, commanded respectively by
Lieutenants-General Faik and Reiss Ahmed Pasha.
The brigade commanders are Hussein Avni Pasha
and Hakif Bey to the first, Shahin Pasha and Mahomed
Bey to the second division. Opposed to this force is
Tergukassoff, just inside the Russian frontier, with
detachments at Igdyr and Koolpi. He has with
him, as far as I can learn, twelve battalions of infantry,

five regiments of cavalry, and thirty-two guns; but it is rumoured that reinforcements, in the shape of one complete division, are within three days' march of him. If this is the case, it will fare badly with Ismail Pasha, who, although he was following Tergukassoff with a force double that of the Russians, never once dared attack in the retreat from Zaidikan.

I have been much amused by a perusal of Turkish official telegrams of this campaign. Mukhtar Pasha, reporting the engagement of Khaliass, states that after thirty-three hours' hard fighting the Russian army was cut in two, and fled in disorder, pursued by him. In point of fact, the fight lasted eight hours, during which time eight battalions of Tergukassoff's army held their ground against Mukhtar's division of nineteen battalions, and though they fell back to Zaidikan on the following day, the Turks never advanced from Khaliass until the 27th, when the Russians effected a most masterly retreat through Kara Kilissa and Dijadin to Igdyr. The Turkish general so far failed in his duty as to have to report to the Commander-in-Chief that he was ignorant of the route pursued by Tergu-kassoff, and the feat performed by that dashing and intrepid officer in relieving the garrison of Bayazid in the face of a force of double his own strength within one fortnight of the time he was reported as fleeing before the Turkish right wing, with his army demoralised and his guns buried, shows that Ismail Pasha must have overrated considerably his success at Kara Kilissa and Zaidikan. I am assured by an English gentleman who accompanied the Turkish troops in this march, that the only Russian corpses he saw by the road were those disinterred by Kurds from the burial-ground at Zaidikan, so I can scarcely credit the report that the infection from decomposing bodies was the cause of the slowness of Ismail's advance. Turning again to the operations of this corps from the date of our leaving the camp at Zewin on the 30th of June, until the 14th of July, when Loris Melikoff made a reconnaissance in front of our camp at Vezinkui, not a shot was exchanged between Mukhtar Pasha's forces and the Russians. The official despatches which say that the Russians had been defeated and driven successively out of Mellidooz, Sara Kamysh, and Beghli Ahmed, are utterly false. We not only did not come into collision, but we never came in sight of the Russians at those places. The sympathy that one naturally feels for the Turks in their gallant struggle in Armenia is deadened by the braggadocio and childish conceit indulged in by all ranks regarding their successes. The withdrawal of a Russian reconnaissance after its object has been fully effected is construed into a great victory ; its losses are multiplied by hundreds, and the enemy openly vilified as cowards and barbarians. With all this Mukhtar Pasha, and very wisely too, never ventures to oppose these reconnaissances in the plains, declines absolutely to hazard his army by attacking, and is unable to bring forward one instance of oppression or cruelty practised by the Russians in this country. As to reports of cruelty, I may mention that on the 28th ult., during the reconnaissance to the west of the Yagni Tepe, the Cossacks carried off a number of carts. The owners, complaining to Loris Melikoff that they were poor men, and would be ruined if he confiscated their goods, he assured them that if the carts were private property they should be released, and he immediately sent a *parlementaire* to the Mushir to inquire into the truth of their statement, and on learning that it was true, he allowed the men to take their *arabas* back to Kars. I am glad this act of courtesy produced a like civility on our part, as Mukhtar Pasha at once returned some cattle captured by his patrols.

I notice that Mr. Gibson Bowles, in *The Times* of the 8th of July, states that Ahmed Vefyk Pasha has reported to him that ambulances have been purchased with money sent by the Stafford House Committee and despatched to Asia Minor. I can assure the members of that body, who have so liberally sacrificed time and money in the good cause of relieving the sufferings of the sick and wounded of the Turkish army, that up to this day not one single ambulance or one single bale of medical comforts has reached Mukhtar Pasha's head-quarters. I have this moment returned from the hospital, where I have conversed with the only two qualified doctors in this camp, and they have not even heard of such help having been despatched from Constantinople. It is true that two English doctors, Messrs. Casson and Featherstonhaugh, are at Erzeroum, where, aided by our consul, Mr. Zohrab, his son, a boy of sixteen, and the American missionaries, they are working nobly among the wounded, who have been neglected in the most cruel manner. The British public should know the treatment that these English doctors received in Constantinople, where Ahmed Vefyk Pasha refused them any assistance or money, and where the English residents had to make a subscription in order that these gentlemen should have funds in hand to enable them to commence their labours on arrival

at Erzeroum.* I have learnt from the highest authority
that the most urgent representations were made to the
Stafford House Committee by gentlemen whose position
and past careers place them beyond suspicion, as well
as firm friends of the Turks, begging that in no case
might distributions of money be left to any Ottoman officials. These representations have been steadily
disregarded, and the result now is that on this 3rd day
of August there is an army of 35,000 men without a
litter, without one single ambulance wagon, without one
case of surgical instruments, and, neither here nor at Kars,
nor at Erzeroum, has a shilling of the money so nobly
subscribed by the English public been received. Would
that I had the pen of Dr. Russell to describe the
harrowing scenes I have witnessed, and the still more
terrible stories I have heard of wounded men left in
hospital for their wounds to mortify, rather than
Turkish bigotry and Turkish fanaticism should so far
relent as to permit amputation; men with undressed
wounds left to find their way to the nearest hospital,
forty miles from the scene of battle; maimed soldiers,
unable to walk, crawling on hands and knees to the
nearest well to slake their burning thirst and then to
die! The only gleam of sunshine to relieve this ghastly
picture is the patient endurance, the uncomplaining
fortitude, the noble heroism with which the poor sufferers have borne their terrible agonies. It was heart-

---

* This statement was contradicted in public print by Dr. Dickson, the
surgeon to the Constantinople Embassy; but I have subsequently seen and
conversed with the promoter of this subscription, who states that £60 were
by this means handed over to Dr. Casson, and Dr. Casson himself assured
me that had it not been for the generosity of a certain section of the
English community in Pera he would have been unable to start his
hospital in Erzeroum.

rending to pass by group after group of wounded, and to feel how utterly powerless I was to help. I have written and telegraphed strongly on this subject, and have not hesitated to blame the Administration, who are alone at fault ; and for this reason my letters have been detained and my telegrams suppressed. Is it to be wondered at that a man, with one drop of human kindness in his breast, could pass through the scenes I have feebly attempted to describe, and not boil over with indignation at the conduct of a Government which treats its soldiers worse than it does its dumb cattle—fails to clothe them, fails to pay them, and then, when sick and wounded, leaves them utterly uncared for ?

CHAPTER XIV.

MOSLEM AND CHRISTIAN.

Return to Erzeroum—Russians evacuate Ani—Incompetency of Commanders of Turkish Right and Left Wings—Christian Harvest and Moslem Reapers—Disinterred Russians—Behaviour of Kurds in Head-quarter Camp, and in the Right Column—English Hospital at Erzeroum—War Preparations at Erzeroum—Ani once more reoccupied—Conduct of the Russians in Armenia—The Kurds of Shoragel, Mehded, and Youssouf Bey—The Kurds in Alishgird—At Moosh—At Bitlis—In Van—The Treatment of American Missionaries—Of Armenian Villages—Apathy or Sympathy of Ismail Pasha—Skirmish at Taouskin—Another at Hiersai Bulak—Engagement on 18th August—Preparations for a Winter Campaign—War Taxes, and prompt Payment of subordinate Officials.

ERZEROUM, *August 13th.*

GENERAL Loris Melikoff's unaccountable inactivity and the rumoured advance of a Russian column on Olti, induced me to leave the head-quarter camp and to return to Erzeroum, where I shall be in a better position to learn the truth regarding the operations of the Turkish right and left wings, and be enabled, should occasion require, to move out to join any force which may become involved in actual hostilities.

At dawn on the 5th inst. we were somewhat astonished to hear that the Russian division, which in my last I told you had taken up a very strong position to the north of the ruins of Ani, had during the night fallen back across the Arpa River, and encamped near Kizil Kilissa. The reason for this retrograde movement is involved in obscurity, for, with a Russian force there,

Mukhtar Pasha's right was most seriously threatened, and any attempts by him to thwart an attack on either Kars or Vezinkui would most assuredly have been defeated by a demonstration by this body. Their retirement across the river thus left his right flank free, and was hailed by the Turks as another proof of the dread in which they were held by the Muscovites.

This movement certainly did not lead me to anticipate any immediate action on the part of the central Russian column, and coupled with the reported arrival of reinforcements, both with Tergukassoff's forces at Igdyr, and Komaroff's at Ardahan, forced me to the conclusion that the Grand Duke would throw forward his now strengthened right and left wings by Olti and Bayazid on Erzeroum, and endeavour, by cutting off Mukhtar's retreat to that place, to force him into Kars. This, of course, is a mere supposition, but the fact is that both the Olti and Bayazid roads are guarded by comparatively small bodies of troops, under generals whose knowledge of the art of war, and whose aptitude for command, can only be represented by a negative quantity; and as this is as well known in the Grand Duke's tent as in Mukhtar Pasha's, it would not surprise me any moment to hear of a strong Russian advance on this place, and of the Turkish Commander-in-Chief being forced into Kars, where, of course, his fine army would be useless for all further operations during this campaign, or to hear of the central Russian column interposing between Mukhtar Pasha and that fortress, consequently severing him from his base, placing him in an extremely hazardous situation, and eventually compelling him to fight his way through them to Erzeroum, or to lay down his arms.

The march from Kars to this place presented no features worthy of record, except that the villagers were busy cutting an extremely rich barley crop, the Mahomedans profiting by the absence of the Christians to appropriate their untouched fields. I followed the route taken by the Russian army in its retreat from Zewin with a view of ascertaining from the villagers themselves the extent of the "atrocities" inflicted by Loris Melikoff's troops. Passing through Vezinkui, the site of a Russian encampment, Azatkui, Vairan Kale, Tchiflekkui, Beghli Ahmed (a Christian village), I halted the first day at Kotanli. At this latter place the Russian division, marching on Zewin, made their first halt from Kars. At none of the villages, with the exception of Kotanli, could I hear of any cruelty or oppression. Everything taken was paid for—it is true, in rouble notes, but a ready sale was found for them to the Armenian merchants of Kars and Erzeroum. At Kotanli a man complained to me that a bullock had been taken from his herd by some Cossacks for which no payment was made. The deserted state of Beghli Ahmed I have before described to you. It bore the same appearance now. The neat fields ready for the sickle were being cut by Mahomedans from the neighbouring villages, who were loud in their indignation at the conduct of the Circassians and Kurds who followed the Turkish army.

On the second day I made a march of 42 miles, passing Ali Sophi, Kirk Punar, Sara Kamysh, through the pass of that name, over the Mellidooz plateau by Kara Orghan to Zewin. At none of these places could I find any traces of Russian cruelties, but the ghastly sight I met on the site of the Russian encampment at Mellidooz will ever live in my memory. The graves of their dead had been opened, and seventeen corpses, stripped of the clothes in which their comrades had buried them, lay exposed, naked, mutilated, and rotting, to the sight of the passer-by. This fact has been reported by so many, and officially so by our Consul at Erzeroum, that I feel I am repeating an oft-told tale when I write this pitiable and deplorable tale of outrage. I found some villagers who were willing for a small sum to re-inter the bodies. These men told me that this act of sacrilege had been committed, for the sake of the clothing, by Kurds, who thought it a pity it should be wasted. The crimes of these men are glossed over or else attributed to the Russians by their clansman, Mushir Kurd Ismail Pasha, late Vali of this place, and now commander of the Turkish right wing. In spite of Mukhtar Pasha's stringent and oft-repeated orders for the summary execution of the instigators of the Bayazid massacre, the blame of this foul act of treachery has been laid at the door of the Mahome-dan inhabitants of that town, while Sheik Jelalu-deen has been allowed to go scathless. Ferik Faik Pasha, too, through whose negligence and supineness the act was committed, still holds the command of a division, although a month ago the Commander-in-Chief sent orders for his suspension and trial. As long as the Turkish Government permit Ismail Pasha and Faik Pasha to retain their commands, and allow Sheik Jelaludeen to go free, so long does it connive at the atrocities committed by the Kurds, and is itself respon-sible for the lives of those who have been thus cruelly murdered.

I have been unable to obtain any confirmation of Ismail Pasha's reports of Russian atrocities in the

Alishgird plain. Although I have conversed with a great number of inhabitants, both Mahomedan and Armenian, they one and all maintain that they were treated with consideration by Tergukassoff's column, and that it was not until the Russians had fallen back from Zaidikan that they were exposed to the cruelties spoken of by Kurd Ismail Pasha, and these acts were one and all committed by Kurds, not by Russians. I myself can testify to the manner in which Loris Melikoff's column behaved to the inhabitants. It is high time that the Foreign Office should publish Sir Arnold Kemball's reports on the subject to the people of England.

It is only just, on the other hand, to state that with Mukhtar Pasha's column the Kurds and Circassians have been kept well in hand. Marauding and plundering have been promptly and severely punished; and though it is possible that this severe discipline may be attributable in no small degree to the presence of our military *attaché* at Turkish head-quarters, yet the Commander-in-Chief deserves more credit for restraining his irregular levies than he does even for the successful issue of this part of his campaign.

Prior to leaving the head-quarter camp I visited the field-hospital, with the view of ascertaining whether any stores had been received since the commencement of the war, either from the Stafford House or Red Cross Societies. I was positively assured by the Commander-in-Chief, by Yusuf Bey, the principal medical officer, and by Dr. Schoeps, the surgeon in charge of the field-hospital, that nothing whatever had been received from any English society. The state of the hospital was most pitiable : there was no hospital bedding or blankets ;

drugs were at their lowest ebb; there was one case of instruments (received only after the battle of Eshek Khaliass; there was no iron among the stores in any shape or form, no quinine, no splints, and but a very limited quantity of bandages. On my informing Dr. Schoeps that Ahmed Vefyk Pasha had assured the Stafford House Committee that he himself had purchased and sent out stores, blankets, litters, and ambulance-carts, he said that nothing whatever had been received from Constantinople for this army corps, except a gratuity of two medjidies to each wounded man in Kars and forty cases of empty medicine-phials. In order that I might have official authority for this statement, Sir Arnold Kemball was good enough to speak both to Mukhtar Pasha and to Dr. Yusuf Bey on the subject, and they both declared that no stores at all had been received from Ahmed Vefyk Pasha, or from any English society. On my arrival here I called on Dr. Casson, who assured me that, so far from Ahmed Vefyk having afforded him any assistance either in stores or money, he had deliberately declined doing so, and that had it not been for the liberality of the English at Constantinople and at Erzeroum, he would have been quite unable to commence work here, owing to want of funds. I am afraid I must take exception to Mr. Gibson Bowles's statement, or else must include myself on the roll of the " worst-informed of correspondents." Ahmed Vefyk's statement that he held receipts for the blankets issued to the Turkish soldiers was received with ridicule, a brigade-commander telling me, with a smile, that he could get receipts for any number of them from any major in his brigade. All I can say is, that I have spoken to the Commander-in-Chief, to both divisional and to two brigade-commanders of the 4th army corps, and they deny the receipt of anything whatever from Ahmed Vefyk. I am aware that he himself declined to furnish a statement of his expenditure to an officer in the employ of the Stafford House Committee, and absolutely refused either money or stores to Drs. Casson and Featherstonhaugh when they were passing through Constantinople for Erzeroum, and with a show of some rudeness, said :—

"We do not want a paltry £20,000 or £30,000 ; our hospitals are splendidly supplied. They need nothing in the way of medicines, instruments, or ambulance-trains. What we want is a universal subscription throughout England. Let every man, woman, and child show sympathy for our cause by subscribing even sixpence—that is what we want."

Where the money intrusted to Ahmed Vefyk Pasha has gone to I do not pretend to say, but this I can say, and with certainty too, that not a single penny of it has come to the 4th Turkish army corps, that at this moment there is not a litter or an ambulance-wagon at the head-quarters of the army, and that the field-hospital is almost without medical stores of any kind.

I have since learnt that the stores purchased by Ahmed Vefyk were sent to Batoum and Trebizond. It seems odd, however, that in spite of the numerous appeals made in the columns of *The Times* and other papers, no efforts should have been made by this gentleman to forward stores to Erzeroum and Kars, where even at the outbreak of the war heavy fighting was anticipated.

Mr. Layard has taken exception to my statements as to the hospitals in the Turkish army. The evidence of

my own eyes, coupled with the knowledge that every
word I have written must be borne out by the despatches of our gallant military *attaché*, Sir Arnold
Kemball, as well as by our Consul at Erzeroum, Mr.
Zohrab, and by Doctors Casson and Featherstonhaugh,
who repeatedly spoke to me of the difficulty they encountered in Pera on their way to the front, induce me
to adhere to the above text.

It is a pleasure to turn from the scene of criminal
carelessness and mismanagement daily visible in the
Turkish hospital to the clean, well-ordered, admirably-
organised establishment under the charge of Doctors
Casson and Featherstonhaugh, who have been sent
out here at the sole expense of that philanthropic noble-
man Lord Blantyre. These gentlemen were kind enough
to permit me to accompany them on their morning visit
to their hospital yesterday morning, and though I am
not one of those who care for ghastly sights, and must
plead guilty to a feeling of nauseating anguish when I
look upon the agonies that soldiers daily suffer, yet it
was with no small feeling of national pride that I noted
the comfortable beds, the snowy sheets, the clean
bandages, the cheerful, willing bearing of the patients
themselves, all showing such a marked difference to the
surroundings of the neighbouring Turkish hospitals.
When I contrasted the womanly gentleness and kindly
firmness with which my countrymen performed their
labour of love, with the perfunctory, indolent manner
with which the Turkish surgeons attend to their
patients, I did not wonder at the statement I had
so constantly heard as to the piteous entreaties of
wounded men to be transferred to the "Ingliz" hospital.
Through the liberality of Mr. Layard, Lady Kemball

and other English ladies in Constantinople, these gentlemen were enabled to provide themselves with many
comforts hitherto unknown in Turkish hospitals; but
their means are now at a very low ebb, and unless they
receive speedy and liberal support from a generous
English public their sphere of usefulness will be much
curtailed. Is it too late to reiterate the injunction that
funds should be sent direct to the officers themselves,
and on no account should they be permitted to pass
through the hands of any Turkish official? I forward
a letter to you from Dr. Casson, which will corroborate
all I have said as to the obstacles thrown in his way by
the Ottoman authorities, and will, I trust, prove to
even the most advanced philo-Turk that to trust in the
honesty of a Turkish official is to trust, indeed, in a
broken reed.

The new Governor of Erzeroum seems a man of a
very different stamp from Kurd Ismail Pasha. A
soldier by education, he has busied himself in frequent
brigade parade-days, in seeing personally to the repair
of the fortifications, to the mounting of the artillery,
which now has nearly all arrived from Trebizond. He
has made an excellent gun-road over the Devi Boyun
Pass into the Passin Plain, and has placed a number of
heavy field-pieces in the earthworks on that position;
so if the Russians ever find themselves within striking
distance of Erzeroum, they will meet with a very different
reception from what would have awaited them had they
pushed boldly on in June, when there was absolutely
nothing to prevent them marching into the town.

As I close this, a rumour reaches me, from an
authentic source, that the Russians have re-occupied Ani,
after a sharp engagement with Mukhtar Pasha's troops,

T

in which his cavalry were worsted, and that a brigade, amounting to four battalions of infantry, two batteries of artillery, and one regiment of cavalry, marching down from Ardahan, have occupied Zaim, or Yenikui, the site of their head-quarters during the recent siege. I hope to be able to send you particulars of these operations in my next.

ERZEROUM, *August 20th.*

Having accompanied Mukhtar Pasha's army in the advance from Zewin to the Russian frontier, I have been enabled to speak from personal experience as to the conduct of his troops on the line of march, and I must confess that, with the exception of a few cases of pillage, and one of murder, committed by Kurds and Circassians, the villagers were left unmolested, the country presenting no signs whatever of having witnessed the passage of the two armies. There is no doubt that the presence of Sir Arnold Kemball influenced the Turkish Commander-in-Chief in promptly repressing all acts of marauders. That the severity meted out to the offenders was unlooked for and unwelcome, may be judged from the fact that on Mukhtar Pasha hanging a man for murder, 1,100 of his irregular comrades deserted.

My statements as to the moderation shown by the Russians, both in their advance to the Soghanly Range and their retreat to Kharrak-Darrah, have been borne out by the despatches of the Turkish General, who only instanced one act of severity on their part—viz., the treatment of the Kurds of Shoregel. I can safely assert that not a single village their armies passed through was in the slightest degree damaged, and

although I made the minutest inquiries on the two
journeys I have made over the road, I have only been
able to ascertain one instance of property having been
taken without having been paid for, and that was at
Kotanli, where a bullock was carried off by the Cossacks.
As, however, I lost a horse from this village when the
Russians were not in the neighbourhood, it is more
than possible that the theft was the work of Moslem
thieves, who abound in the valley of the Kars Tchai.

As Mukhtar Pasha himself brought to the notice of
the Porte the treatment of the Kurds of Shoregel, and
as the Ottoman Government has communicated his
despatch to their representatives abroad, I have made
inquiries into the matter, and am enabled to give you some
particulars as to their past history and relations both
with the Turkish and Russian Governments, which
may in some way palliate the conduct of Loris Melikoff
towards them. The inhabitants of the Shoregel district,
which lies due east of Kars, are either Turkish peasants
or Karakapaks—emigrants from Persia. Prior to
Paskiewitch's invasion of 1828 the population was
entirely Armenian, but now very few Christian families
remain, the most part having abandoned their homesteads
and fled to Russia in 1829. The chief family in this
district is that of Khatoon Oghoulleri, and the head of
this family is Ismail Pasha, the late Governor-General of
Erzeroum, commonly known as Kurd Ismail Pasha, a
name of course derived from his Kurdish origin. This
family, owing to several of its members holding positions
under Government, has constituted itself the ruling
power in the district, the other Mahomedans being
virtually slaves of the Khatoon Oghoulleris. After
the Crimean war, Mehded Bey, the elder brother of Kurd

T 2

Ismail Pasha, collected a band of chosen spirits, and commenced a system of brigandage along the frontier, pillaging Russian and Turk alike. His wealth was a means of silencing all opposition on the part of the Governors of Kars, who recognised in him a turbulent spirit, likely to raise disturbances in their province, were his vocation to be interfered with, and they were only too willing to secure peace in their vilayet by the simple expedient of filling their own coffers. His depredations, however, grew so bold, that they reached the ears of the authorities in Constantinople, and they, learning of his power, and the difficulty there would be in repressing his band effectually, made him Kaimakam, or lieutenant-governor, of the Shoregel district, very much on the same reasoning that after the Mahsood Vaziri campaign of 1861 a famous robber chieftain, Futteh Roz, was made commandant of the British outpost of Mortaza. From the date of this appointment the name of Mehded Bey ceased to be a terror in the Kars district, but his occupation in Turkey was gone. He commenced brigandage on a more extended scale in Russian territory, and a lengthened correspondence ensued between the Governor-General of the Caucasus and the Governor-General of Erzeroum; dissensions rose to such a pitch that remonstrances on the conduct of Mehded Bey were addressed by the Russian ambassador to the Ottoman Government, and it was proved beyond doubt that on more than one occasion, members of his band who had been arrested by Turkish police, while robbing caravans on the main Persian route, had been released by the Kars and Erzeroum Pashas, under circumstances that savoured very much of bribery. At length Sir Robert Dalyell, late Consul at Erzeroum, took the matter up, on some English subject having laid a complaint before him, and on his earnest representations Mehded Bey was removed from his appointment. But until his death robberies, though on a smaller scale, continued; and I hear on authority that the people taken of Shoregel by Loris Melikoff are members of Mehded Bey's band, which has not yet been broken up.

It is a well-known fact, and I have it from an officer high on the Commander-in-Chief's staff, that Youssouf Bey, son of the late Mehded Bey, and nephew of Kurd Ismail Pasha, has been bought over by the Russians, and since the commencement of the war has been supplying them with grain. This man is an inhabitant of the village of Digor, and only a few days before I left the camp a party of Russians proceeded to that place to pay Youssouf Bey a friendly visit, who, fearing that a knowledge of the enemy being so close to the rear of his camp might come to the ears of the Marshal, determined to take the bull by the horns, so, warning them of their danger, he galloped off to Mukhtar Pasha's camp, and told him that a body of Cossacks were attacking Digor. The Commander-in-Chief, knowing Youssouf Bey's character, was not disturbed by this news; he merely detached Mustafa Safvet Pasha with some cavalry to drive them off, and warned the Kurd that it was only his relationship to Ismail Hakhi Pasha that saved him from the hangman's knot.

I give you a brief list of some of the atrocities committed by Kurds in the Van, Bitlis, and Alashgird districts. The majority of these, I am aware, have been reported by our energetic Consul, Mr. Zohrab, to her Majesty's Government; but I trust for that reason they

will not be the less interesting to the British public.
A complete list it is impossible for me to obtain, but
from all sides—from Turk and Armenian alike—I hear
piteous tales of the desolation that reigns throughout
Kurdistan—villages deserted, towns abandoned, trade
at a standstill, harvest ready for the sickle, but none to
gather it in, husbands mourning their dishonoured
wives, parents their murdered children ; and this is not
the work of a Power whose policy of selfish aggression
no man can defend, but the ghastly acts of Turkey's
irregular soldiery on Turkey's most peaceable inhabitants, acts the perpetrators of which are well known,
and yet are allowed to go unpunished.

On the 28th of June, on Tergukassoff falling back
from Zaidikan, Ismail Pasha's irregular cavalry, instead
of following up the Russians, proceeded to scour the
country in small bands, pillaging and destroying all the
Christian villages in the Alashgird plain.   Fortunate it
was that upwards of 3,000 Armenians placed themselves
under the protection of the Russian general (himself an
Armenian), and under his escort passed safely into Russian
territory, or the loss of life would have been ten times
as great as it now proves to be.   In Jeranos, Utch
Kilissa, Kaya Beg, Moola Suliman, Ahmadkoi, Kara
Kilissa, and Kheshishkui, all Armenian houses were
destroyed, and the few remaining Christians ruthlessly
put to the sword.   In the church at Utch Kilissa
ten men who had sought refuge there were brutally
murdered.   I have conversed with an Armenian priest
of that place, who indignantly denies that this was
committed by Russians—a statement made by Ismail
Pasha, and circulated by the Porte to the European
Powers—and who solemnly assures me this was the

work of Kurds after the Russians had passed through. Some of these irregulars, under the command of Hassaranli, of Sofi Agha, proceeded to Kaya Beg, midway between Kara Kilissa and Moola Suliman, and there killed Johannes Kehya, the head man of the village, and with him one Serkis, a merchant from Bitlis. They then went on to Moola Suliman, and killed an Armenian merchant named Ampassoon, having robbed him first of all his property, completely destroying the place, as well as the neighbouring village of Ahmad, where, together with some Circassians, they slaughtered all the cattle. At Kara Kilissa four Armenians found hiding were murdered, their wives violated and then killed, under circumstances of the most atrocious nature.

In the neighbourhood of Moosh, one Moussa Bey, a son of Mirza Bey, a Kurd from near Van, has been ravaging the country at the head of a small body of cavalry. The villages of Moolah Akjam, Hadogan, and Kharkui, having been first pillaged, were set on fire. At Ardouk he extracted £60, and at Ingrakam £40 from the head men of the village, under pretence of sparing them from destruction, and straightway set the places on fire. He then proceeded to a Mussulman village called Norashen, and hearing that an Armenian merchant of Bitlis was passing through, robbed him of all his goods, to the value of 30,000 piastres, and then ordered his men to murder him. At Khartz this monster entered the house of the Armenian priest, who had lately brought his bride to his father's home. Binding the old man and his son together with cords, this inhuman scoundrel ravished the poor girl before their eyes, and then gave orders for the murder of the three.

I can write no more. A bare recital of the horrors

committed by these demons is sufficient to call for their condign punishment. The subject is too painful to need any colouring, were my feeble pen enabled to give it. Suffice to say, that the town of Bayazid, having been pillaged, and more than 1,100 people slain, is now a heap of ruins.

Bitlis is entirely deserted—not a shop open in the bazaar. The villages of Philirieh and Ishmirondagh in its immediate neighbourhood have been completely devastated. In Van and its immediate neighbourhood they have been guilty of the greatest excesses. The American missionaries for months have been living on the lake in boats, fearing each day would be their last. The governor of the district, an able and humane man, has afforded them all the protection in his power, but he at last, for fear of exciting the Kurds against himself, was obliged to beg them to leave the place, when they took refuge in an Armenian monastery on the lake. From these gentlemen I received a long account not only of their own sufferings, but of the cruelties practised on all Christians in their districts. I am aware I shall be told that the Kurds were instigated by Russian gold, with a view of exciting European indignation against the Porte, but as the leaders of these gangs of murderers, Sheik Jelaludeen, Obaidulah and Pekas, Fakim Effendi, Sheik Tell and Osman of Sert, and Tahir Bey of Van, all served against the Russians, under the command of Kurd Ismail Pasha, this accusation falls to the ground. On the 4th of May, the Kurdish volunteers commenced to enter the city of Van, in obedience to the summons of their clansman Ismail; *en route* they committed much damage, attacking a caravan of cotton-merchants returning from Persia. and after completely looting the loads, they murdered in sheer wantonness the three chief men, and gutted the following villages: Khoosp, Pertag, Kuzilja, Noorkui, Dulozen, Nakhta. In Avgugli, they burst open the church, in which the women and children had been placed for safety, and violated them all, leaving them naked. The people of Latwantz and Shahbaghir shared the same fate. In Jaim, Sheik Jelaludeen's men, headed by their fanatical leader, seized everything of value, and compelling the villagers themselves to carry the goods, drove them off to their mountains. Out of 600 who started, only 400 finally reached Van in safety; the greater part of the absentees were virgins and young boys, doubtless kept for the worst form of slavery. This gang also attacked the village of Kordjotz, violating the women, and sending off all the virgins to their hills; entering the church they burned the Bible and sacred pictures; placing the communion-cup on the altar, they in turn defiled it, and divided the church plate amongst themselves. In sheer wantonness they emptied all the flour and oil they could find in the village into the streets, and mixing baskets full of manure with them, kneaded the whole together. They then attacked the vineyard of the head man, Melikian, cutting down all the trees, leaving it a mere wreck. Passing on to Kharbobitz, they performed similar acts of barbarism, and again at Kharagoons the church was desecrated and spoiled, women violated in the very streets; the Hooseeh monastery in the neighbourhood was attacked, the graves of the elders dug up, and, on these savages finding no treasure in them, used as latrines. Between Van and the Persian border, in the neighbourhood of Bashkala, the following villages were attacked and looted, all boys and young women carried off, whilst the remainder, stripped naked, were driven into the fields amidst the jeers of their Moslem tormentors : Soladeer, Vank-ki-kui, Bazingird, Eringanee, Hatchpodan, Kharodan, Malkaven, Arag, and Baz, were all thus treated ; in the first-named, some show of resistance being offered, fourteen men were slain.

Sheik Obaidulah's men rivalled their comrades under the flag of Jelaludeen ; these latter operated between Van and Faik Pasha's camp. They attacked and robbed the villages of Shakbahgi, and Adnagantz, carrying off all boys and virgins. At Kushartz they did the same, and killing 500 sheep, left them to rot in the streets, and then fired the place. Khosp, Jarashin, and Asdvadsadsan, Boghatz and Aregh suffered in like manner ; the churches were despoiled and desecrated, graves dug up, young of both sexes carried off, what grain they could not transport was destroyed, and the inhabitants driven naked into the fields, to gaze with horror on their burning homesteads.

The monastery of St. Bartholomew, the richest in the district, was attacked by Ali Khan's horsemen, and completely destroyed—its valuable treasury broken open, and its contents distributed amongst the robbers. A number of women and children from the neighbouring villages had taken refuge in the building. The most desirable of these were carried off, and a priest, in endeavouring to defend his daughter, was murdered. The monastery was completely destroyed, the grave of the saint, its founder, was dug up, his bones scattered to the winds, and his resting-place defiled.

Early in June a body of men coming up to reinforce Jelaludeen attacked and looted the village of Dushag ; amongst other acts of villany, the wife of the priest was violated in turns by a gang of men, before his eyes. The poor woman died from the injuries she received; and having mutilated the husband in the most grievous manner, they left him to die. Lesk, Hawantz, Shahbahgi, and Pergal were treated in like manner—women violated, whilst the young of both sexes were driven off into the most hopeless captivity.

In spite of Mukhtar Pasha's energetic remonstrances, the perpetrators of these outrages are allowed to go free, and the man who shelters and screens these miscreants is retained in his command by the Ottoman Government. As long as Kurd Ismail Pasha is at the head of a Turkish force, so long will the Kurds be allowed to carry on their war of creeds with impunity.

Should the Russians obtain reinforcements, I dread to think what may happen, for the rank and file will doubtless burn to avenge their murdered comrades of Bayazid, the desecrated graves of Zaidikan and Mellidooz, and the war, which hitherto (with the exception of the conduct of the Turkish irregular soldiery) has been carried on in a chivalrous manner, will be stained with excesses on both sides, and, like all wars in which religion is made use of as the incentive to fight, will be sanguinary and awful in the extreme.

ERZEROUM, *Aug. 24th.*

I am happy to be able to announce that on the 15th inst. orders were received from the Seraskier for the assembling of a court-martial here to try Hussein Sabri Pasha, late commandant of Ardahan, and Faik Pasha, the general of the Van division. The condition of the Armenians in the country through which Ismail Pasha's army has passed is pitiable in the extreme. Out of

122 villages in the Alashgird plain, all but nine are
entirely deserted, as I told you in my last. The few
Christians who had not availed themselves of Russian
protection were, on the retreat of Tergukassoff, bar-
barously murdered, and a number of hamlets were
burnt down. In the Moosh district several villages
were destroyed and many of the inhabitants killed.
The town of Bayazid and neighbouring villages shared
the same fate. In the majority of these places, men,
women, and children have been put to death under
circumstances of most atrocious cruelty. In spite of
many of these outrages having been clearly traced to
the followers of Sheik Jelaludeen, and in spite of the
cold-blooded murder of the Russian prisoners of war
being attributable to his instigation and actually perpetrated by his own men under his own eyes, it seems
more than probable that this monster will escape justice
altogether, as Kurd Ismail Pasha, the fanatical commandant of the Turkish right wing, has now reported
that the massacre of the Russians and of the Armenians
in Bayazid was the act of the Mahomedan inhabitants of
the place, not of the Kurds, although it has been proved
most conclusively that Jelaludeen did instigate, and his
men did carry out, this act of foul treachery; and, to
the shame of the Ottoman Government, this monster is
still an honoured guest in the camp of Kurd Ismail Pasha.

Mushir Ismail Pasha, commanding the army at
Bayazid, moved his camp on the 3rd inst. to Varpoz,
and subsequently to Zor, with the view of being better
able to observe Tergukassoff's movements. On the 11th
inst., being informed that a party of Russian cavalry
were at Taouskui employed in removing the inhabitants
to the interior to protect them from the Kurds, Ismail

at daybreak moved down on the place with one regiment of cavalry, 2,000 irregular Kurds, eight battalions
of infantry, and three guns. The village, being fourteen
miles from the Turkish camp, was not reached until 10
a.m., by which time five squadrons were seen escorting a
large convoy of country carts, horses, and cattle away
from Taouskui. On the approach of the Turks the
Russian cavalry formed line to the right, leaving one
squadron *écheloned* about half a mile in the rear, and
covered their front with dismounted skirmishers. They
then retired their main body by alternate squadrons
from the left. Ismail Pasha's Kurds, Arabs, and Bashi-
Bazouks made no pretence of closing even with the
Russian skirmishers, and, of course, his infantry and
cavalry did not appear on the field in time to be of use;
consequently, the Russians were enabled to draw off
their heavy convoy with the loss of only one man killed,
the Turkish loss amounting to ten. Captain M'Calmont,
of the 7th Hussars, who was present on the field, says,
in a letter to me, that nothing could have been prettier
than the manner in which the Russian commander
handled his men, and he commented in forcible terms
on the want of dash and utter absence of discipline and
order among the irregular cavalry of the Turks, who al!
displayed an irresistible longing to move to the rear
directly the Russian skirmishers opened fire. He owns
that, considering the Turks outnumbered their opponents by more than six to one, and considering that the
Russians effected their object of moving off a heavy
convoy with comparatively little loss, the affair at
Taouskui does not reflect much credit either on Ismail
Pasha's generalship or the valour of his troops.

On the 16th the Turkish right wing again had a

skirmish with Tergukassoff's cavalry. At dawn Hadji Hassein Pasha, a noted freebooter, whose men have gained an unenviable notoriety by pillaging the Christian villages in the Alashgird plain, was sent, with all the irregular cavalry, numbering upwards of 3,000, supported by one infantry regiment, under Colonel Hakif Bey, to Hiersai Bulak, fourteen miles south-east of Moussin, to which place Ismail had moved subsequently to the engagement on the 11th. The Cossack vedettes, being far outnumbered, evacuated the village and fell back, covering their retreat by dismounted skirmishers. As usual, the Turkish infantry were late on the field, and the irregular cavalry would not face the Cossacks, who retired rapidly through the villages of Mula Ahmed and Gulyan. Just beyond the latter Russian reinforcements were met, and the retreating Cossacks then faced about and made a vigorous onslaught on the Kurds, who retired in much confusion, losing some ten men killed. The Russians, however, did not push their success, for Shahin Pasha's brigade, which, on the sound of firing, had moved out from camp, now came up, and deploying in support of Hakif Bey's battalions, effectually checked pursuit and covered the retreat of the Kurds.

On the 18th there was a sharp engagement between the Russian main army and Mukhtar Pasha's forces. At about eight a.m. the Russians were seen advancing in five columns from their camps at Gadikler and Kharrak-Darrah; the strongest, which was on the extreme right, moved towards the Yagni Tepe, evidently with a view of preventing the Vezinkui division, under Hussein Hami Pasha, moving to the assistance of the main body. The defence of the front was intrusted to

Mahomed Nadjib Pasha, while the Commander-in-Chief, with Raschid Pasha's division, proceeded to the support of the Nakharji-Tepe, a knoll on the extreme right, which was threatened by three columns. As yet I have been unable to obtain more than the briefest details of the affair; but it appears that the Russians drew off towards the evening in excellent order, and that although Edhem Pasha and Ghazi Mahomed Pasha, Schamyl's son, attempted to harass their retreat with cavalry, they were unable to effect anything. Mukhtar Pasha himself bears witness to the extreme gallantry displayed by the Russian cavalry under the heaviest artillery fire, and more than one account states that their infantry were magnificently handled. The Russian retreat was slow, and throughout marked with much coolness and decision. What their object was it is most difficult to say, for no single attack was pressed home. Their losses must have been heavy, as ours amounted to more than 400 killed and wounded. It seems extraordinary that the Russian Commander-in-Chief should persist in making fruitless, half-hearted attacks against the Turkish position, which is virtually impregnable against any assault of Loris Melikoff's forces in their present strength.

It is evident the Porte anticipates a winter occupation of the Kars Valley by the Russians, as orders have been received that the engineer officers of this army corps should prepare estimates for the construction of temporary barracks on the Soghanly mountains for an army of 25,000 men. The site has not yet been fixed on, but I believe that opinion is divided between Tcharpakli and Sara Kamysh. Stone, wood, and water are in abundance, and wooden huts could be erected at a small cost at either of these places. Sara Kamysh being in a valley, is well sheltered, and perhaps for this reason is the preferable site, owing to the extreme latitude of the Soghanly range and the heavy snowstorms. The Syrian and Arabian troops will be fairly annihilated, should the Porte determine to keep them hutted during the ensuing cold season.

Orders have been received in the Erzeroum district authorising the Governor to appropriate for the use of the troops seventy-five per cent. of the harvest, leaving the remainder for the support of the inhabitants. This is termed an extra war tax, and is causing the utmost discontent among the rural population, who already have been called upon for contributions far beyond their means. Mahomedans and Christians alike rail at the intolerable exactions of the Government authorities, who pay for nothing that they export in the Sultan's name. Where the money goes is a mystery. With the exception of officers in the highest grade, whose complaints would be likely to reach Constantinople, not a soul in this army has seen pay for two years. A colonel of artillery informed me that no officer or man in his command had received any for forty-seven months. The foreign doctors in the employment of the Porte yesterday brought a most painful case to my notice, where a poor Italian veterinary surgeon was actually dying of starvation in this city, having received no pay, allowances, or rations for twenty-two months. They themselves are many months in arrears, and it is only owing to the untiring exertions of our indefatigable consul, Mr. Zohrab, that they ever receive even their pecuniary compensation in lieu of rations.

Ground between
KARS
AND
ALEXANDROPOL,
to illustrate operations
OF SIEGE OF KARS, BATTLES OF KIZIL TEPE,
YAGNI AND ALADJA.

Scale of English Miles.

London: Cassell, Petter & Galpin.

CHAPTER XV.

TURKISH SUCCESSES.

Battle on 18th August—Attack on the Nakharji-Tepe unsuccessful—Russians
fail to press home any of their Assaults—Turkish Losses—Stripping the
Dead—Skirmishes between Ismail and Tergukassoff at Khalifin and Abazgool
—Battle of Kizil-Tepe—Successful Assault of the Hill by Mehemed Bey—
Gallant Attempt of the Abkhasian Prince to retake it—He is Wounded—
Sheremetieff succeeds to the Command—Melikoff arrives with Reinforcements—Defeat of the Russians—Losses on both Sides—Reinforcements
called for by both Mukhtar and Ismail—Mr. Zohrab's position in Erzeroum
—Paper Organisation of the Ottoman Army and its actual Condition—Drill
and Discipline—Skirmishers and Sentries—Taxation in Armenia—Movements of Ismail Pasha.

ERZEROUM, *September 3rd.*

A SHARP touch of the sun, which has confined me to bed
for the past ten days, prevented me from forwarding you
my usual weekly budget last mail, and repeated attacks
of fever, which retard my recovery, must be my excuse
for a brief letter to-day. I have been enabled to collect
some particulars of the battles near Kars on the 18th
and 25th of August from trustworthy eye-witnesses.
In both of them the Turks were victorious, and in the
latter engagement, where they assaulted the Russian
camp, they proved that they are a match for their opponents in the open field. The result of these victories
has been to instil fresh courage and enthusiasm into
Mukhtar Pasha's troops, to improve the *morale* of his
men—in fact, to double the value of the fighting
strength of his army.

U

It appears that at dawn on the 18th the Russian forces were descried drawn up in the plain between Gadikler and the Turkish camp. Their strength was computed at from forty-two to forty-eight battalions of infantry, 112 guns, and ten regiments of cavalry. They advanced in five columns, making their first attack on the villages of Kharkana and Tainalyk, which were only held by small detachments of irregulars, and, having occupied them, commenced a violent cannonade on the Turkish entrenchments and on the villages of Hadjiveli and Sarbatan, in which were outposts of considerable strength, the defence, however, was not vigorous, and by 8 a.m. the enemy were in possession of Sarbatan, whence, moving their guns into the cover afforded by the banks of the Mazra stream, they opened a violent cannonade on the head-quarter camp. Situated on the slopes above Kharkana, their guns were served most accurately, and although owing to the steep embankments behind them, and the fact that the percussion shells plunging into the soft soil often failed to burst, the losses were not heavy, yet the moral effect of the storm of shells was such as to open Mukhtar's eyes to the fact that his men would not advance under such a deadly fire. They then moved forward a column, with four batteries, and commenced a heavy artillery fire on the Nakharji-Tepe, a conical hill on the extreme right of the Turkish position, which was held by one battalion, strongly entrenched, with three field-pieces in an earthwork. This knoll rises to a height of 800 feet above the plain, the sides are smooth, but very steep, having a gradient of over forty-five degrees, and it can only be approached by a single path in the rear. Thus it may well be considered impregnable; indeed, it seems the Russians

thought so, for they never pressed their attack, merely
contenting themselves with a violent cannonade, which
did but trifling execution, the garrison losing only three
killed and seventeen wounded The majority of the
shells, being necessarily fired at a great elevation and
at a range of 3,000 yards, passed clean over the crest,
bursting harmlessly in the rocky ravines in the rear.
The Russians using only percussion fuses, the projectiles were absolutely harmless to the defenders, who
were reinforced at 10 a.m. by three battalions and
cavalry, under Schamyl's son, and thus defied attack.

While these two columns were threatening the
right front of the camp, it became apparent that the
remainder of the Russian forces were about to prosecute
a determined attack on the Vezinkui position, to which,
on the first appearance of fighting, Mukhtar Pasha had
despatched Major-General Mahomed Nadjib Pasha with
six battalions and two batteries. He took up a position
to the west of the Yagni Tepe, and was promptly sup
ported by Hussein Hami Pasha from Vezinkui, with
twelve battalions and two more batteries, while Edhem
Pasha, with all the regular cavalry and some 3,000
Circassians, also lent his assistance. Opposed to this
force were eight battalions of infantry, four batteries,
and seven regiments of cavalry, the remainder of the
Russian forces being held in reserve. These were some
1,200 yards north of Yagni Tepe, and from 9 a.m.
to 2 p.m. a violent cannonade was kept up from both
sides, but with small results. The Turks held the
ridges connecting the hills, from which the Russians
made but one ineffectual attempt to dislodge them. At
noon Edhem Pasha moved his cavalry round, with the
intention of cutting off the Russian retreat. A regiment

of dragoons charged him in flank, but was repulsed with a loss of fifty killed. Shortly after this, Major-General Shefket Pasha, with a force of eight battalions and two batteries, assaulted and carried the village of Sarbatan. This was effected in conjunction with Ghazi Mahomed's men, who, finding the attack on the Nak-harji-Tepe not likely to be developed, moved round by Tainalyk, and, threatening the flank of the Russian column, compelled it to retire. Following it up, the position of the enemy advancing on Nakharji became dangerous, and these, too, were forced back. Lieutenant-General Hadji Raschid Pasha, marching down on the Yagni Tepe with his division, released by the repulse of the Russian attack on the Nakharji-Tepe, threatened the column operating on the Yagni side. They were compelled to retire, which they did in good order, though losing heavily, leaving, however, only one prisoner—an officer's orderly, with his dead master's horse—in the hands of the Turks. With the retirement of the right Russian column of attack all fighting ceased. The enemy drew off on all sides, and, withdrawing their detached camps from Ani and Parget, concentrated their forces at Kharrak-Darrah and Gadikler. The Turkish losses are estimated at 114 killed and 352 wounded; those of the Russians are unknown. A Prussian doctor present on the field told me he counted between seventy and eighty dead on the ground, and that the contrast between them and the Turkish dead was most marked —the latter fine-bearded men, with excellent shoulders and legs, the former thin, attenuated boys, scarcely able to hold a musket. He remarked also that not a single Russian lay on the ground with a vestige of clothing. The sight of the naked corpses, he said, adds

to the misery of the task the surgeons have to perform.
Surely Turkey might try to prevent, at least, this barbarous custom of despoiling their dead enemies; but,
alas! both officers and men indulge in it, and the senior
officers even lend their sanction to the custom.

From the Turkish right wing we hear of a couple
of small skirmishes—one near the village of Khalifin,
where a detachment of Turks, consisting of four field-
guns, 1,200 cavalry, and three battalions, moved up to
support a cavalry picket which was in difficulties. The
Russians, numbering but two battalions, without artillery, fell back on Igdyr with but slight loss, the Turks
not caring to pursue. Our loss was five killed and
thirty-five wounded. On the same day there was an
affair between the Russian outposts in the vicinity of
Abasgool and Turkish irregulars there. The losses are
not known, but it appears that Ismail Pasha mentions
a noted Kurdish chieftain, Sheik Khalid Effendi, as
among the missing.

The battle of Kizil-Tepe, which resulted in a
complete victory for the Turks, has been followed
up by Mukhtar Pasha entrenching the heights to
the south of the villages of Gadikler, and holding
them with six battalions of infantry and five heavy
guns. I have been enabled to gather the following
details concerning the battle:—The 24th being the
birthday of the Sultan, Abdul Hamid, Mukhtar
Pasha in the evening assembled the commanders of
divisions and brigades, and unfolded to them a plan
he had decided on for signalising the day by a vigorous
onslaught on the enemy. The Russians, as before, were
in three camps, at Kharrak-Darrah, Gadikler, and Ani.
Spies had kept him informed for some days of the

watchword of his foes, and he had also learnt that preparatory to striking a decisive blow at his left, Loris Melikoff had drawn off the majority of the troops from his centre camp, the 39th Division having left it that afternoon, and that he had massed them at Kharrak-Darrah; indeed, it was afterwards ascertained that but one battalion of infantry had been left to hold the Kizil-Tepe hill, whilst three more were in the camp at Bash Gadikler. To the First Division was given the post of honour. The plan unfolded was as follows:—At midnight Captain Mehemed Bey, with his division (Hadji Raschid Pasha, the rightful commander, was in Erzeroum on court-martial duty), was to advance on the Kizil-Tepe. Favoured by the darkness of the night, and accompanied by Circassian spies, who possessed the watchword, it was judged he would gain the summit unperceived, or, at any rate, unsuspected. This movement was to be supported by the Second Division moving on between Kizil-Tepe and Utch Tepe, thus preventing the troops in Ani affording help to their comrades; whilst the main body of cavalry, supported by Hussein Hami's troops from Vezinkui, were to advance by Yagni and Khalif-Oghlou to threaten the Kharrak-Darrah position. The total number of men at Mukhtar's disposal for these operations were fifty-four battalions, eight batteries, and about 6,000 cavalry.

At about 2 a.m. on the 25th Mehemed Bey's division, consisting of thirteen battalions, with three batteries, having pushed forward by Kharkana and Sarbatan, reached the Kizil-Tepe hill, and commenced the ascent on the southern side. The Russians, deceived by the counter-sign being given to their challenge, permitted the advance of the Turks until too late; but on discovering their mistake made a most determined stand. This, however, was of no avail in face of the vastly superior numbers opposed to them, and they were speedily driven off, leaving eighty dead on the summit of the hill. Having gained the crest, and knowing that dawn would see him heavily attacked, Mehemed Bey commenced to entrench his position, and ere day broke had two batteries on the hill well covered in gun-pits, whilst his men had thrown up for themselves very effectual shelter trenches. As soon as it was light the captain opened a heavy fire on the enemy's camp at Gadikler, in which the utmost confusion reigned. The bursting of shells in the midst of the terror-stricken camp-followers only heightened disorder; tents were hurriedly struck, and left lying on the ground, only to entangle the feet of horses passing over them; shopkeepers in the bazaar commenced dismantling their huts, and packing all their portable property in *fourgons*, preparatory to a hasty flight on Alexandropol, whilst staff officers were seen dashing hither and thither, vainly endeavouring to get under arms the few soldiers left in the camp. The sun was scarcely above the horizon ere Loris Melikoff was made aware that his centre was in imminent danger, and his communications with the force at Ani threatened. Hastily getting his division under arms, he despatched Prince Tchavachavadzi (the chief of the Abkhasian race), with all the cavalry and horse artillery, to endeavour to shell the Turks out of their newly-won position. Placing his guns within 2,500 yards of the hill, and supporting them with his dragoons, the prince opened a terrible fire on the Kizil-Tepe. The Turkish loss, however, was comparatively slight, for many of the shells, passing over the crest, fell harmlessly in the gullies beyond, whilst many more, plunging into the soft grassy slope, failed to explode at all. His cavalry, however, were fully exposed to Mehemed Bey's fire, and one regiment, the Nijni Novgorod Dragoons, suffered terribly.

In the meantime Melikoff was advancing, by the road from Karajal to Kizil-Tepe, his men in three columns, he with the left moving straight to Tchava-chavadzi's support. Heimann threatened Sarbatan, whilst Komaroff opposed Hussein Hami at Vezinkui; but before the welcome reinforcements arrived the Abkhasian prince had been struck down grievously wounded, and some confusion was caused by the absence of any general officer with the cavalry. But Sheremetieff, who had advanced from the Bash Gadikler camp with two battalions, assumed command, moved the troops round to the east of the Kizil-Tepe hill, and endeavoured to carry it by assault. Time after time did this gallant officer lead his men up the steep slopes of the Red Knoll, under the deathly storm that rained on them from above; time after time were his men hurled back in confusion. Melikoff at the same time made strenuous efforts to assault the hill from the north, but with like success, whilst all Heimann's efforts to carry Sarbatan, and thus cut Mehemed Bey off from the main camp, were frustrated by the gallantry of Mukhtar Pasha's troops, who, inspired with enthusiasm by their success, redoubled their efforts, and in spite of the murderous artillery fire rained on them from upwards of 100 guns, drove the enemy back on to his main camp at Kharrak-Darrah; indeed, at one time it appeared as if this would be carried, and a scene of the

wildest confusion ensued. Tents were struck, and every
preparation made for a hasty retreat; but owing to the
personal gallantry of Generals Heimann and Komaroff,
who received a severe wound, the men were rallied, and
the Turks compelled to draw off, satisfied with their first
success, the capture of Kizil-Tepe. The Russian official
loss was twelve officers and 237 men killed, thirty-four
officers and 667 men wounded. That of the Turks is
421 killed, and 938 wounded.

Both he and Ismail have sent in the most urgent
requests for reinforcements, especially of artillery. The
only field-battery fully horsed in this neighbourhood
was at the Ghiurji Boghaz, and that, with a battalion
from that place, has been to-day despatched towards
Kars, leaving but one battalion, with one battery
unhorsed, to guard the defile leading to Olti.

Large bands of Circassian and Kurdish deserters are
prowling about the neighbourhood of the town plundering and murdering to the fullest extent they are able.
They are all armed with Government repeating rifles,
and, as there are no troops here, it has been found impossible to check them. Last night a village within
three miles of this was attacked, three men (Mahomedans) murdered, and 120 head of cattle driven away.
It speaks well for the English name, for the Turks'
knowledge of English justice, and still more for the
reputation in which our consul here is held by Mussulman and Christian alike, that the villagers should in
the first instance have come to Mr. Zohrab to beg him
to submit their case to the Pasha of Erzeroum. I am
enabled to state this as a fact, as Mr. Zohrab was in my
rooms when the men came to him with their piteous
tales. I have the more pleasure in making this inci-

dent public as I am aware that there is a very large
party, many of my fellow-countrymen, too, who, having
partaken of our consul's liberal hospitality, do not hesitate openly to bring accusations against him which they
must know to be false. Mr. Zohrab has not hesitated
openly to denounce the system of oppression that exists
in Armenia. He has not hesitated to denounce the
corrupt character of the majority of the Turkish Pashas,
and to show them in their true light to our Minister
at Constantinople. The feeling there being of an eminently Turkophile character, Mr. Zohrab's reports have
been unfavourably received, and doubts have been
thrown on their accuracy. Ask any of the American
missionaries in Armenia if the British consul has not
rather underrated than overrated the barbarities that
are openly committed. Ask them to whom they turn
in danger or difficulty ; ask them to whom they submit
all cases of oppression practised on the Protestants ;
ask them who is accessible at all hours of the day to
Mahomedan and Armenian, English, American, Austrian, or German alike, and they will at once answer,
Mr. Zohrab. To whom do the German doctors turn for
protection when unable to obtain their just pay from
the Turkish Government ? To Mr. Zohrab. He is
secretary and treasurer to the Stafford House Committee
here. He is the interpreter to Lord Blantyre's doctors,
and the instrument through which they obtain permission to perform operations. He is postal agent, house
agent, and forwarding agent to the majority of Englishmen here, and there is not one among us who on
arrival did not meet from him a warm English welcome,
a comfortable meal, and for whom he did not immediately find house-room. I have travelled with him

through the district, and can bear testimony to the way in which the lower classes—the agriculturists—turn to him as a guide and a friend, and welcome him in their villages. Thoroughly acquainted with their language, with their manners and customs, he is at home among them, ever ready and willing to hear their smallest trouble, and never forgetting a promise. Because he openly denounces Turkish rulers and the Turkish Government, because he openly states his conviction, founded on a twenty-three years' acquaintance with this country, that it will be the happiest thing possible for Mahomedan and Christian alike when Armenia passes out of the hands of the Porte, because he boldly repudiates the mendacious statements of Russian atrocities in Asia Minor, and because he has not hesitated to blame the Kurds, and their bigoted, fanatical chief, Ismail Pasha, as being the perpetrators of every outrage committed in the Van and Alashgird district, he is dubbed a Russian agent, and treated with discourtesy and disrespect by those from whom he is entitled to nothing but gratitude and thanks.

I have, in a previous chapter, given the paper organisation of the Turkish army, by which it will be seen that no European State possesses such a perfect military system as the Porte, but on examining into the actual state of affairs we find matters very different.

The Nizam battalions, as a rule, are fully officered, and each one has a surgeon, but the Redifs are very badly off—one officer per company usually being considered quite sufficient to answer every purpose in war. Discipline, in one sense of the word, does not exist, but crime is very rare. Strong drink being forbidden by religion, the Turks, consequently, are a sober, abstemious race, and drunkenness, the curse of European armies, is, I may say, unknown in the rank and file of the Ottoman army. I wish I could say it was equally rare among the officers, but I am forced to confess that, although I have never yet seen a Turkish soldier the worse for liquor, I have seen officers of all grades, from that of lieutenant-general downwards, in a state of intoxication. Articles of war exist, but are rarely called into requisition; more rare still is it for a court-martial to be held. Should a private or subordinate officer commit a crime, the *dictum* of the colonel or *chef du battailon* is sufficient to insure condign punishment; while in the case of an officer of superior grade, court influence or bribery wards off the evil effects of any *faux pas.*

In the matter of drill, I have yet to see a Turkish infantry battalion that could hold its own with our worst militia corps, while their cavalry are totally ignorant of the meaning of the word. To expect a Turkish cavalry soldier to take a fence would be to strike at the root of all their liberty. The artillery is by far the best disciplined and best drilled branch of the service. I have seen batteries walk past in a very creditable manner, but I have never seen them attempt to manœuvre at a faster pace. Of the sappers and miners I can say nothing. In Armenia, at any rate, they are like the snakes in Iceland—"there are none." Drill of all sorts is carried on with as much noise as possible; every bugle or trumpet call is repeated by every officer and non-commissioned officer in the battalion. The consequence is that at all the skirmishing parades the confusion is appalling. A faint attempt to copy the English system has been introduced.

Men skirmish in single rank on the hill-side, but in presence of cavalry invariably in groups. Supports move in the same formation as skirmishers—*i.e.*, either in single rank or in groups—reserves always in column of half companies or companies. Men fire as they please, and they generally please to fire standing. Guard duties are carried on in the most slovenly manner possible. The relief of sentries is never carried on in the presence of a non-commissioned officer, nor do sentries walk "briskly backwards and forwards on their posts in a soldierlike manner," for they never move at all, but stand on the same post until the next man for sentry strolls forward as a relief.

ERZEROUM, *Sept. 7th.*

I am not aware whether an account of the taxation of a country comes legitimately under the head of "war news," but as I have not seen any description of the interior economy of Armenia in any English journals, I am in hopes that the following brief notes may interest some of your readers, bearing as they do on the iniquitous system of government in vogue in this land, explaining in themselves the unequal burden imposed on Christian and Mahomedan, and the reason for the grave discontent that exists among the entire Armenian population. It is a custom sanctioned by usage, if not by law, that all Government servants are exempt from taxation, and as all Mahomedans except the poorer classes hold official appointments, it follows that the greater proportion of the revenues is derived from the lower orders, from those classes, in fact, who in England pay nothing to the State by direct taxation. By far the heaviest and most obnoxious charge is that for "military services." Mahomedans only are called upon to bear arms, but the Christians pay for their exemption a poll-tax of sixteen piastres per annum. I find on inquiry that in the vilayet of Erzeroum this impost has been increased to thirty piastres per annum for the last two years, and that, in addition to this sum, there is a permanent war-tax, which has existed in its present form since 1854, of twenty-five piastres per head on all Christian families.

The tax on house-property amounts to one-third per cent. per annum, but on mills and on shops and houses of business to ten per cent. Every man following a trade or profession pays ten piastres per annum for the privilege of pursuing his calling, while a Medjlis, or committee of merchants, in every city sits annually to fix the amount of profession-tax to be deducted from all men of business. This varies, but rarely is fixed at less than seven per cent. of a man's income, in many cases amounting to as much as fifteen per cent.

Government, again, claim ten per cent. of the harvest, the value of which is computed by an official specially appointed for the purpose. More often, however, the viceroy of a district farms the tax, and the "mooltazim," or speculator, who has purchased this tribute has a great field for extortion. Municipalities claim, in addition to the State exaction of ten per cent., a further sum of one per cent. for city purposes from all townsmen owning arable or meadow land, and this latter is subject to the same impost—viz., ten per cent.—as the harvest is. A charge of three piastres on every sheep and goat above the age of one year is levied at the expiration of each lambing-season. Horses, cattle, camels, and mules are exempt from this tax, but they are subject to a special charge of two and a half per cent. on sale, each sale having to be registered in public market. All wood brought into bazaars for sale, except for fuel, is subject to an impost of two per cent. Permission to erect new buildings has to be obtained from the governor of the township, who invariably exacts a handsome fee for granting a warrant to build, while the unhappy dabbler in bricks and mortar is further mulcted in the sum of ten piastres for every workman employed. Import and export duties, though very heavy, varying from three to fifty per cent., are often evaded by a liberal backsheesh to the Custom-house official. Indeed, many merchants pay a fixed sum per annum to these worthies, in order to insure a prompt clearance of their goods, and to avoid the trouble of Government dues. For the privilege of carrying arms every man (Christians are forbidden to use firearms) is called upon to pay two and a half piastres per annum for each gun he owns, but, I believe, except in towns this tax is never collected.

The proceeds of the harvest-tribute are remitted to Constantinople for State purposes, while the balance of the revenues is kept in the district treasuries for provincial purposes. By this means the governor of a vilayet is responsible for the payment of the officials under him, and each town is nominally called upon to disburse the pay and allowance of the regiments of their murkess or circle; Erzeroum, for instance, paying the Erzeroum battalion, Erzingjan its own battalion, and so on, so that really the Porte is not responsible for the non-payment of its soldiery. The onus rests upon the vali or governor of the district, and to show what a punctual regard they have for the performance of their duties, I may mention that I have conversed with men of nearly every battalion and battery in this army corps, and find that they are from nineteen to forty eight months in arrears.

I was unable in my last to give you more than a few lines referring to the movements of Ismail Pasha's force near Bayazid. It appears from information I have since obtained that he received orders from Mukhtar on the 1st August to move the camp from Narriman, five miles west of Bayazid, to some spot where he could better observe the movements of Tergukassoff's force, which was encamped at Igdyr. These instructions were coupled with the most stringent injunctions that he was on no account to cross the Russian frontier, and that he would be held personally responsible for any outrages committed on Russian subjects by his irregular soldiery. Notwithstanding these express orders, Ismail Pasha moved on the 4th inst. to a place called Arzab, near the Balykly Lake ; on the 5th to the Jila Gedik Pass ; and on the 6th to Zor, about seven miles inside the frontier, and six from Igdyr, where the Russian left wing, numbering, I believe, but twelve battalions of infantry, four batteries, and seven regiments of cavalry, were encamped. As might be supposed, the Kurds at once got loose, and the first day attacked a Christian village in Russian territory, killed seven men, women, and children, besides completely sacking the place. Tergukassoff, on the 11th, sent an escort of cavalry to bring off the Armenian villagers in Taouskui. This brought on the conflict I briefly described in my last, which resulted in the Kurds ignominiously declining to attack a small body of dragoons, less than one-sixth of their own number. Ismail Pasha is most indignant at the Russian General removing the Christians from beyond the reach of his fanatical clansmen, and asserts that he was about to forward a party of men to protect those very villagers from pillage, when Tergukassoff sent his men to escort them farther inside the frontier.

Mukhtar Pasha is, as might be supposed, justly indignant at this deliberate disobeyal of orders on the part of his subordinate, Ismail, more especially as it has led to the pillage of a Christian village in Russian territory, and the cold-blooded murder of inoffensive inhabitants. He has sent down the strictest orders that the offenders, whoever they may be, are to be seized, and, regardless of their rank or position, hanged on the scene of their crime. It is, however, much to be feared that Ismail's fanaticism and his dread of offending his own tribe will lead him to screen the culprits. As yet I have been unable to learn of any men having been executed for participation in the Bayazid massacre, and I know on the authority of an officer recently returned from the army that both Jelaludeen and Faik Pasha, in spite of the Commander-in-Chief's orders, are still at large.

Sir Arnold Kemball has, as usual, shown much determination and promptitude in calling on Mukhtar Pasha for the just and speedy punishment of all the perpetrators of these barbarities; but it is only just to add that the Commander-in-Chief has invariably met our gallant military attaché half-way, and has proved himself throughout this campaign a man determined that no odium of brutality shall mark the track of his army. Loris Melikoff has nothing to fear should his wounded fall into the hands of Mukhtar Pasha.

V

CHAPTER XVI.

ARMENIANS—THE TRUE STORY OF BAYAZID.

Arrival of Stafford House Stores at Erzeroum—State of Hospitals in Main Army and in Right Wing—Turkish Authorities refuse Permission to amputate— Refuse Carriage for Medical Stores—Our Hospitals in Erzeroum—My Ideas of the Armenian—Their Exodus to Russian Territory, caused by Kurdish Atrocities—Denial of this by Kurd Ismail Pasha—Changes in the Turkish Staff—Jealousy of General Kohlmann—Court-martial on Sabri and Faik Pashas—Hussain Avni, and Zarif Mustafa—The true Story of Bayazid— Ferocity of the Kurds—Supineness of Faik Pasha—Neglect of Ismail to Support—Consequent Defeat of the Turks at Bayazid by Tergukassoff— Defence of Mr. Zohrab.

ERZEROUM, *Sept. 9th.*

I THINK I mentioned in one of my previous letters that Lieutenant Malcolm Drummond, R.N., last month brought to this place from Constantinople, at his own expense, several cart-loads of Stafford House stores, which were handed over to Drs. Casson and Featherstonhaugh for distribution to the hospitals here. The former gentleman, taking with him one assistant, has proceeded to Mukhtar Pasha's head-quarters with a large supply of medical comforts, as the only qualified medical practitioners in the camp were some weeks ago ordered into Kars. There has been very severe fighting, entailing heavy losses in killed and wounded on the Turks, so the arrival of Dr. Casson with his English supplies will be most opportune. On all sides I hear stories, from Turkish officials too, speaking of the frightful state of the hospital arrangements at all the

camps and fortified towns in Asia Minor. I myself was
a witness of the discreditable state of things both at
Kars and at Mukhtar Pasha's camp, where the hospitals
were destitute of drugs, where there were no beds for
the patients, and where there was not a single litter or
ambulance for the conveyance of the sick and wounded.
I, consequently, am not surprised to learn from our
officers at Bayazid that there is no hospital in Ismail
Pasha's army, not a single doctor with a corps of
35,000 men, and that sick and wounded have to be
sent into Erzeroum for treatment—a distance of 130
miles. It will scarcely be believed in England, but it
nevertheless is a fact, that here in Armenia, where we
have had upwards of 3,000 wounded in our hospitals,
until the arrival of Lord Blantyre's doctors not a single
case of amputation had been performed. On the day
after reaching Erzeroum, Drs. Casson and Featherstonhaugh went over the hospitals, in company with our
Consul, Mr. Zohrab, and the principal medical officer,
Ismail Bey. They noticed many cases requiring the
use of the knife, and pointed them out to the principal
medical officer, who kept a discreet silence. The following day they were handed over a hospital containing
about 200 patients—wounded men, many of them suffering from wounds inflicted two and a half months
previously. All their hurts were most neatly bandaged,
but on removing these there was scarcely one that was
not suffering from gangrene, and the poor fellows owned
that their wounds had not been looked at for weeks ;
in fact, as Drs. Casson and Featherstonhaugh have both
remarked to me, such cruelty and mismanagement they
could not conceive to have been possible. Having
carefully examined the men committed to their charge,

v 2

the doctors selected eight on whom it was urgently necessary to perform operations. They at once sent to Ismail Bey, who came down to the hospital and flatly refused permission for any amputations to be performed. Mr. Zohrab, our Consul, was present at the interview, which has been recounted to me by all three Englishmen there. Dr. Casson, on hearing this refusal, said, "But the men will die if these operations are not at once performed." Whereupon Ismail Bey replied, "Better that they should die than that they should become burdens on the Sultan as pensioners." Drs. Casson and Featherstonhaugh at once closed the interview by stating that if free permission were not accorded to them to act according to their judgment, they should return to England immediately, and Mr. Zohrab notified his intention of reporting the conversation officially. This frightened Ismail into granting permission for one operation (a slight case) to be performed ; and subsequently, on a renewal of the threat that the English doctors would return, they were permitted to exercise their own discretion in performing amputations. I am happy to say sixteen cases have been carried out successfully in the English hospital, whereas up till to-day not one case has been attempted by other than British surgeons.

I am aware that Mr. Layard has written strongly denouncing Dr. Casson's conduct in asserting that the Turkish Government prefer to lose their soldiers rather than that they should remain burdens on the State as pensioners. With all due deference to the ambassador's superior judgment, I must venture to uphold Dr. Casson's opinion. I have conversed with Turkish doctors, and with foreign doctors in Turkish employ, many of them strong Turkophiles, and they, one and all, have assured me that they have been unable to obtain sanction to a single amputation, and that the reason is as above stated—the senior medical officers are strictly enjoined by Government on no account to permit them. If Mr. Layard would only reflect for one moment, he would see that facts disprove his statement. If the Turkish Government are anxious to save the lives of the gallant men who risked their all, without even hope of reward, to stem the torrent of Russian invasion, why does the Porte not make some efforts to establish hospitals, to organise ambulances, to furnish instruments and medicines? As I have repeatedly stated in my letters, these things do not exist in Asiatic Turkey. With Ismail Pasha's army there is not one doctor. Does that look as if the Ottoman Government was anxious about the lives of its men? In spite of my letter of the 23rd of June, feebly describing the sufferings of the wounded in their march from Taghir and Khaliass to Erzeroum, and my request that litters might be sent out; in spite of Ahmed Vefyk Pasha's letter to the Stafford House committee, that litters and ambulances had been sent to Armenia, there is not one with this army to-day. One more instance, and I have done:—A few days ago a German doctor was ordered to Olti, where there is a force of some 5,000 men and no medical man. This gentleman called on Dr. Casson, and begged from him some stores, as he was being sent without medicines or instruments. Dr. Casson made a selection of three horse-loads of various drugs, instruments, lint, and hospital necessaries. What was his astonishment to learn that Ismail Bey had refused to provide carriage for these things, and had told the German doctor that if he wished to take them he must do so at his own expense. The same state of things exists at Kars, where typhus fever is raging, and where the doctors have been so terribly overworked that all four are on the sick-list with that dread disease. A German doctor in Turkish employ has written me several letters, begging me to use my influence to cause some of the doctors and Stafford House stores so freely distributed throughout European Turkey to be despatched to Kars, where they are far more needed than in Erzeroum.

I mentioned some few weeks ago that we had organised a small fund for the relief of the wounded men in hospital, providing them with such luxuries—meat, tobacco, fruit, &c.—as we could afford, and giving them, on their discharge from hospital, a small gratuity to enable them to go to their homes. Mr. Zohrab, our Consul, who is foremost in all works of charity, and whose goodness to the labouring classes about here, Turks and Christians alike, has given him a position in Erzeroum that few Consuls hold in other Turkish cities, is the honorary treasurer, and he daily visits the hospitals for the purpose of distributing his little doles. Our money is very low; but last mail a handsome donation from Lady Chesterfield gave us a fresh start. Any contributions to this fund should be sent to our Consul here, through Messrs. Coutts or Hanson, to Constantinople, and I can assure you they will be well spent and most gratefully received. Besides assisting the patients, the money is expended in paying the hospital attendants, dressers, night-watchers, and the like; for these men, like all Government servants, have seen no pay for months. It is impossible to expect that they will show even ordinary care and attention to the patients if they are never paid; so now they have been temporarily transferred to our establishment, and are paid regularly every week by Mr. Zohrab. This has had a most beneficial effect. Any man found neglecting his work is dismissed, and the result of prompt payments, firm discipline, and gentle supervision, can be seen in the cheery, willing manner in which all our English hospital attendants perform their work, and may be learnt also from the fact that patients in the other hospitals beg to be transferred to ours whenever vacancies occur.

While writing the above I have been visited by a doctor in Turkish employ, whom I questioned on the subject of amputations. He informs me that they are not absolutely forbidden by the Government, but that the following procedure is laid down, should a surgeon deem a case worthy of operation:—The doctor in charge of the patient makes a report to the principal medical officer, who himself visits the hospital, examines the man, and, if he considers amputation necessary, lays the whole case before the military committee of the district, who decide as to whether the operation shall be performed or not. This doctor informed me that though he has repeatedly during the war applied for permission to amputate, he has invariably been refused by the principal medical officer here; and, after conversation with doctors of all nationalities, I cannot learn of one single instance in which permission to amputate has been accorded by any of the three principal medical officers, either here, at Kars, or at Ardahan. Again, I have ocular evidence that amputation is disapproved of, if not formally forbidden. In this army there are thousands

of officers and men decorated with war-medals for
service in Yemmen, Crete, Servia, Montenegro, and
Herzegovina. Is it possible that, had amputation been
performed, we should not see proudly riding at the
heads of their companies, their regiments, brigades, or
divisions, men whose armless sleeves tell of a life saved
by a judicious use of the knife? After our wars in the
Crimea, in India, in China, and New Zealand, regimental officers might be counted in scores whose looped-
up sleeve told of surgical skill. Scarcely a regiment in
the service did not possess one living evidence that the
British Government, at any rate, encouraged amputation; and a glance at German and French corps to-day
tells the same tale. Who has seen a Turkish officer
similarly situated? I, for one, certainly have not; nor
can I learn of a single instance of amputation having
been performed, except by British doctors, and then only
after the strongest pressure had been brought to bear on
the Turkish authorities.

I have had several opportunities during my recent
visit to Erzeroum of conversing with many of the leading Armenian families in the place on the subject of the
war, of Turkish rule, and of their ideas as to the effect
of any change of Government upon them. These con-
versations have not improved my ideas of the Armenian.
A more selfish, narrow-minded, mean, cringing race, I
fancy, does not exist, the Protestant Armenian being
of a lower type than those who have clung to their
old religion; but both are despicable to a degree. Far
preferable is the agricultural Turk, who bears uncomplain-
ingly the heavy burdens imposed on him in the way of
taxation, sends out all the males of his family between
the ages of sixteen and sixty to fight the common foe

—the hated Moscov—entrusts the gathering of his harvest to the women of his family, and sees ruin, absolute ruin, staring him in the face through the wickedness and corruption of his Pashas, whose ears never hear the maledictions hurled at them by their poorer, suffering fellow-countrymen. As far as I have been able to learn, the bulk of the Armenians would welcome any change. They have been oppressed for centuries, treated with contumely, unable to obtain a hearing in the law-courts, compelled to pay, in addition to the Government taxes (which fall far heavier on the Christian than on the Mahomedan), innumerable unjust levies forced on them by officials against whom there is no redress; and they consequently see that there is no hope for them to obtain an equal footing with Mussulmans in this country. When the Russians, in June, were close on Erzeroum, and the fall of the city was looked on as inevitable, the Armenian might have been seen moving briskly about, as if he longed to welcome the invader, the prowess of whose deeds, the valour of whose men, and the invincibility of whose armies had for years been old wives' tales in every Armenian household. The check at Zewin and the subsequent retirement of both Russian armies caused a revulsion of feeling, and the evil deeds of the Moscov began to be recounted, his tyrannical form of government, his religious intolerance; dim visions of the knout and of Siberia flitted through the Armenian brain, and the question began to be asked whether it would not be better to bear the ills they had than fly to others they knew not of.

The idea of freeing themselves and establishing a "Switzerland in Asia Minor" has never entered their heads, and though since I saw the scheme mooted in your columns I have propounded it to many well-educated, intelligent Armenian gentlemen, they have one and all denounced it as impracticable and absurd. For centuries they have remained a subject race, and so they will remain to the end of the chapter. Those few who have travelled in Europe, and become politicians of a minor character and merchant princes, may have formed wild visions of a kingdom in the mountains of Anatolia, but the idea is scouted with scorn by residents of the country itself. They long for change, that is all; they long to escape from the hateful thraldom of the Turk; they long to be taken in hand by some beneficent, just Government—to them it is immaterial, though they would prefer America, England, or Germany to Russia —and allowed to live peaceably and quietly, tilling their own land, selling their own merchandise, living their own uneventful, unambitious lives, free from all dread of their wives being dishonoured by their Kurdish neighbours, their children carried off into captivity far worse than death, and themselves quite unable to move a finger in self-defence, and powerless to call for justice.

In fact, so strong has this longing for change become, that many of the wealthier families, both here and in the neighbourhood, seeing the chances of Russian occupation diminish, have determined on emigrating; and more than one already, having realised all its property, has gone to America.

That the Armenians are content with Turkish rule is false. Their hatred and dread of it are evident from the fact that upwards of 5,000 families have fled from the Van and Alashgird district and taken refuge in

Russia. I am aware that Ismail Pasha states that these people were forcibly taken away by Tergukassoff in his retreat from Zaidikan. Common sense repels such an idea. We know the Russian General had an army consisting of eight battalions, twenty-four guns, and seven regiments of cavalry, and we know that he was threatened in rear by Faik Pasha with 12,000 and in front by Ismail Pasha with 15,000 men. The despatches of the latter General state that he so closely pursued Tergukassoff, and harassed his retreat so continually, that the advance of his men was impeded owing to the infection arising from dead Russian corpses. This we know how far to believe; for Mr. Williams, an English gentleman, present at the so-called pursuit, states that on the 28th all touch of the Russians was lost, and Ismail Pasha himself reported to the Commander-in-Chief that he did not know which road they had taken. Still, any military man will know that it is a moral impossibility for an army of less than 5,000 to convoy over a hundred miles of ground some 15,000 souls, with all their worldly belongings, in face of an army following them in rear, with one double their strength harassing them in flank. No; I have conversed with many refugees from Alashgird, who came into Erzeroum for safety from the Kurds, and these people—Mahomedans for the most part—inform me that immediately after the battle of Khaliass the Armenian exodus was made, and that Tergukassoff never broke camp at Zaidikan until he was assured of the arrival of the fugitives in safety across the Russian border. In the Van district the Muscovite never appeared. There, in consequence of the barbarities committed by the Kurds, the Christians spontaneously fled—

not, however, until they had suffered terrible losses, and more than 380 young girls and boys had been carried off into the most hopeless slavery one can imagine.

I have not yet heard a Turkish officer attempt to extenuate the conduct of the Kurds; nor have I met one who did not freely own that the Christians were fairly driven out of the country by their revolting outrages. There is one, however, who denies all this, who writes despatches to the Turkish Government, stating that the desolation worked in Van and Alashgird is Russian doing, in spite of the Commander-in-Chief knowing that these despatches are false—for has he not ordered the arrest and trial of Jelaludeen, the greatest offender? —in spite of the Ottoman Government knowing it—for have they not ordered the trial of Faik Pasha, who, by his negligence, contributed to these atrocities? The Porte circulates Ismail Pasha's statements to its Ministers abroad as evidence of Russian cruelty and oppression. I simply state as a fact, after the most careful inquiries from Turkish officers and soldiers, as well as from the Armenians themselves, that the exodus from Van and Alashgird was purely voluntary on the part of the Christians, that it was solely on account of the horrors and barbarities they were daily and hourly subjected to by the Kurds. Ismail Pasha is himself a fanatical Mahomedan, connected with the chief robber clan in Shoregel, and, consequently, is anxious to screen his fellow-clansmen from the effects of their misdeeds.

It is simply a disgrace to Turkey that, after the foul massacre of Russian prisoners at Bayazid, the well-known perpetrators of the murders are not only allowed to go free, but should even remain as the honoured guests of the Commander-in-Chief of the Turkish right wing.

There have been a few changes and promotions in the staff of the army since my last—Ferik Reiss Ahmed Pasha, the commander of the first division of the Van and Alashgird army, has been ordered to Kars temporarily to take command of the garrison during the absence of the recently appointed governor, Mushir Mustafa Memenli Pasha, ordered to Erzeroum to assume the functions of President of the general court-martial assembled for the trial of two general officers. Ferik Hadji Raschid Pasha, commander of the first division of the head-quarters army, and Ferik Faizi Pasha (General Kohlmann, the hero of Zewin Dooz) have both arrived at Erzeroum, nominated members of the same court-martial. Major-General Mustafa Safvet Pasha, at present with Mukhtar Pasha, has been promoted to Lieutenant-General, and nominated to the command of the first division of the Van and Alashgird army; Colonel Hakif Bey, of the staff of the same army, has been promoted to Major-General, and appointed temporarily to the second division of that army, *vice* Ferik Faik Pasha, placed under arrest. Captain Mehmed Bey, the Prussian officer, whose defence of the Emir Oghlou Fort was the one gallant deed performed at Ardahan, and who commanded the column of assault at the recent battle of Kizil-Tepe, where he was wounded, has at last been recommended for promotion to a Major-Generalcy, and is temporarily appointed to the command of Hadji Raschid Pasha's division during that officer's absence on court-martial duty at Erzeroum. It is rumoured, with what truth I know not, that poor old General Kohlmann will not return to his post at Kars;

that the praise so freely bestowed on him for his personal
gallantry and the skilful nature of his dispositions at
the battle of Zewin Dooz, on the 26th of June, has
aroused the jealousy of his Turkish comrades, and that
the Mushir has promised not to employ him again
during the war.　If there is truth in these rumours, the
fine old General will add one more name to the long list
of foreigners who, having spent their best years in the
service of Turkey, are in their old age, or in the hour
of Turkish triumph, thrown aside and forgotten.
General Kohlmann's conduct at the siege of Kars in
1855, the skill and care with which he has organised the
Fourth or Armenian Army Corps, the judgment and
engineering knowledge he brought to bear on the construction of the new fortifications round Batoum, Kars,
and Erzeroum, and finally his brilliant repulse of the
Russians at Zewin Dooz, constitute in all fairness a just
claim for his promotion to the rank of Mushir; but
jealousy of foreigners stands in the way, and Kohlmann
has no more chance of his well-earned Mushirlik than
the last-joined private in the Polish Legion.

The court-martial for the trial of Lieutenant-General
Hussain Sabri Pasha, the Governor of Ardahan, and of
Lieutenant-General Faik Pasha, the officer who permitted the massacres at Bayazid, and finally failed to
prevent the place being relieved by a much inferior
force under Tergukassoff, has assembled; but as the
chief evidence against Sabri Pasha, Captain Mehmed
Bey, is still retained at head-quarters, and as Faik Pasha
has not arrived from Bayazid, the proceedings as yet
must be devoid of interest.　It is generally believed
that both men will escape; but even if they are sentenced to degradation, they know full well that there is

always hope for a Turkish Pasha. Hussain Avni Pasha, tried at Kars in 1855 for peculation, was reduced to the ranks, and a promise extracted by our Minister at Constantinople that he should never be employed under Government again, and yet he died Prime Minister of Turkey, by the hand of a man he had grievously wronged.* Zarif Mustafa Pasha, who commanded at the battle of Kharrak-Darrah in 1855, was tried for losing that battle, and sentenced to degradation to the ranks. He was sent to his home, and in six months was again promoted to the rank of Liva Pasha, or Major-General. So the two prisoners about to be brought to trial need be under no fear as to their fate. If Hussain Sabri Pasha's Court influence was sufficient to obtain for him the command of Ardahan after he had been removed from his post in Montenegro for inefficiency, it will be quite sufficient to keep him from all harm in this little difficulty. As for Faik Pasha, to the shame of the Ottoman Government it must be told that he is not to be tried for permitting the murder of Russian prisoners of war—men whose surrender he had accepted, and whose arms had been laid at his feet—but merely for

---

* My statement concerning Hussain Avni Pasha called forth an indignant remonstrance from General Sir Lintorn Simmons, who characterised the story as "utterly groundless and devoid of all truth." I gave it on what may be considered unimpeachable authority, and I regret that I inserted the word "peculation" in place of "gross debauchery, and habitual insolence to Sir Fenwick Williams." Hussain Avni, I find, was never tried; he was sent under escort to Pera, and there released, subsequently serving with such distinction as could be earned in that mismanaged affair, the expedition to Soukhoum Kaleh. In the Appendix I quote the correspondence that passed between Sir Fenwick Williams, Lord Stratford de Redcliffe, Lord Clarendon, and the Porte on the matter. As the name of one Major Simmons appears in these letters, it is but fair to conclude that Sir Lintorn has forgotten the circumstance.

not preventing the relief of the Bayazid garrison by Tergukassoff.

Although well aware so far back as the 10th July of the actual fact of the Bayazid massacre, I have been unable up till now to obtain any reliable account of the frightful scenes enacted. Now, however, through the courtesy of Sir Arnold Kemball, I have been placed in possession of the main details, which I proceed to give. It appears that on the 14th of June, Lieutenant-General Faik Pasha, in command of the Van division of the Turkish army, having organised his forces, which prior to the outbreak of war were much scattered, advanced from Pergi, on the eastern shore of the Van Lake, on Bayazid (which, as you may remember, was evacuated by Ahmed Nuri Bey on the 30th of May without resistance). The Russian commandant, leaving two companies in the citadel, an old massive masonry building, marched to Teperiskui, some ten miles S.E. of the place, and gave battle to Faik's forces. Being much outnumbered he was worsted, and retired in some confusion into the town, occupying the citadel with his infantry, while the cavalry remained just outside its walls. With the aid of two field-guns the officer commanding the cavalry managed to keep the Turks at bay; but, Faik sending Munib Pasha with two battalions and three mountain guns to occupy a hill about 1,200 yards east of the castle, the Turks were enabled to command the Russian position, and finally rendered it untenable. On the 28th June, their water supply having been cut off, the commandant of the garrison hoisted a white flag, and finally sent an officer out to arrange terms of capitulation. An officer of similar rank was deputed by Faik Pasha, and these two met in a house in the town and drew up the proposed treaty, which received the sanction of both the Russian and Turkish commandants.

At 4 p.m. that afternoon, all preliminaries having been gone through, Faik Pasha betook himself to the three-gun battery to the east of the town, and sent a company of infantry up to the citadel, over which the white flag still flew, to line the road from the gates, in order that the Russian prisoners of war might march between the ranks and so down to the camp prepared for them. At the appointed time the gates were thrown open, and the garrison, unarmed, filed out. Some 200 or more had already passed between the lines of Turkish soldiery, when suddenly a body of Kurds (of whom in a previous letter I have reported there were 8,000 in Faik's forces) rushed on the defenceless men and commenced a wild massacre. In vain did the Turkish regular soldiery interpose; it was all to no purpose; in vain did the Russian officers appeal to their sense of honour, and cry that they were unarmed prisoners of war; demons let loose from hell could have shown no worse devilry. A party dashed on in rear of the column and endeavoured to cut off the Russian retreat to the castle, but, fortunately, some Russian soldiers retaining their presence of mind, and saving their own at the expense of their comrades' lives, closed the gates and opened fire on the hell-hounds outside. It is stated, on Faik Pasha's authority,[*] that he opened fire on these miscreants from his own guns, and thus aided the Russian garrison to disperse them. Suffice it to say that, baulked of their prey in the Russian garrison, of whom it is said 236 were thus massacred, the Kurds unchecked

---

[*] This was subsequently denied by several Turkish officers of high rank present on this occasion.

W

rushed sword in hand into the city, and carried their work of butchery among the defenceless inhabitants. Mussulman and Christian, men and women, children and babes, alike fell victims to their lust of blood. In one church 200 bodies were found. Scarcely one house existed in which there were not two or more corpses—and, shame to Turkey, shame to the name of soldier, Faik Pasha, a lieutenant-general, at the head of six battalions of soldiers, heaven save the mark! never moved a file into the town to check these blood-thirsty scoundrels in their work of slaughter. On the contrary, he moved his personal camp to Teperiskui, retained the Kurds in his service, and re-opened fire on the citadel.

From the Russian account of the siege it appears that the garrison, which consisted of thirty officers and 1,587 men, were reduced to the greatest straits prior to their relief. On the 14th of June, immediately after the engagement at Teperiskui, Faik Pasha, in order to insure submission, cut off the flow of water into the citadel, and the garrison had to depend on the small quantities brought in by men who volunteered for this purpose at night. As early as the 20th of June the ration of liquid was reduced to half-a-pint per diem; at times even this quantity could not be spared, and then the day's order notified : " In consequence of yesterday's sortie for water not having proved success-ful, the sick and wounded will receive one pint, men in health one quarter of a pint, daily." Then again, on dark nights, when the vigilance of the Kurds was not so keen as usual, we have a more cheering order: "From the quantity of water brought in last night, a sufficient quantity will be served out to cook food and bake bread." Provisions soon became as scarce as water, and when a sortie was made to the stream, a party was detached to search the deserted houses for food. Even this did not suffice, and on the 6th of July the commandant, himself confined to his bed by a dangerous wound, issued the following pithy order: "My horse and that of the brigade major to be killed, as the remainder of the biscuit is required for the use of the sick; they are to be roasted, not boiled, so that all the water may be kept for drinking." Of the severity of the bombardment, which lasted twenty-seven days, we may judge from the fact that the garrison lost two officers and 114 men killed, seven officers and 359 men wounded, irrespectively of those massacred by the Kurds. Having no artillery, the commandant was unable to reply to the fire poured upon him from twelve field-guns, which Faik Pasha placed in position on an eminence completely commanding the interior of the work.

On the 6th of July, Ismail Pasha effected a junction with Faik; thus the Turkish forces available for the siege amounted to twenty-eight battalions, but the Kurdish chief was so convinced the place would be starved into submission, that he would not hear of an assault. He, however, sent in a *Parlementaire* to the Russian commander, offering to permit him to march out with all the honours of war, if he would capitulate. As if to add to the indignity of the proceeding, the message was sent in by a corporal, who was told to inform the Turkish General that, having regard to the perfidious manner in which the Ottoman troops behaved on the 19th ult., the garrison preferred death to treating with such inhuman monsters. On the following day another *Parlementaire* was despatched from the Turkish camp,

w 2

but he was fired on; whereupon Ismail retired to his own camp at Moussin, and told Faik to prosecute the siege with all vigour. The supineness of these two Generals enabled Tergukassoff to cut in between them on the 10th of July, and relieve Bayazid.

The sufferings of the Russians, bad as they were prior to the massacre, when want of water, the direst want a garrison can feel, led them to offer to surrender, were now increased a thousandfold. To die of starvation, preserving their honour, was preferable—far preferable —to death at the hands of the murderous villains whom a Turkish General permitted to remain in his army. In spite of the breach of faith of which men in his own command had been guilty, Faik Pasha showed no signs of remorse for an act at which all Europe will stand aghast in horror, no sign of shame at the infamy which must inevitably fall on his own head, no sign of pity for the gallant men inside the château, no sign of acknowledgment of the white flag which still floated over the Russian garrison; but gave orders for the continuance of the bombardment, and exultingly pointed out the accuracy of his own artillery practice, boasting that night after night the stream from which alone the Russians could obtain their supply of water was watched, and that the forlorn hope, which ever and anon made desperate efforts to carry up some drops of the precious liquid to their comrades, were attacked in their gallant mission, and nightly driven back with loss. For twenty-three days did this pitiless warfare continue; for twenty-three days did this gallant band hold out, enduring all the horrors of a siege, enhanced by the far worse terrors of a death from thirst, until on the morning of the 10th of July, Tergukassoff, by a feat which must stand on record as one of the most dashing feats of arms of modern times, with eight battalions, thirty-two guns, and seven regiments of cavalry, cut in between Ismail Pasha with twenty, and Faik Pasha with six battalions and 11,000 regulars, relieved his beleaguered comrades, carried them off, sick and wounded, guns, and munitions of war, and then turning on Faik Pasha, signally defeated him, capturing three guns and 800 prisoners. And what did the infuriated Kurds all this time—the fanatical "Ghazis"—who were to carry death and destruction into Russia under their gallant leader, Kurd Ismail Pasha—the heroic men who did not for a moment hesitate to throw themselves on unarmed prisoners of war, on defenceless women and children? No thought of facing that avenging army, no thought of fighting an armed foe. One glance at the steady advance of the Russian infantry, one look at the squadrons of dragoons sweeping round their rear, and then, casting aside their arms, they fled like sheep from the battle-field.

I will not attempt to criticise the conduct either of Faik Pasha on this horrible occasion, or of the Ottoman Government, for employing such mercenaries. I will merely point out that this massacre occurred on the 19th of June; that Mukhtar Pasha has informed Sir Arnold Kemball that orders have been sent down to suspend Faik Pasha and to try him by court-martial; that Kurd Ismail Fakki Pashi has interceded for him; and that he still commands the 1st Division of the right wing of the Turkish army.

Permit me to say a word in conclusion on a somewhat analogous subject. More than once it has been my pleasant lot to speak of the conduct of our consul,

Mr. Zohrab, during this campaign, and to point out the very prominent position he has taken in endeavouring to allay excitement and calm the passions of the fanatic population of Erzeroum. I am aware that he never glosses over the faults or the crimes of Ottoman officials. For this reason he has been dubbed a hater of the Turk, and I have reason to believe his reports have been regarded as highly coloured. As he has dwelt in this country since he reached manhood, and has a knowledge of Oriental languages, manners, and customs possessed by few, and is moreover a straightforward, honest, gallant, English gentleman, his despatches should possess a peculiar value, and his suggestions be received with the respect due to the well-weighed words of a master of the Armenian question. Without attempting for one moment to deny the numerous faults in the Armenian character, I maintain that no report describing their sufferings and oppressions can be too highly coloured. The conduct of Mr. Zohrab at Kars in 1855, where, as one of that gallant little band of our fellow-countrymen who so bravely defended the place against the repeated assaults of the Russians, he added a fresh name to the list of those who, shedding lustre themselves on the name of England, have been forgotten by their country ; his noble abnegation of self in now daily sacrificing hours of a day already far too short for the work this war imposes on him, in order that he may aid Lord Blantyre's doctors in their task of love and charity ; his never-ceasing endeavours to provide for the comfort of all his countrymen, ay, and of Americans too, official and non-official, whom this crisis has attracted to Erzeroum; and the cool front and cheery demeanour he now exhibits among the scenes of danger, of distress, of suffering, and of sickness, to which his family and himself are daily exposed, compel me to say one word in his defence against the cruel imputations I have heard cast upon him, and to claim for him that meed of sympathy which Englishmen are ever willing to accord to a fellow-countryman who tries to do his duty.

CHAPTER XVII.

WINTER PREPARATIONS.

Ghazi Mukhtar Pasha—Promotion of Captain Mehemet Pasha—Further Plans of the Turkish Commander-in-Chief—Condition of the Erzeroum Garrison—Prospect of Famine—Komaroff's Measures for Defence of Ardahan—Rumoured Reinforcements for Tergukassoff—Winter Clothing for Turkish Troops—The British Ambulance—Reported Violation of the Geneva Convention by the Russians—Conduct of the Turks on the Battle-field—Conduct of the Russians in Ardahan—Explosive Bullets—Desertion of the Circassians—Probability of the Loss seriously affecting Mukhtar—Difficulty of an Advance on Erivan—Successful Raid of Arab Cavalry—Force despatched to Natschevan—Russian Reinforcements—Skirmish at Tcherkgi.

ERZEROUM, 12*th September.*

DURING the last few days we received information that the Sultan has bestowed upon Mukhtar Pasha the title of Ghazi, as a reward for his conduct during the campaign, more especially for his brilliant victory at Kizil-Tepe, on the 25th of August. Captain Mehemet Bey, who led the assault on the Kizil-Tepe Hill, and who previously, as our readers will remember, had shown the most marked gallantry at the defence of Emir Oglou Fort at Ardahan, on the 16th May, was promoted to the rank of Liva Pasha, or major-general. As far as I know, this is the only instance of a foreign officer being promoted by the Turks in this campaign for services in front of the enemy. Mukhtar determined to establish his right to the title of Ghazi, and so evidently resolved to drive the Muscov across the Arpatchai into Russian territory. Ismail Pasha, it will be remembered, succeeded in forcing Tergukassoff back into Georgia, and is

established in such a strong position on the hills in front
of Igdyr, that I doubt the possibility of the Russians
being able to drive him back into Armenia. Mukhtar
is so convinced of the impregnability of his own
position, that he has called up from the right wing six
battalions, and has ordered every available man to be
pushed forward from Erzeroum and from the Ghiurji
Boghaz defile to his camp on the Aladja Dagh, and now
there literally is not a man keeping open communications
between this place and the Turkish advanced columns at
Pennek, Sarbatan, and Igdyr; by massing his forces near
Kars, and throwing himself, with all his strength, on the
flank of Melikoff, Mukhtar is in hopes that he will rid
Armenia of the hated Giaour. His recent victories have
increased the enthusiasm of his men, and he very wisely
stirred the spirit of disaffection in Daghestan, proclamations having been circulated amongst the Abkhasian and
the Mingrelian and Circassian tribes by Ghazi Mahomed
Pasha, the son of Sheik Schamyl, the hereditary prince
of that nation. With the Russians in their own territory and insurrection in the mountainous district between
the Caspian and Black Seas, the work of the spring campaign would be much lightened. The common talk of
the head-quarter staff is of wintering in Tiflis and
Erivan; however, the fact of having denuded his line
of communications of troops somewhat jeopardises the
position of Mukhtar. Erzeroum is garrisoned only by
the Mustahfiz battalions of Koniah and Baiboort and
some 400 volunteer artillery, so that were either of
Mukhtar's columns to be defeated and driven back,
it would necessitate the retirement of the others, otherwise the capital would fall into the hands of the
Russians, and the process of revictualling Kars would

be summarily interfered with. The Turkish armies are now reaping the fruits of having raised levies in Kurdistan, the massacres in the Alashgird Plain, and the horrible atrocities committed in Van, Bitlis, and Moosh having caused a general exodus of the Armenians to Russian territory. The crops, though ripe, are waiting for the sickle; there is none to gather them in but robber horsemen, who wander over the country plundering, ravishing, and murdering wherever they please. The consequence is that there is a prospect of a famine throughout the province.

As in Bulgaria, the steady tillers of the ground are Christian inhabitants. In Mahomedan villages all able-bodied men have been drafted off to fill up the gaps caused by the war, and the harvest is being gathered in by women. All grain is seized by the Government officials for commissariat purposes, and the harvest-tax, instead of being one-tenth, as it usually is, is now increased to three-fourths, the remainder being left for the support of the villagers; but even with these large exactions the supply is most limited, and urgent messages have been forwarded to the vilayets of Sivas and Diarbekir to collect and forward all the grain that can be procured. The difficulty of transport, however, will be very considerable for them. Fortunately the harvest there has been an unusually good one; yet, owing to the absence of pack-animals, all of which have been pressed into the transport service of the army, much delay must occur before the supplies reach these.

Melikoff seems to have been well aware of the danger of Ardahan, and, having received early information of the mobilisation of a column at Pennek for its recapture, took prompt steps to insure its safety.

The Emir Oglou, Dooz, and Ramazan Tabia have been considerably strengthened; several minor earthworks have been razed. The barracks and all masonry buildings in the town which would afford cover for an attacking force have been mined. Telegrams have been sent to Akhalzik for reinforcements to be promptly pushed up, and Komaroff has been directed to hold the place to the last extremity. Hassan Bey, commanding the column at Pennek, seems fully alive to the difficulty of the undertaking, and, I hear, will not move forward until he receives intelligence of the arrival of Dervish Pasha's brigade at Ardanutsch. After the junction, in the event of his still considering the place too formidable to be attacked with the troops at command, Hassan Bey has received instructions to stand fast at Pennek, and bar any attempts of a Russian advance by that road to Erzeroum. There are rumours that Tergukassoff has been reinforced by three regiments of cavalry and a brigade of infantry. It is impossible to say what his actual strength is; but we know that in his adventurous advance on Zaidikan he had only eight battalions at his disposal. It is probable, however, that now he has fourteen battalions of infantry, five batteries, with ten regiments of cavalry. Although this does not amount to more than half the forces of Ismail Pasha, who has twenty-nine battalions, six batteries, and from 6,000 to 10,000 horse, yet the Russians are quite strong enough, under their able and gallant leader, effectually to bar the way to Erivan; and I think it may be safely assumed that Ismail Pasha, who has already tested the metal of Tergukassoff's troops, will abandon his loudly-proclaimed intention of wintering in the capital of Georgia; his army, too, is in the most pitiable state. As regards supplies, the whole district in his vicinity has been completely pillaged by his clansmen, the Kurds, and provisions are nowhere obtainable nearer than Erzeroum, where the authorities very naturally pay more heed to orders sent from the Commander-in-Chief than they do to those from Ismail Hakki. Indeed, it was not until he threatened to fall back on Van, and report that he was obliged to do so owing to the neglect of the Erzeroum officials to replenish his commissariat, that Hassan Pasha awoke to the real urgency of his state.

His army is divided into two divisions, one of which he has sent out under Hakif Pasha to Alkali, while he himself with the remainder of his forces stays at Zor. Active preparations have been made throughout the provinces for a winter campaign; 80,000 suits of new uniform have been ordered by Mukhtar Pasha, and he has shown a prescience rare in the Osmanli, by directing that the whole of the skins of the beasts killed by the commissariat during the campaign are to be sent into Erzeroum, for the purpose of being turned into coats for his troops. This is a measure certainly adopted none too soon, for the majority of the soldiers are in rags and tatters.

Doctors Casson and Buckby are at present at Kars, organising an ambulance corps for the head-quarter column of the Turkish army, whilst Dr. Featherstonhaugh, with two assistants, has been left in charge of the English hospital in this place. Mr. Zohrab, our energetic consul, is busily aiding them in collecting material and means for the ambulance train.

I see in a recent issue of the *Times* that Mukhtar Pasha has formally complained of the Russians having

violated the Geneva Convention during the battle of
the 25th of August by firing upon his ambulances.
As these ambulances consisted of a few " Arabas " or
country carts, of the same pattern as those used for the
transport of artillery and infantry ammunition, as well
as for the general commissariat purposes of the army,
and as they were surmounted merely by a small flag, just
eighteen inches square, it would be difficult for an enemy
to recognise them as hospital institutions ; and I think,
taking into consideration the conduct of the Russians to
the Turkish wounded at Ardahan, we may acquit them
of having wilfully perpetrated the crime which Mukhtar
Pasha lays to their charge. These accusations only
tend to embitter the feud now raging between the
Moslem and the Slav, and throw a blot on the civilisation of both. When the Russians take to exaggerating
the savagery of their opponents, they forget that they
too lay themselves open to a charge of inhuman conduct
in having armed the Bulgarians, in having fomented
insurrections among the Christians in the European
provinces of Turkey, and having repeatedly violated the
armistice during the Servian war, when Turkish water-
bearers were shot down in cold blood by Russian rifle-
men in Servian trenches. When the Turks, as they
have too frequently done in Armenia, accuse the
Russians of crimes which exist only in their own
heated imaginations, they must expect unbiassed spec-
tators to expose their misstatements to the Christian
world. It is generally admitted, indeed there can be no
two sides to this question, that off the battle-field the
Turkish regular soldier has shown no disposition to
commit these so-called atrocities. When under fire, and
under the influences of the excitement of the moment,

the Turk undoubtedly behaves in a somewhat savage manner, and I think from the fact that during this campaign the prisoners taken in various actions may be counted on one's fingers, and the wounded prisoners represented by a negative figure, we shall not be wrong in arriving at the conclusion that the Turk slays all wounded men found on the field of battle; and when we remember that until the year 1826 a reward was offered for the head of every enemy brought to the tent of the Commander-in-Chief, we can scarcely be surprised that the custom is still in vogue. That they strip their dead foes is also an undeniable fact, and that they mutilate the dead in as brutal a manner as the Afghan tribes on the north-west frontier of India, I myself can bear witness to. The atrocities committed off the field of battle, the vengeance wreaked on unoffending Armenian villagers, the desecration of the graves of the Russians, the carrying off of boys and maidens for the most diabolical of purposes, have all been committed by the Kurds. The Russians in general, at any rate, have shown their enemy a good example with reference to the wounded men. The statement of the German doctors, Addler and Weiss, taken prisoners at Ardahan, show that the Turkish wounded were treated with the same kindness and consideration as their own; they received the same pay as they would have done had they been serving with their regiments, but very much more regularly. Their rations were accompanied by an extra allowance of meat and soup as refreshing as it was unusual to the Turkish soldiers, and when reported fit for duty the wounded men were provided with five days' provisions, and permitted to return to Erzeroum.

The stories of explosive bullets which have been

bandied about from side to side during the last few weeks is another of those exaggerations of which both parties may well be ashamed. Any sportsman who is used to the Henry-Martini rifle will know that the express bullet striking on a bone inflicts a wound very similar to that made by the old explosive shell. That there is gun-cotton used in the Turkish bullet, or any explosive material whatever, I can confidently deny. I have examined, I may say, hundreds of their cartridges, both in quarters and in the field. The bullet, I have no hesitation in averring, is exactly the same as our own. I have also picked up some unexploded cartridge-cases belonging both to the Krinker and Berdan rifles, with which the Russian forces are armed. In many of these there was a compressed felt plug in the cup at the base of the ball; but I submitted this plug to test, and it possessed none of the qualities of gun-cotton. Consequently, I am satisfied that, so far as explosive bullets are concerned, the Geneva Convention has been violated by neither party during the present war.

We hear that the Grand Duke has been recently reinforced by a complete division of infantry and seven regiments of cavalry. This increase of horse jeopardises Mukhtar Pasha's position considerably. His large force of cavalry is being rapidly diminished by numerous desertions of both Circassians and Kurds, who arrive here in parties sometimes up to the strength of 150 sabres. A day or two ago we received telegraphic information from Kars that a body of 150 of these gentlemen had quietly deserted from the camp and were returning to their homes. Instructions were forwarded to the governor to send a sufficient force to arrest them.

Accordingly a body of infantry and cavalry was despatched from this place, and they very shortly met the Circassians on the road from Kars. They were promptly disarmed and marched prisoners into the town, where they have been located in one of the empty barracks.

On my asking one of the officers what was meant by this desertion *en masse* of the Circassian horse, he replied, "We get no pay, we get no rations, we get no grain for our horses, we get no warm clothing for ourselves. How can we fight under those circumstances? We have constantly applied to Mukhtar Pasha for some of the arrears of pay due to us, for great-coats, and for blankets for our horses, and to all our appeals we received the answer that it is quite sufficient for a Mahomedan to fight for the Sultan with the hope of receiving a reward in the future world. Unfortunately the hope of the reward hereafter does not fill our stomachs or those of our horses, and so we have returned here and mean to appeal to the Sultan for our just dues." Whether the Sultan antedated the bill I cannot say. This reduction of his cavalry is a very serious thing for Mukhtar, still, in the sense in which we speak of cavalry, it certainly was not of much use. There was not an officer in the whole force who understood the art of reconnoitring. He was never able to depend upon the information brought to him by the cavalry leaders. Although, as a rule, the men were willing enough to face the Cossack horse, they distinctly declined to face either infantry or guns. Indeed, on more than one occasion, their hurry to take up a strong position with the reserve when the Russian artillery opened fire upon them was somewhat ludicrous. As long as Mukhtar Pasha could place two battalions in the field to one that the Russians could show, his weakness in this respect was not so discernible. But now the want of sufficient cavalry forces, the want of the eyes and the ears of the army, will, I fear, prove disastrous to him. Should the Grand Duke succeed in cutting in between the Aladja Dagh and Kars, the loss of the greater portion of the Turkish army will be the inevitable result. However, throughout this campaign the Russians have ignored every principle of war in the most disastrous manner. They have allowed to pass by so many excellent opportunities for striking a fatal blow upon their opponents, that even should Mukhtar be seriously defeated in his present position, I see no reason why he should not be able to retire on the Soghanly range with as large a force as he did in May last. There have been a few minor encounters between Ismail Pasha's troops and Tergukassoff's small division, yet the Kurdish chief, who in April proclaimed to the world his immediate intention of invading Russia with 40,000 clansmen, now fails to cross the twenty miles of ground that intervenes between him and Erivan, and he shows more wisdom in remaining in his position on the Igdyr Hills than he did in despatching his bombastic telegram to the Porte.

The valley of the Araxes as it passes through the Erivan plain is entirely devoted to the cultivation of rice. Those of my readers who are acquainted with the paddy-fields of Bengal will easily understand the difficulty of moving a large army of 35,000 men, with its attendant transport consisting either of *arabas* or pack-animals, across that style of country; by the simple act of cutting a few sluices, Tergukassoff would convert the plain into one large morass, and then I think he would gain a more

x

decided triumph on the plains of Erivan than he did at
Taghir on the 16th July last.

On the 20th of September there was a small cavalry
affair in this vicinity. A squadron of Sulimani irregular
cavalry was detached on reconnoitring duty across the
Araxes. It advanced towards Erivan, and actually cut
in between the outposts on the Alexandropol road. These
appear to have been very inefficiently commanded, for
the detachment succeeded in overpowering the postal
escort, bringing letters from the Grand Duke to Erivan.
The sound of firing brought up one outpost, but the
Arab horse, showing the greatest gallantry, having seized
the letter-bags, charged the enemy's cavalry; and, laden
with the arms of the escort, and leading thirty captured
horses, the Arabian irregulars returned with their booty
to camp.

From these letters we learnt that Tergukassoff had
recently been reinforced by twelve battalions under
General Dewel, but the Grand Duke, anxious to
strengthen his centre as much as possible preparatory
to making a determined assault on Mukhtar's position,
had ordered seven of these battalions to return immediately to Karajal. From the letters also we found that
there was an intention of pushing in a force to cross the
Arpa Tchai, and intervene between the two Turkish
wings. This fact was at once communicated to Mukhtar
Pasha, who detached five battalions and a battery to
Natschevan with orders to entrench themselves there.
On the following day, the 27th of September, Ismail
Pasha endeavoured to seize the village of Tcherkgi.
For this purpose at dawn he sent three battalions
with a half-battery, supported by the remainder of
Hakif's brigade. The village was held only by a

small detachment, but the Russian general at once threw forward eleven battalions, two batteries, and three regiments of cavalry, who opposed the assault of our men. Seeing that they were terribly over-matched, Ismail ordered Lieutenant-General Mustafa Safvet Pasha to support this force with the remainder of his division, and after a brisk cannonade on the Russian position, Hakif Bey's troops were again led forward to the assault. They, however, were driven back, and owing to the impetuosity of the Russian advance, were forced to retire to the hills near Alkali, which Tergukassoff proceeded to storm ; night was coming on, and after two attempts, during which his men were brilliantly repulsed by six Turkish battalions on the hill, Tergukassoff drew off. The Turkish loss was 132 officers and men killed, amongst them being Major Ibrahim Bey.

Ismail Pasha, who throughout the campaign has distinguished himself as much by the inaccuracy of his despatches as by his disinclination to expose himself to danger, and who, evidently, is of opinion that a knowledge of strategy is valueless to a general who has the Koran at his fingers' ends, despatched a flaming report to the Seraskierate, in which he announced that he had signally defeated the Russians, who left 1,100 dead on the field. The want of leaders in the Turkish right wing is very severely felt. If Mukhtar Pasha could spare a skilful, determined man to supersede the Kurdish chief, the campaign would have a very different result. There was a rumour that Captain Mehmed Pasha was to have the command, but the blind jealousy of Europeans will stand in his way, and although he and his brigade (who follow him with a rare

x 2

devotion) are always pushed forward wherever the fighting is thickest, yet it is too much to expect that, sinking their blind conceit in their powers, the Osmanli generals will allow Mukhtar Pasha to carry out this move, so necessary for the successful issue of the campaign.

CHAPTER XVIII.

THE MOSLEM AT THE END OF HIS TETHER.

Skirmish near Zaim—Russians defeated—Plans of the Grand Duke—Mukhtar preparing for a Winter Campaign—His Position near Kars—Skirmish at Natschevan—Battle of the Yagnis on 2nd October—Gallantry of Mehmed Pasha's Brigade—Turkish Success at the Little Yagni—Attack and Capture of the Great Yagni—Repulse of the Russians—Heavy Losses—Misery in Kars—Paucity of Doctors—Hospital Arrangements.

On the 30th of September all things pointed to the fact that the Grand Duke was in receipt of heavy reinforcements, and was evidently determined to assume the offensive. News reached the Turkish camp that Komaroff had been reinforced by a complete division from Akhalzik, and that, feeling his position there to be impregnable, he had detached a brigade of four battalions, one field-battery, and one regiment of cavalry, to reinforce the Russian head-quarters. These men marched by Zarchat, encamped on the 29th to the north of the Arpa Tchai, near Zaim, throwing out pickets in that direction. Hassan Ahmed Bey, who commanded at Pennek, aware of this move, and wishing to prevent the proposed junction, detached a regiment of Arab cavalry to watch the force, at the same time warning the Commander-in-Chief of the march of the Russian brigade, so that it might be attacked by troops moving up from Kars, and annihilated before effecting a junction with its head-quarters at Karajal. The Turkish cavalry regiment reached the banks of the Kars-Tchai simultaneously with the Russian brigade, and with true Oriental negligence the colonel bivouacked his men without even posting one picket. The Russians, aware of the usual custom of the Turks on such occasions, attacked them after nightfall, completely surprised them, and succeeded in cutting up some forty or fifty men before the Arabs were able to escape. The following morning Mukhtar Pasha sent a force under Colonel Tcharkir Bey to avenge the loss that his cavalry had received the preceding evening. The Turkish colonel, placing himself at the head of three regiments of cavalry, at once charged the enemy's position, and in spite of a very heavy fire from their field-battery, succeeded in driving the enemy, in some confusion, as far as Parget, when, on perceiving reinforcements moving out from Karajal, Tcharkir Bey wisely retired. On the following morning, 1st October, the Grand Duke sent forward a cavalry brigade, accompanied by two horse-batteries, to harass Mukhtar's right ; and now commenced that series of operations which were intended to cover the real advance of the Russians. It was evidently the Grand Duke's intention to wear out Mukhtar's men, to reduce his force day by day by slight losses, and, finally, by cutting in between him and Kars, compel him to abandon his forward position on the Russian frontier, to leave Kars, and fall back on his base at Erzeroum. By these means the Grand Duke hoped to be enabled to assault and capture Kars, to drive in the detached brigade at Natschevan, and thus compel Ismail Pasha to execute a retrograde movement— in fact, to begin the campaign entirely anew, advance

on the three old roads of Ardahan, Kars, and Bayazid,
concentrate at the foot of Devi-boyun, and take up his
winter quarters in the capital of Armenia. The
skirmish on the Turkish right was of no importance;
their losses, as losses in sheltered trenches exposed to
artillery fire invariably are, were slight, and the Russians,
receiving as good as they gave, retired at dusk to their
camp.

During the month of September Mukhtar Pasha
employed himself in entrenching the hills of Little
Yagni and Kizil Tepe; on the latter were posted some
heavy siege-guns and the position was altogether one
comparatively impregnable. In fact, the Turks were
making their preparations for the winter campaign. A
site had been selected on the eastern slopes of the
Soghanly for a standing camp. Many Christian inhabitants of Kars had been warned that their houses
would be required for the quarters of the troops; large
supplies of ammunition and provisions had been thrown
into that fortress, not merely for the consumption of
the garrison during winter, but for the consumption of
an army of occupation. From spies Mukhtar learned
that the Russians were employing themselves in like
manner, that huts were springing up at Karajal,
similar to those which the Russians erected during the
campaign of '55, and the remains of which may now be
seen round Kars.

But Mukhtar, doubting the reports of deserters and
spies, disbelieved the story of Russian reinforcements,
and hoped that he would be enabled to drive them back
to their own territory before winter set in, in its real
severity.

The Little Yagni position, having been strengthened

and entrenched, was garrisoned by six battalions ; eight guns were also placed upon it, and it was intrusted to Capt. Mehmed Pasha. Hussain Hami Pasha was in command of the division at Vezinkui with a battalion occupying the Great Yagni hills in his front, whilst Hadji Raschid Pasha, with thirty-four battalions, was holding the slopes of the Aladja, his flank resting on the Nakharji and Olya Tepe. The command of the cavalry division had been vested in Lieut.-General Omar Pasha, a German officer of some distinction, who had recently arrived from Bagdad.

The garrison of Kars, terribly reduced by the many demands made upon it, now consisted of four battalions, and these men, under the superintendence of Hassan Bey, the gallant commandant of artillery, were busy in throwing up four new redoubts, two to the north of the Mookhliss Tabia, two to the east of the Karadagh hill. Now, having given a detailed account of the position of the Turkish armies on the 1st October, I will proceed to describe the operations commencing on the morning of the second. Prior to this, however, I must state that on the 30th September, Ahmed Pasha's brigade at Natschevan was attacked by a Russian brigade of superior strength, which after a sharp engagement was driven back, the Turks suffering a loss of about 250 killed and wounded. At dawn, on the 2nd, a signal-gun boomed out from the Olya Tepe, announcing the fact that the Russians were in motion ; indeed, columns were to be seen advancing *en masse* along the Kars road, towards the Little Yagni, whilst others threatened the whole Turkish front. It was evident that the Grand Duke's intention was to turn Mehmed Pasha out of his post, for by 7 a.m., thirty-four battalions, sixty-one guns, and six regiments of cavalry, were drawn up in line in front of the Little Yagni hills. The cavalry (owing to some absurd blunder on the part of the Russian commander) for a length of time were massed in column, well within the range of Mehmed's guns, and suffered very heavily from the accurate artillery firing brought to bear on them. Following the tactics of their grandfathers, the Russians threw column after column upon the steep slopes of Little Yagni, but, as must inevitably be the case where troops armed with breech-loaders have availed themselves of the spade, the defenders were enabled to repulse every attack upon their front, with the most hideous slaughter.

Mehmed Pasha's heroism inspired his men with the utmost enthusiasm. Although they were but Redifs— soldiers fresh from the plough—they showed all the gallantry of trained veterans; they were, however, for some hours exposed to a galling fire from sixty guns in their front, and suffered most heavily. Mehmed Pasha at last saw that unless aid arrived he would by sheer weight of numbers be driven from the Little Yagni hill; so he despatched urgent messages to Kars for aid. The Russian general, however, seemed to think that his men had had enough of it, for about noon there was a cessation of attacks on this position, and a division numbering fifteen or sixteen battalions with twelve guns moved off to the left for the purpose of seizing the Great Yagni, and thus keeping off the reinforcements which were being moved from the Aladja to the support of the Little Yagni. Whilst this was going on in the left of the Turkish position, a heavy attack developed itself on the right, where two columns of infantry, covered by sixty guns, advanced on Sarbatan, and the easternmost

slopes of the Aladja Dagh.   Hadji Raschid Pasha commanding this position sent forward two brigades under
Mustafa Djavid Pasha and Ibrahim Bey, to repel them.
Obeying the calls of their gallant leaders, the Turks
went at the enemy with the bayonet.   On all sides one
hears of the bravery displayed at this point.   After
fighting the Russians were driven back to the banks of
the Arpa Tchai with terrible losses.   In the meantime
the commandant of Kars had sent out five battalions to
the aid of the gallant Prussian.   Cheered by these reinforcements the Redif soldiers gained courage and practically sealed the issue of the day.   Great Yagni, however,
in spite of the repeated suggestions of the staff, had been
left comparatively undefended, one solitary battalion
numbering scarcely five hundred men manned the
entrenchments on its crest, and although these men
showed heroism that has not been surpassed in this war,
the place was carried after a most obstinate defence ;
three junior officers and thirty-seven men alone escaped
to tell the tale.   The cannonade on the Little Yagni
continued all day long, and before nightfall seven
hundred and fifty men had been removed into Kars.
Ahmed Fazel Pasha,[*] who had superseded Mehmed Pasha
in the command on the arrival of the reinforcements,
received a ball through the thigh, and the command of
the position once more devolved on Mehmed Pasha.
Long after dusk the cannonade on this point continued,
although all actual assaults had long since been dis-
continued.

Well now might the Russians have despaired of success.   All their attacks on the Turkish positions had been

* This officer was amongst the prisoners taken in Kars, and died early
in December from the effects of the wound received on the 2nd October.

repelled with the exception of that on the Great Yagni
Hill, and they were doubtless surprised to find that no
attempts were made by the Turkish Commander-in-Chief
to recapture this ; but Mukhtar was well aware that
there was no necessity for him to waste valuable lives to
effect that which must shortly ensue as a matter of
course.

The losses on both sides were most severe. A doctor
with the Turkish army computed the Ottoman casualties
at 1,000 killed and 3,500 wounded, whilst of the Russians
Mukhtar asserted that 2,800 dead bodies were found on
the slopes of the Little Yagni alone !*

The 3rd of October was spent in desultory artillery
firing between the advanced artillery posts, without
leading to anything more; but the following day, seeing
that the Russians had occupied the Kapack Tepe in
some force, Mukhtar Pasha sent forward Hadji Raschid
Pasha with a strong column to reconnoitre, charging
him most particularly on no account to bring on a
general engagement. Prior to that the Great Yagni
had been evacuated, owing to the extreme difficulty of
supplying the garrison with water.

The arrival of the wounded men in Kars strained the
hospital resources to their utmost. There were but four
doctors in the place fit for duty, and prior to this
engagement there were upwards of 4,000 sick and
wounded in the fortress. For those in England or for
those who have campaigned only with our own armies,
which, as a rule, are so adequately provided with medical
officers, with ambulances, litters, and hospital comforts,
it is difficult to conceive the amount of misery daily to

---

* The Russian official report mentioned 960 killed, 2,400 wounded,
and two missing, while 240 Turkish prisoners remained in their hands.

be seen in the streets of Kars—hospital accommodation existed only for 1,200 men, and even for that number there was not sufficient bedding, nor were there cots for more than 300 patients. The barracks and khans (rest houses for travellers) were speedily filled, and yet scarcely one-half of the wounded were provided even with shelter. In despair, the doctors applied to the commandant for the various masonry Government buildings, but this request was refused, and the victims of Turkey's misgovernment, of Russia's love of aggression, were perforce crowded into the small, ill-ventilated huts which abound in the city, men suffering from typhoid, from dysentery, from scurvy, lay side by side with comrades brought low by shot or bayonet. It was practically impossible for one-fourth of these men to be visited by the doctors, who were fearfully overworked; indeed, it was impossible that the medical men could know where all their patients were housed—fresh cases came daily to notice, and men were hourly found who had been lying for days with undressed wounds, unset limbs.

The Stafford House stores that Dr. Casson brought out from Erzeroum early in September were expended before the battle of the Yagnis, and from a letter I received from a German doctor in Kars, dated the 10th of October, I learnt that they were utterly without carbolic acid, lint, charpie, there were no bandages, no splints, no tourniquets, in the hospitals.

From all quarters, however, the story was the same, the Turkish authorities took no means to provide for the medical requirements of their army, and help from England was not only inadequate, but came too late. The hospitals in Erzeroum were now crowded; but whereas in former days such a thing as a man being discharged fit for duty was never heard of, now, under the skilful and kindly treatment of Dr. Featherstonhaugh and his assistants, men were daily turned out cured. It is a pleasure to read the universal testimony borne to the comfort experienced by the Turkish soldiers in the Blantyre Hospital. Officers and men located in the other buildings used to beg for admission, in order that they, too, might reap the benefits of England's charity. In anticipation of a further increase in the number of such, the Governor of Erzeroum despatched Dr. Galenthay to Erzingjan, with instructions to provide hospital accommodation for a further number of 1,000, in addition to the 1,500 who were sent under the doctor's charge.

At Olti, too, early in October, Dr. Flüss reported that his stores were exhausted and his hospitals full, whilst the same story was repeated at Bayazid. In fact, it was computed by the medical authorities that at this time fourteen per cent. of the whole strength of the Armenian army was on the sick list.

CHAPTER XIX.

TURKISH ADMINISTRATION IN ARMENIA.

Mahomedans Exempted from War Taxation—Christians Forced to Pay—Pensioners of Turkish Government—Irregular Imposts—The Discontent they Cause—The Hadji—The Caimakam and the British Consul—The Police Station at the Mouth of the Ghiurji Boghaz—Mr. Layard and the Danger to India—American Missionaries' Views on Christian Oppression—Turkish Reforms—Her Hospitals—Dr. Casson on Turkish Atrocities—Employment of the Press by the Porte—The Abkhasian Exodus—Treatment of the Bayazid Refugees by the Russians and Persians—Treatment of their own Wounded by Turks—Reduction of Unpaid Salaries.

ERZEROUM, *Sept.* 13*th.*

THE publication of the Government orders relative to the new internal forced loan of 600 million piastres was received with the most marked signs of discontent and dissatisfaction—so much so, indeed, that a deputation of the principal Mahomedans called on the Governor of Erzeroum and pointed out to him that the people in this district were more heavily taxed than in any other part of Asiatic Turkey ; with regard to the war, they were subject to numerous requisitions which those living at a distance from the seat of hostilities were not liable to ; they were called upon to feed any detachments of soldiers passing through their villages, receiving no compensation ; and they were constantly obliged to furnish carts and oxen for the transport of Government material, for which they received no payment. In fact, their demands were so reasonable that

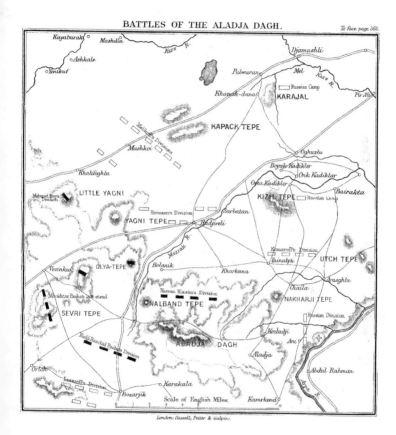

the Governor at once telegraphed to the Porte, who directed that all Mahomedans in the vilayet of Erzeroum should be exempt from the operations of the tax, on condition that they continued to supply horses, carts, and oxen for the transport of munitions of war. Emboldened by this success, the Christians formed a deputation and waited on his Excellency, begging that they, too, might be relieved, as they had already, since the commencement of hostilities, been called upon to pay nine separate money contributions towards the expenses of the war. Hassan Izzet Pasha, however, pointed out to them that they were exempt from military service, that they had all their able-bodied men at home, and were in a position not only to carry on their ordinary business avocations, but also to cut and gather their harvest, which the Mahomedans, owing to the majority of their males being with the army, were unable to do ; and that, although he would forward their petition to the Sublime Porte, he could not hold out much hope of relief.

As is usual in all wars, the effect of this falls with far heavier force on the labouring classes than on any other; the distress rife throughout the district is almost inconceivable. The Pashas and richer people do not feel it, as they take care to draw their pay regularly from the Government Treasury, while the lower officials and the private soldier never see their allowances. These all suffer extremely, more especially the pensioners of the last war—widows of men who fell in 1855, of whom there are still a few dependent on Government bounty for support. Their pensions, small as they are—only 30 piastres a month—have not been paid them this year, and they are consequently plunged in the greatest want and destitution. The people do not complain of the regular taxes, but what they do inveigh against most bitterly are the irregular imposts, from which they have no escape, and which they know full well never go into the Government Treasury. Christians and Mahomedans speak alike on this point, and I have met as many of the latter creed as of the former who state there will be no happiness in Turkey as long as a Pasha exists. I will give you one or two instances to show you the unjust way in which taxes are levied here. These have come under my own personal observation, and I have conversed with the villagers concerned, chiefly Mahomedans, whom, as a rule, I have found more bitter against the system of Pasha rule than their Armenian fellow-countrymen.

In a village some fifteen miles from this, which I have visited three times, dwells a certain Hadji, who is one of the chief men of the place. He is a farmer on a small scale, owns a small plot of land, a few cattle, and is able by the sweat of his brow to earn his own living, and keep his head above water, which comparatively few Turks are. Just after the outbreak of the war, the Caimakam, or sub-governor of his district, called on this man, and demanded a war contribution. The old gentleman gladly consented to give towards the good purpose of driving the hated Giaour out of the kingdom of the Faithful, but did not see his way to the large sum the Caimakam was anxious to extract from him. Appeals were made to his pride as head man of the village, to the odour of sanctity which surrounded him and his family in consequence of his pilgrimage to Mecca, and finally the old gentleman was induced to part with 2,000 piastres in good money, equal to £200, on the express condition that he was not to be called upon for any more war taxes during the present year; but, as the Hadji piteously remarked, "there has not been one single week since then that I have not had to pay towards the war in some shape or another." The first blow that fell upon him was the announcement that he had been drawn for the Mustahfiz, or Reserve troops, and was to join the battalion in Erzeroum. The poor old fellow fled to the British Consul, Mr. Zohrab, who, with his usual kindheartedness, at once went to the palace, explained the old man's case, pointed out that he was over sixty, was the only male in his family, that if he were sent to the front those dependent upon him for support would be plunged into starvation and misery, as their crops would be left standing, and their cattle untended, and that, moreover, he had already served fifteen years in the regular army, had voluntarily given 2,000 piastres to the war fund, and was a just object for the Mushir's benevolence. The pleadings of the British Consul were successful, and the old man, to his delight, was granted exemption. Freed from that trouble, his old friend the Caimakam continued, nevertheless, to make calls upon his purse; his village every week is called upon to furnish a certain number of carts for Government transport; and he, of course, is compelled to pay his share of their cost, varying from ten to thirty piastres a week. As he says, "When and where is this to end? Neither I nor the rest of the agriculturists can go on paying these sums or giving our labour for nothing, and we see nothing before us but ruin and starvation. We help the Government to the best of our power, but Government will not help us;

Y

they only take our money, our young men, our all, and return us not even thanks."

Another instance of oppression, though of a different kind :— In April last the Governor conceived the idea of building a police station at the bridge across the Euphrates, just at the mouth of the Ghiurji Boghaz, and an official was sent to warn the villagers in the immediate vicinity that they would be called upon to contribute £500 towards its construction. They are all small agricultural hamlets, and such a sum was almost beyond the grasp of their intellect. They at once sent a deputation to Ismail Pasha, saying that there were no thieves in the Pass, that they had done without a police station since the commencement of the world, that they were utterly unable to find such a sum among them, and they implored him to reconsider his determination. He refused, and threatened to quarter soldiers in the villages until the money was forthcoming. Thus pressed, the greybeards of the neighbourhood met together, apportioned the various sums to be contributed by each village and by each household, and conveyed the money to Erzeroum. They were then told to collect stones and beams of wood at a certain spot. Workmen were sent out, and the building commenced. It is now finished; I have seen it. It consists of a rectangular, stone, one-storied house, containing but one room 30 by 24 feet; it is 14 ft. in height, unboarded; there are two holes for windows, unglazed; the door consists of a couple of rough planks joined together; the stones are undressed, and no mortar was used in the construction; the roof is a flat mud one—in fact, it is similar to the road-side police stations one sees all over India. The cost, I should say, could not have exceeded 5,000 piastres, especially as the village gave the beams and stones, and many of the villagers were forced to labour on the work. I have conversed with many men who have seen it, and they all say that £30 was the outside sum it cost. What has become of the balance of £500? The answer given by Mussulman and Christian alike is— "It is in this way our Pashas enrich themselves, and grind us down to the dust."

I have read with much interest Mr. Layard's despatch of the 30th of May. With all due deference to the large school of Russophobists who inveigh so loudly against our policy of masterly inactivity in India, I cannot conceive any man who has travelled down the North-West Frontier of the Punjab and viewed the natural ramparts which surround us, and has studied the physical geography of the country beyond them, fearing that the conquest of Armenia, or even the possession of Herat, would endanger the safety of our Indian Empire as long as our rule is as beneficent and as tolerant as it is now, and as long as we have or can put at call 100,000 bayonets, British and native, to man the mouths of the passes in the Suliman Mountains. With regard to the majority of the Christians preferring Turkish to Russian rule, I fear my short experience in this country and my conversation with American missionaries, men as much to be depended upon as Dr. Washbourne, have led me to form a completely opposite opinion. Moslem and Christian alike groan under an intolerable yoke—the yoke of Pashas whose wills are unfettered, whose passions are unbridled, whose vices are beyond description, and whose oppressions are too well known for

y 2

my pen to attempt to describe. Turkey bears a striking resemblance to the Infernal Regions, which good George Herbert said are paved with broken promises ; all her promises of reform have been swept away ; her conduct in this war has been marked by the vilest crimes of which a nation can be guilty. She has not only committed the crime of arming and letting loose bands of undisciplined, fanatical robbers, whose passions, fed by the religious exhortations of their bigoted priests, and strengthened by the proclamations of the Sheikh-ul-Islam, have led, as the Porte knew full well and firmly intended that they should lead, to the brutal massacre of the survivors of the Bulgarian rebellion and the cold-blooded murders of the inoffensive Christians in Armenia. Of worse crimes even than these has Turkey been guilty ; she has been guilty of plunging into a war which she knew would be a bitter and a sanguinary one, and she has made no preparation for the care of the sick and wounded men—of men who pour out their lives like water for the sake of the Prophet and the Sultan. Armies without a single doctor are sent 100 miles from the nearest hospital, and sick and wounded men are left to drag their weary limbs as best they may to the nearest harbour of refuge ; no preparations are made for their transport, no escort sent with them to obtain shelter or food at the various villages *en route ;* they are left unprovided with money to procure themselves even the commonest necessaries of life on the way, and, as Turkish doctors themselves have said to me, only the slightly wounded men ever reach Erzeroum ; and it is the wish, doubtless, of the Government that it should be so, for, as I have before asserted, so I repeat, that it has been deliberately stated by the principal medical officer of Erzeroum, in the presence of three Englishmen, that "the Porte prefers its soldiers to die rather than that they should become pensioners on the State." The conduct of the Ottoman Government goes far to prove there is too much truth in Ismail Bey's statement, and until the hospitals in the Turkish army are put on the same footing as those of other European armies, so long, in my humble opinion, should the condition be annexed to the gifts of English stores and the services of English doctors, that no convalescent man should be permitted to return to the ranks, but should be straightway sent to his home; indeed, I do not see why such conditions should not be annexed in all future wars as the price of the assistance given by all sick and wounded aid societies. At the present time they cease to be charities; in the case of Russia they are auxiliaries to her own excellent hospital arrangements; in the case of Turkey they simply fill a void, for it may be said that medical men and hospitals do not exist here, and so the charitable institutions of England heal the wounds of men in order that they may be the more speedily able to destroy some more of God's creatures. Is this charity? I think not. As Dr. Casson very pertinently remarked to me the other day, "the greatest atrocities to be seen in this country are to be daily witnessed in our hospitals. There you have the most dire outrages that Moslems have ever perpetrated, and they are daily and hourly committed by the Turkish Government on her brave soldiers." If the Porte really meant reform, why did it not take measures for the protection of the Christians in Armenia and Bulgaria; why did it not take steps to procure proper medical assistance for the

300,000 fighting men, who need, God only knows how much, every help that man can afford them ?

The statement that Turkey does not employ the Press to support her cause, which I saw in a recent issue of the *Times* under very high authority, is perfectly unfounded. The Porte does employ the Press, and very largely, too. I know two European journals which are heavily subsidised by the Ottoman Government. I know that divers advantages, some partaking of a very solid character, are offered to correspondents who advocate the Turkish cause, and who forward telegrams dictated by Turkish authorities. I am making no idle accusations now, and I know cases in which credits have been opened at various telegraph offices by the Ottoman Government in favour of their said correspondents. If this is not employing the Press, I know not what is ; in fact, as far as my short journalistic experience goes, I have been astonished at what I have learned since my arrival in Turkey. I knew, at least I was told, that every Turkish official had his price, and that the longest purse obtained the services of the best man. But I was not prepared to learn that the razor cut both ways, and that the Turk knew full well that the European could be bribed too.

The Turkish fleet in the Black Sea has been very busily employed of late in transporting the insurgent Abkhasians from Soukoum Kale to Trebizond. Upwards of 4,000 have been already landed at that port, where they are in a state of the greatest destitution. Removed from their homes—where, at any rate, they had land to till, crops to cut, and wherewithal to earn a livelihood—they had been shipped off penniless to a strange

land, and left stranded in Asia Minor, without money
to provide themselves even with the barest necessaries
of life. Many of these men are Christians, and have
appealed to the American missionary at Trebizond,
laying their hard case before him, and many hundreds
have complained to him that they were actually carried
off against their will, and would gladly even now
return and face the anger of the Russian Government.*
M. Biliotti, our energetic vice-consul at that place, with
the assistance of Mr. Cole, is inquiring into the case,
which, as far as I have been able to learn, reflects but
little credit on the Ottoman Government. What will
become of the poor creatures it is hard to say. There
is no hope that they will receive a money grant from
the Porte to enable them to purchase agricultural
implements, oxen, horses, &c., or that they will be
assisted to build homesteads. I hear that small grants
of land will be made to them, but at the best these
Abkhasians will find that their lines have not been cast
in pleasant places.

It is satisfactory to learn that the survivors of the
Bayazid massacres who fled into Russia to escape the
fury of the Kurds were treated with the greatest
hospitality and kindness by the Mahomedan inhabitants
of Maku and the neighbouring villages, whither they
fled for protection, arriving, many of them, perfectly
naked, having been stripped to the skin by the blood-
thirsty savages, who even now form part of Ismail

* A lengthened correspondence on this subject took place between
Prince Reuss and Mr. Layard on the one hand, and the Porte on the
other. Promises were given by the latter that all Abkhasians who so
willed it should be sent back to Russia; and about 4,000 signified their
wish to return. It is needless to add that the giving the promise, not the
fulfilment of it, satisfied the scruples of the Porte.

Pasha's army. They were provided with food and clothing, and the Russian general at Erivan sent £500 in gold to the governor of Maku to be divided among them, as the town was gutted and burnt by Sheik Jellaladeen's men. Everything of value being destroyed and upwards of 460 Christians, men, women, and children, murdered in cold blood, under circumstances of the most revolting cruelty, it is not to be wondered at that the survivors decline to return to Turkish protection, and announce their intention of settling permanently in Persia or Russia. Some few merchants have returned in the hope of recovering money they had buried, but in every instance, as far as I can learn, they had been forestalled in their search by the Kurds. In the district of Van order has been partially restored. Two battalions from Mussaul and Djezireh have arrived, and the governor, a man of firm and humane temperament, has succeeded in a certain measure in reassuring the Christians of their safety. The American missionaries, after months of wandering in disguise in fear of their lives, have at last been enabled to return to their homes, but are forbidden to pursue their labours, for fear of irritating the Kurds.

Large batches of wounded men have been arriving in Erzeroum during the past few days from Kars, as is usual here; the slighter cases pour in fast, and the hospitals now are deluged with hand wounds, very many of them requiring amputation. Owing to the very strong pressure brought to bear on the principal medical officer, Ismail Bey, Dr. Featherstonhaugh has no difficulty now in procuring the necessary permission for these operations. Yesterday he carried out eight successfully; the poor fellows were overwhelmed with gratitude at the kindness with which they were received in the British hospital, and the extreme care and attention shown them by our surgeons. "There is no pride about the English," said a wounded man to a comrade after Dr. Featherstonhaugh had been busying himself in washing a wounded limb, the hurts of which were much aggravated by the fact that the owner had ignored the principle that cleanliness is next to godliness for some months previous to his wound.

The 1,800 wounded men were sent in from Kars without any doctor to attend on them. So it is not to be wondered at that the mortality *en route* was something frightful. Four Turkish doctors were sent out from Erzeroum to meet these poor fellows on the road, and afford them all the assistance in their power; but of the sixty-five wounded handed over to the care of Dr. Featherstonhaugh, one and all denied that their bandages had been removed since the day they had been first put on. They said, "The doctors came out to be seen, but they did not touch one of us; they just walked about and smoked at Hassan Kale, and never even looked at us." Of course the number of carts was far from sufficient for the large number of men they were supposed to convey, and I am in no way exaggerating when I say that hundreds of men, badly hit too, walked the whole distance from Sarbatan to Erzeroum, 130 miles. No preparations were made for them to receive rations at the various villages on the road; the consequence was that the stronger and healthier were enabled to forage for themselves, while the sick and weakly often and often went without a meal. No money even was distributed among these poor fellows, already upwards of three years in arrears of pay, to enable them to purchase a good meal. And this is the country, forsooth, that is trying to inaugurate reform, and would do so even if not paralysed at its earliest efforts by the wicked aggression of Holy Russia. Turkish reform! When Pashas, Effendis, Cadis, and all the blood-sucking officials have been vigorously suppressed, when the Turkish peasant, Mahomedan or Christian, can freely ventilate his wrongs and obtain justice against his superior in the social scale, then we may hope for reform in Turkey. Has Turkey one whit improved in the last five centuries? No. Her diplomatists have learnt to tell falsehoods with more freedom and more unblushingly; her cruelties and oppressions are practised more vigorously, but more secretly; and she is far more steeped (I mean her higher classes) in vice and barbarism than she was 500 years ago. The lower classes have not improved one whit either. The same depravity and ignorance; the same rude implements that were used 1,000 years ago are used now; the unmuzzled ox treadeth out the corn, guarded by a small boy with a stick to see that the dumb beast does not help himself to the grain; the same low, half-underground mud huts that satisfied their ancestors satisfy the present Turkish peasantry; the same blind faith in the doctrine of Mahomed and absurd belief in the superiority, intellectual and moral, of the followers of the Prophet over all other nations, and the same willing, cheerful endurance under all difficulties, the same free, open hospitality to strangers, exist now in the humbler classes as ten centuries ago. The saving clause in Turkey is, indeed, her poor. They are her nobility. I have met in my travels in this country few Pashas who could, by any means, be made to answer to the term " gentleman ;" but I have met many specimens of Nature's true nobles under the ragged garb of a private of Redifs, or the still more tattered clothing of a Mahomedan villager.

I have in the course of the past few days received visits from two officials high in Government employ in this vilayet, and took the opportunity of questioning them as to the effect the recent order reducing salaries by one-half would have on the *employés* here. They both gave me much the same answer. The order lays down that during the war Government officials will only receive one-half of their salaries ; the remainder will be looked upon as a loan by the Sublime Porte, who will give bonds for the sum, which will be redeemable at the close of hostilities. Both my friends assured me that this order was issued solely for the purpose of standing well in the eyes of certain European Governments. One informed me that he had seen no pay at all for twenty-seven months ; while the other, though forty-three months in arrear, had at his urgent entreaties received one month's pay in April ; but they said the Mushirs and Valis of districts, and Caimakams, or sub-Governors, as well as all Treasury officials, take care to receive not only their pay regularly every month, but to take it in good money, thus making a difference to them of eighty per cent., when we consider the present value of paper money. One of them—from his position he is enabled to speak with certainty on such a theme, and from my knowledge of him, and from the fact that I have never yet detected him in a falsehood, I believe him to be trustworthy—positively assured me that the

Vali of this district took his money from the treasurer every month in gold; that Mushir Mukhtar Pasha, on leaving Erzeroum for Kars in April, took what, according to regulations, he was allowed to take—viz., an advance of six months' pay—and that this was taken in gold, leaving the paltry sum of £1,500 in the Erzeroum Treasury wherewith to carry on the expenses of the war. "If," said these men, "the pay of all Pashas is to be reduced by one-half, a small saving will be effected by Government; but if they are to be permitted, as hitherto, to rob as they please, and only the salaries of small officials are to be mulcted, well, the saving will be *nil;* we are months—nay, years—in arrear, and never hope to see our back pay again, so a reduction of our salaries by one-half will not affect us or men in our position in the slightest degree, and most certainly will not affect Government."

There are one or two errors into which I have fallen in my previous letters, which I now wish to correct. The first is the statement made shortly after the battle of Taghir, to the effect that the Russian General had offered a reward of 2,000 roubles for the capture of any English officer. This rumour was current, not only throughout the Turkish camp, but also in Erzeroum. I, however, treated it as a mere rumour until I saw it stated, as I thought in all seriousness, in a semi-official letter from one of Sir Arnold Kemball's assistants, an officer of a scientific corps, whose connection with a recent high official at Constantinople makes his anti-Russian proclivities a matter of family pride. I have since learnt that this officer made the statement as a joke. It was a joke, however, which I maintain I was justified in placing some credence in, although I must express my regret that I was led into the error of accusing the Russian general, Tergukassoff, who has throughout these operations shown himself a gallant and humane officer, of such a dastardly act as that of offering rewards for the capture of the military attachés of a friendly Power.

The second mistake into which I have fallen has caused some annoyance in the Turkish camp, and although it is a very trivial one, yet I feel it my duty to correct it. In a more recent letter, referring to the barbarous custom of disinterring the Russian dead as practised by the Kurds and Bashi-Bazouks, and of stripping the Russian corpses, I stated that an aide-de-camp of the Turkish commander-in-chief might be seen in the head-quarters camp wearing a Servian officer's coat, thus showing that Turkish officers sanctioned the custom of despoiling the dead. Again I was wrong. The officer in question is not an aide-de-camp of Mukhtar Pasha. He is merely commanding the personal escort of his Excellency, not on his personal staff. The fact, however, remains unaltered that an officer living in Mukhtar Pasha's camp, the daily companion of his aides-de-camp, and one who constantly accompanies the chief himself in his rides, in his walks—one holding a position much sought after in our service—might be daily seen in the uniform patrol jacket of a dead Servian officer. That this custom of despoiling dead enemies is sanctioned by the Turkish authorities I have on the highest authority, and I know that in Servia the Turkish Commander-in-Chief declined to interfere with it.

CHAPTER XX.

THE TURN OF THE TIDE.

Russian Reinforcements—Mukhtar draws in his Men—The Grand Duke occupies the late Turkish advanced Posts—Mukhtar's Confidence—Despondency of Turkish Soldiers—Increased Desertions—Russians learn the Value of a turning Movement—The Battle of the Aladja Dagh—Gallant Defence of the Little Yagni—Loss of the Olya Tepe—Extraordinary Conduct of Men sent to support the Position—Russians occupy the Nalband Tepe—Panic on the Aladja Dagh—Flight to Kars—Scene in the Fortress—Hassan Bey's Exertions—Sanitary State of Kars—Mehmed Pasha evacuates the Little Yagni—Mukhtar's Plans—He falls back on the Araxes—Ismail Pasha also retires—Russian Trophies—Retreat through the Kose Dagh—Evacuation of Kuipri Kui—Energy of Faizi Pasha—Ismail surprised at Hassan Kale—Capture of Captain Creagh—Treatment accorded to him, and to Dr. Casson—Turks fall back on the Devi-boyun—Reinforcements from Constantinople and Batoum.

On the 6th and 7th of October, heavy columns of reinforcements arrived at Karajal, and the Turkish Commander-in-Chief learned from spies that his opponents had been strengthened by two complete divisions. It was impossible now to conceal from himself the fact which he had hitherto strenuously denied, that the Russians were about to commence an offensive movement on a very grand scale. It would have been wise if Mukhtar, even at this late hour, had fallen back on the Soghanly range, leaving in Kars a strong garrison; but he still possessed the firm belief in the qualities of his own soldiers and of his own strategic powers, and felt certain that he would be able even now to hold his own on the slopes of the Aladja Dagh. He however felt that his position was too extended, and that a brigade on the Kizil Tepe still was exposed to capture. Consequently, on the morning of the 8th, he abandoned all his advanced positions, withdrew from the plains of Sarbatan, and concentrated his forces in the position occupied in the early days of August. On the 9th the Grand Duke, taking advantage of the retrograde movement on the part of the Turkish Commander-in-Chief, occupied Kizil Tepe, Sarbatan, Hadji-veli, and the eastern slopes of the Great Yagni. As he thus was exposed to the artillery fire from the whole of the Turkish guns, he pushed forward his own artillery accompanied by strong columns of infantry, and vigorously replied to the Turkish fire, never venturing, however, to assault. At dusk the Russians, who had pressed forward to the left bank of the Mazra stream, now retired to the far side, and bivouacked for the night. On the 10th, the Grand Duke bombarded the Turkish camp from dawn to sunset, threatening it at the same time with the usual dense masses of infantry. The two following days were passed in comparative quietude. On the 12th, the ball opened by the Russians repeating the manœuvre of the preceding week, pouring a most destructive fire into the Turkish shelter trenches, which covered nearly their whole front, and harassing the Osmanli by repeatedly threatening an infantry assault.

Mukhtar, although personally unacquainted with the ground, had always persistently maintained that it was impossible for an army to move round the rear of the Aladja Dagh, and feeling convinced that only small bodies of troops could intervene between him and his right wing at Igdyr, felt safe with the occupation of Natschevan; consequently he thought only of his front.

His flanks and his rear were left comparatively un-defended, and absolutely unreconnoitred. In spite of Mukhtar Pasha's confidence in the security of his position, there was a pretty general feeling throughout the Turkish camp that a turning movement was not only possible, but was really on the *tapis*. A settled conviction of impending danger seems to have fastened itself on the minds of his men. Since the advance from Zewin, they had fought with the courage and boldness of conquerors, with the enthusiasm of men fired by religious exhortations. Now the weight of im-pending danger fastened on them, and they became most despondent. On the night of the 10th October up-wards of 700 deserted. On the morning of the 14th it became known that a Russian division had crossed the Arpa Tchai, and had made its appearance in the vicinity of Bazardjik, and Hadji Raschid Pasha was moved off to oppose this body with twelve battalions of infantry, eighteen guns, and some cavalry. His first attack was successful, and he succeeded in driving Lazaroff's division back on to a small range of hills near Orlok. For a time it seemed as if the impetuosity of the Turkish infantry would carry the day, for there is no doubt Lazaroff's men were thrown into great disorder by the gallantry of the onslaught. Hearing the sound of firing to the south of the Aladja Dagh, the Grand Duke learned that his turning movement had proved so far successful as to necessitate the march of a Turkish division from the main camp on the Aladja Dagh, towards Orlok. Leaving this attack to develop itself, on the morning of the 15th, he advanced with his entire forces to crush the Ottoman army. His right column, which was the strongest, moved *viâ* Kapack on the Little Yagni hill, the troops bivouacking on the Great Yagni, advanced on Vezinkui; those at Hadji-Veli were directed on the Olya Tepe, whilst the division at Sarbatan and on the Kizil Tepe were ordered to assault the camp on the Aladja Dagh.

All day long Captain Mehmed Pasha defended his position on the Little Yagni against the repeated assaults of the enemy. He had with him but ten battalions, six field and four siege guns, whilst his assailant numbered thirty-six battalions and fifty-six guns. The Russians with dogged pertinacity endeavoured to gain the crest of the hill; the Turks, inspired by the valour of their commander, as often repulsed them. On one occasion, shortly before noon, a very powerful assaulting column made a most determined attempt to reach the summit, and for a few moments the place seemed lost. As the Russians poured in over the northern face of the entrenchments the Turks fell back in confusion to the southern slopes of the hill; but Mehmed Pasha, with his usual dauntless courage, placed himself at the head of the Ohf battalion of Mustahfiz, and drove the enemy back at the point of the bayonet, following them up nearly to the foot of the hill.

The fight on the Olya Tepe for a time was conducted with equal gallantry; four battalions holding it behaved in a marked manner. Their losses, however, were most severe, for the Russian artillery, which now fired mostly timed fuses, burst their shells on the summit of the conical hill with deadly accuracy. Mukhtar, forseeing that the loss of this hill meant the loss of the day, made a determined attempt to retain it. He despatched five battalions to its assistance, retiring himself to the Sevri Tepe for the purpose of taking the Russian columns in

z

flank. The leading half-battalion of the brigade, destined for the relief of the Olya Tepe, reached the crest of the hill in safety, but the remainder for some unaccountable cause were seized with a sudden panic; when they were about half-way up, there was no attempt at a disorderly stampede, no breaking the ranks and rushing headlong on their comrades below, but merely reeling from the effects of the sudden rain of shot that burst on them, as they cleared the summit of the Bolanik ravine they turned and retired slowly towards the Aladja Dagh. This strange conduct seems also to have animated the officers. No one seemed capable of taking command, of deploying the men, or of returning a shot to the Russian infantry who were now pressing after them. They never rallied, never made another attempt to reinforce their hardly-stricken, bravely-fighting comrades on the crest, who, seeing the help once so near gradually passing away, lost heart; and as the Russians, emboldened by the failure of the attempt to reinforce the Olya Tepe, pushed up its slopes with redoubled vigour, the Moslems turned and fled. Pushing a few companies up the sides to occupy the hill, the Russian commander continued the pursuit of the five battalions who had recoiled from his fire, and pressing up the Bolanik ravine, by noon had completely cut in between the troops on the Aladja Dagh and those at Vezinkui. Promptly taking advantage of the ground, field guns were dragged up the slopes of the Nalband Tepe, and a heavy fire poured on a division which Mukhtar had hastily collected and placed on the Sevri Tepe.

At the sight of the Russian division strongly established in their midst, a general panic seems to have seized the troops on the Aladja Dagh, who, regardless

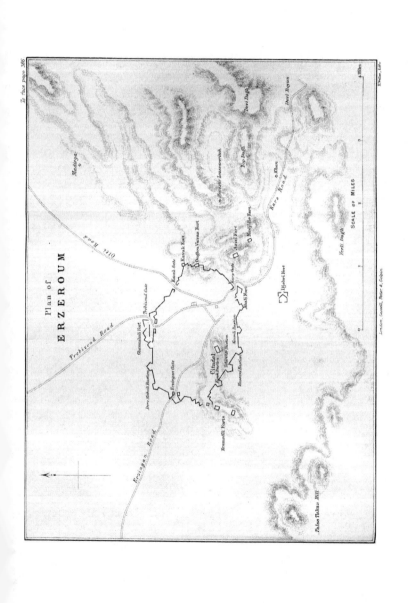

Plan of
ERZEROUM

Trebizond Road

Old Road

Kara Road

Khan

Deri Degh

Deri Boyun

Mosque of Leozootyoobah

Top Degh

Madieye

Mejidie Fort

Aziei Fort

Kavak Fort

Ooghoo Varmas Fort

Kavak Gate

Trebizond Gate

Oosmanbek Fort

Devi-Schooli Bastion

Kratrepe Gate

Citadel
Tchaboolan Bastion
Tchaboolan Bastion

Tabrese Gate

Muzzeli Bastion

Khanli Fort

Ujehri Fort

Yeri Degh

Boonooli Bastion

Krennelli Forts

Fatan Teban Hill

Erzingan Road

SCALE OF MILES

London, Cassell, Petter, & Galpin.

E.Weller, Litho.

of the entreaties and threats of their officers, broke their
ranks and moved rapidly in dense disorganised crowds
in the direction of Kars. Mukhtar vainly endeavoured
to rally the fugitives, whose conduct was already beginning to tell amongst his own men, who were falling
back rapidly; indeed, the panic now appears to have
set in generally amongst the men, as it almost invariably does with Turkish troops when once the flank is
turned, and a frightful scene ensued. The sole aim and
object of one and all seemed to be to reach the friendly
shelter of the fortresses as soon as possible; horse
and foot, officers and men, guns, baggage, wagons, all
dashed forward in one confused mass. Every man for
himself was the cry, and no one hesitated to use whatever arms he had in order to open a path for himself in
the living mass before him.

Mukhtar Pasha showed, as he has invariably shown
throughout the campaign, the greatest gallantry, and
bravely endeavoured to rally his men. Some few, be-
lieving in their chief, still clung to him, and with these
he was able to make a stand on a hill near Vezinkui.
By this means he was enabled to cover the disgraceful
flight of the troops. Hussain Hami Pasha, who was
commanding at Kars, at once moved out a brigade,
who, with fixed bayonets, barred the way. Thus a
certain amount of order was restored among the flying
masses before they entered the city, where the scene
defied description. Women, having thrown off their
veils, thronged the parapets, straining with eager eyes
to watch for the advent of those loved ones never to
return. The Christian merchant, ever mindful of his
worldly goods, was hurriedly gathering his property
together, and removing it to a place of safety. The

z 2

pressed commissariat bullock cart-drivers, heedless of the curses of the Circassians and Kurds, who vainly endeavoured to force their horses through the endless strings of vehicles, were goading on their bullocks in hopes to pass through the fortress and reach the peaceful quiet of their own homes before the stern necessity of war should again compel them to serve a thankless and rapacious government, whilst the Governor, aided by the gallant commandant of artillery, was vainly endeavouring to restore some sort of order amongst the flying masses, who now thronged the entrenchments to the south of the town. In vain did Hassan Bey try to rally these men; in vain did he point to the smoke still wreathing up from the crest of the Little Yagni where Mehmed Pasha still barred the march of the Grand Duke's army. Prayers, threats, exhortations were of no avail, and the brave gunner soon found himself compelled to visit his batteries, and prepare for the renewal of the siege which he foresaw was now about to burst upon him. As far as his own department was concerned he had no fear; the batteries all had been thoroughly repaired; extra traverses had been erected in the works on the eastern and western hills; extra bombproof accommodation had been provided for the garrison of the forts; the number of armed citizens had been largely increased; he had received reinforcements of trained artillery, and he had more than 800 rounds per gun in the magazine; but the sanitary condition of the place was worse than ever. Typhoid was raging amongst the sick and wounded, and though supplies of food were abundant, there was no firewood, nor was there fodder for the cavalry or artillery horses.

Mehmed Pasha was enabled to retain possession of

the Little Yagni Hill; but at nightfall, perceiving that
the whole of the Turkish positions except his own were
in the hands of the enemy, and that there was no hope
of receiving further support, made preparations for eva-
cuating it, dismantling the guns, and carrying off their
breech pieces. At midnight he retired unperceived and
unmolested into Kars, where he found Mukhtar Pasha
and Hami Pasha (who had been re-appointed commandant on the 5th October), together with all the
senior officers, in the Tahmasp Battery, making arrangements for the future of the campaign, which
seemed dark enough. The Commander-in-Chief, on
receiving the reports of staff officers, found that not
more than 13,000 men fit to bear arms could be collected, and he was well aware that, unless he could
throw a force between Kars and Erzeroum, there was
not a man to bar the Russian advance on that city; he
determined, therefore, to leave Hussain Hami Pasha with
10,000 men to hold the place, while he himself, with
the remaining 3,000, would fall back on the Soghanly.
He at once telegraphed to Ismail Pasha, who was in
Russian territory, near Igdyr, ordering him to retire
immediately on Kuipri Kui. This retrograde movement caused much surprise in the camp of the Kurdish
chief, for on the 16th instant, two days before he
received Mukhtar Pasha's telegram, Tergukassoff had
fired a salute of 121 guns, on learning the news of the
Grand Duke's victory. Ismail Hakki, with that facility
for invention which has characterised him throughout
the campaign, published an order to his men that
Tergukassoff had received intelligence of an insurrection in Russia, the Panslavonic conspirators having
dethroned Alexander, and proclaimed the Czarewitch in

his stead.   On the 17th, however, Ismail Pasha learned
the true cause of this rejoicing, and discovered that
Mukhtar had been routed and compelled to abandon his
advanced position.   At daybreak on the 19th, the
Kurdish chief, having destroyed all his spare ammunition
and commissariat stores by fire, detached six battalions
and a battery to Bayazid, while he himself with
the remaining twenty-two battalions and thirty-three
guns fell back on the Araxes.   At mid-day on the 16th,
Mukhtar, being unable to learn any tidings of the
division under Raschid Pasha, came to the unwelcome
conclusion that the whole of the troops on the Aladja
Dagh had fallen into the hands of the enemy.   In
this he was not far wrong, as it transpired that, with
the exception of thirteen battalions, who were enabled
to cut their way towards Khagisman, and who in
driblets afterwards rejoined the force, the whole of the
infantry, cavalry, artillery, commissariat, and hospital
equipments, with large trains of baggage animals, had
fallen into the hands of the victors.

Nine thousand men, 56 guns, upwards of 3,000 pack
animals, with seven pashas were prisoners in the Russian
camp.   Among these were Hadji Raschid Pasha, the
commander of the division ; Hassan Kiazim Pasha, chief
of the staff, together with his five *aides-de-camp ;* Shefket
and Mustafa Pashas, brigade commanders ; and Omar
Pasha, the German renegade in command of the cavalry
division.   Thus, taking into consideration the serious
losses his army had sustained, and remembering that he
must retain sufficient men to form the nucleus of a
force destined to defend Erzeroum, Mukhtar was enabled
to leave with Hami Pasha, in Kars, the remnants only
of thirty battalions, numbering barely 10,000 men.   The

hospitals, as I said before, were crowded with sick, and it is computed that there were no less than between six and eight thousand men unfit for duty in the fortress. At mid-day on the 16th, Mukhtar fell back on the village of Yeni Skui, reaching it on the 18th. He had with him then ten battalions, numbering about 3,000 bayonets, and ten mountain guns. The Grand Duke having made arrangements for the despatch of the prisoners to Goomri, detached General Heimann with two divisions to follow up Mukhtar Pasha. Lazaroff was directed to move on Magardjik, and thus cut off the communications between Erzeroum and Kars. On the 27th, owing to the rapid pursuit of Heimann, Mukhtar was forced to fall back on Kuipri Kui, where he effected a junction with Ismail Pasha, who had succeeded in traversing the Alishgird plains, avoiding the pursuit of Tergukassoff's strong cavalry force. In passing through the defiles of the Kose Dagh range Ismail Pasha divided his force into two columns, in order the quicker to pass this obstacle. The left column marching by Moola Suliman and Taikhojeh, was attacked on the 26th by a brigade of Cossacks, but owing to the steadiness of the infantry commander in charge of the rear guard the Russians were beaten off. Learning from Ismail Pasha that Tergukassoff was also in hot pursuit, Ahmed Mukhtar determined to abandon Kuipri Kui and fall back on the Devi-boyun. In this he was wise, for the field-works erected to cover the bridge were completely commanded on the northern and eastern faces, and so were not calculated to enable the Turkish commander to make a stand behind them. Another reason, doubtless, for this decision was that his men, as also Ismail Hakki's troops, were much demoralised, and it was a matter of question whether they would face the Russians in the plain ; so that Mukhtar wished to traverse the five-and-twenty miles constituting the Passin Plain unexposed to the attacks of the large Russian cavalry force in his rear.

Leaving Ismail in command of the combined divisions, numbering scarcely 13,000 bayonets, Mukhtar pushed on towards Erzeroum, directing his lieutenant to retire at once on Hassan Kale. This movement was carried out none too quickly, for at 4 p.m. on the 28th, just three hours after the Turks evacuated the place, the Russian advanced guard occupied Kuipri Kui, finding large quantities of grain which the Osmanli had forgotten to destroy.

Mukhtar, on reaching the Devi-boyun ridge, defending the south-eastern entrance to the capital, found that Faizi Pasha had not been idle. Immediately on receipt of the intelligence of Mukhtar's reverse and disaster, which the gallant old Hungarian had long predicted, he set to work to place Erzeroum in as complete a state of defence as was possible with the scanty means at his command. He had hurriedly collected all the able-bodied men in the city, convalescents as well as civilians, armed them, and sent them up to the batteries on the Devi Dagh range ; but even with this precaution he was not enabled to place more than 3,000 men on that position. He, however, had contrived to send up forty guns, the majority of them Krupp's breech-loading siege guns ; the entrenchments had been much improved, redoubts had been thrown up on the advanced spurs, and every inch of the road from the Nabi Tchai was swept by a cross fire from the heights above. Ismail Pasha, although well aware that he was being pursued by three divisions of Russian infantry and by vastly superior forces of cavalry, with true Oriental negligence, bivouacked his men in the plain to the south of Hassan Kale, without throwing out one single picket. Many men, more particularly the superior officers, entered the village, and slept in the numerous khans inside the old battlemented walls. Heimann's advanced guard discovered and reported this fact; the general in command immediately determined to surprise the Turkish bivouac that night. Moving a force by Ogomi to the north of the place, so as to take the sleeping Turks in flank, he himself about midnight advanced straight on the town. Another panic, another flight, was the inevitable result. Disturbed in their sleep by the sound of firing in their immediate vicinity, the Turks sprang to their feet. All thoughts of defence were at an end; men abandoned their arms, gunners abandoned their guns, commissariat drivers their carts, and all dashed in headlong confusion along the road to Khooroodjook. Many hundreds were cut down by the Cossacks, who dashed in upon the unarmed fugitives, hundreds more were taken prisoners in the town of Hassan Kale, amongst them being Captain Creagh, late of the 1st Royals, who, after being robbed of everything he possessed by the Cossacks, was taken a prisoner to General Heimann. That officer, with much courtesy, expressed his regret at the somewhat rough treatment the gallant captain had received, which, however, under the circumstances, was perfectly unavoidable, and at once gave him a permit to return to the Turkish camp at Erzeroum. I think this little incident deserves to be recorded. I doubt whether any British general would have treated a newspaper correspondent in the same manner. And surely when we hear of the treatment to which Doctors

Casson and Buckby were subjected in Melikoff's camp, Heimann's conduct is worthy of all praise. These two doctors had in August proceeded from Erzeroum to the head-quarter camp for the purpose of organising hospital and ambulance corps at the front. Whilst there, Dr. Buckby had been stricken down by typhoid fever, and was consequently, owing to prostration, unable to accompany Mukhtar Pasha in his retreat from Kars on the 17th October. When he was sufficiently recovered to bear the fatigues of the journey, he and his comrade determined to endeavour to reach Erzeroum; but shortly after commencing their march they were met by Cossack patrols, and led into the Russian camp. Their request to be permitted to pass on to the Turkish head-quarters was refused; and, in a military point of view, Melikoff, I humbly submit, was justified in so acting: but the treatment they received from Russian subordinate officials can only be stigmatised as brutal. Yet it was scarcely on a par with that meted out to Dr. Armand Leslie and his companions in Europe.

The fugitives from Hassan Kale were checked in their flight by some of the troops at Khooroodjook, who, on the noise of the firing, promptly turned out, and advanced in its direction. Ismail Pasha was thus enabled on the 29th to effect a junction with Mukhtar Pasha on the crest of the Devi-boyun.

Urgent telegrams had been sent to Constantinople for all available help, and on reaching Erzeroum, Mukhtar Pasha received the welcome intelligence that Dervish Pasha had been enabled to send him five battalions from Batoum, which were already on the march from Trebizond, and that twelve more battalions,

with two batteries, were *en route* from Constantinople.
Prior to the arrival of these men, Mukhtar Pasha was
enabled to place in position on the Devi-boyun ridge
about 16,000 men and sixty guns, and with these he
seemed confident that he should be able to repel all
attacks that Heimann might make on him. He was under
the impression that the Russian forces opposed to him
amounted to only twenty-two battalions, fifty-six guns,
and seven regiments of cavalry, whereas, with the
arrival of Tergukassoff's troops, the Russians had no
less than forty-eight battalions, ninety-six guns, and
twelve regiments of cavalry on the eastern slopes of
the Devi Dagh. As may be imagined, the *morale* of
Mukhtar's troops had been much affected by the
recent defeat and flight. Mukhtar showed the greatest
energy and gallantry in endeavouring to repair the
irreparable mistake he committed in pushing so far
forward from Kars, and mixing freely with his men
endeavoured to rally their spirits. In this he was aided
by the cheery bearing of his two foreign generals,
Faizi and Mehmed Pashas.

CHAPTER XXI.

OPERATIONS ROUND ERZEROUM.

Turks strengthen both Erzeroum and the Devi-boyun—Heimann attacks Mukhtar—Great Gallantry of Mehmed Pasha—Faizi holds the Turkish Right—Heimann tries a Ruse—Faizi tries to rally the Osmanli—Flight to Erzeroum—Turkish Losses—Mukhtar Pasha encourages his Men—His Refusal to surrender—Russians invest Erzeroum—They construct a Redoubt on the Tope Dagh—Relative Defensive Value of Erzeroum and Kars—Heimann's ill-judged Attempt to Assault the place—Gallantry of Tarnaieff—Capture of the Medjidieh Lunette—Mehmed Bey retakes it—Death of Tarnaieff—Failure of the Attack on the Kremedli Fort—Coolness of the English—Mr. Zohrab—Dr. Featherstonhaugh—Reginald and Percy Zohrab—Conduct of Turks to Wounded—The Gentle Ladies of Erzeroum—Mutilation of Russian Dead.

THE first three days of November were spent by the Turks in strengthening the works, both at Erzeroum and the Devi-boyun. The recent heavy falls of snow made advance from Olti a matter of such difficulty, that Mukhtar Pasha considered it impossible for the Ardahan column to turn his left flank. He, however, posted a small detachment in the Ghiurji Boghaz, and on the suggestion of Faizi Pasha, the Euphrates was dammed up to the north of Erzeroum, so as to convert its valley into one large morass. On the morning of the 4th of November, Heimann advanced from Khoo-roodjook with the intention of forcing Mukhtar out of his strong position.

Profiting by the lesson taught him at Zewin on the 25th of June, and by the repulse of the many frontal attacks he had so gallantly led during this campaign, Heimann at last appeared convinced that to gain a position defended by breechloaders and spades, he must either attempt a strong flanking movement, or draw the Turks out of their entrenchments by stratagem. It is more than probable that this was suggested to him by Tergukassoff, who throughout the campaign had shown himself a thorough master of the art of tactics; indeed, few living generals could handle troops better than this general has done. Heimann determined on this occasion to try both a turning movement and a ruse, so during the night of the 3rd of November he sent off a strong column along the mountain road towards Partak, and another column towards Nabi Kui. These were directed to conceal themselves in the numerous ravines on either flank of the road leading up to the Turkish position.

Mukhtar's troops were divided into three divisions. The right, under the command of Faizi Pasha, held the high ground above the village of Topalack. It had been strongly entrenched, and on it two or more redoubts had been placed. The centre was under the command of Mukhtar Pasha himself, whilst the left column, under Captain Mehmed Pasha, occupied a flat-topped conical hill, which enfiladed the whole Turkish front, and commanded all the ground in its vicinity. This was the key of the position, and Heimann sent forward a strong body of troops to endeavour to seize it. The gallant Prussian succeeded in repelling all these attacks; but towards mid-day, owing to very severe losses, he was obliged to apply to the Commander-in-Chief for assistance. Mukhtar Pasha, appreciating the danger, detached three battalions and two batteries to reinforce his left. Two of these battalions Mehmed placed on the crest of the hill, and threw the guns with the other battery slightly forward on some rising ground to his left, thus completely raking the Russian attacking columns. These movements seem to have been so far successful that all idea of carrying Mehmed Pasha's position was abandoned by the Russian general, and their columns withdrew out of range.

Success seemed certain for the Turks, and more so when, at about 2 p.m., a strong cavalry division was seen advancing up the Persian road, straight on their entrenchments. Mukhtar at once sent an infantry column, supported by two horse artillery batteries, down the road to drive these adventurous horsemen back. With loud cheers the Turks leapt out of their entrenchments, and dashed down the hill, halting now and then to pour volleys at long ranges into the Russian cavalry. Some of these were already dismounted, and plied the Turkish infantry as they advanced with a sharp fusilade. This only drew them further into the trap, for the Cossacks now began to retire, and the Turks pressed on in all haste. Soon they reached the Nabi Tchai, when, suddenly, from either flank sprang up thousands of footmen, who, pouring volley after volley into the astonished Turks, dashed in at them with the bayonet. Mukhtar now saw his mistake. His advanced brigades turned, and in much confusion endeavoured to regain the safety of their entrenchments ; but the Russians were already between them and the works. Hundreds of gallant Osmanli were shot down in brave but ineffectual attempts to hew their way through the dense masses of Russian infantry, whilst hundreds more sullenly threw down their arms and gave themselves up as prisoners. Mukhtar could not but see that the ambuscade must prove fatal; however, with that heroism which he has shown throughout the campaign, he at once placed himself at the head of two battalions, and endeavoured to stem the torrent of advancing Russians. It was too late, however; the contagion had spread, and the majority of the troops in the centre, regardless of their commander's personal example, of his entreaties, his orders, regardless of the threats of their own officers, turned and fled towards Erzeroum. In vain did Faizi Pasha endeavour to rally these men; it was in vain he pointed out that if they would only cling to the hill on the right above Topalack they would be enabled to enfilade the Russian advance, and at any rate check their pursuit. It was of no use. As long as the sun shines brightly the Turk will fight to the death, but he is a bad player at a losing game.

The scene on the road leading down to Erzeroum defied all description. Large convoys of commissariat cattle blocked the road, and through these Circassian and Kurdish horsemen endeavoured to cleave a way, while the infantry, rushing over the low hills on either flank, sought the safety of the town. Mehmed Pasha and Faizi Pasha, the two European officers commanding the flanks, behaved with the greatest gallantry. The steady front showed by their men did, in fact, check the rapid advance of the whole of the Russian force, and thus delayed the capture of Erzeroum. Had the panic spread to their men, there is no doubt that Heimann could have passed over the Devi-boyun, reached and entered the capital of Armenia that night. The Governor, hearing of the defeat, closed the gates of the city in order to prevent the fugitives rushing in, and as he feared pillaging the town; but at about midnight, the excitement having to a certain extent calmed down, strong guards were placed at the gates and the men allowed to file slowly in. All the barracks in the place were filled with sick and wounded men, so that there was no accommodation for the fugitives, whilst to add to their other horrors a heavy sleet commenced at about 11 p.m. The streets were crowded with famished, panic-stricken soldiers, who, wearied with the hardships they had recently undergone, sank exhausted into the mud and endeavoured to seek comfort in sleep. Where Mukhtar Pasha went that night no one knows. Shortly after midnight, Faizi and Mehmed Pasha reached the city ; the former drew off his guns, and managed to escape unperceived by the enemy. Mehmed Pasha, however, was not so fortunate ; he was followed up in his retreat by a Russian brigade, and had to contest every inch of the way from the Devi-boyun to the Pasha Punar, some three miles from the walls. The following morning the Russians could be distinctly distinguished on the crest of the Devi Dagh mountains, busily engaged in throwing up redoubts, and preparing for the bombardment of the city. It is very difficult to estimate what the Turkish losses were, but it may be safely assumed that 3,000 prisoners and 42 guns were left in the hands of the enemy, while between 2,500 and 3,000 men were either killed or wounded.*

This was a severe blow to Mukhtar Pasha, quenching, as it did, the last hope of being able to undertake the offensive during the campaign. He, however, busied himself to raise the fallen spirits of his men. He daily visited the fortifications, addressing some few words of spirited encouragement to his soldiers. He

---

* Mukhtar Pasha acknowledged to 1,000 men killed.

assembled a council of war in the palace, to which he invited the leading Mahomedans and Christian inhabitants, and there explained to them the real state of the case. Fired by the enthusiasm of their chief, and prompted by the hope that large reinforcements would speedily arrive, these announced their determination of aiding him with all their ability in the defence of the city. On the 6th inst. a *parlementaire* arrived from the Russian general, and demanded a surrender of the place. To this Mukhtar returned an answer that Erzeroum belonged to the Sultan and not to him, and that until he received instructions from his royal master he was unable to return a reply. He at once despatched a telegram to Constantinople informing the Porte of the very warlike feeling amongst the inhabitants, and his own determination to lay down his life rather than resign his charge.

On the following day he received an answer directing him to defend the place to the last man and the last cartridge. A note to this effect was despatched to General Heimann, who informed Mukhtar Pasha that he would give him three days' grace, and if at the expiration of that time he did not surrender, he should commence the bombardment.

On the 7th inst. the Russians busied themselves in throwing up a redoubt on the hills to the eastern face of the town. From what we learn, this must have been a large work some 200 yards in length, with a parapet ten feet in height, and a ditch in front. It was situated about 2,500 yards from the Tope Dagh, and completely dominated the city. All day and all night men were employed in its construction. Mukhtar's forces were too weak for him to attempt to prevent the erection of these

A A

siege works. He could do nothing but collect supplies and make all arrangements for withstanding the assault, which he knew would not be long delayed. Erzeroum is perhaps better adapted for this purpose than Kars : the enceinte is of strong profile, and cannot be carried until it has been breached. The perimeter is about three miles, whereas that of Kars is almost ten, and the entrenchments of Kars, as we have already seen, owing to their weak profile, can easily be carried by assault. On the walls of Erzeroum there are mounted upwards of 150 Krupp siege guns, many of them being eighteen centimeters in calibre. The garrison, including armed inhabitants, of whom there are several thousands, cannot be less than 20,000. This gives four men per yard for the defence of the walls, which would render an assault an extremely hazardous undertaking.

On the morning of the 9th November, General Heimann made an ill-judged attempt to carry the outworks by storm. Columns were directed upon the Azizi position on the south-east, on Kremedli Fort, to the south-west ; but owing to the darkness of the night, or the treachery of the spies, the attacks were not delivered simultaneously, and so resulted in failure.

It appears that during the evening of the 8th November there was a council of war in General Heimann's tent, on the crest of the Devi Dagh range, to consider and discuss the best means of capturing Erzeroum. All saw that a most favourable opportunity had been lost on the 4th November, when in all probability if Mukhtar had been promptly followed up, the place would have surrendered without a struggle. However, several causes combined to make this movement particularly hazardous at that moment. In the

first place, a severe snow-storm came on as the sun went
down, which much impeded the advance ; in the next,
the feat of crossing a mountain-range 8,000 feet above
sea-level, by a single road, with an army of 50,000 men
and 120 guns, is not one lightly to be undertaken ; and
lastly, the Russians were thoroughly worn out after their
late long and rapid marches. So Heimann judged it
inexpedient to risk an assault on the 5th November.
At this meeting in the Russian commander's tent,
a staff officer named Tarnaieff, a man of Armenian
extraction, who had distinguished himself on more
than one occasion during the campaign, and who
was personally acquainted with the city of Erzeroum,*
volunteered to undertake the capture of the outlying
Azizi works, if he were entrusted with the command
of three battalions, and were supported by a complete
brigade. His views at first were scouted as ridiculous,
but so earnest was the young lieutenant-colonel, and so
fired by enthusiasm, that at last he succeeded in im-
pressing his opinion on the minds of the senior officers.
Heimann himself, a bold, daring leader, had readily
fallen in with them, but the more cautious divisional
generals, mindful of recent disasters against fieldworks
defended by the breech-loader, dissuaded him for some
time from countenancing Tarnaieff's proposal. In the
end, however, the young Armenian carried his point,
and arrangements were made, not only for carrying out

* Tarnaieff was for some years employed in the Russian Consulate at
Erzeroum, nominally as a dragoman. The fact that carefully prepared
plans of all the works were found on his body, proves the real nature of
his employment, and that the capture of Erzeroum had for many years
been determined on. The act of employing staff officers as dragomans in
the consulates of fortified towns, is a novel feature in diplomacy, one that
redounds more to the far-sightedness of the Russian Government than to
its honour.

the attack on the Azizi outworks, which command the whole eastern system of fortifications, and virtually constitute the key of the position, but also for supporting it by a simultaneous attack on the south-western face near the Kremedli redoubt.

At midnight the Russian columns paraded—the right, consisting of ten battalions, near the Loussa-voritch Monastery, destined for the attack on the Azizi, whilst the left column of sixteen battalions assembled on the Yerli Dagh, to the south of the town. Tarnaieff with three battalions led the right column of attack, being supported by seven more battalions under a general of brigade. These were left some two miles in rear, and covered by the darkness. The brave young colonel moved silently onward, accompanied by one field battery, until he arrived within about three-quarters of a mile of the fort. Here he deployed his men, and dropping two battalions, with instructions to push on directly they heard the firing commence, he crept noiselessly on. His men were provided with scaling-ladders, and he determined to throw the ladder party on the salient angle of the Medjidieh lunette, whilst he with the remainder of the battalion entered the work through the open gorge.

From Turkish sources we learn that before break of day a sentry in the Medjidieh lunette, an outwork of the Azizi fort, hearing what he took to be the approach of a large column of troops, reported the matter to the officer of the guard, who declined to believe the man's statement. As dawn broke, the garrison of the lunette learned that the sentry had not been mistaken, for two bodies of Russian troops suddenly entered the work, one from the parapet in the front, one from the open

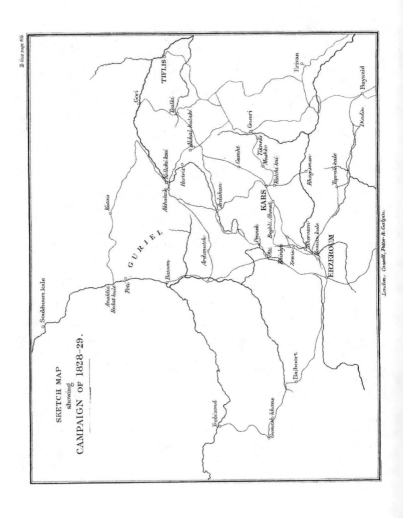

SKETCH MAP
showing
CAMPAIGN OF 1828-29.

TIFLIS

Gori

Tsalki

Akhal-kalaki

Akhalzik

Hertwiz

Tskhi-kui

Ardahan

KARS

Gumbt

Tiknesh
Moubkis

Hadshi-kui

Gumri

Erivan

Khagisman

Toprak-kale

Bayazid

Ivedin

GURIEL

Katais

Ardanutsh

Penek

Baghli-Ahmed

Oltu

Zewin
Rarrarn

Hassan-kale

ERZEROUM

Peki

Batoom

Anaklia
Redut-kale

Soudhoum-kale

Trebizond

Gümish-khana

Baiboort

London: Cassell, Petter & Galpin.

gorge in the rear, and before the men could even seize their arms, the place was in the possession of the Russians. Captain Mehemed Pasha, commanding Azizi, which is about 1,200 yards in the rear of these outworks, hearing a disturbance, with that promptitude and gallantry that have characterised him throughout the campaign, placed himself immediately at the head of half a battalion of one of the new regiments recently arrived from Trebizond, and proceeded to ascertain the cause. On approaching the Medjidieh fort, he at once saw it was in the hands of the enemy. Without giving the matter a thought, he fixed bayonets and straightway charged them. A sanguinary hand-to-hand fight took place inside, but such was the impetuosity of the onslaught that the Russians were fairly driven out of the work, not before they had removed the garrison, consisting of twenty officers and 500 men. Tarnaieff's reserve battalions now made a desperate effort to retake the lunette, and the sound of the firing was now to be distinctly heard in the city. The big guns of Azizi opened upon the Russian columns with terrible effect. Awakened to a sense of their real danger, thousands of citizens, stirred with frenzy by the wild exhortations of the Moolahs (who thundered forth their anathemas on the hated Giaour from every minaret), dashed up to the citadel, where arms were hurriedly distributed.

By 7 a.m. the whole road from the Tabreez Gate to the Azizi was crowded with a mass of armed men proceeding to defend the city. With this welcome re-inforcement Mehmed Pasha was not only enabled to repel all the Russian attacks, but towards the afternoon had so far gained the ascendency that, delivering one more impetuous bayonet charge, he hurled the Russians back from the lunette, and then drove them inch by inch up to the walls of the Tope Dagh redoubt.

To turn to the Russian column of attack on the south-east, descending the Yerli Dagh, instead of keeping along the crest and moving down the easternmost slopes of the Palantukan range, it found itself discovered, and under a heavy fire from both the Djebri and Ahali forts long before they had approached their goal. Further advance was useless. The Kremedli is a permanent work, and to endeavour to carry it by storm must only have ended in disaster and disgrace, so Heimann very wisely recalled the column, which at about 2 p.m. fell back on Topalack. The casualties here were very small. Had the commander of the detachment been enabled to reach the Kremedli unnoticed, in all probability Erzeroum would have fallen, for, attacked on both sides, Mukhtar would not have been able to devote the whole of the garrison to the repulse of the gallantly-led attack on the Medjidieh lunette.

Mukhtar Pasha, on the first sound of firing, had proceeded to the Azizi fort, and himself directed the fire of the heavy guns on the Russian columns. The gallantry of the Turks was most marked, and augured badly for any Russian columns that might endeavour to assault their stronghold; but no less marked was the conduct of Dr. Featherstonhaugh, who, aided by Reginald and Percy Zohrab, sons of the worthy British consul of the place, went about regardless of the hail of bullets, binding up the wounds and helping the stricken men to a place of safety. These two English youths were on the field of battle carrying out their humane work until long after midnight, when they proceeded to the English Hospital, there to make all necessary arrangements for the large number of men waiting admission. They were not alone in their work of charity, for the consul himself, accompanied by his eldest son, a lad of eighteen, and by the old consular cavasse, Mustafa, who has been a faithful servant of Her Majesty for upwards of forty years, were equally busy on the battle-field, superintending the conveyance of the wounded to a place of safety, and endeavouring to save Russian prisoners. In this humane work Mr. Zohrab nearly lost his life. A Turkish soldier, foiled in his attempts to plunge his bayonet into the body of an already badly wounded Russian, turned on the consul, and threatened to bayonet him. The timely arrival of a Turkish officer saved the life of one of the best men in the consular service.

And now I have to place on record one of those acts of cold-blooded atrocity which, alas! have been furnished in such ghastly quantities by the present war. Directly it became known in the city of Erzeroum that the fortunes of the day rested with the Osmanli, bands of women trooped up to the field armed with knives, hatchets, choppers, whatever household weapons came first to their hands, and then commenced a system of mutilations which it does not do to dwell on. Suffice to say that from Englishmen, who visited the battle-field on the following day, I learn that nearly every Russian found lying on the ground was decapitated and subjected to nameless outrage, and that the appearance of the wounds proved that many of them were inflicted on still living men.

The gallant Tarnaieff, who was wounded early in the day, surrendered to a Turkish officer, but this was not sufficient to save his life: his dead body, mutilated in the cruellest manner, was found in the Medjidieh lunette the following day, clad merely in a silk shirt dyed crimson with the life-blood of the brave young Armenian. Heimann, on learning from others present that he had been wounded and had surrendered himself a prisoner, sent in a *parlementaire* to Mukhtar Pasha, offering any two Turkish officers in exchange for the hero of the day, but the Turkish Commander-in-Chief was compelled to return answer that no such officer was to be found amongst the prisoners. Some few Russians, including one officer, were taken alive, owing to the exertions of the gallant little Captain Mehmed Pasha, to whom belonged the honour of the day. His prompt attack on the Medjidieh lunette before the Russian supports had time to arrive was the sole cause of success. His personal bravery on this, as on every other occasion in which he has been engaged during the war, extorted the admiration of all who saw him; he certainly well earned his promotion to the grade of lieutenant-general, which it is rumoured Mukhtar has recommended him for.

The Turkish casualties in this engagement were exceedingly heavy, about 700 killed and 1,500 wounded, whilst twenty officers and 500 men were left prisoners in the hands of the enemy. But the Russian loss must have been far heavier. Three hundred dead bodies were left in the interior of the Medjidieh fort, and Captain Mehmed Pasha may be trusted to have given a very good account of the columns whom he broke and pursued to Tope Dagh. The Russians, having failed in their attempt to carry the outworks, and having learnt that reinforcements were daily arriving from Trebizond, determined completely to invest the place. To effect this, a road was made over the Devi Dagh range, *viá* Partek, to Tsitawankh, in the Euphrates valley, and by this means bodies of cavalry were enabled to pass over the range and occupy Madirga. In obedience to directions received from the ambassador at Constantinople, Sir Arnold Kemball, who throughout the campaign had been present wherever the fighting was thickest, and wherever the danger was greatest, now left Erzeroum, and took up his head-quarters at Baiboort, midway to Trebizond. The only British officer left in the place was Mr. Zohrab, the consul, who, however, was quite at home in a besieged town. November, 1877, will seem to him but a counterpart of November, 1855, when, as secretary and interpreter to Sir Fenwick Williams, he aided in the heroic defence of Kars.

CHAPTER XXII.

THE THIRD CAPTURE OF KARS BY THE RUSSIANS.

Siege of Kars—Capture of Fort Hafiz Pasha—Russians Move their Head-
quarters—Projected Assault of the Place—Detail of Attacking Columns—
Success of Lazaroff on the Right—Death of Count Grabbe in front of the
Kanli Tabia—Capture of all Works on the Plains—Capture of Karadagh
and Citadel—Hussain Hami Pasha escapes—The Majority of the Garrison
surrender—Grand Duke enters the Place in Triumph—Melikoff moves
towards Erzeroum—His Column forced to fall back from Olti—Komaroff
moves to Ardahan—Thence to Ardanutsch—Skirmish there—Condition of
Erzeroum—Treachery at Kars—Hussain Bey, Commandant of Artillery—
Osman the Renegade—Hassain's Visits to the Russian Camp—The Circassian Letter Carrier—His Death—Abandonment of the Hafiz Pasha
Tabia—Escape of Hami Pasha—The Man whom the Russian General
allowed to wear his Sword—Like Father like Son.

To turn now to the main Russian column, under the
immediate command of the Grand Duke Michael, which
after the battle of the Aladja Dagh had been established
at Kharrak-Darrah with a division at Magardjik, having
cleared his camp of all sick, wounded, and the many
thousand prisoners, who were all sent into Goomri, and
having ordered up the siege train from that place, he
determined once more to open the siege of Kars.

Lazaroff was accordingly directed to commence siege
batteries at Magardjik, whilst one division was moved
to Vezinkui, with instructions to bombard the eastern
face of the town. The Grand Duke himself on the 10th
inst. moved round from Karajal to Vairan Kale, the spot
which Mouravieff selected in 1855 for his head-quarters
camp. During this march the Russian flank was exposed
to the attack of the enemy, and Hami Pasha was not
slow to take advantage of it. Moving out the greater

portion of his garrison, he attacked the Russian division on the line of march, and threw it into some confusion. But Melikoff quickly rallied his men, and turning on the Turks, drove them at the point of the bayonet back into their entrenchments. So sudden was the onslaught and so rapid the flight, that for some time the Russians were in undisputed possession of Hafiz Pasha's fort, and were enabled, before the garrison recovered their surprise, to dismantle the guns and remove the breech-pieces. As there had been no intention of carrying the place by assault, this Russian column was unsupported, and consequently forced to retire from the position it had so successfully and gallantly won. The next day the Grand Duke sent a *parlementaire* to the city to demand its surrender, but Hussain Hami Pasha declined to discuss the subject, and threatened to fire on any party venturing on a similar errand. The following day, on the 12th of November, the Russian batteries commenced to bombard the forts on the southern and eastern faces of the city.

The Grand Duke had now adopted the plan followed by Paskiewitch in 1828, by Mouravieff in 1855, viz., that of commencing siege operations on the southern face of the fortress. In May and June the mistake was committed of bombarding the place from the north, when it was found that the works situated on lofty hills suffered little or no damage; the siege batteries now covered an arc of a circle, stretching from Komadsor on the right bank of the Kars stream, through Karadjuren, Magardjik, and Azatkui, to the foot of the hills west of Vezinkui; their fire was directed against all the southern forts, which comprise the Suwarri, the westernmost, the Kanli, Faizi Bey, and Hafiz Pasha; the magazines and town must also have suffered from the bombardment, whereas in the first so-called siege they escaped scathless.

On the 16th the Hafiz Pasha fort was silenced, the guns had been dismantled, and breech-pieces removed during the attack on the 10th; and it is supposed that the new breech-pieces of Kars workmanship were scarcely calculated to stand the same test as Herr Krupp's handiwork. The effect of this success was to leave the south-eastern angle of the work entirely undefended; and on the 17th the Grand Duke, after assembling a council of war, determined to assault the place—the smallness of the garrison, the large extent of front, with scarcely a man available for every three yards of parapet, the state of demoralisation to which the men had been reduced since the recent defeats, the fact that typhoid was raging inside the city, and that there was dissension amongst the Turkish generals, were quite sufficient reasons to induce the Grand Duke to attempt an assault, and gave him every hope of success. It was well known in the Russian camp that the entrenchments connecting the various works were of very slight profile, that the obstacles in front were scarcely calculated to delay an assaulting column for five minutes, that many of the so-called forts had open gorges, and that few had flanking defences for their ditches.

On the night of the 17th the columns were told off for the attack : that on the extreme right advancing from Vezinkui was to threaten the Karadagh works, whilst it was to seize the Hafiz Pasha fort, and then climbing up the southern slopes of the Kara Dagh, take the Ziaret Tabia in reverse; this was composed of the 40th Division, under the command of Lazaroff, he who successfully

carried out the turning movement at the battle of the
Aladja Dagh. The central column, which extended from
Magardjik to Komadsor on the Kars Tchai, was under
Count Grabbe; it consisted of fourteen battalions,
drawn from the 19th Division, the Moscow grenadiers
and the Caucasian rifles. This force was destined to
attack the Kanli and Suwarri forts to the south of
the place. On the left bank of the Kars Tchai,
General Roop, with the remainder of the Moscow
grenadiers, was directed to attack the Tahmasp fort,
whilst Komaroff, with the Ardahan brigade, was told
off to capture the Mukhliss Tabia. Three storming
columns, as it were, surrounded the whole fortress;
they numbered forty-four battalions, exclusive of reserve,
and assuming each battalion to be but 600 strong, the
attacking force amounted to 26,400 men, exclusive of
artillery and engineers, whereas the garrison did not
amount to one-half that number. One hundred and
forty-four field guns accompanied the assaulting column,
and did admirable service.

Under cover of a very heavy fire from fifty-two
siege guns, the columns advanced, those on the south
and east with orders to carry the works opposed to
them at all cost; those on the west and north with
orders only to make a very serious demonstration,
without pushing an actual assault.

Each column was accompanied by a ladder party,
but with the fatality that usually attends such detachments, the ladders were far too short, and heavy loss of
life was the consequence.

Lazaroff's column, moving on the Hafiz Pasha Tabia,
carried it with comparatively little loss, the troops
holding it, having no artillery, hastily abandoning the

place. Moving the greater portion of his division to the right, he swept the entrenchments clean, and straightway proceeded to climb the steep rocky slopes of the Kara Dagh hill. This was accomplished without loss, for the assailants were sheltered from the fire of the guns on the crest, and the forts on the plain were too much occupied in their own defence to spare a thought for the Karadagh.

As one brigade of Lazaroff's 40th Division advanced on the Ziaret Tabia, the only work with a closed gorge on the crest of the Kara Dagh, the other moved on to the citadel, an antiquated masonry work, capable of making a stubborn defence against infantry assailants, but quite precluded from defending itself against troops accompanied by guns. Its artillery consisted of one muzzle-loading rifled gun, and three field-pieces. It was garrisoned by a couple of companies of Redif artillerymen, who speedily took to flight, and the citadel, with its vast stores of small arms, ammunition, ordnance stores, magazines, &c., fell into the hands of the Russians. At about the same time the Ziaret Tabia was carried, and this commanding the Kara Dagh redoubt and the Karapatlak battery, speedily led to their capture.

To turn to the central column under Count Grabbe, a brigade moved on the Suwarri, whilst a second undertook the capture of the Kanli fort; the Suwarri, held by an Arab Redif battalion, was captured with slight loss, but the Kanli Tabia, held by Anatolian Nizams, made a most determined resistance. Count Grabbe was killed in leading the assault, and more than one attack was hurled back with heavy slaughter. The officer who succeeded to the command, a colonel of engineers, instead of trying a frontal attack, worked round to the gorge, closed by a masonry block-house. The massive gates were blown in, and the garrison were offered two alternatives : that the redoubt in which they had taken refuge should be subjected to dynamite experiments, or that they should surrender unconditionally. After a short parley, the place was given up; thus the citadel and the works on the southern and eastern faces were in the hands of the Russians. In the meantime, General Roop, finding the fire opposed to him very slight, pushed up to the walls of the Tahmasp Tabia, which after a slight skirmish was captured.

A large portion of the garrison now endeavoured to cut their way out of the works, but Komaroff's infantry and Prince Tchavachavadzi's dragoons opposed and captured by far the greater number. It is a curious coincidence that Mukhtar Pasha reported both these officers as killed in the battle of Kizil-Tepe on the 25th August, yet they sufficiently survived to take part in the crowning act of the campaign! Both had been very severely wounded in the Kizil-Tepe fight.

The commandant, Hussain Hami Pasha, succeeded in escaping, together with some few horsemen,* but by noon on Sunday, the 18th, the whole of the garrison, numbering about 12,000 men, several Pashas, 257 siege and sixty field guns, were in the hands of the victors, besides vast quantities of provisions, ammunition, &c.

On Monday, the 19th, the Grand Duke entered the

---

* It is worthy of note that Sabri Pasha, commandant at Ardahan, and Hami Pasha, commandant of Kars, both served under Mukhtar Pasha in Montenegro ; that they were at his request removed from their commands for incompetence during the campaign of 1876; that when he succeeded to the charge of the Fourth Army Corps, he found these two most worthless gentlemen in command of the two chief fortresses in Asia; that both should have unsuccessfully defended their trusts, and that both should have escaped scatheless !

city, receiving the homage of the chief inhabitants, Mahomedan and Christian, and on the following day the Turkish prisoners were moved under escort to Alexandropol, a civil governor was appointed over the city, native inhabitants enrolled as police, and quiet reigned around. Melikoff, with two divisions and the siege train, consisting of fifty-two guns, immediately marched for Erzeroum with the object of aiding Heimann, who, being provided only with field guns, was quite prevented from commencing the siege of a fortress which mounted upwards of 150 heavy Krupp guns on its walls. Moving by Tcharpakli and Bardez, Melikoff tried to push a brigade to Olti, and there enter the Erzeroum valley by the Ghiurji Boghaz, and Euphrates valley simultaneously as by the Devi Boyun, but the rugged nature of the road and heavy falls of snow prevented this column reaching Olti. It accordingly returned, and with the Commander-in-Chief entered the Passin plain, where they found all Heimann's troops located. Failing in his rash attempt to carry the Azizi works by storm, Heimann had detached a brigade to Madirga, about five miles north-east of Erzeroum, to prevent the garrison obtaining supplies from the numerous villages in the Euphrates valley. To support this detachment he had constructed a road *viâ* Partak to Kiossa Mahomed, but the Turks had burnt this last-named village, and destroyed his road. Typhoid fever, too, had broken out with much virulence in his army, and he was now giving his men that rest they had so long needed.

Simultaneously with Melikoff's move to the south-west, the Grand Duke had detached Komaroff with his old brigade on Ardahan, with orders to settle the civil and military administration of that district, and then marching *viâ* Ardanutsch and Artvin, suppress *en route* all attempts at a rising in Lazistan, push down the banks of the Tchoruk Su, and co-operate with Oklobjia at Batoum.

Ardahan, over which the Russians had kept a firm grip since its capture in May, needed no further supervision, so Komaroff, in spite of the terrible weather and bad state of the roads, pushed on towards Batoum encountering a band of Lazi irregulars at Ardanutsch, where it may be remembered on the 28th of June he fought a similar fight on the self-same spot. After a sharp engagement, in which his losses were most insignificant, he swept these undisciplined bands before him and occupied Ardanutsch, which he placed under the jurisdiction of the governor of Ardahan.

Erzeroum in the meantime had been profiting by Heimann's inability to prosecute the siege with vigour : reinforcements both of men and guns came up from Batoum, from Trebizond, and from Constantinople. Large supplies of food were procured from Erzingjan, and the neighbouring villages in the Euphrates valley. All inhabitants not volunteering to bear arms were summarily expelled the city, and Mukhtar dismantled their houses to increase his stock of firewood. Mainly owing to the lack of vigilance of the Russian cavalry commander, the Turkish general was enabled to employ the many mills (forty-three in number) in the immediate vicinity of the city in grinding the large stores of wheat Faizi Pasha had providentially collected.

By the end of November it was calculated that Mukhtar had about three men for the defence of every yard of front, and that he had upwards of four months'

B B

full provisions for these men. His great want was in cavalry, and his cavalry general, Moussa Pasha, a Russian deserter of the name of Kondukoff, was a man whom the Commander-in-Chief distrusted, and the men openly abused.

There seems to be no doubt that Kars was to a certain extent captured by bribery—that is, that the key of the work, the Hafiz Pasha Tabia, on the southeast corner of the fortification, was purposely left undefended. I have once or twice in these pages spoken of Hassan Bey, the Commandant of Artillery, as a man of much ability; he served for many years in England in studying artillery at Woolwich, and flattered himself that he knew the temper of the English nation towards the Turks. It was amusing to hear his opinion of the utter selfishness that marked our conduct in all matters pertaining to our Foreign policy; and he did not hesitate to impute the basest motives to all Englishmen who did not openly uphold the Osmanli in all their doings.

During the first siege, in June and July, Hassan Bey behaved with much zeal and gallantry. It was not until after the battle of the Aladja Dagh, when every one saw that the game in Armenia was lost, that suspicion attached itself to him, and then not until he had begged to be permitted to accompany a flag of truce to the Russian camp for the ostensible purpose of learning the strength and disposition of the enemy's forces.

From several sources I have gathered the following story, which may be relied on as giving the truth regarding the "Fall of Kars:"

A certain European doctor in Pera, owing to incompatibility of temper, obtained a divorce from his wife, who, preferring the honour of reigning in a harem to the privilege of sitting at the table of an Englishman, espoused one Kibrisli Mahomed Pasha. Within a short period of the second marriage this lady gave birth to a son, who was received into the Mahomedan Church, and named Osman. The youth became a fluent French and English scholar, was educated at the Military School of Constantinople, and, after entering the service, was attached to the Embassy in Paris as military pupil. He also visited England, and made himself thoroughly acquainted with the organisation of the various European armies. On his return to Constantinople he was promoted to the grade of major on the staff, and appointed to Van, where he remained for some years. Owing to an unfortunate quarrel with the Governor, he fell into temporary disgrace, and on the outbreak of the war tendered his sword to the Russian Government. His services were eagerly accepted, and he was given a high appointment on the Intelligence Branch of the staff of the Caucasus, for which his previous training peculiarly fitted him.

Whilst on the staff in Armenia Osman Bey had many opportunities of forming an acquaintance with Hassam Bey, colonel of artillery, and then commandant of the citadel at Erzeroum. Their European education and common knowledge of English drew the bond closer, and the higher Ottoman officials in Erzeroum remarked that they held aloof from Turkish officers, and mixed much in the society of the Europeans in the place, being frequent guests at the house of Mr. Obermüller, the Russian consul.

Mukhtar Pasha was well aware that Osman Bey was in Melikoff's camp, and that through him the Russians had obtained an accurate knowledge of the organisation of the Ottoman Forces, and of the construction of the various fortresses. He, however, placed much confidence in Hassan Bey, but did not consider his services sufficient to warrant his promotion to the rank of Liva Pasha, or general of brigade. This fancied act of injustice rankled in the mind of the "patriot," and is supposed to have been the cause of his disaffection.

It appears that early in November Hassan Bey volunteered to take a flag of truce to the Russian camp and ascertain their exact strength, also what troops they had detached in pursuit of Mukhtar Pasha. He was granted permission, and visited Lazaroff's camp, in the vicinity of Magardjik. He returned to Kars with the story that Osman Bey was there, very disgusted with the treatment received at the hands of the Moscovs, and anxious to rejoin the Crescent; that the Russians were not numerous, had no siege guns, and that no fear need be entertained for the safety of Kars. On the 10th of November, it will be remembered, that a sortie of the garrison was repulsed with much slaughter, the Turks being driven back with such impetuosity that the Russians seized the Hafiz Pasha Tabia, and dismantled the guns. The following day, before commencing the bombardment, the Grand Duke sent a flag of truce to Hami Pasha, demanding the surrender of the place, which was indignantly rejected. On the 12th Hassan Bey once more volunteered to visit the Russian camp, and ascertain if they were in a position to bombard or assault the town. He returned again, stating they were very weak, quite unable to risk an assault, and he suggested that there was no necessity to repair or occupy the Hafiz Pasha Tabia. On the 13th the bombardment commenced, and the next day a Circassian was seized endeavouring to pass the sentries at night with a letter from Osman Bey, in the Russian head-quarters at Vairan Kale, to Hassan Bey. Though written in Turkish, it was couched in such ambiguous phraseology that it was found impossible to attach any meaning to it. Hassan Bey, when sent for, denied all knowledge of its contents, but urged that the man should be put to death. He denied that the letter was for him. Being a man of great force of character—quite the leading spirit of the place—he was listened to. The Circassian was thrown from the citadel cliff, and the commandant of artillery went about his work as usual—he carried his point. The Hafiz Pasha Tabia was left undefended by guns, and on the first assault was captured. The column then was enabled unopposed to scale the southern cliffs of the Kara Dagh, and to seize both the works on its summit and the citadel with absolutely no loss. The commandant of the fortress managed to escape, but amongst the prisoners was Hassan Bey, who now may be seen an honoured guest in the camp of the Grand Duke—the only Turkish officer who is permitted to wear his sword. The evidence is but circumstantial; but the links of the chain seem strongly riveted together, and I fancy would be considered sufficient in any court to justify the death of the Turkish gunner. A strange feature in the history of the case is that Hassan Bey's father sold Varna to the Russians in 1828.

CHAPTER XXIII.

PASKIEWITCH'S CAMPAIGN IN 1828–29.

Paskiewitch's Forces—Doubts about Persia—Pankratieff watches her at Khoi—
Brigade for the Circassians—The Russian Plans—Their Three Columns—
Their Strength and Leaders—Inability to Siege Erzeroum in one Campaign
—Cross the Frontier 14th June—Detail of Army of Czar—Of that of
the Sultan—Kars captured 23rd June—Akhalkalaki, 24th July—Hert-
witz, 26th July—Akhalzik, 16th August—Ardahan taken same Day—
Aitzkui, 18th August—Russian Right Column captures Bayazid—The
Russian General cantons his Army in Armenia—Turkish Spring Prepara-
tions—Endeavour to recapture Akhalzik—Massacre of Christians—19th
May, 1829, Paskiewitch rejoins the Army—11th June, he advances—19th,
Battle of Zewin—20th, Battle of Mellidooz—28th, Erzeroum surrenders—
Treaty of Adrianople.

A BRIEF account of the campaign of 1828-29 will be
a fitting sequel to this story of the war of 1877. To
the general reader, it will be one more proof of the truth
of the old adage, "History repeats itself." To the
military student, it will be a proof that it does not do
in these days of the breech-loader and the spade to re-
hearse the tactics of our fathers ; and that, after all, as
Napoleon pithily expressed it, "God favours the heaviest
battalions."

In December, 1827, Russia then being at war with
Persia, the feud between the Sultan and the Czar that
had been slumbering for many years broke out. Hastily
concluding a peace with the Shah on the 6th February,
Paskiewitch, the Governor-General and Commander-in-
Chief of the Caucasus, commenced preparations for the

subjugation of Armenia. Irrespective of the natural wish to extend her conquests completely round the Black Sea, a campaign in Anatolia necessarily must form a portion of the plan of any war waged between the Porte and Russia. The vast resources Turkey possesses in her Asiatic provinces enable the Sultan to recruit his forces to an almost unlimited extent from the hardy mountaineers of Armenia, consequently the aim and object of the Russian War Minister is, by decisively attacking the Ottoman on this side, to hinder men from being despatched to Europe to swell the armies there.

The forces at the disposal of Paskiewitch for his operations amounted at this time to

> 51 battalions of infantry,
> 11 squadrons of cavalry,
> 17 regiments of Cossacks,
> 12½ batteries of artillery, numbering 154 guns.

The policy of Persia, in spite of the recent peace, was still undefined, and it was thought more than probable she would take advantage of the fact of Russia's complications, and once more declare war. She had only just ceded to the Czar two rich provinces, and paid a very heavy war contribution, so Paskiewitch deemed it advisable to be quite prepared for her entering into an alliance offensive and defensive with the Turk. To guard against any coalition of troops, the Russian general organised a corps under Pankratieff, consisting of six battalions, two regiments of Cossacks, and sixteen guns, which he posted at Khoi, in Persian territory, be it minded.

Another evil has to be guarded against in all wars between Russia and Turkey, and that is insurrection in the Caucasian provinces. They were, it was known, ripe

for revolt, and it was rumoured Mahomedan emissaries
had been travelling through the Abkhasian and Mingrelian country, endeavouring to incite the people to
rise. To guard against this, Paskiewitch occupied the
Caucasian country with fifteen battalions, three squadrons of cavalry, forty-two guns, and four regiments of
Cossacks.

Thus there were left for the expeditionary army—

> 30 battalions,
> 8 squadrons of cavalry,
> 11 regiments of Cossacks,
> 96 guns.

The ports of Poti and Batoum were, as for many
years they had been, the object of Russia's desire; consequently, Paskiewitch detailed one column to act on
the shores of the Black Sea whilst, with the remainder
of his army, he determined to operate in two columns:
the main or central one advancing by the Allaghoz
chain was to reduce the frontier towns of Akhalzik,
Akhalkalaki, Hertwitz, Kars, and Ardahan; whilst the
left corps, pushing across the Ararat range, was to
subjugate the province of Bayazid, and guard the flank
against the attacks of the Kurds, who, it was known,
attracted by "loot," would swoop down from Van and
Moosh. In fact, the corps operating on Poti and on
Bayazid were acting as wings of the main army advancing into Armenia.

The right, or Batoum army, was placed under the
command of Major-General Hesse, and consisted of—

> 8 battalions of infantry,
> 14 field guns,
> 1 regiment of Cossacks.

The left, or Bayazid column, was under the order of Tchavachavadzi, the reigning prince of the Abkhasians, and numbered—

>   3 battalions of infantry,
>   8 field pieces,
>   1 regiment of Cossacks.

Whilst at Natschevan, keeping open free communication between the left wing and main army were posted 2 battalions.

Paskiewitch himself commanded the main column, which was to be massed in the neighbourhood of Goomri, and amounted to

>   18 battalions of infantry,
>   9 squadrons of cavalry,
>   7 regiments of Cossacks,
>   56 field guns.

The Russian commander felt that his forces were too weak for him to hope to reduce Erzeroum in one campaign, for prior to an advance across the Soghanly range, it would be necessary to seize all the fortified places, many of them very strongly garrisoned, in the provinces of Kars, of Akhalzik, and of Bayazid. He therefore determined to devote his whole time to subjugate these districts, leaving the conquest of Armenia to the following year.

There were many reasons in favour of Goomri being chosen as the base of operations in Armenia. In the first place, the ground between it and Kars was open, and feasible for the movements of large bodies of troops ; in the second place, it enabled a blow to be struck at one of the main Turkish fortresses, without exposing the Russian frontier to the danger of an attack; and thirdly, it threatened the flank of any army advancing by the Soghanly range to the relief of Ardahan or Akhalzik. There were other minor reasons, too, which led to the selection of Goomri: it was in a central position, and easily furnished with supplies; the siege train, quartered at Erivan, could more easily be moved by this road than any other; and lastly, the subjugation of Kars gave the Russians possession of the large valley watered by the Kars and Arpa rivers, with abundance of grain and forage.

Then, as now, the Ottoman organisation was ill-adapted for offensive warfare, and it never seemed to have struck Paskiewitch that the Turks could plan a counter-stroke.

Prior to commencing operations, the Russian Commander-in-Chief threw forward a detachment under Major-General Popoff to Suram, to guard the defiles of Bordjom. This force numbered

3 battalions,
608 Cossacks,
4 guns,

and formed a connecting link with Hesse's troops on the Batoum line. Thus on the 12th of June, all preparations being complete, Paskiewitch massed his troops at Goomri, which now consisted of but

15 battalions of infantry,
8 squadrons of cavalry,
6 regiments of Cossacks,
52 guns.

DISTRIBUTION OF RUSSIAN ARMY, 12th JUNE, 1825.

Designation of Column.	Infantry.	Cav.	Guns.
Major-General Hesse. Black Sea Column - .	4,541	462	14
Major-General Popoff. Bordjom Flanking Column	1,180	608	4
General Paskiewitch. Central or Main Column. Chief of the Staff—General Von Sacken. Quartermaster-General—Colonel Valkhovski.			
1st Brigade Infantry, Major-General Mouravieff	2,511	...	...
2nd ,, ,, ,, ,, Bergmann	2,562	...	...
3rd ,, ,, ,, ,, Korolkoff	3,488	...	...
Cavalry Brigade, Colonel Rarevsky - - -	...	3,346	...
Artillery ,, General Gillenschmidet - .	...	...	70
Major-General Prince Tchavachavadzi. Left or Armenian Column - - - - - -	2,151	336	8
General Merlini. Left Central or Natschevan -	1,730	47	2
General Pankratieff. Corps of Observation on Persian Frontier - - - - - -	2,691	715	16
Total - .	20,854	5,514	114

Great pains were taken to arrange a good commissariat establishment, the organisation of which the Commander-in-Chief himself took in hand ; and in May he had already succeeded in collecting at Goomri—

> Government wagons - - - 530
> Hired arabas - - - - - 540
> Pack animals - - - - - 2,250

Whilst in the vast storehouses at Goomri and in its immediate vicinity, he had stored for transport—

> 12,000 sacks of biscuits
> 1,000 ,, barley
> 4,000 ,, wheat
> 4,000 casks of salt meat
> 1,100 gallons of brandy.

More than 3,000 men were hired to assist in
the commissariat train; an extremely liberal scale of
wages, coupled with firm supervision, ensured good
work.

Field hospitals were established, one at Goomri for
300; one at Tsalki for 200 sick. An ambulance train
for the movable columns was organised, numbering
sixty-six specially-constructed *fourgons;* there were two
companies of trained hospital orderlies to aid the
surgeons in their work, whilst a large corps of litter-
bearers were also organised.

Let me turn now to the Turkish army, of which, I
regret to say, I can find no such detailed account as of
the Russian. The most strenuous exertions were made,
not only to strengthen the garrisons of all the fortresses,
but also to organise an army for offensive operations.
For this purpose—during the early spring—the chief of
the Karakapaks reconnoitred the whole course of the
Arpa river, as well as the passes through the Bordjom
range, all of which were held by strong detachments
of irregular troops.

Akhalkalaki was held by 1,000 Lazi volunteers;
Ardahan was occupied by upwards of 2,000 regular
soldiers; Akhalzik was reinforced by a large detachment
of cavalry; and Kars, considered the key of Armenia,
besides being furnished with a garrison of 15,000
infantry to man the walls, was further strengthened
by a brigade of 3,000 cavalry, with fourteen field
guns. Van was garrisoned by 1,500 men; Bayazid by
1,000; whilst a corps of 40,000 was being organised
by Halib Pasha with which to take the offensive. The
religious feeling of the multitude being worked upon by
the Moolahs, recruits came forward in great numbers,

and it seemed as if the Porte would be able to crush the Russian forces by sheer dint of numbers.

On the 14th of June, Paskiewitch, advancing from Goomri, crossed the Arpa Tchai, carrying with him in his vast commissariat train forty days' provisions. He halted that day at Tikhniss, in Turkish territory, and the next morning moved to Maskni, encountering slight opposition from a small party of Turkish horse.

A brief reconnaissance of the fortress of Kars induced the Russian general to determine on attacking Kars on the southern face, the northern and eastern being too precipitous to admit of assault, or of the construction of regular siege works. Moreover, the occupation of ground on the south-east face cuts off communication more completely with Erzeroum. Consequently, on the 17th, Paskiewitch moved *viâ* Azatkui to Magardjik, where he halted for the night, and the following day advanced to Kitcik-kui; but during this march his flank was exposed to attack, and the Turkish commander was not slow to take advantage of the opportunity presented him: he made a vigorous sortie, which for some time promised success; but the conduct of his irregular Kurds and Karakapaks threw the main force into confusion, and he was eventually compelled to retire with heavy loss, the casualties amongst the Russians amounting to twelve killed and thirty-nine wounded.

On the 20th of June the siege park reached Paskiewitch, and enabled him to commence his offensive operations against the city. At the same time he was aware that Kiossa Mahomed Pasha was advancing in all haste to relieve the fortress, so he threw up some field works on the banks of the Kars river to guard his left flank.

On the 22nd of June, covering the work by a feigned attack on the citadel, Paskiewitch opened his first parallel, and on the 23rd assaulted the place on the south and south-western faces with numerous columns. At 8 a.m. he was in possession of the enceinte, when the Pasha surrendered the citadel with 151 guns, and 11,000 men became prisoners of war. Kiossa Mahomed Pasha, hearing of the fall of Kars, abandoned his intention of crossing the Soghanly, and moved north towards Hoonkiar-Dooz. Paskiewitch now determined to capture Akhalkalaki. For this purpose he left Kars, with a strong garrison, under General Bergmann, and on the 17th of July, moving to Zaim, and thence, by the eastern shore of Lake Tchildar, to Ghegh Dagh. On the 22nd, he sent Colonel Abukoff to the commander of the fortress of Akhalkalaki with a flag of truce, to demand the surrender of the place. This was fired on, and that officer killed. On the 24th, Paskiewitch assaulted the town, and captured it, with fourteen guns and 300 men. The Russian soldiers, infuriated at the conduct of the Turks for having fired on their flag of truce, slew upwards of 600 men. Without losing a moment of time, the Russian General detached the chief of his staff, General Sacken, to Hertweiz, which surrendered without firing a shot. Thirteen guns and 300 men fell with the place. General Hesse, in the meantime, with the right column, had captured Poti, with forty-three guns, thirteen standards, and 2,000 men. By the capture of Akhalkalaki and Kars the routes by the Bordjom mountains and Arpa-Tchai were now opened to the Russians ; and on the 26th of July reinforcements reached Paskiewitch from Tsalki and Goomri. On the 1st of August, the Russian Commander learnt that the Osmanli forces had reached Ardahan and were moving forward to attack him. The Russian, nothing loath to accept battle, advanced towards Akhalzik, reaching Koltchi-kui on the 3rd inst. On the 5th, he attacked the Turks and drove them back, but Kiossa Mahomed Pasha was able to effect his junction with the garrison of Akhalzik, where now were encamped 30,000 men. On the 9th, after a hard battle, in which the Russians were victorious, the Turks abandoned their guns and fled towards Ardahan. On the 10th, Paskiewitch commenced the siege of Akhalzik, and by the 12th had completed the investment of the place. On the 15th, breach-batteries were opened, and on the 16th of August, after a desperate fight, the place was captured. The garrison fought with the most determined valour, and it is computed that upwards of 5,000 men were slain in its defence. Out of 400 artillerymen who manned the guns on its walls, but fifty were left to tell the tale. Thirteen hundred Lazis out of a body of 1,800 recently raised were slain. Sixty-seven guns, and fifty-two standards, were captured; the Russian loss being only 128 killed and 495 wounded. In consequence of the heroism displayed by the defence, Paskiewitch permitted the garrison of the citadel to march out with all the honours of war. On the 18th, the Russian Marshal determined to reduce Aitzkui, and despatched Colonel Vidbelski, with five companies and six guns, to effect this. The place surrendered, with twenty-four pieces of artillery, without attempting a defence.

In the meantime orders had been sent to Bergmann,

in Kars, to move on Ardahan, and the Commander-in-Chief, on the 18th inst., directed Mouravieff to march for the same place. This officer, however, learnt on his road there that the fortress had capitulated to Bergmann on the 16th inst. The left column in the meantime had been equally successful. Having subjugated the whole province of Bayazid, with the exception of the citadel, which was left masked, Prince Tchavachavadzi had marched as far as Toprak Kale. He had been re-inforced by two battalions and four guns from Khoi, and Bergmann had also sent a force down from Kars to keep open communications with him. On the 20th September, the Prince, finding that his flank was threatened by the Pasha of Moosh, at the head of a large body of Kurds, determined to recapture Bayazid, and hold it. For this purpose he returned, attacked and defeated a body of 3,000 Kurds, who were covering the place, when the garrison fled, and with the loss of but ten men Bayazid, with its twelve guns and three standards, fell into the hands of the Russians.

Early in September, the Prince, having made all arrangements for the government of the province, advanced into the Alashgird plain, seized the fort of Toprak Kale, which had been occupied by Kurds during his absence, and busied himself with collecting supplies on the fertile district.

On the 19th inst., the Pasha of Moosh having advanced to Grakon, the Prince determined to attack him, and on the following day defeated him, with a loss of 600 men, his own casualties amounting to sixty-seven. On the 28th, finding that the Pasha of Van was rousing all the Kurds in his district, and fearing that his communications might be cut off, he retired on

Bayazid. Winter now setting in, Paskiewitch felt that his forces were far too weak to attempt the subjugation of Erzeroum in one campaign. He therefore left strong garrisons in the principal towns, and returned with the main portion of his army to Russian territory. General Berbutoff was left in command at Akhalzik with 2,300 infantry, 326 cavalry, and four guns. Bergmann was left at Kars with 2,400 infantry, and 280 cavalry, and twelve guns; whilst Pankratieff occupied Bayazid and the neighbouring towns with 8,000 men, 376 cavalry, and eighteen guns. Thus, with a force of 20,000 infantry, 5,000 cavalry, and ninety-six guns, Paskiewitch had completely conquered the provinces of Kars, Akhalzik, Bayazid, and Poti in the short space of five months, had captured three fortresses and several fortified towns, 313 guns, and 8,000 prisoners graced the Russian General's triumph, whilst his own casualties only amounted to 3,200 killed and wounded. As may be imagined, the greatest consternation reigned at Constantinople. On learning of the reverses in Armenia, the generals in command were immediately disgraced, and two new officers who were in favour at court were sent to supersede them.

Every effort was made to raise the army in Anatolia. Envoys were sent to Persia to endeavour to draw her into the war, and emissaries were despatched to Abkhasia, Ghuriel, and Mingrelia, to stir up revolt there.

The plan of the new Turkish Generals Salegh and Hakki Pashas was as follows. An army of 80,000 men and 66 guns was to be massed at Erzeroum, and advanced *via* the Soghanly range on Kars; whilst a second army of 50,000 men and 50 guns was to be massed on Van to act on the Russian flank.

c c

In February, Paskiewitch heard that the Turks were advancing on Akhalzik, and he at once detached Mouravieff to Suram with six battalions and eighteen guns to cover that fortress, whilst General Hesse was directed to suppress the insurrection in Ghuriel as promptly as possible.

On the 28th of February, Osman Bey entered the city of Akhalzik. The garrison retired into the citadel, and there succeeded in keeping him at bay. The Turks, with their usual ferocity, commenced a system of carnage, and, as at Bayazid in these latter days, so at Akhalzik in 1829, every Christian inhabitant was slain.

Mouravieff in the meantime pushed forward with all vigour to relieve the place, and on the 28th attacked the Turks, defeated them with a loss of 3,000 men, and relieved the garrison.

Hesse, after some sharp skirmishes in which his casualties amounted to 187 men, succeeded in suppressing the rebellion in Ghuriel. The snow having cleared away, and the roads being tolerably practicable for troops, in April Paskiewitch determined to renew his operations for the subjugation of Erzeroum. Pankratieff, at Bayazid, was directed to proceed with four battalions and twelve guns to Katchewenk on the Arpa-Tchai, whilst Paskiewitch, on the 19th of May, having settled the difficulty with Persia, rejoined headquarters at Akhalkalaki, and none too soon, for he here learnt that the Turks had 15,000 men near Ardahan, marching to the relief of that fortress, whilst 50,000 men were at Hassan Kale, on the western slopes of the Soghanly Dagh.

On the 25th of May, Pankratieff was directed to march on Karadjuran, near Kars, to cover that fortress. Paskiewitch at the same time pushed forward to Beghli Ahmed. Salegh Pasha had now reached the Soghanly. Finding that the majority of the Russians were at Kars, he determined to move towards Akhalzik, Mouravieff was sent to counteract this movement to Tsurskab; and on the 2nd of June this general attacked the Turkish forces, defeated them, and took one gun and 1,200 prisoners. The Osmanli being thus checked on their advance on the northern road, Paskiewitch felt free to concentrate all his troops and advance on Erzeroum. This movement was carried out in three columns, the right under the command of Mouravieff, the left under the command of Pankratieff, and the third under the Commander-in-Chief; the two roads leading from Kars and Erzeroum diverge at Kotanli and meet again at Kuipri Kui, the first or southernmost road passing through Sara Kamysh, Mellidooz, and Khorassan, whilst the second or northernmost road passes by Deli Mussa, Kara Orghan, and Zewin. Salegh Pasha, at the head of the main body of the Turkish army, barred the northernmost road on the Zewin Dooz; whilst Hakki Pasha, with 1,300 infantry, 7,000 cavalry, and sixteen guns, took up the entrenched position on the Mellidooz plateau. Just where the road ascends from the Sara Kamysh defile, a knoll in the centre of the plateau commands all the roads, and this was strongly entrenched by the Turks. On the 11th of June, Paskiewitch, who determined to advance by the northern road, sent forward strong parties of cavalry to patrol the Sara Kamysh defile, and thus drew off attention from his main attack. Burtsoff, with 2,000 infantry, was now sent into the defile, whilst the Commander-in-Chief, with 14,000 men and fifty guns, moved towards the Tchakir Baba. On the 13th of June, Burtsoff made a

c c 2

threatened attack on Hakki Pasha's camp. Fearing assault, this general drew in all the outposts, and thus the Russian Commander-in-Chief was enabled to cross the Soghanly Range without firing a shot. On the 17th inst., however, Osman Pasha, with 1,200 men, was detached to Bardez to reconnoitre, and on the 17th he was attacked by Mouravieff and driven back, not on his own army, but on Salegh Pasha's forces at Zewin. Further concealment now was useless, and Paskiewitch determined to attack the Turkish Commander-in-Chief, who was posted on the Zewin plateau with 40,000 men. Pankratieff was sent to the left bank of the Chansu to prevent Hakki Pasha falling back and joining his chief, and Burtsoff was warned to attack the Mellidooz position directly the Turks showed any disposition to abandon it. On the 19th, Paskiewitch, passing through Kanli, descended towards Zewin; Salegh Pasha advanced to meet him, but was driven back into his entrenched position, which was immediately attacked by the Russians, who drove the Turks off in complete disorder, captured 500 prisoners, and twelve guns. The following day, Paskiewitch, leaving a force at Zewin, and crossing the Chansu, ascended by Kara Orghan to attack Hakki Pasha at Mellidooz. After a sharp fight, the Turks were defeated, the commander and fifteen guns being taken.

Being aware that promptitude constitutes half the battle in fighting with Oriental nations, Paskiewitch immediately set off in pursuit of the Turks, and on the 23rd inst. reached Kuipri Kui, which he found to have been abandoned. He at once placed himself at the head of a flying column of cavalry, eighteen horse-artillery guns, and dashed on Hassan Kale. So close was the

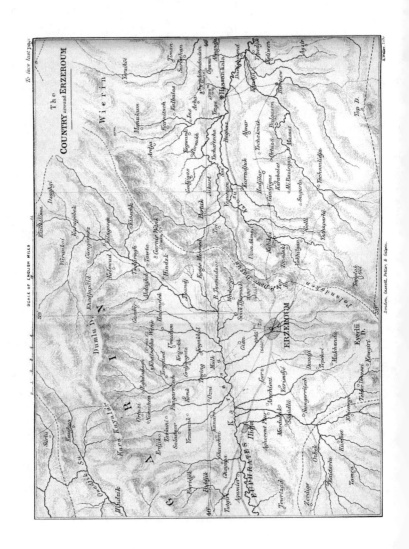

The
COUNTRY around ERZEROUM

SCALE OF ENGLISH MILES

London, Cassell, Petter, & Galpin.

pursuit, that Selegh Pasha had only just time to escape from the place, leaving twenty-nine guns in the hands of the Russians. On the 24th the whole of the Russian army concentrated at Hassan Kale, and a *parlementaire* was sent in to the Governor of Erzeroum, demanding its surrender. This was refused; so on the 25th Paskiewitch advanced to the Nabitchai stream, and on the 27th seized the Devi Boyun heights unmolested. On the 28th the city surrendered, a slight skirmish taking place between the excited soldiery in the citadel and the Russian troops as they entered the town, 150 guns, four Pashas, and about eight thousand prisoners falling into the hands of the Russian General. Thus, in five short weeks from the commencement of the campaign, Paskiewitch had been enabled to effect his object. He subsequently advanced towards Trebizond, and occupied Baiboort. Insurrections among the Lazis, however, broke out, and this, coupled with the badness of the roads, prevented him advancing further than Gumish Khane. In August, the treaty of Adrianople having been signed, the Russians evacuated all the conquered provinces with the exception of Akhalzik, Akhalkalaki, and Kars.

The frontier-line was laid down afresh, and has remained unaltered since those days. In the war of 1855, Kars capitulated to Mouravieff, Paskiewitch's lieutenant; but by the Treaty of Paris, in 1856, it was again ceded to the Turks. It is not my province to speculate on the future of Armenia, but I doubt if an instance has occurred in the history of any nation of a province twice conquered at the point of the sword, having been twice ceded by a stroke of the pen.

APPENDIX A.

ORGANISATION OF TURKISH ARMY.

1. Tabular Statement of Regular Troops on War Footing.

2.   ,,   ,,   Reserve Troops, completely organised.

3.   ,,   ,,   Field Artillery.

4.   ,,   ,,   Cavalry.

5.   ,,   ,,   Siege Artillery.

6.   ,,   ,,   Regular Infantry.

7.   ,,   ,,   Reserve Troops without cadres.

8.   ,,   ,,   Engineers.

9. Establishment of Battery of Horse Artillery.

10.   ,,   ,,   Field Artillery.

11.   ,,   ,,   Mountain Artillery.

12.   ,,   Cavalry Regiment.

13.   ,,   Company of Engineers.

14.   ,,   Regiment of Infantry.

15. Scale of Pay of Officers.

16.   ,,   ,,   Non-commissioned Officers and Men.

17. Tabular Statement of Military Districts.

TABULAR STATEMENT OF THE REGULAR OR NIZAM FORCE OF THE TURKISH ARMY WHEN PLACED ON A WAR FOOTING BY CALLING OUT OF THE ICHTAYAT OR 1ST RESERVE TROOPS.

No. of Corps	Head-quarters of Corps d'Armée.	INFANTRY				CAVALRY			ARTILLERY								ENGINEERS		GRAND TOTAL			
		Battalions	Men	Horses	Mn. Guns	Squadrons	Men	Horses	Field					Garrison			Cos.	Men	Men	Horses	Field Guns	Siege Guns
									Batteries	Men	Horses	Mules	Guns	Cos.	Men	Guns						
1st	Constantinople	28	23,828	693	14	37	6,037	6,535	39	6,911	7,548	293	234	144	21,600	500	40	7,480	65,856	15,069	248	500
2nd	Shumla	24	20,424	594	12	24	3,860	4,176	14	2,436	2,627	119	84	20	3,000	1,253	2	374	30,094	7,516	96	374
3rd	Monastir ...	41	34,354	985	16	24	3,860	4,176	17	2,769	2,702	281	102	21	3,150	731	1	187	44,320	8,144	118	731
4th	Erzeroum ...	24	20,424	594	12	24	3,860	4,176	14	2,436	2,627	119	84	24	3,672	574	1	187	31,962	7,516	96	574
5th	Damascus ...	24	20,424	594	12	24	3,860	4,176	14	2,436	2,627	119	84	3	450	149	1	187	27,357	7,516	96	149
6th	Bagdad	20	17,020	495	10	12	1,930	2,088	14	2,436	2,627	119	84	2	300	—	1	187	21,873	5,329	94	—
7th	Yemmen ...	20	17,020	495	10	—	—	—	6	911	999	79	36	5	750	204	1	187	18,898	1,474	46	204
	Total ...	181	153,494	4,450	86	145	23,407	25,327	118	20,335	21,757	1,129	708	219	32,922	3,411	47	8,789	240,360	52,564	794	2,532

TOTAL FIELD ARMY. { Infantry ... ... 153,494 / Cavalry ... ... 23,407 / Engineers ... ... 8,789 / Artillery ... ... 20,335 }   Guns... ... 794

TABULAR STATEMENT OF RESERVE TROOPS OF THE TURKISH ARMY,
THE BATTALIONS, REGIMENTS, AND BATTERIES OF WHICH ARE FULLY OFFICERED AND EQUIPPED.

No. of Corps	Head-quarters of Corps d'Armée	1st Ban Redif					2nd Ban Redif					Mustahfiz					Grand Total		
		No. of Battalions	Infantry	Cavalry	Artillery	Total	No. of Battalions	Infantry	Cavalry	Artillery	Total	No. of Battalions	Infantry	Cavalry	Artillery	Total	Infantry	Cavalry	Artillery
1st	Constantinople	28	22,400	377	753	23,530	28	22,400	1,229	1,216	24,845	28	22,400	3,511	8,274	24,165	77,200	5,117	10,243
2nd	Shumla	24	19,200	1,061	1,353	21,614	24	19,200	1,401	3,874	24,475	24	19,200	3,566	7,797	20,563	47,600	5,968	8,793
3rd	Monastir	32	25,600	1,947	2,524	30,071	32	25,600	889	1,638	28,127	24	19,200	1,964	4,681	25,745	70,400	4,800	8,843
4th	Erzeroum	24	19,200	314	984	20,498	24	19,600	1,387	1,736	22,723	24	19,200	1,023	1,565	21,788	47,000	2,724	3,285
5th	Damascus	24	19,200	966	2,045	23,211	24	19,600	690	753	21,043	24	19,200	330	370	19,900	47,000	1,986	3,168
6th	Bagdad	5	4,000	2,000	2,060	8,060	—	—	1,410	2,509	3,919	—	—	1,350	1,603	2,953	4,000	5,859	6,272
7th	Yemmen	—	—	—	—	—	—	—	—	—	—	—	—	—	—	—	—	—	—
...	Black Sea Coast	12	9,600	—	—	9,600	12	9,600	—	—	9,600	12	9,600	—	—	9,600	28,800	—	—
	Total ...	149	119,200	6,665	9,719	136,584	144	116,000	7,006	11,726	134,732	136	108,800	11,744	24,290	144,734	322,000	26,454	40,604

TABULAR STATEMENT OF FIELD ARTILLERY IN THE TURKISH ARMY.

N.B.—The Mountain Guns in three batteries of the 4th, 5th, and 6th Army Corps are kept in store.

No. of Corps d'Armée.	Head-quarters of Corps d'Armée.	No. of Batteries.			Strength of Batteries.				Guns.			Wagons.		
		Horse.	Field.	Mountain.	Men.	Horses. Saddle.	Draught.	Mules.	4-Pdrs.	6-Pdrs.	Mountain Guns.	Ammunition Wagons.	Baggage Wagons.	Forage.
1st	Constantinople...	9	27	2	5,495	1,834	5,526	230	108	108	12	216	38	36
2nd	Shumla	3	9	1	2,436	637	1,926	119	36	36	6	126	13	13
3rd	Monastir ...	3	9	4	2,769	712	1,926	286	36	36	24	126	13	13
4th	Erzeroum... ...	3	9	4	2,436	637	1,926	119	36	36	24	126	13	13
5th	Damascus ...	3	9	4	2,436	637	1,926	119	36	36	24	126	13	13
6th	Bagdad	3	9	4	2,436	637	1,926	119	36	36	24	126	13	13
7th	Yemmen	—	5	1	941	150	750	48	30	—	6	90	5	5
	Total ...	24	77	20	18,949	5,244	15,906	1,040	318	288	120	930	108	106

TABULAR STRENGTH OF REGULAR CAVALRY OF TURKISH ARMY.

Number of Corps d'Armée.	Head-quarters of Corps d'Armée.	Number.		Effective Strength.						
		Regiments.	Squadrons.	Combatants.		Staff.		Total.		
				Men.	Horses.	Men.	Horses.	Men.	Horses.	
1st	Constantinople	7	37	5,735	6,142	302	393	6,037	6,535	N.B.—The Effective strength of a Squadron is 152 men and horses.
2nd	Shumla ...	4	24	3,720	3,984	140	192	3,860	4,176	
3rd	Monastir ...	4	24	3,720	3,984	140	192	3,860	4,176	
4th	Erzeroum ..	4	24	3,720	3,984	140	192	3,860	4,176	
5th	Damascus ...	4	24	3,720	3,984	140	192	3,860	4,176	
6th	Bagdad ...	2	12	1,860	1,992	70	96	1,930	2,088	
7th	Yemmen ...	...	...	...	...	...	...	...	...	In course of formation.
	Total Strength	25	145	22,475	24,070	932	1,257	23,407	25,327	

TABULAR STATEMENT OF SIEGE ARTILLERY IN TURKISH ARMY.

No. of Corps d'Armée.	Head-quarters of Army Corps.	Effective of a Company.		No. of Companies.	Total Strength.		Siege Guns.	
		Officers.	Men.		Officers	Men.		
1st	Constantinople ...	3	150	96	288	14,400	500	N.B.—This Force is capable of expansion—Redif and Mustahfiz gunners being drafted into it in time of war to almost an unlimited amount.
2nd	Shumla ...	3	150	20	60	3,000	1,253	
3rd	Monastir ...	3	150	21	63	3,150	731	
4th	Erzeroum ...	3	150	24	72	3,600	874	
5th	Damascus ...	3	150	3	9	450	149	
6th	Bagdad ...	...	...	...	...	...	...	
7th	Yemmen ...	3	150	5	15	750	204	
	Total Strength ...	18	900	169	507	25,350	3,711	

TABULAR STRENGTH OF THE REGULAR OR NIZAM INFANTRY.

No. of Corps.	Corps D'Armée.	Regiments.	Battalions.	INFANTRY OF THE LINE.							CHASSEURS.				TOTAL.		
				Battalions.		Staff.		Total.			Battalions.	Effectives.		Mountain Guns.	Total Strength.		Mountain Guns.
				Men.	Horses.	Men.	Horses.	Men.	Horses.	Battalions.		Men.	Horses.		Men.	Horses.	
1st	Constantinople ...	7	21	17,367	399	595	105	17,962	504	7		5,866	189	14	23,828	693	14
2nd	Shumla	6	18	14,886	342	510	90	15,396	432	6		5,028	162	12	20,424	594	12
3rd	Monastir	10	33	26,900	649	850	150	27,750	769	8		6,604	216	16	34,354	985	16
4th	Erzeroum ...	6	18	14,886	342	510	90	15,396	432	6		5,028	162	12	20,424	594	12
5th	Damascus ...	6	18	14,886	342	510	90	15,396	432	6		5,028	162	12	20,424	594	12
6th	Bagdad	5	15	12,405	285	425	75	12,830	360	5		4,190	135	10	17,020	495	10
7th	Yemmen ...	5	15	12,405	285	425	75	12,830	360	5		4,190	135	10	17,020	495	10
		45	138	113,735	2,644	3,825	675	117,560	3,289	43		35,934	1,161	86	153,494	4,450	86

TABULAR STATEMENT OF THE TERRITORIAL RESERVE ARMY, ORGANISED INTO BATTALIONS, BUT WITHOUT OFFICERS.

No. of Corps d'Armée.	Head-quarters of Corps d'Armée.	1st Reserve.		2nd Reserve.		3rd Reserve.		Total.	
		Battalions.	Strength.	Battalions.	Strength.	Battalions.	Strength.	Battalions.	Strength.
1st	Constantinople	28	22,400	21	16,800	147	117,600	196	156,800
2nd	Shumla	54	43,200	36	28,800	120	96,000	210	168,000
3rd	Monastir	40	32,000	32	25,600	102	81,600	174	139,200
4th	Erzeroum	66	52,800	36	28,800	66	52,800	168	134,400
5th	Damascus	18	14,400	30	24,000	24	19,200	72	57,600
6th	Bagdad	10	8,000	10	8,000	24	19,200	44	35,200
7th	Yemmen	...	...	...	...	...	...	...	...
...	Black Sea Levies	12	9,600	18	14,400	3	2,400	33	26,400
	Total	228	182,400	183	146,400	486	388,800	897	717,600

TABULAR STATEMENT OF ENGINEERS IN THE TURKISH ARMY.

No. of Corps.	Head-quarters of Corps d'Armée.	No. of Companies.	Strength.		Total.
			Officers.	Men.	
1st	Constantinople ...	40	240	7,240	7,480
2nd	Shumla	2	12	362	374
3rd	Monastir	1	6	181	187
4th	Erzeroum ...	1	6	181	187
5th	Damascus ...	1	6	181	187
6th	Bagdad ...	1	6	181	187
7th	Yemmen ...	1	6	181	187
		47	282	8,507	8,789

Establishment of a Battery of Horse Artillery.

	Men.	Saddle Horses.	Draught Horses.	Mules.
Captain	1	1	...	...
Secretary...	...	...	...	...
First Lieutenant... ...	1	1	...	...
Second Lieutenants ...	2	2	...	...
Sergeant-Major	1	1	...	...
Sergeants	8	8	...	...
Quartermaster-Sergeant ..	1	1	...	...
Bombadiers	12	6	...	...
Gunners	54	54	...	...
Drivers	42	...	60	...
Trumpeters	3	3	...	...
Water-carrier	1	1	...	...
Ordnance Corps Private .	1	1	...	5
Farriers	2	2	...	...
Saddler	1	1	...	...
Wagon-maker	1	...	...	...
Carpenter	1	...	...	...
Armourer	1	...	...	...
	133	82	60	5

A Battery has Six Guns (either of four or six Pfünd weight), Krupp's steel breech-loading guns; one Ammunition Wagon, one Baggage Wagon, one Forge, completes the establishment.

ESTABLISHMENT OF A BATTERY OF FIELD ARTILLERY.

—	Men.	Saddle Horses.	Draught Horses.	Mules.
Captain	1	1	...	...
First Lieutenant ...	1	1	...	...
Second Lieutenants ...	2	2	...	...
Sergeant-Major	1	1	...	...
Sergeants...	8	8	...	...
Quartermaster-Sergeant ...	1	...	...	...
Bombadiers	12	...	...	...
Gunners	54	...	...	...
Drivers	42	...	60	...
Trumpeters	3	3	...	...
Water-carrier	1	...	...	1
Ordnance Corps Private...	1	1	...	5
Farrier	1	1	...	...
Wheelwright	1	...	...	...
Carpenter...	1	...	...	...
Armourer	1	...	...	...
Saddler	1	1	...	...
	132	19	60	6

The Battery has Six Guns. As a rule these are Krupp's steel breech-loading six-Pfünder rifled pieces. Some batteries are armed with the four-Pfünder. One Ammunition Wagon, one Baggage Wagon, one Forge, completes the establishment.

D D

ESTABLISHMENT OF A MOUNTAIN BATTERY.

	Men.	Saddle Horses.	Mules.
Captain	1	1	...
First Lieutenant	1	1	...
Second Lieutenants... ...	2	2	...
Sergeant-Major	1	...	...
Sergeants	8	...	...
Quartermaster-Sergeant ...	1	...	...
Bombadiers	12	...	...
Gunners	36	...	...
Drivers	18	...	18
Trumpeters	3	...	...
Water-carrier	1	...	1
Ordnance Corps Private ...	1	1	5
Farrier	1	...	...
Saddlemaker	1	...	...
Wheelwright	1	...	...
Carpenter	1	...	...
Armourer	1	...	...
	90	5	24

ESTABLISHMENT OF A TURKISH CAVALRY REGIMENT.

	Regimental Strength.		Squadron Strength.	
	Men.	Horses.	Men.	Horses.
Colonel	1	3	...	...
Lieutenant-Colonel ...	1	2	...	...
Squadron Commanders ...	2	4	...	...
Major on the Staff ...	1	2	...	...
Regimental Secretary ...	1	2	...	...
Adjutants-Major... ...	2	4	...	...
Secretary of 2nd Class ...	1	2	...	...
Assistant Secretary ...	1	1	...	...
Paymasters	2	2	...	...
Standard-bearer	1	2	...	...
Veterinary Surgeons ...	3	4	...	...
Physician ranking with Lieut.-Colonel	1	2	...	...
Physicians ranking with Major	2	2	...	...
Physicians ranking with Adjutant-Major ...	2	2	...	...
Physician ranking with Captains	1	1	...	...
Surgeons of the 1st Class..	1	1	...	...
,, ,, 2nd Class..	2	2	...	...
Armourer	1	1	...	...
Master Saddler	1	1	...	...
,, Farrier	1	1	...	...
Riding Master	1	1	...	...
First Captains	6	6	1	1
Second Captains	6	6	1	1
First Lieutenants ...	6	6	1	1
Second Lieutenants ...	6	6	1	1
Sub-Lieutenants	12	12	2	2
Sergeants...	60	60	10	10
Corporals...	96	96	16	16
Privates	672	672	112	112
Water-carriers	12	12	2	2
Musicians	30	30	5	5
Saddlers	6	6	1	1
Total strength ...	941	954	152	152

ESTABLISHMENT OF A COMPANY OF ENGINEERS.

Major in Command	1
Secretary	1
Paymaster	1
Surgeon	1
Captains	2
First Lieutenant	1
Second Lieutenant	1
Sub-Lieutenant	1
Sergeant-Major	1
Sergeants	12
Quartermaster-Sergeant	1
Corporals	12
Privates	144
Musicians	3
Wheelwright	1
Carpenter	1
Saddler	1
Water-carriers	2
	187

Although laid down in the Hatti-Houmayoun of 1869, Engineers do not exist in all the corps of the Turkish army. In the fourth there were none, except a few mechanics in Erzeroum. Nominally each corps has a battalion of eight companies, the first, or Constantinople army, having three battalions, one a pontoon corps, the other two sappers.

ESTABLISHMENT OF A TURKISH INFANTRY REGIMENT.

	Regimental Staff.	Chasseur Batallion.	First Batallion.	Second Batallion.	Third Batallion.	Company Organisation.
Colonel	1	...	...	...	...	...
Lieutenant-Colonel	1	...	...	...	...	...
Chief of Batallions...	...	1	1	1	1	...
Major on the Staff...	1	...	...	...	...	...
Paymaster-in-Chief	1	...	...	...	...	...
Regimental Secretary	1	...	...	...	...	...
Adjutants-Major	...	2	2	2	2	...
Batallion Secretaries	...	1	1	1	1	...
Assistant Secretaries	...	1	1	1	1	...
Paymasters of Batallions	...	1	1	1	1	...
Standard-bearer	1	...	...	..	...	...
Regimental Physician	1	...	...	...	...	...
Doctor ranking with Chief of Batallion	...	1	1	1	1	...
Physician to Right Half Batallion	...	1	1	...	...	...
„ to Left Half Batallion ...	...	...	...	1	1	...
„ ranking as Captain ...	...	1	...	...	1	...
Surgeon-in-Chief	...	1	1	...	...	...
Assistant Surgeons	...	...	...	1	1	...
Armourers	...	1	1	1	1	...
Regimental Musicians	80	...	...	...	...	...
Batallion Musicians	...	33	33	33	33	4
Captains	...	8	8	8	8	1
Lieutenants	...	8	8	8	8	1
Sub-Lieutenants	...	8	8	8	8	1
Sergeants-Major	...	8	8	8	8	1
Sergeants	...	40	32	32	32	4
Corporals	...	64	64	64	64	8
Privates	...	640	640	640	640	80
Water-carriers	...	8	8	8	8	1
Total strength ...	87	828	819	819	819	101

ANNUAL SCALE OF PAY RECEIVED BY THE OFFICERS OF THE
TURKISH ARMY.

GRADE.	£	s.	d.	
Marshal Commanding First Corps .	5,637	12	6	
,, ,, other Corps	5,421	2	6	
Lieutenant-General of all arms ...	1,302	3	4	
Major-General ,, ...	725	2	6	
Colonel ,, ...	391	7	6	
Lieutenant-Colonel ,, ...	269	1	8	
Chief of Battalion or Squadron ...	197	14	2	
Major on the Staff	133	19	2	Commissioned
Regimental Paymaster	131	10	0	Officers.
Adjutant-Major of Right Wing or				
Squadron	110	8	4	
Regimental Secretary	97	19	6	
Adjutant-Major of Left Wing ...	92	9	2	
Battalion Secretary	91	11	8	
,, Paymaster	65	18	4	
,, Assistant Secretary ...	65	18	4	
CAVALRY.				
First Captain	73	15	10	
Second Captain	62	0	10	
First Lieutenant	55	13	4	
Second Lieutenant	51	4	2	
Sub-Lieutenant of First Class ...	48	10	0	
,, ,, Second Class ...	44	16	8	
ARTILLERY.				
Captain	70	11	8	Subordinate
First Lieutenant	53	19	6	Officers.
Second Lieutenant	49	7	6	
Third Lieutenant	47	10	10	
INFANTRY.				
Captain	70	11	8	
Lieutenant	53	19	6	
Sub-Lieutenant	49	7	6	

MONTHLY SCALE OF PAY OF NON-COMMISSIONED OFFICERS AND MEN.

ARTILLERY.	£	s.	d.
Sergeant-Major of Battalion	0	13	9
Battery Sergeant-Major	0	10	6
,, Quartermaster-Sergeant	0	8	9
Corporal	0	7	8
Gunner of Horse Artillery	0	6	5
,, Field or Garrison Artillery	0	5	9
Corporal of Drivers	0	8	4
Farrier Sergeant	0	13	6
Saddler Sergeant	0	12	2
Magazine Sergeant	0	15	3
Sergeant of Water-carriers	0	10	6
Water-carrier	0	7	6
Trumpet-Major	0	13	8
Trumpeter	0	7	6

CAVALRY.			
Regimental Sergeant-Major	0	12	3
Quartermaster-Sergeant	0	9	1
Troop Sergeant-Major	0	8	4
Corporal	0	7	6
Private	0	6	4
Farrier Sergeant	0	13	6
Saddler Sergeant	0	12	2
Corporal of Water-carriers	0	8	4
Water-carrier	0	7	6
Regimental Trumpet-Major	0	13	6
Squadron Trumpet-Major	0	8	4
Trumpeter	0	7	6

INFANTRY.			
Battalion Sergeant-Major	0	13	8
Quartermaster-Sergeant	0	10	6
Sergeant	0	9	0
Corporal	0	7	6
Private	0	5	9
Water-carrier	0	5	9
Bugle-Major of Regiment	0	13	6
Battalion Bugle-Major	0	10	6
Bugler...	0	8	2
Drummer or Fifer	0	5	9

TABULATED STATEMENT, SHOWING NUMBER OF BATTALIONS AND MEN FURNISHED BY EACH MILITARY DISTRICT TO THE RESERVE INFANTRY.

No. of Corps.	Head-quarters of Army Corps.	Head-quarters of Military Districts.	First Reserve. No. of Batts.		Second Reserve. No. of Batts.		Third Reserve. No. of Batts.		Total. No. of Batts.		Total No. of Men.
			With Cadres.	Without Cadres.	With Cadres.	Without Cadres.	With Cadres.	Without Cadres.	With Cadres.	Without Cadres.	
1st	Constantinople	Ismidt	4	4	4	3	4	21	12	28	32,000
		Broussa	4	4	4	3	4	21	12	28	32,000
		Konieh	4	4	4	3	4	21	12	28	32,000
		Kaisariak	4	4	4	3	4	21	12	28	32,000
		Kara Hissar	4	4	4	3	4	21	12	28	32,000
		Isbarta	4	4	4	3	4	21	12	28	32,000
		Kale Sultanieh	4	4	4	3	4	21	12	28	32,000
											224,000
2nd	Shumla	Shumla	4	9	4	6	4	20	12	35	37,600
		Adrianople	4	9	4	6	4	20	12	35	37,600
		Sofia	4	9	4	6	4	20	12	35	37,600
		Boli	4	9	4	6	4	20	12	35	37,600
		Angora	4	9	4	6	4	20	12	35	37,600
		Tchorum	4	9	4	6	4	20	12	35	37,600
											225,600
3rd	Monastir	Monastir	4	5	4	4	4	17	12	26	30,400
		Janina	4	5	4	4	4	17	12	26	30,400
		Uskub	4	5	4	4	4	17	12	26	30,400
		Drania	4	5	4	4	4	17	12	26	30,400
		Smyrna	4	5	4	4	4	17	12	26	30,400
		Aidin	4	5	4	4	4	17	12	26	30,400
		Seraievo	4	5	4	4	...	...	8	9	13,600
		Travnik	4	5	4	4	...	...	8	9	13,600
											209,600

Corps	Army		City										Men	Total
4th	Erzeroum	...	Kharpoot	...	4	11	4	6	4	11	12	28	32,000	192,000
			Sivas	...	4	11	4	6	4	11	12	28	32,000	
			Erzeroum	...	4	11	4	6	4	11	12	28	32,000	
			Kars	...	4	11	4	6	4	11	12	28	32,000	
			Van	...	4	11	4	6	4	11	12	28	32,000	
			Diarbekir	...	4	11	4	6	4	11	12	28	32,000	
5th	Damascus	...	Damascus	...	4'	3	4	5	4	4	12	13	19,200	115,200
			Jerusalem	...	4	3	4	5	4	4	12	13	19,200	
			Beyrout	...	4	3	4	5	4	4	12	13	19,200	
			Antioch	...	4	3	4	5	4	4	12	13	19,200	
			Aleppo	...	4	3	4	5	4	4	12	13	19,200	
			Adana	...	...	...	...	...	...	...	...	...	...	
6th	Bagdad	...	Bagdad	...	1	2	...	2	...	1	1	5	4,800	24,000
			Kerkouk	...	1	2	...	2	...	1	1	5	4,800	
			Solimanieh	...	1	2	...	2	...	1	1	5	4,800	
			Morsaul	...	1	2	...	2	...	1	1	5	4,800	
			Hillah	...	1	2	...	2	...	1	1	5	4,800	
			Bassora	...	...	...	...	...	...	...	...	...	...	
7th	Yemmen (in course of formation)	...	...	...	...	...	...	...	...	...	...	...	...	...
...	Coast Army of Black Sea	...	Trebizond	...	4	4	4	6	4	1	12	11	18,400	55,200
			Tireboli	...	4	4	4	6	4	1	12	11	18,400	
			Samsoon	...	4	4	4	6	4	1	12	11	18,400	

APPENDIX B.

RUSSIAN ARMY ORGANISATION.

1. Cavalry Organisation.
2. Artillery   „
3. Engineer   „
4. Infantry   „
5. Pay of Officers.
6.   „   Non-Commissioned Officers and Men.
7. General Statement of Russian Forces.

The cavalry of the Russian army consists of two divisions of cavalry of the Guard, seven of the Line, and one of the Caucasus; the first division of the Guard contains seven regiments, that of the Caucasus four, all other six regiments. Each is composed of four squadrons; thus there are 56 regiments, or 224 squadrons, of regular cavalry in the army. With the exception of those of the Guard and of the Caucasus, each division consists of two regiments of dragoons, two of lancers, and two of hussars.

All dragoons, and the rear rank in hussar and lancer regiments, are armed with Berdan's breech-loading carbine. Cuirassiers, hussars, and lancers, and all non-commissioned officers, with Smith and Wesson's breech-loading revolver. Dragoons are armed with a long rifle of the Krinker converted pattern—eventually they will be served out with Berdan's—they carry 32 rounds each. All mounted troops wear a sabre, varying in shape and weight for the different branches.

There are two establishments for cavalry, namely, the War, and the Peace; in the former there are 128 men per squadron, in the latter 112 men.

Authorised War Establishment of a Russian Cavalry Regiment.

	Regiment.	Squadron.
Officer Commanding	1	...
Lieutenant-Colonels	2	...
Regimental Adjutant	1	...
„ Paymaster	1	...
„ Quartermaster	1	...
„ Instructor at Arms	1	...
Officer commanding Non-Combatants	1	...
Trumpet-Major	1	...
Senior Surgeon	1	...
Junior Surgeon	1	...
Veterinary Surgeon	1	...
Chaplain	1	...
Squadron Commander	4	1
Captain	4	1
Staff-Captain	4	1
Lieutenants	8	2
Cornets	8	2
Senior Sergeants-Major	4	1
Cadets	8	2
Junior Sergeants-Major	16	4
Non-commissioned Officers	56	14
Trumpeters	16	4
Privates	672	168
Officers' Servants	28	7
	841	207

Artillery Organisation.

The generally recognised constitution of a brigade of artillery is four batteries of eight guns each. To each division of infantry there is attached a brigade, consisting of two 9-pfünders and two 4-pfünders. The Grenadier Artillery Brigade of the Caucasus has three mountain batteries in addition, and 19th, 20th, and 21st Caucasian Divisions have an extra 4-pfünder battery attached to them.

The Horse Artillery Brigade of the Guard consists of five 4-pfünder batteries. The other seven Horse Brigades have but two batteries of the same calibre : there are thus—

48 Batteries, rifled	9-pfünders,
105 „ „	4-pfünders,
4 „ „	3-pfünders,
18 Horse Batteries, rifled ...	4-pfünders,

and it is intended to raise 50 mitrailleuse batteries. The guns are mostly bronze, Krupp's breech-loaders, the weight of the 4-pfünders being $6\frac{3}{4}$ cwt., of the 9-pfünders, $12\frac{1}{4}$. The smaller gun carries 130, the larger 120 rounds of ammunition. The fuzes are mostly percussion; the time-fuze is, however, being rapidly introduced into the service. The larger gun is frequently used as a siege piece, its projectile weighing 30 lbs. All non-commissioned officers and gunners are armed with short dragoon sword and breech-loading revolver, for which they carry 12 rounds in a small pouch.

AUTHORISED ESTABLISHMENT OF BATTERIES OF RUSSIAN FIELD ARTILLERY.

	Officers				Non-Com. Officers				Privates							Total	Horses				Guns	Carriages					Ammunition Boxes.
	Lieutenant-Colonel.	Captain.	Lieutenant.	Sub-Lieutenant.	Sergeant-Major.	Cadet.	Senior N.-Com. Officer.	Junior N.-Com. Officer.	Bombardier.	Laboratory Men.	Gunners.	Trumpeters.	Drivers.	Officers' Servants.			Riding.	Artillery.	Train.	Total.		Ammunition.	Provision.	Park.	Sanitary.	Others.	
4-P. Horse Battery ...	1	2	2	2	1	2	8	16	8	50	200	4	12	6	314		161	146	17	324	8	16	2	4	1	1	...
4-P. Field Battery ..	1	1	2	2	1	2	8	16	8	40	140	4	12	6	243		17	126	17	160	8	16	2	4	1	1	...
9-P. ,, ,, ...	1	1	2	2	1	2	8	16	8	50	190	4	13	6	304		17	180	17	214	8	24	2	5	1	1	...
3-P. Mountain ...	1	1	2	2	1	2	8	11	8	30	145	4	80	6	301		8	120	66	194	8	...	...	...	...	...	112
Mitrailleuse ...	1	1	2	2	1	2	8	16	8	30	110	4	12	6	203		25	98	17	140	8	8	2	4	1	1	...

Organisation of Engineers.

The Corps of Engineers in the Russian army consists of " Sappers and Miners" and "Pontoniers;" the former include engineer field parks, siege parks, telegraph parks, whilst the latter merely the bridging corps. There are 11 battalions of sappers, and six half-battalions of pontoniers; each of these latter carries sufficient pontoon boats to make a bridge 700 feet in length. As in the infantry, so in the sappers, each battalion is composed of four companies; the peace and war establishment being entirely distinct.

Authorised Establishment of a Battalion of Sappers and Miners.

	Battalion.	Company.
Colonel Commanding	1	...
Lieutenant-Colonel	1	...
Battalion Adjutant	1	...
,, Paymaster	1	...
,, Quartermaster	1	...
Instructor in Arms	1	...
Administrative Officers	2	...
Battalion Drummer	1	...
,, Bugler	1	...
Senior Surgeon	1	...
Junior ,, ...	1	...
Captains	4	1
Subalterns	16	4
Cadets	4	1
Sergeants-Major	4	1
Senior Non-Commissioned Officers	16	4
Junior ,, ,, ...	56	14
Sappers and Miners	832	208
Drummers	12	3
Buglers	12	3
Officers' Servants	20	5
	988	244

AUTHORISED WAR ESTABLISHMENT OF A HALF-BATTALION OF
PONTONIERS.

————	Half Battalion.	Company.
Colonel Commanding	1	...
Battalion Adjutant	1	...
„ Paymaster and Quartermaster ...	1	...
„ Drummer	1	...
„ Bugler	1	...
Senior Surgeon	1	...
Veterinary Surgeon	1	...
Captains	2	1
Lieutenants	2	1
Sub-Lieutenants...	2	1
Ensigns	2	1
Sergeants-Major...	2	1
Senior Non-Commissioned Officers	10	5
Junior „ „	28	14
Pontoniers	240	120
Drivers	120	60
Drummers	6	3
Buglers	6	3
Officers' Servants	8	4
	435	214

Russian Infantry.

The Infantry of the Russian army consists of three divisions of Guards, four of Grenadiers, 41 of the Line, and seven brigades of Rifles; each division is composed of four regiments, those of the Guards numbered according to their division, those of the Grenadiers from 1 to 16, whilst those of the Line run from 1 to 164; the regiments of regular Rifles are styled numerically from 1 to 20; the brigades of Turkestan and the Caucasus have territorial designations.

Each regiment is composed of three battalions except in the case of those from 73 to 84 inclusive, which have four battalions. These are again subdivided into five companies, four of the Line, one of Rifles—these latter companies, on service, are amalgamated and form an extra battalion styled the Combined Rifle Battalion.

Battalions have four separate establishments, viz. :—

1. The War Establishment.
2. The Increased Peace Establishment.
3. The Peace Establishment.
4. The Cadre Establishment.

I have only given the war strength of all branches in this appendix, none other being necessary for the purposes of this work.

The total strength of the Russian infantry is 188 regiments, consisting of 580 battalions, with 32 rifle battalions in addition, making a total of 612 battalions of the regular army; but there are also 48 frontier battalions of irregular troops.

Eventually the whole of the infantry will be armed with the Berdan rifle, which as yet, however, has only been served out to the division of the Guard, Grenadier division, and Rifle battalions. The Krinka and Carle rifles now are the principal weapons in use. Every soldier carries, in two pouches, 60 rounds. Forty rounds in addition are carried by the regimental train, and 60 more by the army reserve train. Non-commissioned officers of line battalions, and all ranks in the Guard and Grenadier divisions, carry a short, two-edged sword in addition to the bayonet, which is invariably fixed when troops are on the move.

E E

SCALE OF ANNUAL PAY AND TABLE MONEY OF OFFICERS.

	Ordinary Pay						War Pay						Table Money	
	Old Guard.		New Guard, Artillery, and Engineers.		Cavalry and Infantry of Line.		Old Guard.		New Guard, Artillery, and Engineers.		Cavalry and Infantry of Line.			
	£	s.	£	s.	£	s.	£	s.	£	s.	£	s.	£	s
General	297	17	297	17	297	17	446	15	446	15	446	15	315	11
Lieutenant-General ...	238	6	238	16	238	6	357	8	357	8	357	8	315	11
Major-General ...	178	14	178	14	178	14	268	1	268	1	268	1	315	11
Colonel	120	15	120	15	120	15	181	2	181	2	181	2	193	4
Lieutenant-Colonel ...	...		93	8	93	8	...		140	1	140	1	...	
Major	...		...		77	6	...		...		115	18	...	
Captain	93	8	77	6	64	8	140	1	115	18	96	12	...	
2nd Captain	77	6	64	8	59	11	115	18	96	12	89	7	...	
Lieutenant	64	8	59	11	54	15	96	12	89	7	82	2	...	
Sub-Lieutenant ...	59	11	54	15	51	10	89	7	82	2	77	6	...	
Ensign or Cornet ...	54	15	51	10	48	6	82	2	77	6	72	9	...	

N.B.—The following command allowances are also granted:—

		£	s
Officer Commanding Battalion ...	}	90	3
,, ,, Squadron		22	4
,, ,, Battery		86	8
,, ,, Company		17	8

PAY OF NON-COMMISSIONED OFFICERS AND MEN.

	GUARD.				LINE.			
	Annual Pay.			Daily Pay.		Annual Pay.		Daily Pay.
	£	s.	d.	£	s.	d.	£	s.	d.	£	s.	d.
Sergeant-Major ...	5	15	11	0	0	$3\frac{3}{4}$	3	17	3	0	0	$2\frac{1}{2}$
Senior Non-Commissioned Officer	2	15	7	0	0	$1\frac{3}{4}$	0	14	9	0	0	$0\frac{1}{2}$
Junior Non-Commissioned Officer	2	14	8	0	0	$1\frac{3}{4}$	0	13	3	0	0	$0\frac{5}{12}$
Bombardier and Lance-Corporal	1	0	9	0	0	$0\frac{3}{4}$	0	9	2	0	0	$0\frac{1}{3}$
Private, Drummer, and Bugler ...	0	13	$0\frac{1}{2}$	0	0	$0\frac{4}{9}$	0	8	8	0	0	$0\frac{1}{4}$

In addition to the above the men receive a "mess allowance," varying in amount, but averaging about $1\frac{1}{4}$d. per diem, and the following rations free—

Flour	...	...	...	...	2 lbs.
Barley	...	...	...	...	$\frac{1}{4}$ „
Salt	...	...	...	...	$\frac{1}{4}$ oz.

Authorised Establishment of Infantry Regiment, Battalion, and Company of the Russian Army.

	Regiment.	Battalion.	Company.
Regimental Staff.			
Major-General	...	...	...
Field Officer for Interior Economy ...	1	...	...
Executive Field Officer	1	...	...
Regimental Adjutants	3	...	...
Paymaster	1	...	...
Quartermaster	1	...	...
Instructor in Arms	1	...	...
Officer in Command of Non-combatants	1	...	...
Regimental Drummer	1	...	...
,, Bugler	1	...	...
Senior Surgeon	1	...	...
Junior Surgeons	4	...	...
Chaplains	2	...	...
Battalion Staff.			
Colonels	4	1	...
Battalion Adjutants	4	1	...
,, Drummers	4	1	...
,, Buglers	4	1	...
Captains	20	5	1
Lieutenants	20	5	1
Sub-Lieutenants	20	5	1
Ensigns	20	5	1
Cadets	20	5	1
Sergeants-Major	20	5	1
Senior Non-Commissioned Officers ...	80	20	4
Junior ,, ,, ...	240	60	12
Corporals...	400	100	20
Privates	2,960	740	148
Drummers	60	15	3
Buglers	60	15	3
Officers' Servants	80	20	4
	4,034	1,004	200

N.B.—Each Company is provided with the following tools:—12 hatchets, 6 shovels, 3 picks, 3 axes, 1 scythe.

APPENDIX C.

MEMORANDUM ON THE NATURE OF THE ARMENIAN THEATRE OF WAR, AS REGARDS REQUIREMENTS FOR MILITARY PURPOSES.

ROADS.

Trebizond to Erzeroum.—An excellent hill-road, of an average width of twenty-seven feet : it passes over ranges of a height of 8,000 feet, consequently the gradients in many places are steep, but are practicable everywhere for heavy guns.   Bridges.—All the streams are bridged over, and culverts thrown over small mountain torrents.   The bridges do not admit of guns or wheeled vehicles passing each other.   The stages, which are dealt with further on, are somewhat longer than we consider an average march, but there is good accommodation for troops at each.

Erzeroum to Kars.—By no means such a good road as that from Trebizond.   The ascent to the Devi-Boyun is steep ; but lately it has been eased off, and an excellent gun-road now crosses the range : through the Passin plain the road is excellent.   Cavalry and infantry could march with a wide front on either flank as far as Khorassan.   Across the Soghanly range there are four roads, dealt with later in this Appendix.   Neither of these is metalled, nor are streams bridged : that *viâ* Ala-kilissa, Bardez, and Tcharpakli is the best, but both by it and the Mellidooz, guns can be freely moved.

Erzeroum to Ardahan.—Merely a hill-road, practicable for field artillery after some engineering labour.   Between Lisgaf and Olti there are two routes, that by Id and Narriman being the easier.

Erzeroum to Bayazid.—This branches off from the Kars road at Kuipri-Kui, where it crosses the Araxes by a fine masonry bridge.   The Kose Dagh range may be traversed by four routes, that from Delibaba to Zaidikan being the one most generally used, but all are practicable for field-guns.

SUPPLIES.

Armenia is a land flowing with milk and honey, with many flocks and herds.   As in India, so here, there is no dearth of meat; large quantities of cattle may be procured in every village—goats and sheep principally in the mountainous country, kine in the plains ; fowls also in abundance.

Grain.—Maize, wheat, barley, and oats are cultivated, the Alashgird, Passin, and Kars plains being the richest districts.   For a large force the country mills are not numerous enough to turn out sufficient flour ; handmills should therefore be carried.

Forage.—In abundance : the grass and clover are particularly rich, especially on the slopes of the Allaghoz and Soghanly ranges.

Fruit.—Grapes, nectarines, peaches, apples, pears, mulberries, filberts, walnuts, melons, are found in various parts, the Thortoom and Khagisman districts being perhaps the most famed.

Vegetables.—Potatoes in and round Trebizond ; beans, pumpkins, vegetable marrows, turnips, carrots, onions, in nearly every village.

Firewood.—Only to be found in the mountainous regions near Trebizond, and the Soghanly.   Tezek, or compressed manure, is greatly used for fuel.   Its manufacture occupies the Armenians all the winter, but quantities sufficient for a large force could not be found.

Strong Drinks.—There is a fair claret to be procured in bulk at Kharpoot; the supplies at other places are small, being imported from Europe.   Indeed, such things as wine and brandy can only be procured at the large towns.

Tobacco.—In any quantity, but not good.

Water.—Plentiful and good; but the Turkish soldier and camp-follower require more supervision even than natives of India to keep the supply undefiled.

TRANSPORT.

Arabas, similar to the Indian bullock-cart, of either two or four bullocks.   These and pack-ponies could be procured in, I may say, unlimited quantities by employing local agents. Mules are dear and not easily found.

ACCOMMODATION.

The mud, flat-roofed houses, which form the majority of the dwelling-places in Armenia, are not very pleasant quarters, but are preferable to a bivouac in the rain. There are many places enumerated in the accompanying Road Report, which contain two-storeyed houses, airy and substantial, admirably adapted for field hospitals or barracks.

CLIMATE.

Most variable, on account of the changes of altitude as the traveller passes over the road. Commencing at sea-level at Trebizond, two high ranges of 6,000 and 8,500 feet are crossed before reaching Erzeroum, 6,100 ; there the Devi-Boyun, upwards of 8,000 feet, is traversed, and the Araxes followed, until it drops to 5,000 ; the Soghanly again rises to 8,200, and a further descent to Kars once more brings the aneroid down to 5,600. Thus, warm clothing is necessary, for even in the height of summer, when the glass reminds one of July in the Punjab, the nights are piercingly cold ; indeed, the inhabitants wear furs all the year round. The winter is most severe. Snow to a depth of several feet covers the ground, rendering locomotion a matter of much difficulty and danger.

ROUTES.

Route No. 1.—Trebizond to Erzeroum.

st Stage, Djevizlik ; distance, 18 miles.—Road excellent ; a slight ascent the whole way. Water and grazing in abundance. Djevizlik is a village containing about 80 stone houses ; there is a good deal of fruit in the vicinity during the season. Supplies of all sorts to be obtained in any quantity in giving short notice. There is a post-horse station here, and fair Armenian accommodation for the traveller.

2nd Stage, Khamsikui ; distance, 16 miles.—Road good ; still an ascent. The village contains about 100 houses, scattered a good deal. Water and grazing in abundance ; also fuel. Supplies in large quantities on giving short notice. Excellent accommodation for the traveller in one of the many stone khans which abound in the village. There is also a post-horse station.

Khamsikui to Zigana ; distance, 21 miles.—Over a very stiff mountain range. The road, though good, is very steep, and it is a long stage for wheeled vehicles or guns. There is

(*Trebizond to Erzeroum.*)

no water on the crest, but on the greater part of the road there is both grass and fuel in abundance. Zigana is a village of about 150 houses, well cultivated, and capable of affording supplies for a large body of troops. It is a post-horse station.

Zigana to Gumesh Khaneh ; distance, 27 miles.— A stiff descent to Ardasat, about 12 miles. This is situated in a peculiarly wild-looking valley. Supplies of all sorts plentiful, and excellent accommodation to be found in the village, which is a post-horse station. Fuel is the only article necessary for troops about which there would be any difficulty. From Ardasat to Gumesh Khaneh the road follows the course of the stream. This last-named village contains about 450 houses. There are silver mines in the neighbourhood ; and the neat, white-washed shingled roofs give an air of comfort to the town rarely seen in a Turkish place. Supplies of all sorts to be had in abundance. There is a post-horse station, a post office, a telegraph office, and a functionary styled a Caimakam in the village.

Gumesh Khaneh to Khadrak ; distance, 27 miles.—Road good ; for the first 20 miles it winds along the banks of the river, then, ascending the water-

(Trebizond to Erzeroum.)

shed, passes through Murad-Khaneh, a small village inhabited by robbers, and shepherds who possess numerous flocks of small mountain sheep, and then descends to Khadrak, a small, unimportant hamlet, where supplies would not be found in any quantity; accommodation for travellers bad; firewood scarce. This is a post-horse station.

Khadrak to Baiboort; distance, 15 miles.—Road good; a general descent to the town, which is by far the most important on the route from Trebizond to Erzeroum. There is a post office, telegraph office, post-horse station, and Caimakam here. Supplies of all sorts to be had in abundance, except fuel. The inhabitants are a wild, lawless race, and likely to prove obnoxious to European troops in the place. There is an old castle which dominates the town, but it is of no value in these days; nor is there any position in the immediate neighbourhood capable of being converted into a standpoint.

Baiboort to Kop; distance, 15 miles.—Road good, though steep. Ascending the northern spur of the Kop Dagh, the halting-place is a small group of huts, with very bad accommodation. Water plentiful; supplies and fuel scanty. A post-horse station.

Kop to Farna-kapan ; distance, 16 miles.—Road good, but very steep, crossing the Kop Dagh, nearly 9,000 feet above sea-level. The stage, which is also a post-horse station, consists of a small hamlet. Supplies very scanty ; accommodation bad.

Farna-kapan to Karabooyuk ; distance, 16 miles.—Road good and level. The halting-place consists of a khan, where only very small quantities could be obtained. There are villages in the vicinity whence supplies could be obtained. The water supply is from a spring opposite the khan, and would have to be carefully guarded. This is a post-horse station.

Karabooyuk to Erzeroum ; distance 27 miles.—Passing through Ilidja, famous for its hot springs. This village is of considerable size, and would furnish supplies to a large extent. Fuel is the most scarce commodity.

Route No. 2.—Erzeroum to Kars.

Erzeroum to Hassan Kale ; distance, 20 miles.—Road good, crossing the Devi Dagh by a newly-made gun road,* 16 feet in width, at 5 miles ; then descending to the Passin plain, passing through the village of Khooroodjook, which possesses large flocks and herds. Hassan Kale is an old

---

* This road, I hear, has fallen into a terrible state owing to the amount of traffic over it, and is now anything but a "gun road."

(*Erzeroum to Kars.*)

walled town, containing about 6,000 souls. There is a very picturesque though useless castle here. Supplies in large quantities, but there would be difficulty for fuel for a large force. There are hot springs here, much resorted to by scrofulous and rheumatic people. Being on a branch of the Araxes, there is an endless water supply, and very good fishing in the neighbourhood.

Hassan Kale to Kuipri-Kui ; distance, 10 miles.—Road good and quite
(*On the Araxes River.*) flat; the village contains about 300 houses. Supplies, except fuel, would be obtainable in fair quantities, and the neighbouring villages would afford a vast number of cattle and sheep. The roads here diverge to Kars and Bayazid.

KuipriKui to Khorassan ; distance, 20 miles, along the left bank of
(*On the Araxes River.*) the Araxes.—Excellent grazing ground in the vicinity. Khorassan is a large village with flocks, herds, and an admirable water supply. Very good accommodation for the traveller ; fuel scarce.

Khorassan to Mezingird.—Ascending the southern slopes of the Soghanly Dagh ; road fair, practicable for guns ; but at this stage supplies scarce, with the exception of firewood, which can be had in abundance. There is difficulty about water here ; the stream is very small.

Mezingird to Sara Kamysh ; distance, 18 miles.—Road quite practicable for guns ; first ascends to the Mellidooz plateau, then down into the Sara Kamysh defile. There are several Circassian villages in the neighbourhood of this halting-place, whence supplies could be procured. Water and firewood in abundance ; accommodation limited, but the vast pine forests offer every facility for the bivouac of troops.

Sara Kamysh to Kotanli ; distance 20 miles.—Road level and good. The village is rich in flocks and herds ; there is a very good camping-ground on the left bank of the Kars Tchai. Fuel is scarce.

Kotanli to Kars ; distance, 25 miles.—Road good ; crosses the Kars Tchai twice, which is always fordable, passing through several villages, the populations of which are devoted to agriculture. Fuel in the whole valley is scarce, as it all has to be procured from the Soghanly Range.

Route No. 3.—Erzeroum to Kars (another Route).

Erzeroum to Hassan Kale.—Same as before.

Hassan Kale to Kuipri-Kui.— Do.

Kuipri-Kui to Ala-Kilissa; distance, 18 miles.—Road quite practicable for guns ; ascends the western slopes of the Soghanly. The village is insignificant, and supplies scanty ; water plentiful; camping-ground cramped.

Ala-Kilissa to Zewin; distance, 16 miles.—Road good. Water plentiful; supplies and accommodation very scanty. Camping ground good.

Zewin to Mellidooz; distance, 15 miles.—Large camping-ground. Water at some distance; supplies nil. Nearest village, Mezingird, 3 miles.

Mellidooz to Sara Kamysh; distance, 16 miles.—As route No. 2.

Sara Kamysh to Kotanli.—As route No. 2.

Kotanli to Kars.—As before.

Route No. 4.—*Erzeroum to Kars.*

Erzeroum to Hassan Kale.—Same as before.

Hassan Kale to Kuipri-Kui.—   Do.

Kuipri-Kui to Ala-Kilissa.—   Do.

Ala-Kilissa to Yeni-Kui; distance, 20 miles.—Road practicable for guns. Small village, but with notice supplies could be procured from places in the neighbourhood. Water good; fuel limited.

Yeni-Kui to Bardez; distance, 15 miles.—Road good. Camping-ground fair; fuel and supplies plentiful.

Bardez to Tcharpakli; distance, 20 miles.—Road practicable for guns. A small village with a limited quantity of supplies. Water and fuel plentiful.

Tcharpakli to Kotanli; distance, 16 miles.—Road excellent.

Kotanli to Kars.—As in other routes.

Route No. 5.—*Erzeroum to Olti.*

Erzeroum to Hindsk; distance, 13 miles.—Through the Euphrates valley; road excellent. A small village, but in such a closely-populated district that supplies can be obtained in great quantity; fuel scarce;

(Erzeroum to Olti.)   grazing and water in abundance.

Hindsk to Lisgaf; distance, 20 miles.—Road bad, practicable for pack, *not wheeled carriage*, though after some engineering labour guns could be moved on it. Here is the Ghiurji Boghaz, a defile most difficult to defend, easy to turn. Supplies of cattle, sheep, fuel, forage, and water in abundance.

Lisgaf to Id; distance, 16 miles.—Road good. Supplies fair; collections could be made after short notice.

Id to Olti; distance, 20 miles.—Passing through Narriman, still keeping to the stream. Supplies plentiful; accommodation good.

The following Table of Altitudes may be of interest to some of my readers, illustrating the extreme variation of temperature to which we were exposed, and the difficulties that stand in the way of military operations:—

Trebizond	sea-level.	Zewin Dooz	...	6,500 feet.
Zigana	5,200 feet.	Eshek-Khaliass		7,800 „
Kop Dagh	8,000 „	Taghir		7,400 „
Erzeroum	6,150 „	Mellidooz		8,600 „
Hindsk	6,200 „	Mezingird	.....	7,800 „
Kara-Kobeg	... 6,600 „	Sara Kamysh	...	7,500 „
Lisgaf	6,800 „	Kirk Punar	...	6,800 „
Kutumar	6,700 „	Vairan Kale	...	6,400 „
Kntuman	8,000 „	Kars (town)	...	5,800 „
Hemron Dooz	... 9,000 „	Kars (citadel)	...	6,130 „
Knipri-Kui	5,600 „	Vezinkui		6,400 „
Khorassan	5,300 „	Aladja Dagh	...	8,500 „
Deli-baba	6,600 „			

APPENDIX D.

CORRESPONDENCE published in the Blue Book relating to the "Defence and Capitulation of Kars," having reference to Hussain Avni Pasha:—

Despatch No. 16—D. Therapia, September 27, 1854, from Lord Stratford de Redcliffe to the Earl of Clarendon—announces the appointment of Hussain Pasha as Chief of the Staff, to Shukri Pasha, the newly-nominated Commander-in-Chief in Armenia.

Despatch No. 60—D. Erzeroum, November 17, 1854, from Colonel Fenwick Williams to the Earl of Clarendon—complains of the conduct of both Shukri Pasha and Hussain Pasha towards him.

Enclosure No. 3 in above despatch.—Colonel Williams complains of the studied incivility of Hussain Pasha.

Despatch No. 62—D. Foreign Office, December 29, 1854, from Lord Clarendon to Lord Stratford de Redcliffe—insisting that General Williams must be upheld, and demanding that the most stringent instructions be sent by the Porte to the Mushir in Armenia to avoid a recurrence of the affronts to which General Williams is exposed from Shukri and Hussain Pashas.

Despatch No. 66 and Enclosures—D. Erzeroum, December 8, 1854, from Colonel Williams to Lord Stratford de Redcliffe—complains still more strongly of the "*insolence*" of Shukri and Hussain Pashas.

Despatch No. 69—D. Constantinople, December 14, 1854, from Lord Stratford de Redcliffe to Lord Clarendon—announces that the Porte has reprimanded Shukri and Hussain Pashas, and empowered Vassif Pasha to dismiss them.

F F

Despatch No. 165—D. Erzeroum, February 25, 1855, General Williams to Earl of Clarendon—announces that Vassif Pasha has placed Hussain Pasha under arrest.

Enclosure No. 2, in 165—

Charges against Liva Hussain Pasha, Chief of the Staff.—" As the British Commissioner to the army at Kars, I charge Liva Hussain Pasha, the Chief of the Staff, with the following instances of disregard for the English Government, and of personal contempt towards me.

" 1.—On his arrival at the camp of Kars, he began by making alterations in the defences of that place, and by causing considerable movements of troops, without informing me of his object or instructions ; and on my resenting this neglect, he told me, in presence of Kerim Pasha, that ' he had received his orders as to what was necessary to be done.'

" 2.—For having from that day continued to treat me with contempt and silence, this conduct being pursued towards a friendly Commissioner, sent to communicate to his Government all intelligence necessary to enable that Government to assist the Porte.

" 3.—For habitual drunkenness and debauchery, evincing his sympathy for Shukri Pasha as regards that officer's disrespect towards me, and a fellowship for that Ferik in all those vices which degrade the military profession and lower the dignity of man.

" (Signed)   W. F. WILLIAMS.

" *Erzeroum, February* 25, 1855."

Despatch No. 176 — D. Constantinople, March 21, 1855, from Lord Stratford de Redcliffe to Lord Clarendon—reports that the Seraskier disapproves of the arrest of Shukri and Hussain Pashas ; and further states that whatever may have been their demerits at Kars, yet they served with distinction under Omar Pasha.

N.B.—It was whilst serving with Omar Pasha that Major Lintorn Simmons formed that acquaintance with Hussain Pasha which induced him to deny the fact of the disgrace in 1855.

Enclosure No. 2, in Despatch No. 179, from Brigadier-General Williams to Kerim Pasha.—Announcing the departure of Hussain Pasha for Constantinople to undergo *trial.*

Enclosure No. 3, in Despatch No. 187—D. Erzeroum, March 20, 1855, from Brigadier-General Williams to Earl Clarendon—

"It is also notorious that the Pashas in question, Shukri and Hussain, had given themselves up to such habitual drunkenness and dissipation, that, besides their having become a bad example to the Sultan's troops, and a disgrace to their fellow officers, they were never by day, in consequence of their nocturnal gambling and debauchery, in a fit state of mind to transact the business of the Council." * * *

Hussain Pasha made no secret of his dissipated conduct; and on one occasion the people of his quarter of the town were exasperated to such a degree, that they would have actually made an attack on his house had they not known that the Mushir was about to arrive; and they therefore decided on laying a formal complaint before His Excellency.

Despatch No. 213—D. Constantinople, May 17, 1855, from Lord Stratford de Redcliffe to the Earl of Clarendon—reports that neither Shukri nor Hussain Pashas have been submitted to any judicial proceeding, and that Omar Pasha has applied for the services of the latter.

Enclosure No. 1, in Despatch No. 213.—The Seraskier states that so far from charges existing against Hussain Pasha, he has been much praised by the Commander-in-Chief at Kars; and that, on the express demand of Omar Pasha, he was to be sent to the army of Eupatoria.

Despatch No. 228—D. Constantinople, June 14, 1855, Lord Stratford de Redcliffe to Earl of Clarendon—reports the determination of the Seraskierate to release Hussain and Shukri Pashas, and to send the former to Omar Pasha's staff.

Despatch No. 236—237, on the same subject.—Lieutenant-Colonel Simmons urges that Omar Pasha was unaware that charges had been preferred against Hussain Pasha when he applied for his services, and states that Omar Pasha wishes his appointment to be delayed until the charges shall have been inquired into.

Mr. Zohrab, in a letter to me dated Erzeroum, December 7th, 1877, says, "I think Sir Lintorn Simmons' memory is at fault. I was the medium of communication between Sir Fenwick Williams and Hussain Avni Pasha, saw him under arrest, translated the charges that were to be preferred against him, and know that he was released on reaching Constantinople. He was subsequently employed with Sir Lintorn Simmons in Asia, and murdered last year."

Although I was in error in accusing Hussain Avni of peculation, I think these extracts prove that my story was not "utterly groundless," and to clear myself from the imputation of rashly listening to Armenian stories, I publish the above.

They prove that the Porte then, as now, in the case of Chefket Pasha, paid little attention to the requests of the British Government for the punishment of evil doers, Lord Stratford notwithstanding.

THE END.

CASSELL PETTER & GALPIN, BELLE SAUVAGE WORKS, LONDON, E.C.

CHEAP EDITION, extra crown 8vo, cloth, 7s. 6d.

A RIDE TO KHIVA.

TRAVELS AND ADVENTURES IN CENTRAL ASIA,

By CAPTAIN BURNABY.

With Large Maps showing Districts traversed, &c.

"Captain Burnaby has published a charming and instructive book at an opportune moment."—*Times.*

"It is the best compliment we can pay the writer that we lay the book down with a wish that there were more of it. There are comparatively few volumes of travel about which the same could be said."—*Scotsman.*

"Captain Burnaby's book is emphatically the book of the season, appearing not only at just the right nick of time, when all eyes are turned to the East, and universal interest attaches to the attitude of Russia, but being, besides, singularly refreshing, outspoken, and unique."—*Irish Times.*

"Captain Burnaby's book is interesting throughout. It contains much useful information, and a spirit of light humour pervades the whole volume. His description of his ride on a camel crossed in love is so amusing that it leaves a feeling of want behind; insomuch that we confess we should have intensely relished witnessing his discomfiture ourselves."—*Army and Navy Gazette.*

"From the first page to the last there is no dull writing in the book. It possesses the charm and ease of good conversation, and carries the reader along with all the dash of the Ride it records."—*World.*

"The book charms like a novel, and yet bears the impress of truth on every page. We hear a good deal about 'the book of the season,' but if ever the term was rightly applied it is to 'A Ride to Khiva.'"—*Field.*

"Captain Burnaby's 'Ride to Khiva,' which has come forth most opportunely, combines the freshness of youth with the vigour of manhood, and deserves a high rank among the books of travel. We can only close the book with a recommendation of its contents to all who would understand fairly and impartially the question between Turk and Russ."—*Daily Telegraph.*

"All this makes the book equally fitted to interest politicians and to delight young ladies, and at once place it in every drawing-room in London, and command for it a place on the shelves of every library in the country."—*Vanity Fair.*

Cassell Petter & Galpin, Ludgate Hill, London ; Paris and New York.

In One Volume, demy 8vo, with large Coloured MAP, **£1 1s.**

EGYPT AS IT IS.

By J. C. McCOAN,

Late Editor of the "Levant Herald."

" We can recommend 'Egypt as It Is' as supplying a want which is much felt—a truthful and able account of the country."—*Athenæum*.

" Mr. McCoan, our latest and most comprehensive informant." — *Mr. Gladstone in the Nineteenth Century*.

" Mr. McCoan has succeeded in producing a book of extraordinary freshness and power."—*Daily Telegraph*.

" This practically useful work has appeared at an opportune time, and is well calculated to inform its readers correctly on many important matters, as to which in all probability they have hitherto formed a completely erroneous judgment. —*Army and Navy Gazette*.

" We regard this as *the* book of the year, because in style, in matter, and in arrangement it is excellent. The style is spirited, clear, and racy. The reader is borne along as though he were reading a novel, and at every turn the volume sparkles with keen and incisive remarks. As to the value of the matter we can speak in the highest terms."—*Financier*.

" There is probably no other book in the English language—none at least of recent publication—written with the same object, and embodying the like amount and kind of information. Mr. McCoan's volume embodies an immense mass of well-digested information, and at the present time, when British relations with Egypt are daily becoming closer, it may be welcomed as a work of great utility and value."—*Scotsman*.

" Mr. McCoan's ably-written work on Egypt is very opportune. Its commerce, finances, cultivable area, minerals, population, are now all things about which a lively interest is felt. Mr. McCoan's work supplies the required information with fulness."—*Leeds Mercury*.

" A very complete and most interesting account of Egypt as it is. In separate chapters the author deals with the history, the population, the cities and towns, the relations of Egypt and the Porte, administration, finance, commerce, agriculture, climate, the Suez Canal, manufacture, and many other features."— *Liverpool Albion*.

Cassell Petter & Galpin, Ludgate Hill, London ; Paris and New York.

2

RUSSIA.

By D. MACKENZIE WALLACE, M.A.

" Undoubtedly the best book written on modern Russia by a foreigner, and one of the best books ever written on that country by either foreigner or native."— *Times.*

" Mr. Wallace's book deserves a cordial welcome, as much for the opportuneness of its publication as for its intrinsic excellence."—*Quarterly Review.*

" This very complete and thoroughly interesting work appeals to many classes of readers. It is full of information ; it abounds in views on every question which has agitated Russian society in modern times ; and it contains a large number of clever characteristic sketches of Russians of all classes and conditions."—*The Pall Mall Gazette.*

" What Mr. Wallace says about the Eastern Question is likely to be read with special interest just now, as conveying the opinions of one who is exceptionally qualified to speak upon the subject, not only by knowledge of a most rare kind, but also by a singular capacity for seeing both sides of a question."—*Academy.*

" As an account of the social and political condition of Russia this book may truly be pronounced the best yet published in the English language. It is, moreover, written in a style so clear and buoyant, and its contents are so well arranged, that the reader's interest is kept up, without any sense of weariness, to the end."— *Guardian.*

" Le livre de M. Wallace, que ses compatriots liront avec plaisir et profit, ne laissera pas d'avoir son utilité pour les Russes eux-mêmes, qui y trouveront souvent plus d'impartialité que dans les jugements de leurs propres auteurs."—*Journal des Debats.*

" Das rechte buch zur rechten zeit."—*Frankfurter Zeitung.*

We congratulate the author on having written a book of which it may be said that, as to its topic, it has, in the French phrase, *fait époque ;* it has made a difference in the intelligence with which a very important subject may be regarded." —*New York Nation.*

Cassell Petter & Galpin, Ludgate Hill, London ; Paris and New York.

In One Volume, Demy 8vo, with MAPS, price **21s.**

TURKEY IN EUROPE,

By Lieut.-Colonel JAMES BAKER.

"Col. James Baker has given us the best and most instructive book we have yet seen on Turkey in Europe."—*Edinburgh Quarterly Review.*

"Colonel Baker has worked up with diligence, and recapitulated with brevity and distinctness, all that he could learn as to the ethnology, migrations, conquests, and defeats of Bulgarians, Greeks, Turks, Albanians, Servians, and Montenegrins. He has put together all the facts he could collect as to the educational, judicial, financial, military, and naval systems of Turkey. Of all that he speaks of from personal knowledge he is a trustworthy witness, calm, shrewd, and impartial. Of all that he speaks of from historical and other printed documents, he is a trustworthy compiler, intelligent, concise, and rapid. As a traveller, Colonel Baker inserts the usual traveller's stories, to give variety and relief to his statistics and his discussions."—*Saturday Review.*

"It is impossible to imagine any work on European Turkey more complete in its information, more circumspect in its judgments, more comprehensive in its view, more thorough and accurate in its facts."—*World.*

"The Author deals with almost every question which has arisen in connexion with European Turkey, and he gives a great deal of interesting information on the subject of travelling, farming, the manners and customs of Jews and Gipsies in Turkey, the work done by the American Missionaries, the plan of education at Robert College, and so on."—*Athenæum.*

"In the description of men and manners the humorous is pleasantly blended with the appreciative, while that of landscape and scenery is vivid and unconstrained."—*Academy.*

"Colonel Baker's Book is very exceptionally valuable on three grounds : first, because of the glimpses it gives of the social and domestic conditions of the inhabitants ; secondly, on account of the practical information it contains about Turkish agriculture ; and, thirdly, for Colonel Baker's account of the organization and condition of the Turkish military forces."—*Scotsman.*

"We can heartily recommend the work to our readers as a pleasant, entertaining, and instructive account of a country important to the first degree at the present moment, but one of which a great deal too little is known."—*Live Stock Journal.*

Cassell Petter & Galpin, Ludgate Hill, London ; Paris and New York.

4

Cassell Petter & Galpin's Volumes.

England : Her People, Polity, and Pursuits.

By T. H. S. ESCOTT. Two Vols., Demy 8vo, cloth, 24s.

The English Army: Its Past History, Present

Condition, and Future Prospects. By Major ARTHUR GRIFFITHS, Author of "Memorials of Millbank," "The Queen's Shilling," &c. &c. Demy 8vo, cloth, 21s.

The French Revolutionary Epoch.

A History of France from the Beginning of the First Revolution to the End of the Second Empire. By HENRI VAN LAUN, Author of "The History of French Literature." Two Vols., demy 8vo, 24s.

The Family Physician.

A Modern Manual of Domestic Medicine. By PHYSICIANS and SURGEONS of the Principal London Hospitals. Royal 8vo, cloth, 21s.

This Work has been specially prepared with a view to placing in the hands of Families a Comprehensive and Practical Guide to the Treatment of Sickness and Disease. Each Section is written by an Eminent Physician or Surgeon, who has made such Section the subject of his special study and practice.

Pleasant Spots Around Oxford.

By ALFRED RIMMER, Author of "Ancient Streets and Home-steads," with numerous Original Woodcuts. Extra fcap. 4to, cloth gilt, gilt edges, 21s.

The Magazine of Art. VOLUME I.

With an Etching for Frontispiece by L. LOWENSTAM, from a Picture by FRANZ HALS, and containing Full-page Engravings of Pictures by Sir F. LEIGHTON, P.R.A., P. H. CALDERON, R.A., W. C. T. DOBSON, R.A., A. ELMORE, R.A., T. FAED, R.A., Sir JOHN GILBERT, R.A., F. GOODALL, R.A., Sir EDWIN LANDSEER, R.A., J. E. MILLAIS, R.A., J. PETTIE, R.A., J. PHILLIP, R.A., E. M. WARD, R.A., G. F. WATTS, R.A., W. F. YEAMES, R.A., J. B. BURGESS, A.R.A., VICAT COLE, A.R.A., J. E. HODGSON, A.R.A., FRANK HOLL, A.R.A., H. S. MARKS, A.R.A., &c. &c. Extra crown 4to, cloth, gilt edges, 7s. 6d.

Picturesque Europe. VOLS. I. to IV.

Each containing Thirteen Exquisite Steel Plates from Original Drawings and nearly 200 Original Illustrations. With Descriptive Letterpress. Royal 4to, cloth, gilt edges, £2 2s.; morocco, £5 5s. ea.

Vols. I. and II. of PICTURESQUE EUROPE contain Great Britain and Ireland complete, and can be obtained bound together in One Vol., whole bound, extra gilt, gilt edges, £5 5s.

Cassell Petter & Galpin: Ludgate Hill, London; Paris; and New York.

THE NEW BIBLE COMMENTARY.

New Testament Commentary for English

Readers. Edited by C. J. ELLICOTT, D.D., Lord Bishop of Gloucester and Bristol.

VOL. I. contains THE FOUR GOSPELS, price £1 1s.

VOL. II. contains THE ACTS OF THE APOSTLES, ROMANS, CORINTHIANS, and GALATIANS, price £1 1s.

VOL. III. contains the REMAINING BOOKS of the New Testament, price £1 1s.

The Life of Christ.

By the Rev. F. W. FARRAR, D.D., F.R.S., Canon of Westminster, and Chaplain in Ordinary to the Queen.

Illustrated Edition. With about 300 Illustrations, Coloured Map, and Steel Title, extra crown 4to, elegantly bound in cloth, gilt edges, 21s.; calf or morocco, £2 2s.

Library Edition. Complete in Two Volumes, cloth, price 24s.; morocco, £2 2s.

The Half-Guinea Illustrated Bible.

Containing 900 Original Illustrations specially executed for this Edition from Original Photographs and other Authentic Sources. Printed in clear, readable type, with Reference. 1,248 pages, crown 4to size. Strongly bound in cloth, 10s. 6d. *Also in Leather bindings in great variety.*

The Bible Educator.

Edited by the Rev. E. H. PLUMPTRE, D.D., assisted by some of our most Eminent Scholars and Divines. With about 400 Illustrations and Maps. Complete in Four Volumes, extra crown 4to, cloth, 6s. each; or in Two Double Volumes, cloth, 21s.; library binding, £1 4s.; half-calf, marbled edges, 31s. 6d.

Some Difficulties of Belief.

By the Rev. T. TEIGNMOUTH SHORE, M.A., Incumbent of Berkeley Chapel, Mayfair, Hon. Chaplain to the Queen. Crown 8vo, cloth, 6s.

The Life of the World to Come, and other

Subjects. By the Rev. T. TEIGNMOUTH SHORE, M.A., Incumbent of Berkeley Chapel, Mayfair, Hon. Chaplain to the Queen. Crown 8vo, 240 pages, cloth, 5s.

Some Present Dangers of the Church of

England, and other Papers. By C. J. ELLICOTT, D.D., Lord Bishop of Gloucester and Bristol. Crown 8vo, cloth gilt, price 2s. 6d.

Cassell Petter & Galpin: Ludgate Hill, London; Paris; and New York.

The King's Secret.

By the DUC DE BROGLIE. Being the Secret Correspondence of Louis XV. with his Diplomatic Agents, from 1752 to 1774. Two Volumes, demy 8vo, cloth, 24s.

New Greece.

By LEWIS SERGEANT. Demy 8vo, with Two Maps, 21s.

"Mr. Sergeant's work is not that of a traveller ; it comes to us with higher claims. It is a combination of the historical, the economic, and the political. There is no work which can be compared with Mr. Sergeant's for the comprehensiveness with which it states what is known as the Greek Question."—*British Quarterly Review.*

Russia.

By D. MACKENZIE WALLACE, M.A., Member of the Imperial Russian Geographical Society. *Cheap Edition*, in One Vol., with Two Maps, 10s. 6d. *Library Edition*, Two Vols., with Maps, 24s.

"Undoubtedly the best book written on modern Russia by a foreigner, and one of the best books ever written on that country by either foreigner or native."—*Times.*

Armenia, and the Campaign of 1877.

By C. B. NORMAN, late Special Correspondent of *The Times* at the Seat of War. With specially-prepared Maps. Cloth, £1 1s.

"The book is the best we have seen on the subject."—*Scotsman.*

Egypt as It Is.

By J. C. McCOAN, late Editor of the *Levant Herald.* Demy 8vo, cloth, with Map, £1 1s.

"Supplies a want which is much felt—a detailed and a truthful and able account of the country as it is in its moral, material, and economical aspect."—*Athenæum.*

Turkey in Europe.

By Lieut.-Col. JAMES BAKER. Demy 8vo, with Maps, £1 1s.

"Col. James Baker has given us the best and most instructive book we have yet seen on Turkey in Europe."—*Edinburgh Quarterly Review.*

A Ride to Khiva.

By CAPTAIN BURNABY. *Cheap Edition.* With Maps, 7s. 6d.

The Great Thirst Land. A Ride through

Natal, Orange Free State, Transvaal, Kalahari. By PARKER GILLMORE (" Ubique "). *Cheap Edition*, with Map, 7s. 6d.

England, Cassell's History of.

From the Earliest Period to the Present Time. With about 2,000 Illustrations. NEW TONED PAPER EDITION. Complete in Nine Vols., cloth, each, 9s. Library Edition, bound in brown cloth, gilt tops, £4 10s.

United States, Cassell's History of the.

With 600 Illustrations and Maps. 1,950 pages, extra crown 4to. Complete in Three Vols., cloth, £1 7s.; or in library binding, £1 10s.

India, Cassell's History of.

With about 400 Maps, Plans. and Illustrations. 1,188 pages, extra crown 4to. Complete in Two Vols., cloth, 18s.; or in library binding, £1.

The War between France and Germany, Cassell's

History of. With 500 Engravings and Plans of the Battle-fields. Complete in Two Volumes. Extra crown 4to, cloth, 18s.; or bound in half-calf, 30s.

Russo-Turkish War, Cassell's History of.

VOL. I. By the Author of CASSELL'S HISTORY OF THE FRANCO-GERMAN WAR. With about 300 ILLUSTRATIONS. Extra crown 4to, cloth, 9s. (*To be completed in Two Vols.*)

British Battles on Land and Sea.

By JAMES GRANT, Author of the "Romance of War," &c. With about 600 Illustrations. Complete in Three Vols., extra crown 4to, cloth, £1 7s.; or in library binding, £1 10s.

Old and New London. A Narrative of its History,

its People, and its Places. In Volumes, each containing 200 Illustrations. Complete in Six Vols., price 9s. each; or in library binding, the set of Six Vols., £3.

The History of Protestantism.

By the Rev. J. A. WYLIE, LL.D. With upwards of 600 Original Illustrations. 1,940 pages, extra crown 4to. Complete in Three Vols., cloth, £1 7s.; or in library binding, £1 10s.

Decisive Events in History.

By THOMAS ARCHER. With Sixteen Original Illustrations. Extra fcap. 4to, cloth gilt, 5s.

This Work has been prepared for the use of students in private and public schools, and gives, in a succinct and readable form, the leading events in the world's history. The historical records are written in a condensed and incisive, yet comprehensive style, and are accompanied by full-page original illustrations, executed with strict regard to the accuracy of detail. These characteristic illustrations will, it is believed, help not only to impress on the pupil's attention the important episodes which they respectively represent, and so promote an enduring interest in the particular event described, but will tend to create a more enlarged interest in the wider range of historical study.

Cassell Petter & Galpin: Ludgate Hill, London; Paris; and New York.

The Book of the Horse.

With Hints on Horsemanship, the Management of the Stable, Breeding, Breaking, and Training for the Road, the Park, and the Field. By SAMUEL SIDNEY. With Twenty-five *fac-simile* Coloured Plates from Original Paintings, and 100 Wood Engravings. Demy 4to, cloth, gilt edges, 31s. 6d. ; half-morocco, £2 2s.

The Book of Poultry.

By L. WRIGHT. With Fifty exquisite Coloured Portraits of Prize Birds painted from Life, and numerous Wood Engravings. Demy 4to, 600 pages, cloth, gilt edges, 31s. 6d.; half-morocco, £2 2s.

The Book of Pigeons.

By ROBERT FULTON, assisted by the most Eminent Fanciers. Edited and Arranged by LEWIS WRIGHT. With Fifty life-like Coloured Plates, and numerous Engravings on Wood. Demy 4to, cloth bevelled, gilt edges, £1 11s. 6d. ; half-morocco, £2 2s.

The Book of Birds.

Translated from the Text of Dr. BREHM, by Prof. T. RYMER JONES, F.R.S. With 400 Wood Engravings, and Forty Coloured Plates from Original Designs by F. W. KEYL. Four Vols., 4to, cloth, 7s. 6d.; gilt edges, 10s. 6d. each. Or Two Vols., cloth, gilt edges, £1 10s.; half-calf, £2 2s.

Cassell's Dictionary of Cookery.

With Numerous Engravings and Full-page Coloured Plates. Containing about 9,000 Recipes. 1,280 pages, royal 8vo, half-roan, 15s.

The Domestic Dictionary.

An Encyclopædia for the Household. 1,280 pages, royal 8vo, half-roan, 15s.

Cassell's Household Guide.

New and Revised Edition. A Comprehensive Guide to Every Department of Practical Life. With Illustrations on nearly every page, and COLOURED PLATES. Complete in Four Vols., 6s. each.

The Diseases of Women: Their Causes,

Symptoms, and Treatment. By A Physician. Extra fcap. 8vo, cloth, 6s.

A Handbook of Nursing, for the Home and

for the Hospital. By CATHERINE J. WOOD. Cloth, 3s. 6d.

Cassell Petter & Galpin: Ludgate Hill, London; Paris; and New York.

Familiar Wild Flowers.

FIRST SERIES. By F. E. HULME, F.L.S., F.S.A. With Forty Full-page Coloured Plates and Descriptive Text, together with a Concise Scientific Summary. Crown 8vo, cloth gilt, gilt edges, in cardboard box, 12s. 6d.

Science for All.

VOL. I. Edited by Dr. ROBERT BROWN, M.A., F.L.S., &c., assisted by eminent Scientific Writers. Vol. I. contains about 350 Illustrations and Diagrams. Extra crown 4to, cloth, price 9s.

The Races of Mankind.

By ROBERT BROWN, M.A., Ph.D., F.L.S., F.R.G.S. Complete in Four Vols., containing upwards of 500 Illustrations. Extra crown 4to, cloth gilt, 6s. per Vol. ; or Two Double Vols., £1 1s.

The Countries of the World.

By ROBERT BROWN, M.A., Ph.D., F.L.S., F.R.G.S. Vols. I., II., and III., with 130 Illustrations and Maps. Ex. crown 4to, cloth, 7s. 6d. each.

The Sea: Its Stirring Story of Adventure,

Peril, and Heroism. By F. WHYMPER, Author of "Travels in Alaska," &c. VOL. I., with upwards of 100 Original Illustrations executed specially for the Work. Extra crown 4to, cloth, 7s. 6d.

Great Industries of Great Britain.

VOL. I. With about 130 Illustrations. Extra crown 4to, 320 pages, cloth, 7s. 6d.

Cassell's New Natural History.

Edited by P. MARTIN DUNCAN, M.D., F.R.S., Professor of Geology, King's College, London, assisted by Eminent Scientific Writers. Illustrated throughout. Vols. I. and II. now ready, 9s. each.

The World of the Sea.

Translated from the French of MOQUIN TANDON, by the Rev. H. MARTYN-HART, M.A. Illustrated. Cloth, 10s. 6d.

Transformations of Insects.

By P. MARTIN DUNCAN, M.D., F.R.S. With 240 highly-finished Engravings. *New and Cheaper Edition.* Demy 8vo, cloth, 7s. 6d.

The Great Painters of Christendom, from

CIMABUE to WILKIE. By JOHN FORBES-ROBERTSON. Illustrated throughout with carefully-executed Engravings of the Masterpieces of the several Painters. Royal 4to, cloth elegant, gilt edges, £3 3s.

"Comprises the history of all that is splendid and admirable in the painter's art."—*Times.*

The Leopold Shakspere.

The Poet's Works, in Chronological Order, from the Text of Professor DELIUS, with "Edward the Third" and "The Two Noble Kinsmen," and an Introduction by F. J. FURNIVALL. With about 400 Illustrations. 1,184 pages. Small 4to, 10s. 6d. Dedicated by permission to H.R.H. PRINCE LEOPOLD.

Royal Quarto Shakespeare.

Edited by CHARLES and MARY COWDEN CLARKE, and containing about 600 Illustrations by H. C. SELOUS. Printed in new large type on royal 4to paper. Complete in Three Vols., cloth gilt, gilt edges, £3 3s.; morocco, £6 6s.

The Practical Dictionary of Mechanics.

Containing 15,000 Drawings of Machinery, Instruments, and Tools in use by every Profession and Trade, with Comprehensive and TECHNICAL DESCRIPTION of each Subject. Complete in Three Volumes, 2,880 pages, super-royal 8vo, cloth, £3 3s.; half-morocco, £3 15s.

The Doré Fine Art Volumes,

Published by CASSELL PETTER & GALPIN, comprise—

	£	s.	d.		£	s.	d.
The Doré Scripture Gallery	5	10	0	Don Quixote . .	1	10	0
The Doré Gallery .	5	5	0	La Fontaine's Fables	1	10	0
The Doré Bible . .	4	4	0	The Wandering Jew .	1	1	0
Milton's Paradise Lost	2	10	0	The Days of Chivalry	0	10	6
Dante's Inferno . .	2	10	0	Fairy Tales Told Again	0	5	0
Purgatorio and Paradiso	2	10	0				

** Also kept in morocco bindings suitable for Presentation.

Louis Figuier's Popular Scientific Works.

New and Cheaper Editions. Containing all the Original Illustrations, the TEXT REVISED AND CORRECTED, price 7s. 6d. each :—

The Human Race. Revised by ROBERT WILSON.
Mammalia. Revised by Professor E. PERCEVAL WRIGHT, M.D.
The World Before the Deluge. Revised by W. H. BRISTOW, F.R.S.
The Ocean World. Revised by Prof. E. PERCEVAL WRIGHT, M.D.
Reptiles and Birds. Revised by Captain PARKER GILLMORE.
The Insect World. Revised by Professor DUNCAN, M.D., F.R.S.
The Vegetable World. Revised by an Eminent Botanist.

Cassell Petter & Galpin : Ludgate Hill, London ; Paris ; and New York.

Shorter English Poems.

By Professor HENRY MORLEY. Being Vol. I. of CASSELL'S LIBRARY OF ENGLISH LITERATURE. Containing the Leading Characteristic Shorter Poems of English Literature, from the Earliest Period to the Present Time, with upwards of 200 Illustrations. Extra crown 4to, 512 pages, cloth, 12s. 6d.

Illustrations of English Religion.

By PROFESSOR HENRY MORLEY. Being Vol. II. of CASSELL'S LIBRARY OF ENGLISH LITERATURE. Illustrated throughout with Engravings from Original MSS., &c. Ex. crown 4to, cloth, 11s. 6d.

English Plays.

By Professor HENRY MORLEY. Being VOL. III. of THE LIBRARY OF ENGLISH LITERATURE. With Engravings from Original MSS., &c. Extra crown 4to, cloth, 11s. 6d.

A First Sketch of English Literature.

By Professor HENRY MORLEY. Crown 8vo, 912 pages, cloth, 7s. 6d.

Dictionary of English Literature.

Being a Comprehensive Guide to English Authors and their Works. By W. DAVENPORT ADAMS. 720 pages, extra fcap. 4to, cloth, 15s.

Dictionary of Phrase and Fable.

Giving the Derivation, Source, or Origin of Common Phrases, Allusions, and Words that have a Tale to Tell. By the Rev. Dr. BREWER. Demy 8vo, 1,000 pages, cloth, 7s. 6d.

Sketching from Nature in Water-Colours.

By AARON PENLEY. With Illustrations in Chromo-Lithography, after Original Water-Colour Drawings. Super-royal 4to, cloth, 15s.

Principles of Ornamental Art.

By F. E. HULME, F.L.S., F.S.A., Art Master in Marlborough College. With over 400 Designs. Royal 4to, cloth, 25s.

Studies in Design.

For Builders, Architects, Designers, House Decorators, and Manufacturers. By CHRISTOPHER DRESSER, Ph.D., F.L.S., &c. Consisting of Sixty Original Designs by the Author, accompanied by Descriptive Letterpress. Demy folio, cloth, £3 3s.

CASSELL PETTER & GALPIN'S COMPLETE CATALOGUE, *containing a List of Several Hundred Volumes, including Bibles and Religious Works, Fine Art Volumes, Children's Books, Dictionaries, Educational Works, Handbooks and Guides, History, Natural History, Household and Domestic Treatises, Science, Serials, Travels, &c. &c., sent post free on application.*

Cassell Petter & Galpin: Ludgate Hill, London; Paris; and New York.

Made in the USA